Mark Twain and Medicine

Mark Twain and His Circle Series
Tom Quirk, editor

Mark Twain and Medicine

"ANY MUMMERY WILL CURE"

● ● K. Patrick Ober ● ●

UNIVERSITY OF MISSOURI PRESS ● COLUMBIA AND LONDON

Copyright © 2003 by
The Curators of the University of Missouri
University of Missouri Press, Columbia, Missouri 65201
Printed and bound in the United States of America
All rights reserved
5 4 3 2 1   07 06 05 04 03

Library of Congress Cataloging-in-Publication Data

Ober, K. Patrick.
    Mark Twain and medicine: any mummery will cure / K. Patrick Ober.
        p.   cm. — (Mark Twain and his circle series)
    Includes bibliographical references and index.
    ISBN 0-8262-1502-5 (alk. paper)
    1. Twain, Mark, 1835–1910—Knowledge—Medicine. 2. Literature and
    medicine—United States—History—19th century. 3. Medicine—United
    States—History—19th century. 4. Medicine in literature. I. Title.
    II. Series.
    PS1342.M43 O24   2003
    818'.409—dc22   2003015504

 ∞™   This paper meets the requirements of the
American National Standard for Permanence of Paper
for Printed Library Materials, Z39.48, 1984.

Designer: Jennifer Cropp
Typesetter: Phoenix Type, Inc.
Printer and binder: Thomson-Shore, Inc.
Typefaces: Palatino, Bordeaux, and Bodoni

For Cathy,
with love and devotion

● ● *and* ● ●

For Chris and Rebecca,
with love, pride, and admiration

"Any mummery will cure, if the patient's faith is strong in it"

Mark Twain, *A Connecticut Yankee in King Arthur's Court*

Contents

Acknowledgments

This book owes its existence to a box of cereal. It may have been a box of Cheerios, or it might have been a box of Wheaties. I was probably not any more than ten years old at the time the cereal box exerted its influence, and I can no longer remember the name of the cereal. I do remember that Cheerios and Wheaties were the staples of our breakfast table when I was a boy in Conrad, Iowa, so the credit belongs to General Mills in any case. At that time, General Mills encouraged American mothers to purchase a "literary classic" for their children—they simply had to clip a coupon from the cereal box and mail it in, attached to a dollar bill. I had the good fortune of having a mother—Maridale Ober—who believed that such things were important. She had lived through the Great Depression and World War II in her native England, and as a relatively new American citizen she wanted the best for her children. She had dropped out of school at the age of fourteen to support her own family after her father's death, and the education of her children was a high priority for her. I remain eternally grateful.

By sheer chance, it was decided that I would receive *Adventures of Huckleberry Finn* and my brother Mark would get *Swiss Family Robinson*. Huck had a profound impact on me. The words in the book were difficult for a young reader, and the dialect was tricky to work through. The story and its implications, of course, were magnificent. Of greater importance to me at the time, it was a real hardcover book, and it was *mine*.

I rarely read any book more than once. Huck is the exception. I don't know how many times I have read *Huckleberry Finn*. I learn something new each time I read it. I have become a Huck Finn addict. The modest bookcase in my living room has seven different editions of *Huckleberry Finn*. Every time I buy a new one, I emphatically explain to my wife, Cathy (who is saintly in her patience!), that there should never be a reason for me to buy another Huck. Ever. And then...I find yet another edition, distinct from any other that I own, with annotations or introductions or footnotes or commentaries or illustrations that are not contained in any of the editions of Huck that are already in my possession. So I buy another one. No family can have too many Huckleberry Finns, I explain to Cathy. (Sadly, my original $1 Huck is nowhere to be found, lost in the time warp between childhood and middle life that takes away so many things of value.)

My mother introduced me to Mark Twain. My father was responsible for bringing the wonders of biology, science, and medicine into my life. Dr. Jess Ober grew up as an Iowa farmboy. He too knew the Great Depression and the importance of hard work. World War II introduced him to my mother, and the GI Bill permitted him to pursue an education in veterinary medicine that would not have been possible otherwise. He deserves a position of honor for his contributions to my accomplishments. His gifts were those that can come from only the best of fathers. His wry sense of humor and his unflagging commitment to fairness and honesty became the definition of the way that life should be lived. He has been a role model for integrity. His willingness to include his young son in the activities of his veterinary practice provided an introduction to the mysterious world of medicine. His belief in the importance of education helped define a career.

Mark Ober and Susie Ober are the remarkable siblings who brought companionship and joy to my growing-up years. Their notable accomplishments are an ongoing source of inspiration and great pride for me. Mostly, they are just wonderful people. I am honored to be a recipient of their love.

I would be remiss not to recognize the contributions of the inspired teachers at Brandon (Florida) High School and Michigan State University. They are responsible for most of what I know about the world beyond medicine. Their lessons were taught well and were essential to my ability to write this very nonmedical book about medicine, Mark Twain, and all the other things in life that are far greater than medicine.

And, of course, there are the numerous people who are responsible for my education in medicine. The faculty of the University of Florida College of Medicine deserves the formal recognition, although even greater credit goes to the individual members of my medical school class who exerted a profound influence on my own medical maturation. Dr. Jon Smally deserves special recognition for being a model of unwavering integrity. He has a no-nonsense approach to those things in life that are important, combined with a humorous impertinence toward everything that isn't. He does not tolerate fools, nor anyone else who takes himself too seriously. He has always had the ability to make me laugh until the tears flow; there are few pleasures in life that are greater than that. I'm not sure I would have made it through medical school without his humor. (On other occasions, I feared I would not make it out of medical school *because* of his humor.) Mark Twain would enjoy the company of Jon Smally.

So, that was the preparation I have had for writing this book. Preparation alone cannot accomplish anything, however, unless the environment is suitable. I have had the distinct advantage of being affiliated with Wake Forest University since 1974. The university and its medical center have provided a world of academic excellence in a supportive and caring environment that could not have been equaled anywhere else in the country. I am grateful to those who taught me what is important about medicine and life, starting with the first frightening day of my internship. My colleagues are remarkable people. The residents in the Department of Internal Medicine have been sources of inspiration and role models in their own right. Special thanks go to the chairmen who have defined my career. Dr. Joe Johnson was brave enough to support Dr. Emery Miller's decision to hire me as an inexperienced clinician. Dr. Bill Hazzard had the confidence to trust me in running the department's educational activities. Dr. Bill Applegate, a remarkable friend from the day we met, has been absolutely fabulous as the willing Huck Finn to my Tom Sawyer. Wake Forest has provided me with superb role models who have been articulate in their humanism and in their insights into the human condition. They have willingly shared not only their appreciation of the lessons of the past but also their visions of the promises of the future. Dr. Robert Prichard, Dr. Jack Felts, and Dr. Cash McCall are among those who have had the greatest influence. The outstanding resources of the Coy C. Carpenter Library and its talented staff have been essential contributors to my research.

And then, of course, there are the medical students. They are my greatest pleasure. They are remarkably bright, challenging, devoted, altruistic, motivated, dedicated, diligent, meticulous, sensitive, sensible, and questioning . . . *always* questioning. It is humbling to realize how much better a person the students have made me, compared to what I would have been without them. Most of them are smarter than me. Their commitment is remarkable. Every one inspires me. They have made my medical career a pure joy. Mark Twain bashed medical students once or twice along the way, but that was because he never had the privilege of meeting a Wake Forest medical student.

No one deserves more recognition than my patients, though. They have taught me more about medicine, and more about the joys and challenges of being a human being, than I could ever explain in words. It is an honor to be allowed to be a part of their lives. Perhaps this would be a good time for me to make a confession to my patients. Those of you who have been so grateful when I have helped you get better were probably going to get better anyway. You didn't really need me at all. Sorry. I used to feel guilty when patients gave me credit for their recovery on the occasions when my only contribution, essentially, was to give them the encouragement that they *would* get better. I do not feel guilty about such things anymore; I have since understood that most of what I do as a physician is related to the process of hope-giving that is known as placebo effect. My patients teach me more about it every day, especially when *my* own confidence in it wavers so that I don't provide them with the full dose they need. Mark Twain understood about the value of faith in healing far better than I did when I started out as a doctor. What my patients have taught me, and what Mark Twain has explained to me, is most of my reason for writing this book. For most illnesses, the greatest benefit occurs when it becomes obvious that one human being cares for another. Caring for another human being is a good thing for a doctor to do. My patients are wonderful people, and it would be easy to care about them even if I were not their doctor (well, most of them, anyway), but being a doctor provides me with the necessary mystique to make the healing work. I may need to apologize, however, to the patients I have *not* helped. My failures are not because I didn't try. Sometimes therapeutic failures occur because the patient has a bad disease that medical science is not yet capable of treating (the fact of which does not make it any less frustrating for either one of us). Sometimes medical interventions do not work because the patient does not suffer from a disease of the physical body (even though the symptoms arise in the physical body). Many patients suffer from an affliction of the spirit, and it is difficult for doctors and patients to figure that one out, much less agree on what all of that really means, or what to do about it. This book talks a lot about such afflictions because they contributed greatly to Mark Twain's understanding of how medicine works.

The intersection of faith and healing and hope and medical care is a tricky one, but it was a central feature of Mark Twain's medical world, just as it is essential to medical practice of the twenty-first century. Pure science and pure faith are mutually exclusive. Challengingly, medicine is neither a pure science nor an absolute art form, but a blend of both; this fact makes it feasible (and, indeed, essential) for every physician to sort out the combination of science and "faith-healing" that can provide the greatest benefit for any single patient. My late colleague Bryant Kendrick played a critical role in my education about the role of spirituality in health and healing. Terry Matthews and Danny Leonard have enhanced my understanding of the power of religious belief through their words, and even more through their personal demonstrations that all spirituality begins with an attitude of caring toward every human being.

I am grateful to all of those who helped me track down information about Dr. Joseph McDowell, McDowell's Medical College, and McDowell's Cave. Valuable information was provided by Charles Boewe, Charles J. DeCroix, B. J. Gooch, Terri Nappier, Deb Rule, Jo Schaper, Bob Smith, Henry Sweets, and H. Dwight Weaver. I am indebted to Gretchen Sharlow and the other organizers of "Elmira 2001" who allowed me as a Mark Twain "unknown" to present my paper on Dr. McDowell at the Fourth International Conference on the State of Mark Twain Studies. The warm, supportive reception of my presentation in Elmira gave me further stimulus to continue with this book, which was still in a fledgling state at the time. My Elmira presentation is the basis of the chapter on McDowell in this book, and I particularly would like to acknowledge the support of Thomas Tenney for selecting my work on McDowell for inclusion in the *Mark Twain Journal*.

The "godfather" of this book, without question, is Kent Rasmussen. Early in the course of putting the medical world of Mark Twain onto paper, I consulted Kent to take advantage of his editing skills and his encyclopedic knowledge of everything that is Twainian. His recommendations resulted in considerable improvement of an early draft, and his ongoing input has been essential to the sculpting of the final draft. Kent's continuing encouragement and faultless guidance at every step allowed me to keep my focus and maintain the energy required to bring this project to conclusion. Victor Doyno deserves recognition for thoughtfully reviewing and substantially improving a draft of the book and giving me invaluable insights into the world of Mark Twain academics and the publishing industry. In addition, I am grateful for the innumerable occasions when Vic's editing provided me with the "right word" when I had written "almost the right word." Barbara Schmidt's review and feedback were of exceptional aid and are greatly appreciated. Gretchen Sharlow's review of the manuscript was equally useful. Robert Hirst and his colleagues at the Mark Twain Project in Berkeley have my everlasting thanks for the scholarly work they have done through the years in bringing Mark Twain to the public in a fashion that is unprecedented and unequaled; they are truly a national treasure, and this book could not exist without their work. Margaret Moore at the Mark Twain House in Hartford, Heather Wade of the Chemung County (New York) Historical Society in Elmira, and Philip Skroska at the Bernard Becker Medical Library of the Washington University School of Medicine in St. Louis have been helpful and gracious in guiding me to important resources. I am indebted to so many for all the assistance I have received. I take full responsibility, however, for any errors of fact or awkwardness of expression that remain.

The greatest credit for the creation of *Mark Twain and Medicine*, however, should go to my wife, Cathy, and to my children, Christopher and Rebecca. They have all been good sports throughout the many years of my obsession with Mark Twain. They have been delightful companions on my treks to Hannibal, Elmira, and Hartford in search of Mark Twain. They have been models of patience as I lingered behind in the places where Twain experienced the joys of boyhood, wrote his masterpieces, and shed his tears. My family understood my passion for personally owning a piece of paper that was not only touched, but actually autographed, by the very same hand that created Tom Sawyer and Huckleberry Finn. My family contributed the time and support that I needed to write this book. My name is on the title page, but in truth this book was created by Cathy and Chris and Rebecca Ober. Thanks.

Abbreviated Titles for Frequently Cited Works

A large number of Mark Twain references were used in writing this book. This creates the challenge of providing adequate designations of the sources of the numerous quotations without overloading the book with annoyingly repetitive citations. To optimize the flow of the narrative while simultaneously allowing the reader to be aware of the origin of a given quotation, the following abbreviations are used to refer to individual works of Mark Twain. This approach has been developed by the Mark Twain Project to clarify communication pertaining to Twain's work and is commonly utilized in compilations of Twain material.

Amer. Claim.	*The American Claimant.* New York: Charles L. Webster and Co., 1892.
Autob/MTA	*The Autobiography of Mark Twain.* Ed. Charles Neider. New York: Harper and Row, 1959.
Autob/NAR	*Mark Twain's Own Autobiography: The Chapters from the North American Review.* Ed. Michael J. Kiskis. Madison: University of Wisconsin Press, 1990.
Buff. Express	*Mark Twain at the "Buffalo Express."* Ed. Joseph B. McCullough and Janice McIntire-Strasburg. DeKalb: Northern Illinois University Press, 1999.
Christian Sci.	*Christian Science.* New York and London: Harper and Brothers, 1907.

Cl. of Call   *Clemens of the "Call": Mark Twain in San Francisco.*
                       Ed. Edgar M. Branch. Berkeley: University of
                       California Press, 1969.

Complete Essays   *The Complete Essays of Mark Twain.* Ed. Charles
                       Neider. Garden City, N.Y.: Doubleday and Co.,
                       1963.

Conn. Yankee   *A Connecticut Yankee in King Arthur's Court.* New
                       York: Charles L. Webster and Co., 1889.

CT-1   *Mark Twain: Collected Tales, Sketches, Speeches, and
                       Essays, 1852–1890.* Ed. Louis J. Budd. New York:
                       Library of America, 1992.

CT-2   *Mark Twain: Collected Tales, Sketches, Speeches, and
                       Essays, 1891–1910.* Ed. Louis J. Budd. New York:
                       Library of America, 1992.

ET&S-1   *Early Tales and Sketches, Volume 1, 1851–1864.*
                       Ed. Edgar Marquess Branch and Robert H. Hirst.
                       Berkeley: University of California Press, 1979.

Foll. Equat.   *Following the Equator.* Hartford: American Publish-
                       ing Co., 1897.

Gilded Age   *The Gilded Age.* With Charles Dudley Warner.
                       Hartford: American Publishing Co., 1873.

Hadleyburg   *The Man That Corrupted Hadleyburg and Other
                       Stories and Essays.* New York: Harper and Brothers,
                       1900.

HH&T   *Mark Twain's Hannibal, Huck and Tom.* Ed. Walter
                       Blair. Berkeley: University of California Press,
                       1969.

Huck Finn   *Adventures of Huckleberry Finn.* New York:
                       Charles L. Webster and Co., 1885.

Inds.   *Huck Finn and Tom Sawyer among the Indians and
                       Other Unfinished Stories.* Berkeley: University of
                       California Press, 1989.

Inn. Abroad   *The Innocents Abroad.* Hartford: American
                       Publishing Co., 1869.

Life on Miss.	*Life on the Mississippi.* Boston: James R. Osgood and Co., 1883.
Ltrs-2	*Mark Twain's Letters, Volume 2, 1867–1868.* Ed. Harriet Elinor Smith, Richard Bucci, and Lin Salamo. Berkeley: University of California Press, 1990.
Ltrs-3	*Mark Twain's Letters, Volume 3, 1869.* Ed. Victor Fischer, Michael B. Frank, and Dahlia Armon. Berkeley: University of California Press, 1992.
Ltrs-4	*Mark Twain's Letters, Volume 4, 1870–1871.* Ed. Victor Fischer, Michael B. Frank, and Lin Salamo. Berkeley: University of California Press, 1995.
Ltrs-Earth	*Letters from the Earth.* Ed. Bernard DeVoto. New York: Perennial Library, Harper and Row, 1974.
Ltrs-Howells (Sel.)	*Selected Mark Twain–Howells Letters, 1872–1910.* Ed. Frederick Anderson, William M. Gibson, and Henry Nash Smith. Cambridge: Belknap Press of Harvard University Press, 1967.
Ltrs-Love	*The Love Letters of Mark Twain.* Ed. Dixon Wecter. New York: Harper and Brothers, 1949.
Ltrs-Microfilm-1	*Microfilm Edition of Mark Twain's Manuscript Letters Now in the Mark Twain Papers, The Bancroft Library.* Ed. Anh Quynh Bui et al. 11 vols. Berkeley: Bancroft Library, 2001.
Ltrs-Microfilm-2	*Microfilm Edition of Mark Twain's Previously Unpublished Letters.* Ed. Anh Quynh Bui et al. 8 vols. Berkeley: Bancroft Library, 2001.
Ltrs/Paine	*Mark Twain's Letters.* Ed. Alfred Bigelow Paine. 2 vols. New York: Harper and Brothers, 1917.
Ltr-Pötzel	Letter to Eduard Pötzel, October 2, 1897. In Robert H. Hirst, "'Permission to Drink Anything': Mark Twain's Letters to Eduard Pötzel." *Bancroftiana* 121 (fall 2002): 10.
Ltrs-Rogers	*Mark Twain's Correspondence with Henry Huttleston Rogers, 1893–1909.* Ed. Lewis Leary. Berkeley: University of California Press, 1969.

£1m Bank-note   *The Million Pound Bank Note and Other New Stories.*
                    New York: Charles L. Webster and Co., 1893.

MTBM   *Mark Twain, Business Man.* Ed. Samuel Charles
                    Webster. Boston: Little, Brown and Co., 1946.

MTP   Mark Twain Papers. Mark Twain Project,
                    University of California, Berkeley.

MT Speaking   *Mark Twain Speaking.* Ed. Paul Fatout. Iowa City:
                    University of Iowa Press, 1976.

Mys. Stranger Mss. *Mark Twain's Mysterious Stranger Manuscripts.*
                    Ed. William M. Gibson. Berkeley: University of
                    California Press, 1969.

N&J-1   *Mark Twain's Notebooks and Journals, Volume I,*
                    1855–1873. Ed. Frederick Anderson, Michael B.
                    Frank, and Kenneth M. Sanderson. Berkeley:
                    University of California Press, 1975.

N&J-2   *Mark Twain's Notebooks and Journals, Volume II,*
                    1877–1883. Ed. Frederick Anderson, Lin Salamo,
                    and Bernard L. Stein. Berkeley: University of
                    California Press, 1975.

N&J-3   *Mark Twain's Notebooks and Journals, Volume III,*
                    1883–1891. Ed. Robert Pack Browning, Michael
                    Frank, and Lin Salamo. Berkeley: University of
                    California Press, 1979.

PW&TET   *Pudd'nhead Wilson and Those Extraordinary Twins.*
                    Hartford: American Publishing Co., 1894.

Rough. It   *Roughing It.* Hartford: American Publishing Co.,
                    1872.

SWE   *The Stolen White Elephant, Etc.* Boston: James R.
                    Osgood and Co., 1882.

$30k Bequest   *The $30,000 Bequest and Other Stories.* New York:
                    Harper and Brothers, 1906.

Tom Sawyer   *The Adventures of Tom Sawyer.* Hartford: American
                    Publishing Co., 1876.

Tramp Abroad

A Tramp Abroad. Hartford: American Publishing Co., 1880.

WIM&OPW

What Is Man? and Other Philosophical Writings. Ed. Paul Baender. Berkeley: University of California Press, 1973.

WWD&OSW

Mark Twain's Which Was the Dream? and Other Symbolic Writings of the Later Years. Ed. John S. Tuckey. Berkeley: University of California Press, 1968.

Mark Twain and Medicine

• • Introduction • •

It always puzzled me how Mark Twain could manage to have an opinion on every incident, accident, invention, or disease in the world.

—Clara Clemens, *My Father, Mark Twain*

Mark Twain had opinions on everything, and he certainly had a lot to say about American medicine.

Mark Twain, of course, was the public persona of the man who was Samuel Clemens in his private life. Attempts to make clear distinctions between the private Samuel Clemens and the public Mark Twain have been all but impossible, and the title of Justin Kaplan's Pulitzer Prize–winning biography, *Mr. Clemens and Mark Twain,* is a testimony to the dual nature of this very complex man.

Toward the end of his life, Samuel Clemens received an honorary medical degree from the New York Postgraduate Medical College, and in 1909 he took advantage of the recognition to briefly put aside his identities as Mr. Clemens and Mark Twain and speak as "Dr. Clemens."[1] It is obvious that he enjoyed presenting himself as the caricatured image of a physician.

Gentlemen and doctors:
   This is the first opportunity I have had to thank the Post Graduate for the honorary membership conferred upon me two years ago; a

distinction which is a real distinction, and which I prize as highly as anyone could. I am glad to be among my own kind tonight. I was once a sharpshooter, but now I practice a much higher and equally as deadly a profession. It wasn't so very long ago that I became a member of your cult, and for the time I've been in the business my record is one that can't be scoffed at...

When the distinction of an honorary membership in the Post Graduate College was conferred upon me, I felt it my duty to put aside other matters for a time and qualify myself for the position before beginning to practice. I have been practicing now for seven months. When I settled on my farm in Connecticut in June I found the community very thinly settled—and since I have been engaged in practice it has become more thinly settled still. This gratifies me, as indicating that I am making an impression on my community. I suppose it is the same with all of you.

...I know one thing—we've improved things ever so much up there; when we started in, seven months ago, there were lots and lots of sick people. There aren't any now. (*MT Speaking*, 631–36)

The speech he gave at that particular dinner at Delmonico's was aimed at entertaining his medical audience. It was far from the first time that "Dr. Clemens" had expressed his opinions on medical subjects, however, and many of his previous comments had not been found quite as amusing by the medical professionals of his day. Through the span of his lifetime, Clemens/Twain suffered from many ailments, pursued many methods of medical care, and made many observations (publicly as Twain, privately as Clemens) about the substance and nature of medicine as he experienced it. Some of his commentary was made by the public figure Mark Twain through his books, stories, and speeches. Other commentary of equal importance was made by the private citizen Samuel Clemens in his personal letters. The fascinating man who was first Mr. Clemens and then Mark Twain eventually developed a third entity of Dr. Clemens, thanks to the honor bestowed upon him by the New York Postgraduate Medicine School. It is not particularly important how seriously we take his honorary election into the medical profession. More crucial, I believe, is the insight that can be gained from better understanding the largely overlooked medical aspects of his life; without this knowledge, it is impossible to fully know Mark Twain.

There is no question that Samuel Clemens was an insightful political observer and social critic who described and defined his era as no other person has done before or since. He became an American icon. People

listened to every word he spoke, read every word he wrote, noticed everything he did, and even gave him credit for doing things he did not do.
For example, only Samuel Clemens could become famous for getting
sick when he was not sick: "James Ross Clemens, a cousin of mine, was
seriously ill two or three weeks ago in London, but is well now. The
report of my illness grew out of his illness; the report of my death was
an exaggeration."[2]

Clemens lived at a time when the world of medicine was splintered
into sects and fiefdoms, each one certain of its own value, and each battling the others for primacy. He had personal experience with many of
the competing medical systems of the nineteenth century; his commentaries provide a unique perspective on American medicine and the revolution in medical systems that he saw and experienced firsthand. His
personal perspective, as he expressed it in his fiction, speeches, and letters,
is as unique, insightful, and entertaining (and sometimes as disturbing)
as his commentary on any other topic that became a subject of fascination for him. His evaluation of the medical practices of his era provides a
fresh, humanistic, and personalized viewpoint of the dramatic changes
that occurred through the nineteenth century and into the first decade of
the twentieth.

This book has been written for three interrelated audiences, with three
overlapping goals in mind, creating a state of affairs that by necessity
reflects my own interests, experiences, and abilities:

(1) For the Mark Twain enthusiast, I hope to explain and clarify the
medical events and beliefs that affected so much of Sam Clemens's personal behavior and influenced so much of Mark Twain's writing. He loved
to use the imagery of medicine. He described a lake's surface as being
"small-poxed with rain-splashes" (*Ltrs/Paine*, 2:711); he wrote about de-
serted western towns that looked "as languid as a consumptive girl"
(*Rough. It*, 197); he characterized a small beat-up piano as "a clattery,
wheezy, asthmatic thing, certainly the very worst miscarriage in the way
of a piano that the world has seen," a piano so bad that "five or six
dejected and homesick ladies approached it doubtingly, gave it a single
inquiring thump, and retired with the lockjaw" (*Tramp Abroad*, 341). He
found that medical terms were useful for literary criticism: "*Deerslayer* is
not a work of art . . . in truth, it seems to me that *Deerslayer* is just simply
a literary *delirium tremens*."[3] And then there was the matter of the dis-
appointing oyster stew: "The oysters were small and could have been
mistaken for tonsils which had been removed to put a stop to throat diseases" (*WWD&OSW*, 298). The literary considerations, however, pale in

contrast to the much more substantial aspects of medicine's impact on Samuel Clemens. From an early age, Clemens came to understand that life was a battle against disease and death, and he realized that it was a battle he would ultimately lose. In the meantime, he experimented with virtually every available form of medical therapy he could find, in the hope that he could somehow gain an advantage over illness. I do not believe that the Clemens/Twain dichotomy can be fully understood without an appreciation of the great impact medical issues had on his life.

(2) For those who periodically and innocently subject themselves to the care of physicians, and for those who find themselves functioning in the role of physicians,[4] my goal is to share some of the often overlooked but extremely witty, perceptive, insightful, and not infrequently caustic medical observations of one of history's most brilliant writers. When he was pestered by an autograph seeker who asked for an entire autographed letter, Clemens took advantage of a chance to barb the medical profession: "I said writing was my trade, my bread-and-butter; I said it was not fair to ask a man to give away samples of his trade; would he ask the blacksmith for a horseshoe? would he ask the doctor for a corpse?"[5] Clemens could be as annoyed with his doctor as anyone else: "That doctor had half an idea that there is something the matter with my brain. . . . Doctors do know so little and they do charge so much for it."[6] There is much entertainment (and even more truth) to be had from reading the words written about medicine by Samuel Clemens. As George Bernard Shaw once observed, Clemens was "in very much the same position as myself. He has to put things in such a way as to make people who would otherwise hang him believe he is joking."[7]

(3) For those who might have little interest in the history of Mark Twain or in the evolution of modern medicine, the fact remains that Samuel Clemens continues to be a leading spokesman for all of humanity. He was never capable of looking at the world in exactly the same way anyone else did, and the rich record of his written words gives us an opportunity to juxtapose Clemens's world of the nineteenth century with the world of modern medicine. My hope is that this book will represent more than just another bit of interesting history about a past century. My intent is to go beyond explaining about cholera epidemics in the Mississippi valley to Twain experts and to go further than reminding medical people that Twain wrote some funny stuff about the measles (if they should ever choose to read something nonmedical again). I have structured this book so that it might give Samuel Clemens an opportunity to explain some extremely important things to all of us, in a way that only he can do. As

a practicing physician, I see three patients who will benefit most from the "art of medicine" for every one who can be helped by the "science of medicine"; human suffering can arise from many causes other than diseases of the physical body, and this fact is a recurring theme in Clemens's writing, just as it was a recurring theme in his personal life. As a medical educator, I am sometimes concerned about the difficulties that many students and physicians experience in truly understanding what it means to be a worried and distressed human. I believe that Clemens gained a wonderful comprehension of these issues, and that he still has much to tell us about ourselves, even in the twenty-first century. I think Clemens developed a tremendous amount of insight as he came to understand the fears that make us all susceptible to pursuing illogical medical therapies, and he probably figured this out before just about anyone else did. I hope that exploring these issues will help put the health, hope, and humanitarianism of Samuel Clemens (and all of the rest of us) in perspective and add value to this work beyond its factual and historical content.

Clemens's comments on medicine and physicians were complex and served a variety of purposes.[8] He used his own childhood experiences with the medical care of the American frontier (which included folk medicine, quackery, and snake-oil remedies) to add color to his fiction. Sam Clemens converted his boyhood in Hannibal into the story of Tom Sawyer. If all of the medical issues and medical references were removed from *The Adventures of Tom Sawyer*, Tom Sawyer would not have had any adventures. The opportunity to make some money by selling a cadaver to the local medical school took Injun Joe, Muff Potter, and Dr. Robinson to the local graveyard with the plan of digging up a fresh cadaver; an even newer corpse was created in the process when Injun Joe murdered Dr. Robinson. Tom and Huck observed the murder, but only because they had been independently drawn to the cemetery in pursuit of a popular folk cure for warts. In a sense, the tensions of the graveyard scene were created by the unexpected commingling of two incompatible medical systems—the boys were pulled to the cemetery by their trust in primitive medical folklore, even as the grave robbers were attracted to the same site in response to the needs of scientific medicine for anatomic study material. The clash caused by this juxtaposition of conflicting systems was *the* recurring theme of Clemens's personal medical life—mainstream medicine was always present, but it always seemed a bit flawed and always somewhat less desirable than it should have been. Traditional medicine was always tainted by the aura of Injun Joe. If doctors have to depend upon the Injun Joes of the world to rob graves for them so that they can learn something about anatomy, might it not be better to avoid traditional medical care altogether? After all, if boys can cure their warts themselves by using a dead cat in a graveyard at midnight, why should anyone employ a doctor who had to learn his craft by using a body dug out of the grave in the middle of the night?

The major medical themes in *Tom Sawyer* reflect Samuel Clemens's personal medical experience. People die, and death is never pretty—Dr. Robinson is murdered and Injun Joe starves to death in the cave. Clemens reminds us repetitively, however, that there is something worse than death—the sometimes disabling misery that is produced by *worrying about* death. Tom was so distressed by the undefined illness of Becky Thatcher that, for a while, he forgot about the murder of Dr. Robinson. It seemed that Aunt Polly's purpose in life was to worry incessantly about Tom's health, and her anxiety led her to subject him to every alternative medical therapy that she knew about in her passion to keep him well. The nineteenth century was the age of patent medicines and hydrotherapy, and these therapies are important components of the story of Tom Sawyer.

The story of Tom Sawyer has an underlying theme in which the innocence of childhood is declared to be an exalted state. It is this innocence that makes the world a desirable and pleasurable place. In such a simple world, the lack of medical knowledge is not a handicap but instead is a significant advantage that contributes quality to life. When Tom picks a pansy for his sweetheart Becky, he symbolically buttons the flower inside his jacket, near his heart—"or next to his stomach, possibly, for he was not much posted in anatomy, and not hypercritical, anyway" (*Tom Sawyer*, 37). Becky is equally innocent until she peeks at the mysterious book that is kept under lock and key by Mr. Dobbins, the schoolmaster whose "unsatisfied ambition [and] darling of his desires was, to be a doctor." As Becky picks up the book, she finds that "the title-page—Professor somebody's 'Anatomy'—carried no information to her mind," but as she looks through the book she comes "at once upon a handsomely engraved and colored frontispiece—a human figure, stark naked" (*Tom Sawyer*, 162). Some of Becky's innocence is gone. Medical knowledge can become frightening when it destroys the innocence of the learner.

Clemens's boyhood is the basis of *Tom Sawyer*, but it is also a central feature of *Adventures of Huckleberry Finn*. In both *Tom Sawyer* and *Huckleberry Finn*, Sam Clemens wrote American medical history. He skillfully blended the world of medicine into the larger picture of life in the nineteenth century, as when Huckleberry Finn describes some of the reading material that could be found in the homes of the Mississippi valley. "There was some books, too, piled up perfectly exact, on each corner of the table. One was a big family Bible full of pictures. One was . . . Dr. Gunn's Family Medicine, which told you all about what to do if a body was sick or dead" (*Huck Finn*, 137). The book Huck referred to was *Gunn's Domestic Medicine, or Poor Man's Friend, in the Hours of Affliction, Pain and Sickness.* First published in 1830, it was the leading domestic medical reference in the West, a "do-it-yourself" book, written so that the average citizen could do his own doctoring without resorting to a physician. Dr. John C. Gunn claimed that his book covered all aspects of medicine, and he assured the reader that his book was an accurate guide for any type of medical treatment or surgical procedure a person might ever need. It described how roots and herbs could be used to cure disease. Even surgical procedures such as amputations of arms and legs could be done by any man by following the simple instructions in the book, "unless he be an idiot or an absolute fool," according to Gunn. To perform an amputation, as he explained, nothing was required beyond some common household items (including a carving knife, penknife, and shoemaker's awl), and no particular skills were needed except "firmness and common dexterity." The greatest difficulty in doing an amputation was in knowing *when* to amputate, but Gunn assured the reader that even the most skilled surgeons had difficulty in making *that* determination.[9]

Clemens loved wordplay in general, and medical terminology gave him unique opportunities to have fun with language. He took advantage of the word *carbuncle* on more than one occasion. This now somewhat outdated term can refer either to a gem (specifically a garnet that has been cut *en cabochon* to optimally demonstrate the stone's color, as in Sir Arthur Conan Doyle's 1892 Sherlock Holmes story "The Blue Carbuncle") or to a large, painful, draining abscess. Clemens was prone to develop abscesses, especially when he traveled long distances by horseback, and he took advantage of the word's two meanings to generate some light comedy in *Following the Equator,* a travel book in which he recounted the details of his trip around the world. "The dictionary says a carbuncle is a kind of jewel. Humor is out of place in a dictionary" (*Foll. Equat.*, 25). Humor, of course, was *not* out of place in anything Samuel Clemens wrote. On his trip to Australia and New Zealand in 1895, Clemens bragged to reporters in Adelaide that he had smuggled a carbuncle past the customs officers. His concealed carbuncle was treated by Dr. Thomas Fitzgerald, the first Australian to be knighted for eminence in medicine. Fitzgerald's therapy included freezing and lancing the abscess, injection of opium, and a prescription for plasters, which were applied by Clemens's wife, Livy.[10] Clemens remarked, "I wish I had been born with false teeth and a false liver and false carbuncles. I should get along better" (*Foll. Equat.*, 315).

As inquisitive as he was in general, there were always some things Sam Clemens preferred *not* to know, and many of these were related to medical issues. He realized that knowledge always comes at a price, and any education that can remove some of the mystery of life is also capable of taking away some of the pleasure. When he was learning the trade of steamboat pilot on the Mississippi River, he was required to "know every trifling feature that bordered the great river as familiarly as [he] knew the letters of the alphabet." In doing so, he achieved a great accomplishment, but at a tremendous personal cost. Clemens found that, through his knowledge, he "had lost something which could never be restored . . . the grace, the beauty, the poetry had gone out of the majestic river!" (*Life on Miss.*, 119). He compared his own experiences in learning about the Mississippi River to the detailed education that is needed to become a physician. As he reflected on how his own understanding of the details of the Mississippi robbed him of his awareness of the majesty of the great river, Clemens came to suspect that a medical education might cause physicians to experience a similar loss of appreciation for the wonders of life. He suspected that a doctor's education could destroy the mystique that underlies the sense of awe most humans feel toward life. Sam Clemens understood that the magician's trick stops being magic at the moment the audience is able to see how the rabbit got into the hat, as he wrote in a letter to the *Alta California* in 1867:

> I am thankful that the good God creates us all ignorant. I am glad that when we change His plans in this regard, we have to do it at our own risk. It is a gratification to me to know that I am ignorant of art, and ignorant also of surgery. Because people who understand art find nothing in pictures but blemishes, and surgeons and anatomists see no beautiful women in all their lives, but only a ghastly stack of bones with Latin names to them, and a network of nerves and muscles and tissues inflamed by disease. The very point in a picture that fascinates me with its beauty, is to the cultured artist a monstrous crime against the laws of coloring; and the very flush that charms me in a lovely face, is, to the critical surgeon, nothing but a sign hung out to advertise a decaying lung. Accursed be all such knowledge. I want none of it.[11]

Clemens had a tendency to return to themes that were of particular importance to him, and the same concerns were still weighing on his mind two years later when he wrote a review of "Midsummer Night's Dream" for the *Buffalo Express:* "I suppose if I were a doctor I would see consumption where ignorant people only saw and admired a blush on a handsome face; and I might see a death warrant in what another man took for a beautiful complexion; and I suppose that in cases where the ignorant were charmed with what seemed a romantic languor, I would say, 'Blue mass is what she wants—the young woman's liver is out of order'" *(Buff. Express,* 96).[12]

Unlike Clemens's use of medical topics in *Tom Sawyer,* which was largely autobiographical, some of his medical writing was more that of burlesque. As with much of his writing, humor and criticism were frequently intertwined in his medical observations. Stereotypical features of physicians could be targets of Clemens's ridicule, as when he wrote about a physician's poor handwriting on a prescription in *Those Extraordinary Twins:* "Dr. Claypool laid down his pen and read the result of his labors aloud, carefully and deliberately, for the battery must be constructed on the premises by the family, and mistakes could occur; for he wrote a doctor's hand—the hand which from the beginning of time has been so disastrous to the apothecary and so profitable to the undertaker" *(PW&TET,* 411).

However, many of Clemens's humorous observations were based on real-life events he found to be anything but amusing. His observation on fictitious Dr. Claypool's poor penmanship was written in 1892, but it may have been based on an event that occurred in 1864. At that time, when Clemens was a reporter for the San Francisco *Daily Morning Call,* he reported on a jury case in which some druggists were sued for making a prescription error. Clemens's attitude was more irate than amused.

> The truth of the matter is, that in ninety-nine cases out of a hundred of these mistakes in putting up prescriptions, the whole blame lies with the prescribing physicians, who, like a majority of lawyers, and many preachers, write a most abominable scrawl, which might be deciphered by a dozen experts as many different ways, and each one sustain his version by the manuscript.... It would be a good thing for the world at large, however unprofessional it might be, if medical men were required by law to write out in full the ingredients named in their prescriptions. Let them adhere to the Latin, or Fejee, if they choose, but discard abbreviations, and form their letters as if they had been to school

one day in their lives, so as to avoid the possibility of mistakes on that account. (*Cl. of Call*, 192–93)

In general, Clemens respected and trusted individual physicians, especially for their support, solace, and comfort, although his aphorisms sometimes contained a bit of a sting: "How welcome is the face of the doctor, in the time of uncertainty when you can't tell for sure just where you are going to."[13] Other comments about doctors expressed a sincere appreciation for acts of kindness and caring, as evidenced in an 1886 letter to his mother: "Don't you suppose I remember gratefully how tender the doctor was with Jean when she hurt her arm, and how quickly he got the pain out of the hurt, whereas I supposed it was going to last at least an hour? No, I don't forget some things as easily as I do others" (*Ltrs/Paine*, 2:470–71).

In 1873, Clemens's wife, Olivia, needed medical attention while the Clemenses were visiting Edinburgh. Clemens sought out a well-known physician and the author of *Rab and His Friends*, Dr. John Brown, who at that time was a total stranger to Clemens. A close friendship developed between Clemens and the man with the "noble and beautiful soul" who was "beloved by everybody in Scotland." Clemens and his family accompanied Brown on his daily rounds for a period of six weeks. The Clemenses would bring books to read while Brown checked on his patients; Brown routinely provided a basket of grapes for Clemens and his family. Clemens was amused by a remark that Dr. Brown made the first time he stepped out of his carriage to visit a patient: "Entertain yourselves while I go in here and reduce the population." As far as Samuel Clemens was concerned, "Dr. John" was "the loveliest creature in the world" (*Autob/MTA*, 194–97).

As much as he respected individual physicians, however, Sam Clemens could be quite cynical about medical practitioners collectively, especially when they were ostentatious, self-serving, or dishonest. He had no use for any doctor whose level of arrogance eclipsed his level of competence. He was not reticent about declaring his disgust for the type of physician who "looms vague and vast in the solemn garb of an awful 'respectability,'—and away up on top of that, he piles the impressive grandeur of a Physician's Diploma. Oh, this fine old 'respectable' dodge— how many trusting communities have I seen it bring to grief!" (*Buff. Express*, 162).

Clemens was always interested in politics, too, and this included the politics of medicine. By the time of his birth in 1835, the political forces

This photograph of Samuel and Livy Clemens with Dr. John Brown was taken in Edinburgh in August or September 1873. Family friend Clara Spaulding is seated at the left, holding Clemens's daughter Susy. Courtesy of the Mark Twain House, Hartford, Connecticut.

of Jacksonian democracy had created an era of unregulated medical practice in the United States; licensure laws were virtually nonexistent, and any citizen who wished to do so was allowed to practice medicine. Regular ("allopathic") medicine was in competition with two dozen or more other sects, including homeopathic medicine, botanical medicine, and hydropathic medicine. Although allopathy presented itself as the "scientific" branch of medicine and proclaimed the other sects to be "quackery," allopathy was a toxic system with no proven benefit over its competitors. Clemens criticized every system of health care, but he also believed that some salutary features could be found in most of the medical movements of the day. He had a love-hate relationship with all of the medical systems of his era, according to his friend and biographer William Dean Howells.

> An interesting phase of his psychology in this business was not only his admiration for the masterly policy of the Christian Science hierarchy, but his willingness to allow the miracles of its healers to be tried on his friends and family, if they wished it. He had a tender heart for the whole generation of empirics, as well as the newer sorts of scientians, but he seemed to base his faith in them largely upon the failure of the regulars rather than upon their own successes, which also he believed in. He was recurrently, but not insistently, desirous that you should try their strange magics when you were going to try the familiar medicines.[14]

Life had a way of playing cruel jokes on Sam Clemens. He loved the wordplay of medicine. In *The American Claimant* (published in 1892) he presented the burlesque possibility that a physician might use medical terminology as a source for the names of his children.[15] "Isn't Doctor Snodgrass your father, and isn't Zylobalsamum your brother... and isn't your name Spinal Meningitis, and isn't your father a doctor and an idiot, like all the family for generations, and doesn't he name all his children after poisons and pestilences and abnormal anatomical eccentricities of the human body?" (*Amer. Claim.*, 264–65). In 1896, Clemens's older daughter, Susy, died of meningitis at the age of twenty-four. He blamed her death on the incompetence of her doctors, even though in truth there was no available treatment that could have saved her. His distress was still obvious in a letter he wrote to Henry Rogers in 1900. "I am not afraid of doctors in ordinary or trifling ailments, but in a serious case I should not allow any one to persuade me to call one. Our Susy died of cerebrospinal menengitis—and as soon as it manifested itself, her physicians gave her up. It was assassination through ignorance" (*Ltrs-Rogers*, 425–26). For Samuel Clemens, the "Spinal Meningitis" that had started as a clever joke in 1892 returned four years later to become one of the most devastating tragedies of his life.

Through the years, Clemens found that the mainstream medical care system usually failed to help him and his family in the ways he had hoped. His repeated failures in gaining the desired medical outcomes from traditional medicine seemed to kindle his enthusiasm for pursuing the alternative care approaches of his era. As a result, he exposed himself and his family to many of the numerous medical care systems available to him, and he clearly enjoyed having the freedom to do so. As biographer Justin Kaplan notes, Clemens was "something of a faddist, and he looked for miraculous cures through hydrotherapy, osteopathic manipulation, electric treatments, mind cure and mind science, health foods, and such homemade nostra as a daily shampoo with strong soap to keep his hair from falling out."[16]

What was the driving force behind all this sampling of medical offerings? Samuel Clemens was a typical citizen of America in the nineteenth century, constantly surrounded by reminders of illness and death. The proximity of illness and the hovering specter of death were steadfast features of the time. Clemens, the most famous man of his era, hoped to beat the system. He had no intent of passively allowing others to decide his medical care—he believed he was perfectly capable of comparing the options and choosing the system that was best for him. He opposed restriction of medical care choices, and he accused physicians of having ulterior motives whenever they tried to block their competitors from getting licensure: "The physicians think they are moved by regard for the best interests of the public. Isn't there a little touch of self-interest back of it all? . . . The objection is, people are curing people without a license and you are afraid it will bust up business. You ought to compromise so you can all get a chance at these people around here" (*MT Speaking*, 387–88). To his disappointment, he eventually discovered that the alternative treatments he supported so strongly were no better than the methods of traditional practitioners. Each promising new system he tried turned out to be another version of fool's gold.

Clemens's approach to medical care was eclectic, but he was unquestionably an advocate of the scientific advances that were being made by traditional medicine. His private beliefs, however, did not always coincide with his public commentary. The private observations of Samuel Clemens sometimes clashed with the public words of Mark Twain. The complexity of his medical opinions is illustrated in the way that Clemens/ Twain dealt with the topic of vaccination. In 1871, in a letter that was obviously personal in nature, Samuel Clemens encouraged his wife, Livy, to get vaccinated against smallpox.

Get vaccinated—*right away*—no matter if you were vaccinated 6 months ago—the theory is, *keep* doing it—for if it *takes* it shows you *needed* it—& if it don't take it is *proof* that you did *not* need it—but the only safety is to apply the test, once a year. Small pox is everywhere—doctors think it will become an epidemic. Here it is $25 fine if you are not vaccinated within the next 10 days. Mine takes splendidly—arm right sore. Attend to this, my child. (*Ltrs-4*, 521)

In 1892, Samuel Clemens wrote a personal letter to his sister-in-law Susan Crane in which the subject of vaccination came up again, but not in the solicitous manner of his letter to Livy. In the letter to Susan Crane, vaccination was of interest only because it set up a joke, and the personal comments of Sam Clemens resembled the kind of statement that might be made publicly by Mark Twain: "The Paris Herald has created a public interest by inoculating one of its correspondents with cholera. A man said yesterday he wished to God they would inoculate *all* of them. Yes, the interest is quite general and strong, and much hope is felt" (*Ltrs/Paine*, 2:569).

In a far more serious tone, Clemens (writing as pure Mark Twain) found it useful to use the subject of vaccination to demonstrate the duplicity of American physicians in dealing with Chinese immigrants. In his role as a champion of the unempowered and disenfranchised, Clemens was aware that the limitations in knowledge, sophistication, and financial resources of recent immigrants made them potential victims of a medical care system that could create obstacles as frustrating and baffling as those produced by any other bureaucratic structure. Physicians were using a universal requirement for vaccination to take advantage of immigrants (including those who did not need to be vaccinated) while charging exorbitant fees. Clemens protested this activity in "Goldsmith's Friend Abroad Again," a series of fictional letters from a recent Chinese immigrant to a friend at home.

[H]e said, wait a minute—I must be vaccinated to prevent my taking the small-pox. I smiled and said I had already had the small-pox, as he could see by the marks, and so I need not wait to be "vaccinated," as he called it. But he said it was the law, and I must be vaccinated anyhow. The doctor would never let me pass, for the law obliged him to vaccinate all Chinamen and charge them *ten dollars apiece* for it, and I might be sure that no doctor who would be the servant of that law would let a fee slip through his fingers to accommodate any absurd fool who had seen fit to have the disease in some other country. And

presently the doctor came and did his work and took my last penny—
my ten dollars which were the hard savings of nearly a year and a half
of labor and privation. Ah, if the lawmakers had only known there
were plenty of doctors in the city glad of a chance to vaccinate people
for a dollar or two, they would never have put the price up so high
against a poor friendless Irish, or Italian, or Chinese pauper fleeing to
the good land to escape hunger and hard times.[17]

The story of Samuel Clemens and his pursuit of the best available medical care is one that merits telling. It is, in part, the complex story of the
personal medical experiences of a quintessential American who lived
when disease and death came early—and often without warning. More
important, it is also a story of personal discovery in which Clemens came
to understand the importance of hope, trust, and belief in the healing
process. In so doing, he discovered the differences between the science
of medicine (which was very rudimentary in his day) and the art of medicine (which is ultimately at the foundation of the healing process). He
understood the role of the interaction between doctor and patient in the
healing process. He was willing to make fun of the behavior of haughty
physicians whose interest in showing off their erudition seemed to super-
sede any desire to help their patients, such as the fictitious doctor in
Those Extraordinary Twins who was "by long odds the most learned physician in the town, and quite well aware of it," the type of doctor who
"liked to show off when he had an audience" by using the gibberish of
medical jargon:

> Without going too much into detail, madam—for you would probably
> not understand it anyway—I concede that great care is going to be
> necessary here; otherwise exudation of the aesophagus is nearly sure
> to ensue, and this will be followed by ossification and extradition of
> the maxillaris superioris, which must decompose the granular surfaces
> of the great infusorial ganglionic system, thus obstructing the action of
> the posterior varioloid arteries and precipitating compound strangulated
> sorosis of the valvular tissues, and ending unavoidably in the disper-
> sion and combustion of the marsupial fluxes and the consequent embro-
> cation of the bicuspid populo redax referendum rotulorum. (*PW&TET*,
> 407–9)

This is a nonsensical statement that contains fabricated words and made-
up processes, vaguely medical-sounding but meaningless. Considering
that *Those Extraordinary Twins* was first published as an add-on to *The*

Tragedy of Pudd'nhead Wilson under the title *The Comedy of Those Extraordinary Twins,* the preceding quotation might be dismissed as an extended "one-liner" that Clemens wrote in order to get an easy laugh by caricaturing the language of the medical profession. He was not above doing such a thing.

However, there was far more to Samuel Clemens than his skill in writing quips. As was the case with many of his jokes, a far more serious concern was present just below the surface. Clemens understood that physicians were able to view a human being in a fashion that was as coldly dispassionate and mechanistic as the way he had learned to visualize the currents and channels of the Mississippi River. He also knew that a doctor's words had immense impact on the patient's reaction to illness and should be chosen carefully because of their power. He was repulsed by the thought that emotions such as grief and sadness could be trivialized by reducing them to simple mechanical processes.

> There are nerves and muscles in our frames whose functions and whose methods of working it seems a sort of sacrilege to describe by cold physiological names and surgical technicalities.... Fancy a surgeon, with his nippers lifting tendons, muscles, and such things into view, out of the complex machinery of a corpse, and observing, "Now this little nerve quivers—the vibration is imparted to this muscle—from here it is passed to this fibrous substance; here its ingredients are separated by the chemical action of the blood—one part goes to the heart and thrills it with what is popularly termed emotion, another part follows this nerve to the brain and communicates intelligence of a startling character—the third part glides along this passage and touches the spring connected with the fluid receptacles that lie in the rear of the eye. Thus, by this simple and beautiful process, the party is informed that his mother is dead, and he weeps." (*Inn. Abroad,* 301)

Clemens needed just a single word to describe his reaction to anyone who could view a fellow human being in such an impersonal, detached, and mechanistic style: "Horrible!" (*Inn. Abroad,* 301).[18] Few things bothered him more than a person devoid of a sense of humanity. For Clemens, such a person was nothing more than an emotionless machine whose "heart was merely a pump and had no other function" (*Autob/MTA,* 125).

Clemens had a knack for identifying concerns that are timeless. His nineteenth-century complaints about the impersonal and technical orientation of physicians and the depersonalization of health care have been repeated innumerable times by patients of the twentieth and twenty-first centuries. The tone of Clemens's distress resonates in the ongoing criticism that modern medicine is too often practiced in "biological garages where dysfunctional human parts are repaired or replaced."[19] The sophisticated technology of current medical science is extremely seductive, and it becomes easy for a doctor to look at a patient as simply "a bundle of biological matter, a collection of tissues to be rolled in and out of treatment, x-ray, and operating rooms." The greatest shortcoming of modern medicine, some would say, may arise from the fact that "a doctor needs to know nothing about the soul wrapped in those tissues."[20] Clemens's own message is that a physician needs to be as interested in a patient's soul as in its wrappings; this may be the most important gift Clemens has left for the doctors and the patients of the twenty-first century.

Samuel Clemens had a lot to report about illness, health, and the human condition. Even though he encountered the same diseases as everyone else, and even though he suffered from the same phobias, anxieties, illnesses, and fear of death as his contemporaries, he had a better imagination and a greater insight into the human condition than most. He came to understand (far better than most humans—including doctors—*ever* can understand) that humans can suffer from both diseases and illnesses, and that diseases and illnesses are entirely different things.[21] Diseases are disorders of the tissues that arise from within the physical body. Diseases have biological origins that influence the scope, severity, and virulence of the sickness that results. Diseases are not the same things as illnesses, which are the conditions that arise from within the soul. Illnesses are commonly mistaken for diseases, even though illnesses are far less biological in their origins. Instead, illnesses are the afflictions of humanity that are created by the attitudes, beliefs, and expectations of those who suffer from them. Illnesses are influenced by the norms of the society in which they arise.[22] Illnesses and diseases require entirely different kinds of therapy.

From an early age, Clemens understood that "disease" and "illness" are totally different entities—he knew that disease was going to kill him someday, but it was illness that was the cause of most of the suffering he experienced throughout his lifetime. This distinction between the diseases of the body and the illnesses of the spirit was Samuel Clemens's major medical discovery. It is the recurring theme of his medical writing.

As Samuel Clemens came to learn, diseases and illnesses often travel together; they are intertwined, and it is not always easy to distinguish between the two. Diseases and illnesses both cause immense suffering, but they demand different treatments. Diseases are treated with drugs, bandages, splints, radiation, and surgery (which are the therapies of physicians). Such treatments do not work well for illnesses. The effective treatment of illness must be based on compassion and caring and, most important, hope. These powerful therapeutic agents exert their effects on the spirit, not the body, and they are far more difficult than drugs to dose correctly (they cannot be weighed out precisely as milligrams of an active agent on any scientific scale). Some doctors find it as easy to provide this type of support as it is to write a prescription or plan an operation. Others are much less comfortable in dealing with illness than with disease (and so they may not even make an attempt to do so).

Clemens came to understand that alternative medical practitioners excel in treating illnesses (but not diseases). He came to realize that there would always be a role for alternative medicine (because illnesses are more common than diseases). Clemens saw that alternative medical sects rose and fell in popularity with changing perceptions of the cause of illness. Although he lived in a time when most diseases were untreatable, Clemens recognized that the alleviation of human suffering was still possible. He was a medical eclectic who was usually willing to try any method that seemed to offer hope, even if it could not offer cure. He questioned the utility of patent medicines, hydrotherapy, electrotherapy, and faith healing, but he also saw that they could be successful in treating many maladies.

Clemens ultimately concluded that the ability to give hope to the sufferer was the most important thing a doctor could offer a patient. In his book *Christian Science,* he wrote that "there is a mightier benefaction than the healing of the body, and that is the healing of the spirit" (*Christian Sci.,* 268). He also knew that there was more than one way to heal the spirit. Sometimes nothing helped more than having a self-depreciating sense of humor, as Clemens discovered in 1882 when his household was overtaken by a series of infections with the dread scarlet fever: "at the last moment the baby was seized with scarlet fever. . . . A couple of days later, the eldest child was taken down with so fierce a fever that she was soon delirious—not scarlet fever, however. Next, I myself was stretched on the bed with three diseases at once, and all of them fatal. But I never did care for fatal diseases if I could only have privacy and room to express myself concerning them" (*Ltrs/Paine,* 1:422).

And express himself he did. This book relies on the many experiences and observations of Samuel Clemens that reflect on the nature of medicine and medical care. By necessity, the contents are short of encyclopedic in their scope. It is impossible to read or reread any of Clemens's writing without coming across examples of material that could have (and perhaps *should* have) been included in this volume. Undoubtedly, Clemens wrote some wonderful passages that have simply been overlooked. Other observations and descriptions were not included in order to avoid redundancy, consistent with a principle that Clemens himself proclaimed in a letter to William D. Howells: "What do you mean? Relieve a screed that is too light & rollicking, by adding some more of the same sort to its company? If you had a patient who was already suffering with the colic, would it help matters any to drive a nail in his foot & give him the lockjaw?"[23]

The story of Samuel Clemens and medicine is the story of the fear, frustration, and futility of all humanity in its battle against untreatable disease and inescapable death. Clemens knew about the value of a sense of humor, and in *Tom Sawyer* he wrote about the health benefits that can come from having a good laugh: "Such a laugh was money in a man's pocket, because it cut down on the doctor's bills like everything" (*Tom Sawyer*, 230). More important, he discovered the role of hope and caring and compassion in the treatment of illness. Clemens understood that healing the spirit can be as important as healing the body. Through the experiences of his lifetime, he came to understand why alternative medicine sects and ministers and "best friends" may do a better job than traditionally trained physicians in alleviating some types of suffering, and he jotted into his personal notebook a conclusion that encapsulated his view of the entire process of healing: "The physician's is the highest & the worthiest of all occupations—or would be, if human nature did not make superstitions and priests necessary" (*N&J-2*, 500).

Section I ●   ●

LIFE IS SHORT...

Life is short and Art is long;
the Occasion fleeting, Experience fallacious,
and Judgment difficult.

—Hippocrates

The ancient physician Hippocrates encapsulated the challenges of medical practice into a few well-chosen words. First of all, Life is short. Too short. Life is short for the patient. Life is also short for the physician, and especially for the physician who strives to become skilled in his Art, which is the Art of Medicine. It is the Art (if applied wisely) that guides the physician to do what is best for the patient. But the Art is never clear. Amorphous and nebulous, the Art is an accumulation of incomplete knowledge, inexact skills, unpredictable attitudes, and inconsistent experiences. Life is short, and the Art is too long (and too complicated and too uncertain); no individual can fully grasp and understand the Art in the time allotted to a single life. Perhaps, if a physician were permitted to live long enough, he might acquire all the knowledge and skills needed to practice the Art in a satisfactory fashion. But it can never happen. Because Life is always too short. And, when Life is short, the windows of opportunity can close faster than they are opened, and any occasion to help seems to disappear before it can be recognized. Because Life is short, all experience is limited and incomplete and deceptive. It is no surprise that experience is fallacious. And judgment is difficult, always. But Hippocrates' first observation remains the dominant principle: Life is short. This simple fact became Samuel Clemens's first lesson about Life, and was the lesson that influenced all the other lessons that were to follow.

1

A Sickly, Precarious, Tiresome, and Uncertain Child

The day was excessively warm, and my comrade was an invalid; consequently we travelled slowly, and conversed about distressing diseases and such other matters as I thought would be likely to interest a sick man and make him feel cheerful. Instead of commenting on the mild scenery we found on the route, we spoke of the ravages of the cholera in the happy days of our boyhood; instead of talking about the warm weather, we revelled in bilious fever reminiscences; instead of boasting of the extraordinary swiftness of our horse, as most persons similarly situated would have done, we chatted gaily of consumption; and when we caught a glimpse of long white lines of waves rolling in silently upon the distant shore, our hearts were gladdened and our stomachs turned by fond memories of sea-sickness. It was a nice comfortable journey, and I could not have enjoyed it more if I had been sick myself.

—Mark Twain, "Concerning the Answer to that Conundrum"

Samuel Clemens was a child of the American frontier, born in 1835 in a small Missouri village with the unlikely name of Florida. As with all biological occurrences, his singular birth was the culmination of an infinite number of preceding events, each one triggered in turn by processes that were equally unpredictable (if not entirely random) in their origins. The creation of Samuel Clemens depended upon the unique blending of the chromosomes needed to create his distinctive being; the potential variations and permutations of human genetic material are overwhelming, and the odds were heavily weighted against the possibility that Samuel Clemens would ever exist. Even when the laws of chance permitted the appearance of Samuel Clemens, his birth was only an infinitesimally small element of a far grander process with a behavior that was just as biological as the forces that led to his existence—the westward movement of the United States. America's advancing frontier was the exploring edge of a living, mobile, amoeboid organism. In its quest to find life-maintaining sustenance, the young nation advanced across the Mississippi River. Along the way, its vital force ingested any nutrients it needed in order to maintain its high level of energy. The parents of Mark Twain were among those who were sucked into its cytoplasm and carried in the westward flow across the Mississippi. Change was the only thing that was a constant in such an organic environment. Unrelenting challenges arose every minute. Nothing was stable, birth was risky, and survival from one day to the next was a chancy proposition.

Disease and death were daily truths for the settlers of the western frontier, and, in the perverse way of nature, children were particularly susceptible. The *Hannibal Gazette* of June 3, 1847, noted that 25 percent of children in that era were expected to die before their first birthday, and 50 percent would be in their graves by the age of twenty-one. No one was more aware of the precarious nature of life than John Marshall Clemens and Jane Lampton Clemens, the couple who had been chosen by the fates to become the parents of Mark Twain. The medical luck of the Clemens family was no better and no worse than that of any other family, as they saw three of their first five children (they eventually had seven) die before reaching the age of eleven. When the sixth child—Samuel Langhorne Clemens—was born in 1835, this newest addition to the family appeared to be an outstanding candidate for becoming one more early death statistic. Sam Clemens was born prematurely—scrawny, sickly, and puny, he appeared to be a likely loser in the game known as "survival of the fittest," the type of runt who had little chance to make it out of childhood. Samuel Clemens reported that he was so ill at the age of seven that he came "so near going to heaven," although the specific nature of his illness at that time is unknown. No one was ever surprised when he was sick, since it was such a common event; it seemed to be generally accepted that he would be numbered among the half of the population that would not survive to the age of twenty-one. In a fragment of the dictation for his autobiography, he described the effects of one of his childhood illnesses on his family: "I had begun to die; the family were grouped for the function; they were familiar with it; so was I." In fact, Clemens quipped, family members were so accustomed to bedside vigils for him that it was sometimes difficult for them to maintain their attentiveness, and "they often went to sleep when I was dying."[1]

By some miracle, young Sam Clemens managed to beat the odds, and he survived through childhood and well beyond. Even so, he could never escape from being pummeled regularly by inescapable reminders of the fragility of life. He turned out to be a survivor, but he came to know of many others who were not, and those who were closest to him seemed to be the most susceptible to early death. There was the brother he never knew, Pleasant Hannibal Clemens, whose earthly existence lasted only a brief three months in 1825. Then, even before Sam Clemens could make it to his own fourth birthday, he saw "bilious fever" take away the life of Margaret L. Clemens, the sister who was his elder by five years. Two years after her death, six-year-old Sam suffered another blow when a brief illness led to the death of his brother Benjamin, his close comrade and his senior by a mere three years. Sam's younger brother Henry survived his early childhood, only to die at age twenty from burns he received from an explosion of a steamboat. Henry's death took the tragedy of death and personal loss to an even higher level for Sam Clemens. Sam was Henry's role model, and Henry's death by burning was the indirect result of his following Sam into a steamboat career on the Mississippi River. It was painful enough for Sam to see family members die before their time, but such distress did not even begin to compare to the overwhelming anguish that arose from the thought that he may have been personally responsible for the death of a loved one. Henry's death would not be the last time guilt and self-recrimination would play major roles in the way Sam Clemens reacted to the illnesses of those he loved. Watching the deaths of those closest to him, one by one, was more anguish than he could bear, and at some point he made a critical decision. He would no longer passively surrender those closest to him to disease. Family members might get sick, and they might die, but it would not be because he did not try to do *something* for them.

In later years, as Sam Clemens evolved into Mark Twain, he became an expert at self-depreciating humor, and he turned his own shaky beginnings into a retrospective joke upon himself. In an anecdote in his *Autobiography,* he recounted a conversation with his mother that may or may not have actually occurred:

I was always told that I was a sickly and precarious and tiresome
and uncertain child, and lived mainly on allopathic medicines during
the first seven years of my life. I asked my mother about this, in her
old age—she was in her 88th year—and said:
"I suppose that during all that time you were uneasy about me?"
"Yes, the whole time."
"Afraid I wouldn't live?"
After a reflective pause—ostensibly to think out the facts—
"No—afraid you would."
It sounds like plagiarism but it probably wasn't. (*Autob/NAR*, 119)

In truth, Jane Clemens had seen a lot of death, and there can be no
doubt that she *was* fearful that Sam would not live. In fact, so was he. If
Sam Clemens had learned any lesson in the early years of his existence,
he had seen that life was tenuous and fragile, and it could come to an
abrupt and unpleasant end with little warning. If the deaths of his siblings had not already made the precariousness of life obvious enough
for Sam Clemens, the lesson was painfully reinforced at the age of eleven
by the death of his father, John Marshall Clemens. Of the many factors
that would come to influence Samuel Clemens's attitudes toward life and
health and medicine, none were more important than the relationship of
young Sam Clemens to each of his parents and the formative influences
of their distinctly different personalities, philosophies, and attitudes.

Whether or not the quoted conversation between Sam Clemens and
his mother actually occurred is not as important as the picture of Jane
Clemens that is provided by the sketch. Jane Clemens was a woman of
humor and wit and open-mindedness. Her impact on her famous son is
best understood from the perspective of her dramatic contrast to his father, a humorless, dour, inflexible, and unloving man. Clemens's parents
lived at opposite emotional poles, and Jane Clemens was everything that
her husband was not. John Marshall Clemens was traditional and conservative in his roles as storekeeper, businessman, and judge. As a father
he could also be harsh and humorless, a man to fear and loathe. A man
who rarely smiled and never laughed, he was "sternly and irreproach-
ably moral."[2] In striking contrast, Jane Lampton Clemens was warm,
kind, and humanistic. She was her husband's counterbalance—"nontraditional," soft and warmhearted, with a twinkle in her eye and kindness in her heart.

John Marshall Clemens was serious and straitlaced, a lawyer, a judge,
a storekeeper, and a businessman who never reached the level of success

he worked to achieve. John Clemens had few close friends, and those who were closest to him happened to be physicians. Contact with these practitioners probably provided Sam with his first exposures to the world of "traditional" medical practice. These medical acquaintances were as traditional and conservative in attitude as John Clemens himself, and unlikely to be seen as positive images by a young boy in frontier Missouri.

Dr. William Peake was one of John Marshall Clemens's few close friends, and he was considered to be a man of some considerable influence in his community.[3] It does not seem likely, however, that Peake had any significant impact on young Sam Clemens's attitudes about medicine. Clemens remembered him more as a "courtly gentleman of the old school" than as a physician. Peake had been born around 1775, and when Clemens later reminisced about Hannibal personalities of the 1840s, his chief memory of the distinguished physician was that "Peake was very old." The doctor was also very old-fashioned in his style; Clemens observed that Peake "wore high stock, pigtail and up to '40, still wore kneebreeches and buckle-shoes" (*Inds.*, 104). Peake was probably the model for Dr. Stevens, a character in the unfinished sketch "Indiantown," written around 1899. Stevens was one of the "gray gentlemen of the old school" who "still wore queues tied with a bow of black ribbon, broad hats, formidable 'stocks,' broadcloth coats with square and ample tails, wrist-ruffles, bosom-ruffles, black gaiters to the knee, low shoes with silver buckles; and they carried gold-headed canes and took snuff, and when surprised said 'God bless my soul, sir!'" (*WWD&OSW*, 155–56).

Dr. Hugh Meredith (1806–1864) was the Clemens family physician and the man who had the greatest impact on young Sam's impressions of the medical profession. Like Dr. Peake, Dr. Meredith was numbered among the few personal friends of the Clemens family, and he was without doubt the closest business ally of John Marshall Clemens. Meredith, a Pennsylvania native and ex-sailor, was not only an important member of the Clemenses' limited social circle, but (more important for Samuel Clemens's developing understanding of the medical profession) he was also their medical doctor in both Florida and Hannibal. Samuel Clemens remembered him as "that gruff old bass-voiced sailor-man, Doctor Meredith, our family physician."[4]

John Clemens and Dr. Hugh Meredith were closely linked through a series of investments and financial enterprises. The two were involved in numerous unsuccessful projects in the town of Florida—their failures included their attempts to develop a navigation company, a railroad, and an academy. Undaunted by their failures, Meredith accompanied the Clemenses when they moved from Florida to Hannibal in 1839, a move necessitated by the financial problems of John Clemens. In Hannibal, Meredith continued to work on civic improvements with John Clemens (in 1843, they founded the Hannibal Library Institute, which consisted of a modest book collection housed in Dr. Meredith's second-floor office).[5] Samuel Clemens later suggested, tongue in cheek, that the doctor's move to Hannibal had nothing to do with the business relationship between Meredith and his father. Instead, Clemens proposed, his own recurring childhood illnesses were such a reliable source of income for Dr. Meredith that the physician "probably removed from the hamlet of Florida to the village of Hannibal about the same time that we did, in order to keep my custom."[6]

Dr. Meredith's medical partner in Florida was Dr. Thomas Jefferson Chowning, who, at the age of twenty-six, had delivered the premature Sam Clemens.[7] If Clemens can be believed, Meredith and Chowning deserve to be memorialized for the development of what may have been the first prepaid health insurance plan in the United States. By Clemens's description, this innovative approach for the financing of health care expenses (destined to be reborn a century later as the standard method for Americans to pay for their medical treatment) was the invention of this pair of country doctors in the village of Florida, Missouri. (Perhaps the business mind of Meredith was responsible for this invention.) More important, Meredith and Chowning provided Samuel Clemens with his first exposure to allopathic medicine, which was often referred to as the medicine of "heroic measures" because of its aggressive approaches to treatment. Allopathy was the traditional medical practice of his day, the precursor of today's mainstream medical practice, and the far from perfect standard by which Clemens eventually measured all health care systems.

> I remember two of the Florida doctors, Chowning and Meredith. They not only tended an entire family for $25 a year, but furnished the medicines themselves. Good measure, too. Only the largest persons could hold a whole dose. Castor-oil was the principal beverage. The dose was half a dipperful, with half a dipperful of New Orleans molasses added to help it down and make it taste good, which it never did. The next standby was calomel; the next, rhubarb; and the next, jalap. Then they bled the patient, and put mustard-plasters on him. It was a dreadful system, and yet the death-rate was not heavy. The calomel was nearly sure to salivate the patient and cost him some of his teeth. There were no dentists. When teeth became touched with decay or were otherwise

ailing, the doctor knew of but one thing to do: he fetched his tongs and dragged them out. If the jaw remained, it was not his fault. (*Autob/ NAR*, 118)

Although this description of the medical treatments of Clemens's youth carries a ring of exaggeration and embellishment that might suggest it is one of his "tall tales," it is actually a fairly accurate representation of the allopathic medicine that he knew as a child. Allopathy was the mainstream medical practice available to all of the citizens of nineteenth-century America. The therapy of the allopathic doctor was usually harsh, unpleasant, and toxic, and every bit as noxious as Clemens's description suggests. Although these severe treatments were administered in good faith by caring doctors with the intent of helping their patients, they commonly created more health problems than they solved. By doing so, allopathic treatment created a receptive environment for the development of a number of competing alternative medical systems, many of which would be sought by Samuel Clemens in his quest for medical certainty in a world of uncertainty. None of the other options was intrinsically better than allopathy, and Samuel Clemens's exploration of complementary medical sects did not result in any lasting benefit for him or his family. His medical "experiments" did, however, give him considerable insight into the human condition, the meaning of health and disease, and the influence of a person's belief system on the quality of life. None of this would have come about if nineteenth-century allopathic medicine had been less caustic.

2

Allopathic Medicine

Taking Heroic Measures

We had a good doctor, one of them old fashioned industrious kind that don't go fooling around waiting for a sickness to show up and call game and start fair, but gets in ahead, and bleeds you at one end and blisters you at the other, and gives you a dipperful of castor oil and another one of hot salt water with mustard in it, and so gets all your machinery agoing at once, and then sets down with nothing on his mind and plans out the way to handle the case.

—Mark Twain, "Tom Sawyer's Conspiracy"

The allopathic medical practices of the nineteenth century cannot be comprehended without some recognition of the primary challenge faced by practitioners such as Dr. Hugh Meredith. Simply stated, Meredith and his contemporaries did not have any real understanding of the nature or basis of any of the disease processes they encountered. The paradigm of medical practice of that era did not even vaguely resemble medicine of today. There was no "science" in medical science. Treatments were empirical, trial and error, hit or miss. There were no underlying principles to guide therapy. There was no awareness that specific diseases were the result of defined biological processes such as bacterial infections, hormone deficiencies, tissue trauma, chromosomal abnormalities, or immunological disorders. Medical practice was still very much in its dark ages. Medicine had yet to mature to a science that was capable of correlating disease processes with their underlying patho-logical causes. Instead, the medical system of the age employed very generalized theories of total body dysfunction to account for every type of illness.

By the concepts of the day, health and disease were not discrete and well-defined opposites; instead, relative degrees of healthiness and sick-liness coexisted in a treacherously shifting state of unsteady balance. A Cincinnati practitioner of 1848 wrote that "disease is not an entity, or real existence, but is only the organic and functional forces, or powers of life, modified by perversion of activity."[1] The medical condition of every person was always nebulous, slippery, and susceptible to unexpected change for the worse, reflecting the interactions between each person's own constitutional makeup and all of the antagonistic forces of the envi-ronment that continually threatened physiological stability. An important underlying concept was that no body part is truly independent of any other—local and systemic diseases were one and the same, and health and disease were features of the entire organism.

With this fuzzy conceptualization of the cause of disease, it is obvious that therapeutic interventions did not develop from thoughtful experi-mentation in physiology, pathology, and pharmacology. Instead, the treat-ment of disease was based on a system of beliefs and expectations that was centered around emotions, philosophies, individual status, hopes, desires, and a variety of cultural factors. The interactions between patient and healer reflected conventionalized social rituals that had evolved over time. The only requirement was for both parties to share consistent and compatible (but not necessarily identical) systems for explaining what life and health were all about.[2]

No one expected to have prolonged intervals of good health. Every sin-gle daily experience was capable of having some effect on health, and po-tentially unsettling and destabilizing events ran rampant in the life of the average human. As Charles E. Rosenberg noted in a review of nineteenth-century medical practice, "The model of the body and of health and dis-ease ... was all-inclusive, antireductionist—capable of incorporating every aspect of man's life in explaining his physical condition." Events such as teething, puberty, menstrual cycles, and even the change in weather with each new season were among the commonplace processes putting humans at risk for unhealthy imbalance. The body was "a kind of stew pot, or chemico-vital reaction, proceeding calmly only if all its elements remained appropriately balanced ... the body was a city under constant threat of siege."[3]

The role of the physician was to readjust the imbalance by manipulating the intake and outgo of the disordered system. This was achieved through adjusting the balance of the body's fluids and secretions by removing blood, stimulating perspiration or urination, or purging. Specific drugs could not be used to treat specific diseases in a world where specific diseases did not exist; instead, medications were employed for their physiological effects as emetics, purgatives, and diaphoretics. In theory, diseases could be either "sthenic" (strong) or "asthenic" (weak), but in practice virtually all were sthenic and therefore required treatment to decrease the patients' level of animation; sthenic conditions usually occurred in association with an inflammatory ("phlogistic") state, which required "antiphlogistic" therapy to settle down the aroused morbidity. "Draining off excess excitement from the body was not entirely metaphorical,"[4] but in fact was the basis for the use of bloodletting, cathartics, emetics, and counterirritants. Restoring the body's delicate balance was serious business, and "heroic" doses were required so there would be no doubt about the gravity of the treatment.

For the nineteenth-century patient and physician, the presence of disease was overt and obvious. Disease was a *physical* entity. If it could not be seen or felt, it did not exist.[5] There was nothing understated about the swollen joints, bleeding ulcerations, expanding tumors, violent fevers, and excruciating pains that were the calling cards of sickness. This physical reality of disease carried major implications for therapeutics. The goal of therapy was to correct an unbalanced system, and the magnitude of treatment required was determined by the severity of the disease. Unfortunately for the patient, disease was never subtle in the nineteenth century. When treatments were needed to readjust the perturbations in the internal equilibrium, they could not be expected do so in a silent or invisible manner. Just as the presence of disease was obvious, the effects of treatment had to be equally apparent if there was to be any hope that the underlying disease would be neutralized. When the mode of treatment was nothing less than a full assault on a patient with emetics that caused him to vomit horribly, bleeding that accelerated his pulse, purgatives that violently cleansed his bowels, and diaphoretics that made him sweat profusely from every pore, there was never any doubt in a patient's mind that his body's internal workings were being manipulated. He could only pray he would survive the treatment. Clemens was fascinated by a popular eighteenth-century medical textbook ("a majestic literary fossil") that described the utility of bloodletting in the treatment of headaches despite the fact that the death rate from such therapy was extremely high.

According to Clemens, "there is no harm in trying to cure a headache—in our day. You can't do it, but you get more or less entertainment out of trying, and that is something; besides, you live to tell about it, and that is more. A century or so ago you could have had the first of these features in rich variety, but you might fail of the other once—and once would do" (*£1m Bank-note*, 246–47).

The acceptance of this aggressive approach to illness was far from universal. In every community in nineteenth-century America there were adventuresome, free-spirited individuals who were unrestrained by the standard thinking of the time. The frontier had a large population of such people. They had seen too much death and too much suffering and were quick to appreciate the joys of living. They still worried about the health of their loved ones but were not fatalistic in their outlook. They were not afraid to strike out independently and run a few experiments on their own in their attempts to find new ways to protect their families' precious health. Samuel Clemens's mother was one such individual.

Jane Clemens, constantly concerned about the health of her boy Sam, was the object of her son's love and adoration. She was almost always receptive to a joke and eager to laugh. She rarely took herself seriously except when she worried about the well-being of her family. (John Marshall Clemens *always* took himself seriously, even when there was no need to do so.) If John Clemens can be best described as "mainstream," Jane Clemens is the model for "alternative." She was as nontraditional in her attitudes and behavior as her husband was a follower of the conventional. Samuel Clemens's relationship with his father was uncomfortable and emotionless; his mother was his ally, mentor, and confidante. John Clemens's harsh style and cold affect made it easy for the son to reject the values the father held dearest. Jane Clemens was an icon for the unconventional, and she was eager to pursue offbeat and irrational medical systems such as patent medicine and hydropathic medicine in her efforts to keep her family healthy. She was intrigued by a St. Louis doctor who had not bathed for thirty years because of the fear of losing his magnetic force, and in her later years she took homeopathic medicines from a believer in spiritualism.[6]

Samuel Clemens's ebullient love of mischief grew out of his relationship with his mother and was fostered by her willingness to tolerate his pranks and stunts. Jane Clemens was the "Aunt Polly" whose loose and loving discipline allowed her son to play out his "Tom Sawyer" instincts. When he was four or five years of age, Jane Clemens found her son gagging on worms and having "convulsions," which his mother attributed

to an infestation with worms. She gave the boy salt in the hope of eradicating the worm infestation, and her intervention seemed to be successful
in interrupting the seizure. When she told Dr. Meredith about the event,
he was puzzled by it, and he encouraged Jane Clemens to withhold therapy at the next seizure until he could come to evaluate the situation for
himself and satisfy his curiosity. Mrs. Clemens did not appreciate Dr.
Meredith's coldly clinical and dispassionate attitude, and she later asked,
"Did he think that I was going to let the child choke?" The boy had no
recurrent episodes, and the suggestion has been made that young Sam
Clemens just might have put the worms in his mouth as a practical
joke that would create consternation for his mother and amusement for
himself.[7]

Sam Clemens was no one's fool. His "sickly" nature made him the
target for more than his fair share of both traditional and nontraditional
medical approaches. It did not take long for him to figure out that no
system of therapy was particularly effective (but at least the nontraditional approaches seemed at times to be more intriguing). It even seemed
possible that, if enough of them could be sampled, there might be a re-
mote hope of finding a system that actually worked. He learned from Jane
Clemens that the allopathic doctors were always available as a backup
plan if a serious illness should arise,[8] but, more important, he also saw
that his mother was willing to do whatever was necessary to keep her
family healthy and alive.

3

Scarlet Fever Will Be True to You

The doctor said water would kill him, but I knowed that when you are blazing with scarlet fever you don't mind that.

—Mark Twain, "Tom Sawyer's Conspiracy"

If pioneer mothers such as Jane Clemens were predisposed to worry about the health of their children, their greatest fears were of infection. Epidemics of bacterial and viral infections were recurring nineteenth-century nightmares. Infections were common causes of death for children on the frontier. A disease such as measles could spread aggressively and with astounding virulence and often resulted in large numbers of fatalities among the young. There was not much any doctor could do for most of these illnesses, and at times it almost seemed as if the care of a physician might hasten the demise of a child. (This appearance may be the result of some selection bias, as physicians were typically consulted only in the most advanced cases where the likelihood of death was substantial.)

Epidemics were common. Many infectious illnesses were yet to be characterized at the time of Clemens's childhood, but some illnesses had very striking features that led to their accurate description. One of the more frightful ones was yellow fever, an acute viral illness that is transmitted by the bite of a mosquito.[1] Within a few days, its victims develop fever, body aches, headache, nausea, and severe weakness. Liver damage causes the jaundice that gives the disease its name, and bleeding from the gastrointestinal tract commonly follows (at times associated with profuse vomiting of dark blood). The death rate could be as high as 15 to 50 percent. Because of its mosquito vector, yellow fever was predominantly a summertime disease. It was particularly prevalent in coastal cities such as Galveston, Mobile, Charleston, and Baltimore; the virus and the vector and the victims all traveled together on the ships that went from port to port. Epidemics of yellow fever were recurrent in the nineteenth century. New Orleans was the epicenter of infection and had at least a few cases even in the best of years. In 1847, there were 2,259 yellow fever deaths in New Orleans, and 9,000 people (9 percent of the city's population) died from the disease in 1853. The Mississippi River was a conduit that permitted the infection to migrate from its coastal origins and travel upstream by steamship, and severe outbreaks occurred in Vicksburg and Memphis.[2] In *Life on the Mississippi*, Twain mentioned "a desolating visitation of the yellow-fever" in Memphis, where "the people were swept off by hundreds, by thousands; and so great was the reduction caused by flight and by death together, that the population was diminished three-fourths, and so remained for a time" (*Life on Miss.*, 321). Hannibal was ravaged by an epidemic in the winter of 1849–1850, as mentioned in a letter of January 1850 from Clemens's sister Pamela in Hannibal to their brother Orion in St. Louis: "I suppose you have not been attacked with the yellow fever,[3] that by the way is raging so here that it is feared it will carry off nearly half the inhabitants, if it does [not] indeed depopulate the town" (*MTBM*, 15).

One bout of infection seemed to follow another. Attentive mothers such as Jane Clemens were continually reminded of the dangers of infection all around them, and they had to remain relentlessly vigilant to protect the health of their offspring. To make matters worse, Samuel Clemens's mother was not one to hide her emotions. Whenever a new bout of infection appeared, she worried (with good reason) that she was at risk of losing more of her family. Her level of anxiety was obvious to her son, as he described years later in "The Turning Point in My Life":

> When I was twelve and a half years old, my father died. It was in the spring. The summer came, and brought with it an epidemic of measles. For a time, a child died almost every day. The village was paralysed with fright, distress, despair. Children that were not smitten with the disease were imprisoned in their homes to save them from the infection. In the homes there were no cheerful faces, there was no music, there was no singing but of solemn hymns, no voice but of prayer, no

romping was allowed, no noise, no laughter, their family moved spec-
trally about on tiptoe, in a ghostly hush. I was a prisoner. My soul was
steeped in this awful dreariness—and in fear. At some time or other
every day and every night a sudden shiver shook me to the marrow,
and I said to myself, "There, I've got it! and I shall die." Life on these
miserable terms was not worth living, and at last I made up my mind
to get the disease and have it over, one way or the other. (*WIM&
OPW*, 458)

Through this childhood experience, Clemens realized that anxiety itself could be contagious, with the ability to spread like an epidemic in
its own right. He learned that the stress from living under the constant
threat of unpredictable death can seem more dreadful than the distress
caused by the disease itself. Samuel Clemens's commentary in his autobiography suggests that the worry about contracting measles created a
very high level of anguish for his family.

In 1845, when I was ten years old, there was an epidemic of measles in
the town and it made a most alarming slaughter among the little people. There was a funeral almost daily, and the mothers of the town
were nearly demented with fright.[4] My mother was greatly troubled.
She worried over Pamela and Henry and me, and took constant and
extraordinary pains to keep us from coming into contact with the con-
tagion. But upon reflection I believed that her judgment was at fault. It
seemed to me that I could improve upon it if left to my own devices. I
cannot remember now whether I was frightened by the measles or not,
but I clearly remember that I grew very tired of the suspense I suffered
on account of being continually under the threat of death. I remember
that I got so weary of it and so anxious to have the matter settled one
way or the other, and promptly, that this anxiety spoiled my days and
my nights. I had no pleasure in them. I made up my mind to end this
suspense and settle this matter one way or the other and be done with
it. Will Bowen was dangerously ill with the measles and I thought I
would go down there and catch them. (*Autob/NAR*, 216)

This worry about death was a never-ending concern for Samuel
Clemens. His own mortality, an important issue for him even during his
childhood, haunted him through the years, and in many ways it was
the defining medical theme of his life. Clemens made his fear of his own
mortality evident in a letter to Dr. Wilberforce W. Baldwin that was written on May 15, 1904, when Clemens was sixty-nine years old: "I was

born with an incurable disease, so was everybody—the same one that every machine has—and the knowledge of the fact frightens nobody, damages nobody; but the moment a name is given the disease, the whole thing is changed: fright ensues, and horrible depression, and the life that has learned its sentence is not worth the living."[5]

By exposing himself to his infected friend Will Bowen, young Sam Clemens achieved success in his effort to come down with the measles. Surprisingly, he found that his anxiety about dying was diminished after he contracted the very illness that had created the anxiety in the first place. By getting the disease, he had eliminated the last of the variables that were under his control. Fate was now out of his hands. The force that drove Clemens to contract measles was the same force that drives patients to doctors in droves and stimulates large amounts of unnecessary medical testing and intervention. That force is fear. More distress is generated by worrying about the implications of the unknown than in coping with the realities of the known. Clemens also discovered that his active involvement in the determination of his own fate was preferable to lingering in the passive role of a helpless victim. There is comfort in knowing, and Sam Clemens found it easier to "know" that he *was* dying than to worry about whether he *might be* dying.

> It was a good case of measles that resulted. It brought me within a shade of death's door. It brought me to where I no longer felt any interest in anything, but, on the contrary, felt a total absence of interest—which was most placid and tranquil and sweet and delightful and enchanting. I have never enjoyed anything in my life any more than I enjoyed dying that time. I *was*, in effect, dying. The word had been passed and the family notified to assemble around the bed and see me off. I knew them all. There was no doubtfulness in my vision. They were all crying, but that did not affect me. I took but the vaguest interest in it and that merely because I was the centre of all this emotional attention and was gratified by it and vain of it. (*Autob/NAR*, 217)

This experience introduces a defense mechanism used by Clemens to lessen his fear of death. During the many occasions throughout his sickly youth when death was expected to visit, but never arrived, Clemens learned how to create an emotional detachment that allowed him to deny the concept of his own death. Intellectually, the possibility of death could not be disputed. However, he could create an emotional separation from death by making the possibility of dying a surreal out-of-body experience. Death was rendered into an impersonal and nonthreatening event when Clemens made himself an actor in his own personal drama. After he contracted measles, measles could no longer be threatening to him because its dangers had been taken out of his control; the script of the play had already been written, the predetermined outcome would be revealed in the final scene, and his only role was to watch passively and dispassionately as the story unfolded. This approach is demonstrated in *The Adventures of Tom Sawyer* when Tom, Joe Harper, and Huck Finn (who are believed to be drowned) watch the community's response to their "deaths." After seeing the adults search the river for their bodies, Tom secretively observes the mourning of their deaths, and then all the boys go into town to attend their own funeral services. A similar scene takes place in *Adventures of Huckleberry Finn,* as runaway Huck watches from Jackson's Island and sees the efforts to bring his presumably drowned body up from the river's depths. As long as he could observe his own dying, he knew that he was still alive.

Clemens had another reason for not worrying about the measles—his prior experiences had taught him that he would live through his illnesses, even when physicians proclaimed that he was beyond hope of recovery and there was nothing to be done for him. This also turned out to be the case with the measles, as Clemens remembered in his *Autobiography.* "When Doctor Cunningham had made up his mind that nothing more could be done for me he put bags of hot ashes all over me. He put them on my breast, on my wrists, on my ankles; and so, very much to his astonishment—and doubtless to my regret—he dragged me back into this world and set me going again" (*Autob/NAR*, 217).

This anecdote illustrates another observation made by Samuel Clemens in his youth. *All* treatments, no matter how odd or unusual, appeared to work on him. It was common for him to be sick. At times he seemed to be at risk of dying. With each illness, he became the subject of an intervention aimed at changing the natural course of his disease (Jane Clemens was not one to stand by idly and wring her hands when one of her children was sick). And, in all cases, he survived—either *because of* the therapy, if one is a believer in such things, or *in spite of* the therapy, if one has a cynical bent (and there would seem to be little reason to speculate about what Samuel Clemens's orientation would have been). At first glance, it appears that Dr. Cunningham was responsible for bringing the dying Sam Clemens back to life. Actually, it is not clear that Sam Clemens was ever at risk of dying from his case of measles,[6] so it is hard to know how much credit to give to Dr. Cunningham and his hot ashes, or even to guess at what the hot ashes were supposed to accomplish. It is notable that the doctor himself seemed to have little confidence in the effectiveness of his treatment. In spite of this, his patient survived. This episode is representative of Samuel Clemens's interactions with practitioners of traditional medicine during his childhood and throughout his adult life. Doctors used treatments that did not seem to be rational. Doctors openly lacked confidence in their treatments. And yet...their patients tended to get better anyway.

But it was never safe to be too confident. Diseases never stopped coming, and measles was far from being the worst sickness in the world. His mother was distressed about the complications of measles, but Clemens himself worried far more about scarlet fever throughout his lifetime. Scarlet fever is a contagious illness that is defined by its characteristic rash; the rash is result of a specific toxin that is produced by an underlying bacterial infection with streptococcus organisms. The streptococcus is widely distributed in nature and is capable of causing infection in a variety of tissues. Although infections with the streptococcus organism are now generally regarded as relatively benign, with fairly innocuous skin infections and "strep throat" being among the more common examples, this was not the case during Samuel Clemens's lifetime, when streptococcal infections could be devastating and life-threatening (and it seemed as though the streptococcal infections associated with scarlet fever were particularly deadly).

Bacteriology was in its infancy in the nineteenth century, and the streptococcus was not isolated from human tissue until 1874.[7] However, scarlet fever's unique rash made it one of the few infections that could be identified with reasonable accuracy even before its causative bacterial agent was identified. As a result, there is fairly good data about outbreaks of scarlet fever in the nineteenth century. England and Wales suffered an enormous number of deaths as the result of major outbreaks between 1825 and 1885. The strikingly higher mortality from scarlet fever during this interval was associated with poor nutritional conditions. The victims were commonly children. In the last half of the nineteenth century, two-thirds of deaths from scarlet fever in England and Wales occurred among children under the age of five years.[8]

The American experience with scarlet fever epidemics was no different. A Pennsylvania physician described an epidemic that lasted from May until December 1839, with fatalities including a four-month-old infant and a two-year-old child. The illness of the older child started with symptoms of headache, nausea, vomiting, prostration, and "an eruption, of a livid hue." As terrifying as the disease was in its earliest phases, it became even more horrible in its terminal phase as "delirium appeared with the eruption, and in a short time terminated in coma; the cheeks suffused with a livid flush; the eyes dull; dark-colored sloughs appeared on the tonsils; the nose discharged an acrid fluid; the extremities become cold, and death closed the scene."[9]

Parents were terrorized by the infection for good reason. For Americans in the nineteenth century, an outbreak of scarlet fever generated a fear that rivaled the dread associated with epidemics of cholera and plague.[10] The severe apprehension associated with a scarlet fever infection is evident in "Tom Sawyer's Conspiracy," a short novel Clemens began to write in 1897 but never completed. In this story, Tom Sawyer is fearful that his brother, Sid, will interfere with a phony abolitionist scare Tom is planning. Tom hopes to catch measles from his friend Joe Harper, with the expectation that his Aunt Polly would then feel compelled to prevent Sid's exposure to the disease by sending him out of town. Joe's original diagnosis turns out to be incorrect, however, and Tom comes down with scarlet fever instead of the measles he had hoped for. The terror that results from the new diagnosis is staggering. Tom has literally placed his life at risk for the purpose of pulling off his prank. "[T]he doctor found it warn't measles at all, but scarlet fever. When aunt Polly heard it she turned that white she couldn't get her breath, and was that weak she couldn't see her hand before her face, and if they hadn't grabbed her she would have fell. And it just made a panic in the town, too, and there wasn't a woman that had children but was scared out of her life" (*HH&T*, 186).

Due to the aggressively contagious nature of an infection with scarlet fever, and the dire consequences of a scarlet fever outbreak, any evidence of the disease was associated with intense efforts to limit its spread by disinfecting any area that had been exposed to the germ. As Tom explained to Huck Finn, there was no question that scarlet fever was a much more severe disease than measles.

We went for measles. It shows how little we knowed and how blind we was. What good was measles, when you come to look at it? None. As soon as it's over you wash up the things and air out the house and send for the children home again, and a person has been sick all for nothing. But you take the scarlet fever and what do you find? You scour out the place, and burn up every rag when it's over and you're well again, and from that very day no Sid and no Mary can come anear it for six solid useful weeks. Now who thought of scarlet fever for us, Huck, and arranged it, when we was ignorant and didn't know any better than to go for measles? (*HH&T*, 191)

Even those who were fortunate enough to survive an infection with scarlet fever could suffer from the long-term consequences of the disease. In his autobiographical works, Clemens recalled how his boyhood friend Tom Nash developed severe complications from a case of scarlet fever that he contracted after falling through the ice on the Mississippi River.

He took to his bed sick, and had a procession of diseases. The closing one was scarlet-fever, and he came out of it stone deaf. Within a year or two speech departed, of course. But some years later he was taught to talk, after a fashion—one couldn't always make out what it was he was trying to say. Of course he could not modulate his voice, since he couldn't hear himself talk. When he supposed he was talking low and confidentially, you could hear him in Illinois. (*Autob/NAR*, 55)

The streptococcal organisms that are responsible for scarlet fever can cause not only otitis media (infection of the middle ear) but also meningitis. Either one could result in hearing loss.[11] Loss of hearing is only one of many serious complications that can result from meningitis. A comment made by Huck Finn in "Tom Sawyer's Conspiracy" not only displays Clemens's own understanding of the complications of scarlet fever but further suggests that Tom Nash (who was the likely source of Clemens's knowledge about scarlet fever) had become deaf as a result of streptococcal meningitis: "I had had scarlet fever, and come in an ace of going deaf and dumb and blind and baldheaded and idiotic, so they said" (*HH&T*, 186). In his unfinished novel *Which Was It?*—written episodically between 1899 and 1902—Clemens introduced the character Dug Hapgood, who "had had scarlet fever when he was a boy, and it had injured his ear-machinery; the defect had increased with the years until at last he couldn't hear himself talk, and didn't believe anybody else could" (*WWD&OSW*, 196). Clemens also used scarlet fever as a cause of deafness in *Huckleberry Finn*. As the runaway slave Jim travels with Huck on their raft down the Mississippi, Jim confides in Huck about the time he slapped his daughter Elizabeth for disobeying an order, only to discover that the child was deaf and had not heard his command. The girl's deafness had been caused by a severe episode of scarlet fever when she was four years old (*Huck Finn*, 201–2).[12]

The horrors of scarlet fever appear again in "The Chronicle of Young Satan," one of Clemens's manuscript versions of *The Mysterious Stranger.* In this story, Satan shortens a young man's life by causing him to drown, and then argues that the drowning was an act of kindness because it spared the man from suffering from the consequences of scarlet fever: "If I had not done this, Nikolaus would save Lisa; then he would catch cold from his drenching; one of your race's fantastic and desolating scarlet fevers would follow, with pathetic after-effects: for forty-six years he would lie in his bed a paralytic log, deaf, dumb, blind, and praying night and day for the blessed relief of death" (*Mys. Stranger Mss.*, 118).

Scarlet fever was a recurring source of tribulation for Clemens. He wondered whether chronic disability from its more severe consequences (particularly meningitis) might represent a fate worse than death. It could be speculated that this opinion, which is expressed so clearly in *The Chronicle of Young Satan,* was a rationalization by Clemens as he struggled to come to grips with the tragedy of the death of his daughter Susy from meningitis (Susy died in 1896; *Young Satan* was written between 1897 and 1900). In any case, he considered scarlet fever to be one of the worst illnesses that could be transmitted from one person to another. For Sam Clemens, the disease became a metaphor for the injury that can be innocently and unknowingly inflicted by a well-intentioned but ultimately harmful ally, a person who "is like your family physician, who comes and cures the mumps, and leaves the scarlet fever behind" (*Life on Miss.*, 309).

Scarlet fever created problems for Clemens throughout his life. It was always a feared disease, and any infection with scarlet fever led to extensive efforts to disinfect the household involved. In 1882, when his daughter Jean contracted scarlet fever, the fumigation of his house with sulfuric acid ruined three or four hundred dollars of metalwork (*N&J-2*, 508).[13] When the son of his friend William Dean Howells contracted scarlet fever, Clemens wrote a letter to Howells in January 1884 that empathized with Howells's plight. There can be no doubt about Clemens's feeling of dread for the contagious disease that stalked him and his family.

The scarlet fever, once domesticated, is a permanent member of the family. Money may desert you, friends forsake you, enemies grow in-

different to you, but the scarlet fever will be true to you, through thick
and thin, till you be all saved or damned, down to the last one. I say
these things to cheer you. The bare suggestion of scarlet fever in the
family makes me shudder; I believe I would almost rather have Osgood
publish a book for me.[14] (*Ltrs/Paine*, 2:439)

4

THE CHOLERA DAYS OF '49

I am a microbe. A cholera microbe. For me there is comeliness, there
is grace, there is beauty findable, some way or some where, in greater
or lesser degree, in every one of the nationalities that make up the
prodigious germ-world—but at the head I place the cholera-germ. To
me its beauty has no near competitor... the cholera-germ—oldest and
noblest and most puissant of all the race of germs, save only the Plague-
Bacillus, at sound of whose mighty name the nations uncover!

—Mark Twain, "Three Thousand Years among the Microbes"

As Jane Lampton Clemens worried about the health and survival of
her children, one concern overshadowed any anxiety she had about the
risk of measles or scarlet fever. Her dominating worry was cholera, a
highly contagious bacterial infection of the intestinal tract that causes
severe diarrhea and dehydration (and, very often, death). Cholera was
more common and far more deadly than any other infection that regularly visited the Mississippi valley. It traveled up the Mississippi River
every spring, carrying with it a high risk of mortality. Nothing else created such a sense of panic as the arrival of cholera, and the risk of becoming infected with the cholera bacterium loomed as an overwhelming
worry for anyone who lived near the river. The fear of cholera even
played a role in determining the site of Samuel Clemens's birth. When
John Marshall Clemens and Jane Lampton Clemens arrived in Missouri

in 1835, they heard reports of a cholera outbreak in St. Louis and chose to settle instead in the village of Florida, where Samuel Langhorne Clemens would be born later in the same year.[1]

Cholera epidemics took many lives in the Mississippi River valley, and the threat of death from cholera seemed unavoidable. Every year, the infection appeared to originate in New Orleans in the spring and then spread northward up the Mississippi through the summer months. The disease shared the same routes that were favored by yellow fever as it moved from one port to the next, carried by the steamboat traffic. A cholera epidemic in 1851 killed twenty-four Hannibal citizens, and Clemens's older brother Orion reported in a newspaper column in June that steamboats were "burying their passengers at every wood yard, both from cabin and deck."[2] Cholera was one more version of death on the American frontier, an undeniable and inescapable fact of life.

Cholera epidemics were accepted as a normal part of the country's westward development. Hannibal editors were fond of quoting Dr. Benjamin Rush, a signer of the Declaration of Independence and the foremost physician in the United States in the early nineteenth century, who once declared that it was necessary for every new settlement to have a phase of unavoidable illness, "its Bilious period." If Rush was correct, then Hannibal was right on schedule for development, and cholera had been appointed as the town's own version of the plague. Hannibal's location on the river may have been an economic advantage, but villagers learned that it also made the town susceptible to the outbreaks of cholera that traveled by the waterways and left death in their wake. Clemens reported that Hannibal's own Bear Creek was "a famous breeder of chills and fever," and he could remember "one summer when everybody in town had this disease at once" (Life on Miss., 546). The season that he remembered so well was the summer of 1849, a year in which the infection had indeed gotten off to a very early start and moved up the river with aggression. The 1849 cholera death toll was devastating. In St. Louis, there were 4,557 deaths from cholera during the year, compared to 4,046 deaths from all other diseases combined. In the month of July alone, there were 1,895 cholera deaths from the city's total population of 50,000.[3]

The only thing more devastating than cholera's death rate was the fear that came with every new outbreak. Each family found its own way of dealing with the risk of cholera. Many people fled from their homes in the hope of escaping the infection. The Hannibal newspapers offered up varying recommendations for avoiding the disease, with the *Journal*

Benjamin Rush. Courtesy of the National Library of Medicine (B22631).

recommending that "a flannel or woollen belt be worn around the belly," while the *Courier* suggested that "soap and courage" were the best preventatives.[4] Dr. William M. McPheeters of St. Louis, who had extensive experience in treating the victims of the 1849 cholera outbreak, reported that many patients chose intoxication by alcohol as their personal prophylaxis or escape.

Instances are known in which individuals, not having the fear of God before their eyes, went out on Sabbath excursions, defying the cholera, and engaging in all manner of excesses, who would suddenly be taken with the disease and in a few hours hurried into eternity. It is also true that there was an unusually large quantity of alcoholic liquors drunk by all classes of our citizens from the erroneous belief in its prophylactic powers, and the records show an increased number of deaths from mania a potu during the prevalence of the epidemic.[5]

It is obvious that the medical profession's first obstacle in dealing with cholera came from its ignorance of the disease's cause. Cholera had not yet been identified as being infectious in nature, a situation that was not unique to this specific illness. By the medical thinking of the era, disease in general was not attributable to specific causative factors, but instead was the result of poorly defined interactions between the personal characteristics of each patient and vague environmental factors. McPheeters believed that the only real hope of eradicating cholera would be "the withdrawal of the peculiar unknown atmospheric poison which has always given rise to it." Because the disease seemed to be most rampant in the parts of St. Louis that were the dampest, dirtiest, and most crowded, hygienic approaches were initiated whenever cholera struck. In addition to the general cleaning of the city, "bonfires were nightly built in nearly every street and the whole city repeatedly fumigated with tar and sulphur," an approach that undoubtedly created a scene of ghastly smoky terror throughout the city and did nothing to reassure the fainthearted. When the outbreak finally subsided in late 1849, McPheeters noted that the general level of health in St. Louis had become remarkably good, and in keeping with the concept of an environmental (rather that a bacteriological) basis for the epidemic, he suggested that "once the storm of disease had subsided the atmosphere seemed to be purified by its fury and rendered fitter for respiration."[6]

For a nineteenth-century allopathic physician such as McPheeters, ignorance of the cause of a disease was never a reason to abstain from making an effort to cure the illness, and most maladies were attacked with confidence. In the paradigm of medical science of the mid-nineteenth century, it made no sense to differentiate between body and environment, body and mind, or health and morals; all were interwoven into a seamless unity of existence. When different physicians prescribed different drugs for the same disorder, their inconsistent behaviors were not seen as an indictment of an irrational system; instead, the variation in their treatment was viewed as a testimonial to the *art* of medicine. Every physician had to skillfully assess the multiple variables that influenced each individual patient—age, gender, latitude of residence, and season of the year, to name a few—and then determine the most suitable therapy to create the needed action. Any treatment that resulted in the required physiological effect was valid, and medicine could not be standardized into a cookbook approach if each patient was to receive the optimal health care. Regionalism was common in medical practice, as evidenced by the use of allopathy's two mainstays—bloodletting and purging with mercurials. Venesection (the removal of blood from the veins) was more commonly employed in the North, where it was believed that the "inflammatory" nature of disease and the constitutional makeup of patients in the region would benefit most from "depletion." In the South, as the thinking went, the liver was more likely to be exhausted because of the hot climate and malaria; as a result, depletion from bleeding would often be contraindicated, but large doses of mercurials (particularly calomel) were thought to be useful in stimulating the torporous liver.

McPheeters seems to have had more humility than some of his peers, whom he accused of "the most willful misrepresentation" when they declared extraordinary success in treating cholera. He was also less enthusiastic than his colleagues in thinking that medical therapy had much hope for eradicating cholera, stating, "although no skeptic as to the powers of medicine, my experience in the treatment of cholera has taught me how impotent is our art when the disease is malignant." In spite of this recognition of his therapeutic shortcomings, McPheeters was far from bashful about aggressive therapy, and he had an invariable personal rule "to abandon no case as hopeless until death had rendered it absolutely so."[7]

McPheeters never found a satisfactory cholera treatment. He tried all of the standard allopathic measures, including purging. The goal of purging was to cleanse impurities from the system, get rid of foreign substances, and depress the overly stimulated vascular and muscular systems. Purging could be accomplished by induction of vomiting with emetics such as ipecac and tartar emetic, or by stimulating evacuation of the bowel with the use of cathartics. The milder cathartics were laxatives such as tamarind, manna, rhubarb, senna, magnesia, or castor oil. Jalap, calomel, and croton oil were more aggressive and vigorous cathartics. Calomel was an allopathic standard. When Meriwether Lewis and William Clark were chosen by President Thomas Jefferson to search for the Northwest Passage, Lewis (who was to serve as the expedition's physician) called upon Dr. Benjamin Rush in 1803 for medical direction. In discussing the best treatments of the day, Rush emphasized the utility of his own patented pills, known formally as "Rush's pills" but more commonly referred to as "Thunderclappers." Rush considered these "sovereign" for virtually any ailment; they were a mixture of calomel and jalap, each of which was "a purgative of explosive power; the combination was awesome."[8]

Considering that the major morbidity of cholera is the result of profuse fluid loss from the bowel, it now seems illogical, counterintuitive, and perhaps just downright stupid that anyone would treat cholera with a vigorous cathartic such as calomel. Nevertheless, calomel was the central component of the therapeutic plan employed by McPheeters. "Calomel, which is regarded by many as the sheet anchor in the treatment of cholera, was faithfully tried in hundreds of cases," McPheeters explained. "I am not prepared to say that no benefit was derived from its use, but certainly it did not meet my expectations. . . . Not a few instances occurred in which the discharges from the bowels assumed a decidedly bilious character, and some in which even ptyalism was induced, and yet the patients died."[9]

McPheeters also had high hopes for bleeding (another standard depletive allopathic practice) for bringing the cholera epidemic under control. Bloodletting, used for the removal of harmful "humors" even before the time of Hippocrates, was the cornerstone of the "heroic" practices, and the theory was that the withdrawal of a patient's blood would reduce vascular spasm, relieve inflammation, decrease congestion, and (paradoxically) arrest hemorrhage.[10] Benjamin Rush was responsible for much of the popularity of bleeding. Rush, who was America's first surgeon general, blamed all disease on "capillary tension." His doctrine of "unity of fevers" asserted that there was ultimately only one disease and therefore only one cure, the removal of irritation by bleeding and purging. Even though he was criticized by colleagues for bleeding his patients "till they were as pale as Jersey Veal," he was not averse to removing up to 80 percent of the body's blood if needed, and he suggested that unaggressive bloodletting "is like untying a Tyger & not destroying him afterwards." Rush is said to have "shed more blood than any general in history."[11] Blood was removed directly from the veins in quantities ranging from several ounces to several pounds. Bleeding could be done locally through cupping and scarification (a method of applying glass cups and creating a partial vacuum, with the goal of causing enough local tissue injury to promote bleeding). Local bleeding was also accomplished through the application of leeches, especially in areas of external inflammation or on infants who might not tolerate cupping. Twenty million leeches were used annually in France in the 1830s for this reason.

The letting of blood "was practiced without any scientific basis for more than 2,000 years. It was done for the wrong reasons and harmed rather than benefited the patients."[12]

In "A Majestic Literary Fossil," perhaps his most ferocious attack on the principles of allopathic medicine, Clemens lampooned a popular medical text that advocated the use of bloodletting for treatment of patients with headaches. The book was identified by Clemens as the *Dictionary of Medicine* but was actually titled *A Medicinal Dictionary; Including Physic, Surgery, Anatomy, Chymistry, and Botany*. Published in 1743 by the fashionable English physician Dr. Robert James, it contained biographical contributions from Dr. Samuel Johnson.[13] Clemens cited the recommendations of a physician named Bonetus, who not only recommended the liberal application of leeches but in one case went so far as to suggest that he would have ordered an arteriotomy if a skilled surgeon had been available to him. Clemens's comment was that of outrage:

> I looked for "Arteriotomy" in this same Dictionary, and found this definition: "The opening of an Artery with a View of taking away Blood." Here was a person who was being bled in the arms, forehead, nostrils, back, temples, and behind the ears, yet the celebrated Bonetus was not satisfied, but wanted to open an artery "with a View" to insert a pump, probably. "Notwithstanding these Precautions"—he dy'd. No art of speech could more quaintly convey this butcher's innocent surprise. Now that we know what the celebrated Bonetus did when he wanted to relieve a Head-ach, it is no trouble to infer that if he wanted to comfort a man that had a Stomach-ach he disembowelled him. (*£1m Banknote*, 247–48)

Clemens was incensed that the book disregarded the fatal outcome for all twelve patients who had been treated by bleeding for their headaches: "not one of these people got well; yet this obtuse hyena sets down every little gory detail of the several assassinations as complacently as if he was doing a useful and meritorious work in perpetuating the methods of his crimes" (*£1m Bank-note*, 248).

McPheeters's hopes for bleeding as an effective treatment for cholera did not last long. His initial enthusiasm soon gave way as he found it to be anything but beneficial.

> Blood Letting.—No remedies employed by me during the cholera seemed at first to produce such decided and favorable results as the lancet. In some six or eight instances, in which the collapse was almost

complete, and in which all the symptoms of advanced cholera were present, the patients seemed rescued from the jaws of death by free blood letting. In these cases the blood first came drop by drop, and was of dark molasses color, but gradually began to run and ultimately to flow freely.... As the disease progressed, however, the same favorable result did not attend the use of the lancet, and it finally fell into disuse ... my zeal in the use of the remedy flagged, owing to repeated failures.[14]

Fortunately for the allopathic doctor (but unfortunately for his patients), bloodletting was not the only therapy available. Blistering was popular as an alternative "heroic measure" in the therapeutic armamentarium of the regular physician. In this methodology, the physician created a second-degree burn on the patient's skin by the local application of an irritant such as Spanish fly, cantharides, or tartar emetic. This process was an example of the principle known as "counterirritation" in which local treatments were used to overcome disseminated disease processes. The use of counterirritation was based on the nineteenth-century belief in the interdependence of all of the body's parts. The blistering and the irritation, burning, and excoriation of the skin caused by the application of plasters led to the development of infection at the site of the newly traumatized skin. The pus that eventually exuded from the sores was interpreted as irrefutable proof that internal disease was being "drawn" and cleared from deep within the body by the counterirritation process.

Samuel Clemens's familiarity with this form of medical treatment is evident in chapter 18 of *Tom Sawyer*, which contains an illustration entitled "Counter-Irritation." Earlier in the chapter, Becky Thatcher attempts to make Tom jealous by feigning interest in Alfred Temple. When Becky later turns her interest back to Tom, the spurned Alfred retaliates by pouring ink onto a page in Tom's spelling book (*Tom Sawyer*, 157). In Clemens's play on words, Alfred's destructive act can be seen as a literary form of "counterirritation" in which Alfred hopes to "draw" the rage of schoolmaster Dobbins toward Tom Sawyer.

Despite the widespread use of counterirritation by other medical practitioners, McPheeters found the methodology to be no more helpful in the treatment of cholera than anything else he had tried: "Dry cups to the spine and wet cups to the abdomen were also freely used, and the latter with good result, the former not ... mustard plasters, frictions with capsicum, dry mustard and salt, hot bricks, blankets wrung in hot water, etc., etc, were extensively tried but with no effect."[15]

With all of the standard allopathic options eventually found to be in-effectual, one might wonder what Dr. McPheeters finally recommended for treatment of cholera. It may be little surprise to find out that he stayed with what he knew best, and he had nowhere to turn except to invent modifications of the old standards.

> When called to a case in the early stage of the disease, in which there was vomiting, an emetic of salt and mustard mixed and dissolved in warm water was invariably given. This would generally arouse the vomiting, after which a single dose of twenty grains of dry calomel was placed on the back of the tongue and washed down with a small quantity of water. This was followed every fifteen minutes, half hour or hour, according to the circumstances, with a powder consisting of musk, calomel and tannin, each five grains, and camphor, four grains. Injections of acetate of lead and laudanum or a strong infusion of nut galls, after each operation of the bowel and a large blister over the abdomen. If the tendency was to sink, I also gave in addition to the above ten grains of carbonate of ammonia in solution, every fifteen minutes or half hour, according to circumstances.[16]

Although cholera was an expected annual visitor for those who lived in the Mississippi valley, the outbreak of 1849 came ahead of schedule. It actually appeared in December 1848 in New Orleans, where it became epidemic. Following the steamboat traffic up the river, the cholera arrived in St. Louis in January 1849. In early April, a steamboat passenger brought the first case to Hannibal, where six deaths occurred between June 15 and June 19. Three people died on a single day in July, and the disease persisted in Hannibal into August. One of the victims of the summer was Sam Honeyman, the father of one of Sam Clemens's playmates.[17]

Jane Clemens had always worried about her family's health, but her distress undoubtedly rose to new heights as she heard of the epidemic affecting hundreds of innocent people in St. Louis and steadily advancing toward her own loved ones. She had already seen some of her own children die from infections, and she was probably struck with terror with each report that a major epidemic was on its way to Hannibal. Her streak of independence was undoubtedly a factor in her efforts to by-pass the interventions of orthodox medicine, but her anxieties about the toxicity of the allopathic approach to cholera were at the root of her behavior. Nothing in her experiences with allopathic medicine would have given her any reason for hope from traditional physicians. Instead, she would have had every reason to have further concern about the toxicity of allopathic therapy if the cholera should strike her loved ones. Her fear of cholera and her distrust of traditional medicine led her to pursue an "alternative" treatment plan for her family, and her sickliest child, Sam, was chosen to bear the brunt of her medical experimentation (at least as the episode was remembered by Samuel Clemens years later). "Those were the cholera days of '49," Clemens noted in his autobiography: "The people along the Mississippi were paralyzed with fright. Those who could run away, did it. And many died of fright in the flight. Fright killed three persons where the cholera killed one. Those who couldn't flee kept themselves drenched with cholera preventives, and my mother chose Perry Davis's Pain-Killer for me" (*Autob/NAR*, 53).

In choosing Perry Davis's Pain-Killer as the family's cholera preventative, Jane Clemens was also introducing her son to a whole new way of looking at medical therapy.[18]

5

Fire in a Liquid Form

The floor was not carpeted. It had cracks in it and I fed the Pain-Killer to the cracks with very good results—no cholera occurred down below.

—Mark Twain, "Chapters from my Autobiography"

Jane Clemens's decision to rush toward the world of patent medicine as the cholera epidemic drew closer says much about the state of medical care in the mid-nineteenth century. The toxicity and futility of allopathic medicine were widely recognized, and the wisdom of avoiding the services of allopathic physicians was obvious to many Americans. However, it did not seem adequate to replace allopathy with a vacuum—doing nothing at all seemed too empty and too defeatist an approach, especially when a major epidemic was around the corner, and particularly when one was a woman with the tenacious character of Jane Clemens. In medicine, doing nothing is rarely an acceptable approach for a patient, even at times when it truly would be the best approach. Avoiding allopathy was an easy decision for Jane Clemens. More difficult was selecting the best alternative. It turned out to be an important decision in more ways than one. When Samuel Clemens's mother endorsed the least credible of all available medical options by deciding to take the route of patent medicine, she sprang open a Pandora's box of virtually innumerable medical alternatives that her son would chase after for the rest of his life.

Jane Clemens was not the only American who came to put her trust in Perry Davis's Pain-Killer as her family's preventative against cholera. Davis was a schemer and con man of renown, the epitome of the "get rich quick" entrepreneur of the nineteenth century who had mastered the art of translating the health concerns of the population into large sums of money for himself. Born in Dartmouth, Massachusetts, in 1791, Davis was initially trained as a shoemaker. According to his own account, which he undoubtedly embellished for public consumption, he developed a severe respiratory infection in December 1839. His multitude of symptoms included a bad cough, a sore stomach, a poor appetite, night sweats, "piles of the worst kind," and a canker in his mouth. He felt driven to develop a medicine to save himself from the grave, and he was apparently successful in doing so. He decided to name his creation "Pain-Killer" because, reasonably enough, it had killed all of his pains. Davis moved to Providence, Rhode Island, and started a business to manufacture and distribute Pain-Killer. He was an aggressive self-promoter, and his name and picture were on every label.

While making a batch of the Pain-Killer in 1844, so the story goes, Davis sustained severe burns to his face and arms from an explosion of alcohol (which was the major ingredient in his invention). He claimed to have cured his own burns by applying the Pain-Killer, and he further claimed that the Pain-Killer "gave immediate relief" (a most unlikely consequence of pouring alcohol and cayenne pepper onto a burn).[1]

Perry Davis's Pain-Killer was similar to the many other patent medicines in that it contained a considerable quantity of alcohol, an ingredient that was the basis for much of the popularity of such products. Davis used the drama of the explosion to his marketing advantage by hiring an artist to create a drawing of his engulfment in flames. The picture, which was widely publicized, showed a huge can exploding, and the text referred to "Alcohol" with a large "A" (lest there was any question about what the purchaser was *really* getting when he bought the Pain-Killer). Using the defense that the alcohol content was medicinal, Davis proclaimed disingenuously that the Pain-Killer was "a stimulant that will not destroy the soul by creating a taste for liquor." Davis, who contributed money to the temperance movement, stated (with a pride that was either hypocritical or self-deceiving) that the Pain-Killer "has saved many a soul from a drunkard's grave."[2]

The popularity of the Pain-Killer and similar patent medicines was undoubtedly related to their considerable content of alcohol, just as the widespread appeal of other patent medicines was due to their opiate

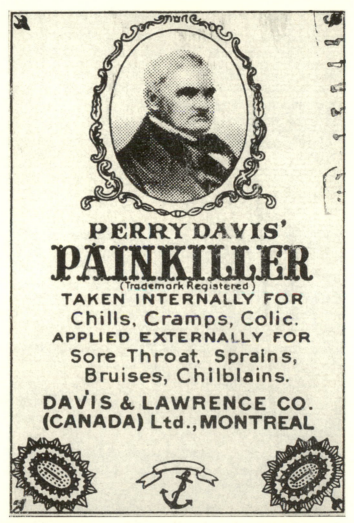

Label from a bottle of Perry Davis's Pain-Killer. Photograph by Louis Davis, Wake Forest University Health Sciences Photography.

content. Information about the content of the different patent medicines was not typically shared with the general public, as the trademark on the medicines allowed their manufacturing process and contents to be kept secret. However, there can be little question that the secret ingredients of the patent medicines contributed greatly to their appeal. For example, the fact that Shiloh's Cure for Consumption was fortified with heroin undoubtedly broadened its market to include many citizens who were nonconsumptive. Kopp's Baby Friend was made of sweetened water and morphine and was advertised as the perfect way to calm down babies. It is not likely that many mothers realized that Mrs. Winslow's Soothing Syrup for teething babies also derived most of its soothing action from its morphine content (one testimonial bragged that the syrup "makes 'em lay like the dead 'til mornin'").

Alcohol was the most predictable solvent, however, and it seemed to become increasingly popular as a constituent of patent therapies as the temperance movement gained momentum. Dr. Kilmer's Swamp Root, touted for its utility in treating occult kidney disease, had a 10.5 percent alcohol content in addition to its 46.5 percent sugar content. Parker's True Tonic was marketed as a reliable cure for alcoholism, and undoubtedly many daughters and wives were impressed by how effectively this tonic discouraged their wayward men from going out and getting drunk, especially when it was taken on a regular basis. (If they had realized that the True Tonic had a 41.6 percent alcohol content, they might have been somewhat less pleased.) Eventually, Americans purchased more alcohol (excluding the sales of ales and beer) in the form of patent medicines than they bought by legal purchase from licensed liquor vendors,[3] and for a while the federal government even considered licensing patent medicine dealers as liquor vendors. The fact that Perry Davis's Pain-Killer was nothing more than a spiced-up alcoholic beverage was undoubtedly a major factor in its widespread popularity. It does seem reasonable to assume, however, that Jane Clemens was naively unaware of its ingredients, and that her own purchases were based on her belief in its claims as a "medicinal" product that would protect her family's health.

The rapid and widespread use of the Pain-Killer is a testimony to Perry Davis's ability as a salesman. The Pain-Killer had been invented in the eastern United States in 1840, but due to its successful promotion it had found its way to Hannibal by 1849 (just in time to help Jane Clemens in her effort to protect her family from the cholera epidemic). Even though it was advertised as a multipurpose remedy, Davis specifically emphasized the Pain-Killer's effectiveness in treating cholera. In his drive to make a buck, he understood the value in playing off the greatest fears of the general population. As he later recounted the successful story of his invention, Davis was particularly proud of the recognition achieved by the Pain-Killer as a nostrum for "the dreaded cholera." He bragged about how the Pain-Killer "was suddenly brought into general notice by the astonishing cures it effected of this terrible disease."[4] Perry Davis's widespread advertisements for the Pain-Killer were found in Hannibal newspapers of 1849 (*ET&S-1*, 470–71). Known Hannibal advertisements of the era promoted the Pain-Killer for external use in the treatment of "bruises, sores, and burns,"[5] but Clemens's numerous references to its fiery potency when ingested are consistent with its marketing as a substance that could be used either internally or externally.

Jane Clemens, always eager to employ the newest and the best in medical therapeutics, made the decision to use the Pain-Killer as a cholera preventative for her family. With alcohol as its major constituent, and additional ingredients that included camphor and cayenne pepper, each fiery dose of Perry Davis's Pain-Killer was unforgettable to its users, and Samuel Clemens's childhood memories of the remedy were not particularly fond ones, as he recalled in his *Autobiography:* "It was a most detestable medicine, Perry Davis's Pain-Killer. Mr. Pavey's negro man, who was a person of good judgment and considerable curiosity, wanted to sample it, and I let him. It was his opinion that it was made of hell-fire" (*Autob/NAR*, 53).

Clemens's early experience with the Pain-Killer was memorable enough that he found a place for it in his fiction, where it burned with similar intensity when Aunt Polly dosed Tom with it in *The Adventures of Tom Sawyer:* "[Aunt Polly] heard of Pain-Killer for the first time. She ordered a lot at once. She tasted it and was filled with gratitude. It was simply fire in a liquid form. . . . She gave Tom a tea-spoonful. . . . The boy could not have shown a wilder, heartier interest, if she had built a fire under him." For his own entertainment, Tom later poured some Pain-Killer down the mouth of Polly's cat Peter. The cat immediately jumped into the air and then "rose on his hind feet and pranced around" before he started running in circles around the room. Peter destroyed everything in his path, all the while squealing and flipping double somersaults before finally leaping out the window to conclude his noisy and destructive melee. When Polly admonished Tom for his act of cruelty to an innocent animal, Tom's defense was that he had given Peter the Pain-Killer out of a sense of pity, because the cat didn't have an aunt. "Because if he'd a had one she'd a burnt him out herself!" Tom explained. "She'd a roasted his bowels out of him 'thout any more feeling than if he was a human!" (*Tom Sawyer*, 109–11).

For Samuel Clemens, Perry Davis's Pain-Killer became the standard by which he judged all noxious therapies. Years later, he suffered some minor injuries when he fell from a carriage during his courtship of Livy Langdon. Livy's sister, Susan Crane, applied a "fiendish successor to Perry Davis's Pain-Killer" to his abrasions. She used "a bottle of some kind of liquid fire whose function was to reduce contusions. . . . She poured this on my head and pawed it around with her hand, stroking and massaging, the fierce stuff dribbling down my backbone and marking its way, inch by inch, with the sensation of a forest fire" (*Autob/MTA*, 188).

The patent medicine industry clearly influenced Clemens's view of the world of medicine. In his youth, his attitude toward patent medicine was largely one of bemusement and mild fascination. As the years went by, however, he became more critical and angry about the obvious manipulation of the public by the drugs' manufacturers. He could not help but notice, however, the striking popularity of patent medicines and the ubiquitous testimonials to their effectiveness. His experiences with the Pain-Killer, and with patent medicine in general, contributed to his eventual cynicism about the public's level of sophistication in making medical choices. He also learned the surprising fact that treatments that cannot possibly be of any benefit *do* indeed seem to help some people's ailments. This observation was the beginning of his insight into the psychology of health and disease, and the insight provided the essential foundation for his later understanding of the nature of healing.

6

PATENT MEDICINE

The Great American Fraud

One million of us, then, die annually. Out of this million ten or twelve thousand are stabbed, shot, drowned, hanged, poisoned, or meet a similarly violent death in some other popular way, such as perishing by kerosene lamp and hoop-skirt conflagrations, getting buried in coal mines, falling off housetops, breaking through church or lecture-room floors, taking patent medicines, or committing suicide in other forms.

—Mark Twain, "The Danger of Lying in Bed"

For independent thinkers such as Jane Clemens, patent medicines had one great advantage above all others. They were sold directly to the public, bypassing the nuisance of consulting a physician. Although they were referred to as proprietary or patent medicines, these remedies were not usually patented but typically were registered under a trademark that maintained the secrecy of their contents and the process of their manufacture. By providing a self-directed approach to medical therapeutics, the marketers of patent medicines took advantage of the reasonable reluctance of many to subject themselves to the drastic approaches of bleeding and purging by the allopathic physicians.

Paradoxically, the belief in the value of a patent medicine could be reinforced if the therapy had effects that resembled the treatments used by the allopathic doctors. For many patients, the most dramatic and memorable actions tended to be those that influenced the activity of the gastrointestinal tract. One advocate of purgation considered the use of laxatives to be "the magnet, the guide, the star of safety" in medical therapy, and he compiled an enormous text that he entitled *The Doctrine of Purgation, Curiosities From Ancient and Modern Literature, From Hippocrates and Other Medical Writers—[citation of 200 names]—Covering a Period of Over 2,000 Years, Proving Purgation Is the Corner-Stone of All Curatives*. A more cynical pharmacist suggested that the real purpose of such medications was "to open men's purses by opening their bowels."[1]

In a sketch ("Enthusiastic Eloquence") that was published in the *San Francisco Chronicle* on June 23, 1865, Clemens created a bizarre juxtaposition of images by suggesting that banjo music had the same effect on him as the gastrointestinal expulsion created by a popular patent medicine known as "Brandreth's Pills": "When you want *genuine music*— music that will come right home to you like a bad quarter, suffuse your system like strychnine whisky, go right through you like Brandreth's pills, ramify your whole constitution like the measles, and break out on your hide like the pin-feather pimples on a picked goose,—when you want all this, just smash your piano, and invoke the glory-beaming banjo!"[2]

Patent medicines appealed to independent spirits like Jane Clemens and played a major part in the medical care of the nineteenth century. Some of the marketing of these products represented quackery at its worst; at other times the drugs were sold in good faith, based on a belief that they *did* actually result in improvement, if not cures, for those who consumed them. In a sense, patent medicines represented a form of faith healing—according to a twentieth-century reviewer, the greatest contribution to the success of patent medicines arose from "the belief of the buyer in the efficacy of the product."[3]

Self-directed health care fit in well with the overall do-it-yourself attitude of nineteenth-century Jacksonian democracy. In an age when all educated experts were viewed with suspicion by the common man, the multitude of nostrums on the market gave each individual extensive liberty in choosing his own medical treatment as only he saw fit. Clemens observed that his mother was particularly predisposed to employ her freedom to sample freely from the patent medicine cornucopia that was available to her as she tried to determine the best available remedies for her family,[4] and she was responsible for his own predilection for exploring alternative medical approaches: "I hold my mother responsible for my desire for experiment. She bought any patent medicine that came along, whether she would need it or not.... When my mother heard of a new cure, she didn't select one from the flock haphazardly. No, she chose judiciously, and chose the one she could spare, which was myself" (*MT Speaking*, 386). Jane Clemens's fascination with patent medicine was immortalized through her son's account of Aunt Polly's enthusiasm for medicating Tom Sawyer: "His aunt was concerned. She began to try all manner of remedies on him. She was one of those people who are infatuated with patent medicines and all new-fangled methods of producing health or mending it. She was an inveterate experimenter in these things. When something fresh in this line came out she was in a fever, right away, to try it; not on herself, for she was never ailing, but on anybody else that came handy" (*Tom Sawyer*, 107–8).

The patent medicine era flourished because of its great appeal to the likes of Jane Clemens, an appeal that was communicated through the development of another great American enterprise—the advertising industry. A pamphlet promoting the benefits of Dr. Bateman's Pectoral Drops is considered to be the first American catalog in print. The patent medicine manufacturers were pioneers in developing and perfecting this classic American art form. The timeless image of the "snake-oil salesman" as the ultimate cliché for deception has become a tribute to the advertising accomplishments of the patent medicine industry (and the fact that P. T. Barnum once wrote patent medicine handbills does not detract from this image). In general, American industry of the era was infantile and trifling, and because of the disproportionate ratio of a strong demand to a limited supply there had been no reason for aggressive or innovative marketing for most manufactured products. The nostrum business was the first industry in which a surplus of cheaply manufactured and easily shipped products quickly arose, and the great surplus of competitive products brought on a need for creative appeals to the general public. The country became inundated with claims of the miraculous effects of Perry Davis's Pain-Killer, not to mention Dr. Pierce's Golden Medical Discovery, Hamlin's Wizard Oil, Doan's Kidney Pills, Holloway's Pills, Dr. Parmenter's Magnetic Oil, Professor Low's Liniment and Worm Syrup, and innumerable other remarkable potions. Sam Clemens was disgusted by the widespread advertising of such remedies by their unscrupulous producers, as he wrote in his notebook: "The surest sign of quack is picture of some ignorant stupid ass in horrible woodcut on a coarse lying, bragging handbill to be treasured by clowns & used in water closets by the rest of the world" (*N&J-1*, 336–37).

The manufacturers of patent medicines also turned to the general public for endorsements. Gushing testimonials from the very believable, sincere, and honest common citizen were a significant component of the marketing effort. The situation was virtually foolproof—most disease is self-limited (with or without intervention), the patent medicines were generally nontoxic, and grateful citizens were pleased to see their pictures in the newspapers along with their words of praise. One newspaper editor advised, "If your brains won't get you into the papers, sign a 'patent medicine' testimonial. Maybe your kidneys will."[5]

The patent medicine craze did not bypass Hannibal, Missouri. The April 20, 1848, issue of the *Hannibal Gazette* contained advertisements for products that promised to cure virtually any ailment known to mankind. Every citizen of Hannibal had the opportunity to learn about Dr. Bragg's Sugar Coated Pills (which could be used to treat "all diseases prevalent in a western and southern climate"), Dr. Larzello's Juno Cordial or Procreative Elixer (for treatment of "impotency and barrenness"), and Dr. McNair's Accoustic Oil (a cure for deafness). If those options did not fit the bill, other choices included Kolmstock's Vermifuge (to eliminate worms), Hay's Liniment (for hemorrhoids), and Genuine Balm of Columbia (to grow hair), not to mention Dr. Connell's Mixture for Gonorrhoea and Gleet. Other available tonics included Dr. Wistar's Balsam of Wild Cherry, Comstock's Concentrated Compound Fluid Extract of Sarsaparilla, Connell's Magical Pain Extractor, Lange's Great Western Indian Panacea, Buchan's Hungarian Balsam of Life, and Dr. Storm's Scotch Cough Candy.[6]

The patent medicine industry of the late nineteenth century symbolized the general spirit of post–Civil War America—an era of greed, self-interest, corruption, and unscrupulous business practices that became permanently identified as "the Gilded Age" after Clemens and Charles Dudley Warner coauthored a novel of the same name. Samuel Clemens not only defined the mood and attitude of this era when he wrote *The Gilded Age*, but he also created the character Colonel Sellers as the embodiment of the patent medicine industry's spirit of pretentiousness and obsession with wealth:

> I've been experimenting (to pass away the time,) on a little preparation for curing sore eyes—a kind of decoction nine-tenths water and the other tenth drugs that don't cost more than a dollar a barrel . . . before many weeks I wager the country will ring with the fame of Eschol Sellers' Infallible Imperial Oriental Optic Liniment and Salvation for Sore Eyes—the Medical Wonder of the Age! Small bottles fifty cents, large ones a dollar. Average cost, five and seven cents for the two sizes . . . You ought to know that if I throw my time and abilities into a patent

medicine, it's a patent medicine whose field of operations is the solid earth!... Annual income—well, God only knows how many millions and millions apiece! (*Gilded Age*, 87–89)[7]

Although the grandiose but bumbling Colonel Sellers was based on James Lampton, a cousin of Clemens's mother, Sellers shared the optimism and enthusiasm of successful Gilded Age entrepreneurs such as Perry Davis. There is no doubt that Davis and similarly minded purveyors of proprietary medicines could make a fortune in the patent medicine business. This fact was not lost on Samuel Clemens. Clemens's fascination with the potential profits of the drug business can be traced to his youth. At the age of twenty, after reading William Lewis Herndon's *Exploration of the Valley of the Amazon, Made Under Direction of the Navy Department (1853–4)*, he made plans to travel to Brazil and explore the Amazon, and perhaps establish a lucrative worldwide coca cartel.

Among the books that interested me in those days was one about the Amazon. The traveler... told an astonishing tale about coca, a vegetable product of miraculous powers; asserting that it was so nourishing and so strength-giving that the native of the mountains of the Madeira region would tramp up-hill and down all day on a pinch of powdered coca and require no other sustenance.
I was fired with a longing to ascend the Amazon. Also with a longing to open up a trade in coca with all the world. During months I dreamed that dream, and tried to contrive ways to get to Para and spring that splendid enterprise upon an unsuspecting planet. (*WIM&OPW*, 459)

This scheme never got off the ground. Clemens started off for the Amazon and did make it as far south as New Orleans, where his desire to become a steamboat pilot replaced his plans to control the cocaine industry.

Samuel Clemens never forgot, however, that there was a great potential for profit in dealing with the gullible, as he suggested in "The Man That Corrupted Hadleyburg": "'Dr.' Harkness... was one of the two very rich men of the place, and Pinkerton was the other. Harkness was proprietor of a mint; that is to say, a popular patent medicine" (*Hadleyburg*, 70).

In 1893, Clemens invented his own patent medicine for treatment of "chilblains" (a now antiquated term for the painful swelling in the hands or feet that follows exposure to cold weather). Clemens proposed the name "Clark's Swift Death to Chilblains" for his creation, which, as he confided to his brother Orion, was nothing more than ordinary kerosene. There was, of course, no "Clark," and Clemens suggested that "Hall's" would do just as well as "Clark's," if Orion preferred. Sam Clemens advised Orion to take out a trademark on the invention and then to start marketing it. ("The one thing necessary to do," advised Sam, "is to add a perfume which will *thoroughly disguise the smell*—& at the same time the *color*, I should suggest.") Samuel Clemens was knowledgeable about the details of sales and profit margins and gave Orion further instruction about preparation of the product: "A gill & less is enough to put in your bottles, I should say—your smallest size—but you could have several sizes—from 50 cents up to what you please. Some remedies are costly because they have to have alcohol in them to prevent freezing. This one doesn't. This one can be prepared for a song & sold at 1000 per cent profit" (*Ltrs-Microfilm-1*, vol. 7, #04332).

It could be argued that Clemens's intent was to cheat the public out of its money. To take plain kerosene, which was a staple in every American household (where it was burned in lamps), throw in some cheap perfume for color and smell, and then sell it in small overpriced bottles—with the intent of generating a 1,000 percent profit—could be viewed as intrinsically dishonest. An alternative argument might be that his proposal was a model of intelligent capitalism at its best. Profit margins aside, it is probably important to observe that Clemens had a great deal of faith in his product and had even used it himself with an excellent outcome: "Mine were the worst chilblains that ever were. I had suffered with them every winter for 22 years when I tried the kerosene oil in 1862. Three saturations cured them until 1864 when they returned, & succumbed to a couple of saturations. They returned in a mild form in '69 & I finished them with one application. They have never come back again" (*Ltrs-Microfilm-1*, vol. 7, #04332).

Clemens continued to experiment on himself with patent medicines throughout his lifetime, and in 1899 he reported that he had found a patent medicine that had done wonders in helping relieve the discomfort of his hemorrhoids. "No physician has ever helped my semi-annual itching piles with even a moment's relief; but I have a rather deadly quack medicine that can do it" (*Ltrs-Rogers*, 406).

In spite of his periodic infatuations with the drug industry, Clemens always came back to the position that the chicanery of the patent medicine business placed it solidly within the domain of the unscrupulous. When he introduced the characters of the Duke and the King in *Adventures of Huckleberry Finn*, he could find no better way to identify them as con artists than to have them proudly proclaim themselves to be sellers of patent medicines. After the King explained that he had "been selling an article to take the tartar off the teeth—and it does take it off, too, and generly the enamel along with it," the Duke responded in kind by noting that he himself had also been known to "do a little in patent medicines . . . oh, I do lots of things—most anything that comes handy, so it ain't work" (*Huck Finn*, 161–62). These characters may have been modeled after the traveling con men who came through Hannibal during Clemens's youth. In 1847, the *Hannibal Journal* identified a visitor to the area as a "Professor of diseases of the eye, from the London Opthalmic Institution." After further interaction with the "Professor," the man's credentials and integrity came into question, as the *Journal* reported in its edition of October 21, 1847:

> A scamp named ROBINSON, and calling himself Doctor, who has been *blowing* about the country for some months past, after managing to get smartly into our debt, left, a few days ago, for parts unknown. He professes to be an oculist, but we conjecture it would puzzle him to tell the difference between fistula in oculo and fistula in *ano* . . . he may infallibly be recognized by his cockney brogue, liverystable *gait*, vulgar manners, and a habit he has, when on horseback, of galloping as if the Devil or the constable was hard after him. He always requires one-third of his pay in advance—a practice . . . which *we* wish we had adopted in our transactions with him.[8]

Although patent medicine represented itself as a form of self-directed therapy for the common man, the industry eagerly tried to bolster its image by seeking testimonials from well-recognized sports heroes, stage stars, military heroes, and national figures such as William Henry Harrison, Martin Van Buren, Andrew Jackson, and the Supreme Court's own John Marshall (who endorsed Gray's Invaluable Patent Ointment). Even as late as 1900, more national advertising money was spent for patent medicines than for any other products.[9]

It should be no surprise that Samuel Clemens, the most recognizable man of his era, was a target of the patent medicine marketers. In November 1905, he received a letter and a four-page circular from J. H. Todd of San Francisco. According to Todd, the circular discussed "Health and Life and how to retain them in the Body as long as you want & wish without Disease-Death, and always in youthful feeling." Todd advised Clemens, "The Age of Reason is now begun & will never end again," and offered to answer any questions Clemens might have "regarding the Truth of Natural Life" (MTP, #34736). The circular was a lengthy advertisement of the virtues of "T. Duffy's Solution, the Elixir of Life," which was designated a "Blood Purifier, Antiseptic, Disease Destroyer" and the "Giver of Life Everlasting." The potion claimed the power to cure everything from acne to whooping cough, including diabetes, dandruff, and tapeworms. "Tumors of the body" were to be treated by applying hot compresses of the solution, taking daily sponge baths with it, and drinking six wineglassfuls of it daily "until cured." Hourly sponge bathing with the solution, combined with ingestion of a wineglassful of the elixir hourly, was recommended for the treatment of typhoid fever and malaria. According to the circular Todd sent Clemens, the "Elixir of Life" was a "CURE of all ailments of the Human, Animal and Fowl," and the only requirement was that the patient maintain "a strict and faithful following of the printed directions for treatment."

Clemens was angered by the solicitation (which undoubtedly brought back memories of his experiences with Perry Davis's Pain-Killer), but he decided against publicly venting his indignation. Instead, he chose to defuse his anger by writing a letter that he never mailed: "A few minutes from now my resentment will have faded & passed, & I shall probably even be praying for you; but while there is yet time I hasten to wish that you may take a dose of your own poison by mistake, & enter swiftly into the damnation which you & all other patent medicine assassins have so remorselessly earned & do so richly deserve." Clemens's opinion of those who profited from the exaggerated claims of patent medicines was straightforward and pulled no punches (at least in his unmailed diatribe): "The person who wrote the advertisements is without doubt the most ignorant person now alive on the planet, also without doubt he is an idiot, an idiot of the 33rd degree, & scion of an ancestral procession of idiots stretching back to the Missing Link" (*Ltrs-Microfilm-2*, vol. 7, #07214).[10]

Clemens was not the only person to recognize a scam when he saw one. The "yellow journalist" Samuel Hopkins Adams intensely attacked the patent medicine business, which he characterized as "The Great American Fraud," in a series of articles published in *Collier's* beginning in October 1905. This was the first significant assault on the patent medicine industry and was followed by a publicity campaign by the American Medical Association (AMA) that reduced the public's confidence in patent drugs even further.[11] These efforts finally exposed the fraudulent advertising of useless products, the peddling of alcohol and opiates in the guise of effective medical treatment, and the extent of the ill-gotten gains taken from a gullible public, setting the stage for the passage of laws that crippled the patent drug market and brought an end to the Great American Fraud.[12]

Clemens himself contributed to the twelfth and final article of Adams's series. In "The Scavengers," Adams attacked those who fraudulently claimed to cure alcoholism or drug addiction when, in truth, they were actually maintaining (and often increasing) their victims' dependency on alcohol, cocaine, or morphine by selling them more of the same. For Adams, these "scavengers" were "leeches of the utmost slime" who lived at "the bottom of the noisome pit of charlatanry." This concluding article, which appeared in the *Collier's* of September 22, 1906, described an incident in which the famous Mark Twain had been taken advantage of by such unscrupulous methods. As reported in Adams's article, Samuel Clemens had sent a servant to the Oppenheimer Institute in New York two years earlier in order to obtain a cure for the man's alcoholism. Within two weeks of the "cure," which had cost Clemens $150, the man showed up at Clemens's home "maudlin drunk." Adams noted that "Mr. Clemens, like most people, dislikes to be buncoed. Unlike most Americans, he is willing to take some trouble on his own account to make trouble for the buncoer."[13]

Indeed, Clemens had been annoyed by the event, and he asked Dr. Isaac Oppenheimer to provide an explanation for the failure of his presumably foolproof program to cure Clemens's butler of his alcoholism. Clemens's anger was intensified by the nature of Oppenheimer's response; Oppenheimer told Clemens that the man was a "dipsomaniac," and that "dipsomania" was an incurable condition. Clemens's own account of the situation can be found in a letter of complaint he wrote to the advisory board of the Oppenheimer Institute: "Dr. Oppenheimer confuses me a little. He says he can cure dipsomania, & in the same breath explains that he can't. Apparently he can cure a dipsomaniac if the dipsomaniac will furnish the necessary auxiliary 'brains'—(resistance-power). That is, the doctor will load the gun if the gun will do the firing. He knows that a dipsomaniac is no such gun, & that the offer is an offer of nothing at all" (*Ltrs-Microfilm-1*, vol. 10, #7191). Adams's article on "The Scavengers" was published ten months after Clemens wrote his letter of complaint to Oppenheimer's advisory board, and Clemens's influence on Adams's exposé is obvious. In the article, Adams repeated Clemens's complaint about the deceitfulness of Oppenheimer's circular argument that the Oppenheimer system was guaranteed to succeed for anyone who would follow his recommendations to the letter. Oppenheimer promised to cure anyone who would follow his directions, but his directions consisted only of the advice to stop drinking alcohol. Oppenheimer had set up his program so that it could never be accused of failing; every relapse was the patient's own fault for not following Oppenheimer's advice!

Clemens recognized that Oppenheimer's methods were just another variation of the patent medicine fraud he had known since childhood. Clemens's desire to "make trouble for the buncoer" led him to seek out Adams and direct Adams's attention toward Oppenheimer's scam. Clemens had no trouble in convincing Adams that Oppenheimer's promise to cure alcoholism was disingenuous, and Adams followed up on Clemens's tip by featuring Oppenheimer as an excellent example of a "scavenger" in the conclusion to his "Great American Fraud" series.[14] It was Clemens's own anger at Oppenheimer's fraud that compelled him to volunteer as a soldier in Adams's national crusade, and Adams reciprocated by reinforcing Clemens's suspicion that the Oppenheimer Institute represented just another version of the patent medicine scam— Adams wrote a letter advising Clemens that "the Oppenheimer crowd has come out openly as nostrum vendors, in their advertising of 'Oppenheimer Tonic'" (MTP, #35520).

As Clemens began to collect more information for Adams to use against Oppenheimer's enterprise, he became curious about why the prominent individuals on the organization's advisory board had allowed their names to be used in support of Oppenheimer's Institute in the first place. He discovered that many of the board members were influential ministers who were deceived by the institute's promise of restoring drunkards to sobriety, and that many of them later withdrew their support when they found out that the operation was a scam. Clemens wrote to a number of them and then passed their responses on to Adams, enabling Adams to list the names of those who "got their fingers burnt pulling other people's chestnuts out of the fire."[15]

Through his investigations, Clemens was dismayed to find that those who had been so eager in their public endorsement of Oppenheimer's operation generally remained publicly silent after they discovered they had been supporting a scam. He attacked this deceit of silence in a letter he addressed to Adams with the intention that Adams would include it in the *Collier's* article (which he did):

Dear Adams—I think that the majority of the illustrious men whom I questioned by mail as to their reasons for recommending Oppenheimer's policy-shop, exhibited themselves as astonishingly careless and dangerous citizens in their replies. They knew that the public believed in them and trusted them, and they were treacherous to that trust, and shamed it. You say that when they discovered how they were being used, they withdrew their names. IN SILENCE. Do you think that that was sufficient? It does not seem so to me. I think that until they repent publicly over their damaged names, the country ought to be ashamed of them as you will see by their letters that they are privately ashamed of themselves. It is certainly laughable—and also pathetic—to see grown-up men act as these illustrious children have acted.[16]

The "Great America Fraud" described by Samuel Adams was but one component of the chicanery of the "Gilded Age" that had been defined by Samuel Clemens. The efforts of Adams and others increased public awareness of the intrinsic worthlessness and the potential harmfulness of patent medicine remedies. Paradoxically, the same newspaper industry that had been responsible for the success of patent medicines through its advertising efforts eventually spearheaded the demise of the patent medicine trade by educating the public. The AMA accelerated the pace of the reform efforts by reprinting Adams's articles in pamphlet form and distributing them widely. The AMA also initiated its own series on quackery and patent medicine fraud in the *Journal of the American Medical Association* and then reprinted its exposés in a three-volume series entitled *Nostrums and Quackery*. The AMA's 1912 list of "Pamphlets on Medical Fakes and Fakers" (which were available to the public at four cents a copy) characterized "Murine Eye Remedy" as "the modern Colonel Sellers."

Although Samuel Hopkins Adams's articles brought the deceptions of the patent medicine racketeers to America's center stage, the reform of the patent medicine industry was a prolonged and gradual process. Initial attempts in the 1880s by some states to pass formula-disclosure bills were blocked by the actions of the patent medicine lobbying organization, the Proprietary Association.[17] This special interest alliance managed to keep proprietary medicines from being defined as drugs in a number of bills that came before Congress. However, a 1904 Senate bill finally had a broad enough definition to include patent medicines as drugs. The Pure Food and Drugs Act of 1906 required that the presence and quantity of substances such as alcohol, cocaine, and opiates be given on the label. As a result, "a lying label [became] illegal instead of merely immoral."[18]

Even so, American entrepreneurs continued to make huge profits by selling patent medicine to unwary consumers. The role of alcohol in the popularity of many patent medicines throughout the nineteenth century and into the twentieth is exemplified by the phenomenal sales of Peruna, which may have been the most prominent proprietary product in the country. In 1936, the AMA reviewed the history of Peruna and noted that the original Peruna "contained about 27 per cent of alcohol and very little else of importance,"[19] and even assays in 1907 and 1910 showed a 20 percent alcohol content. Sold for a dollar a bottle, Peruna cost its millionaire promoter Dr. S. B. Hartman no more than eighteen cents a bottle to produce. Even though Dr. Hartman declared that no one could become intoxicated by taking the prescribed doses of Peruna, reporter and muckraker Samuel Hopkins Adams was of the opinion that the prescribed dose (three wineglassfuls taken over forty-five minutes) "might temporarily alter a prohibitionist's outlook on life." In 1906 the Peruna company "was notified that it either must put some medicine in its 'booze' or it could be sold only in saloons."[20] The response from the Peruna company symbolized the Gilded Age approach to public relations—"Dr. Hartman has always been a strict temperance man himself, and when the government proposition was made to him that he must either manufacture and sell Peruna as an alcoholic beverage or change the formula he was shocked beyond all measure. . . . He could not bring himself to engage in anything that looked like liquor traffic."[21] As the result of Peruna's widespread use as an intoxicant, a derogatory new term for a special type of alcoholic became part of the American vocabulary—the "Peruna drunk." In 1906, Samuel Clemens (who was already fond of making self-depreciating comments about his affinity for cheap cigars) suggested that his lowbrow tastes also predisposed him to using Peruna as his standard alcoholic beverage, as he indicated in a tongue-in-cheek letter of thanks to Andrew Carnegie after Carnegie had sent Clemens some whiskey from Scotland:

> Dear St. Andrew,—The whisky arrived in due course from over the water; last week one bottle of it was extracted from the wood and inserted into me, on the instalment plan, with this result: that I believe it to be the best, smoothest whisky now on the planet. Thanks, oh, thanks: I have discarded Peruna. (*Ltrs/Paine*, 2:789)

In the mid-twentieth century, comedian Groucho Marx discussed the popular alcohol-containing patent medicine Hadacol on his radio program. Marx asked inventor Dudley J. LeBlanc what his product was good for, and LeBlanc replied, "It was good for five and half million for me last year."[22] Additional legislation later in the twentieth century, long after Samuel Clemens's death in 1910, finally put the patent medicine companies out of business. Clemens's poor opinion of the patent medicine industry, and his frustration at the government's unwillingness to close it down sooner, is obvious in a letter he wrote in 1900 to his close friend Reverend Joseph Twichell.

> [W]ith curious and senile inconsistency, the State has allowed the man to choose his own assassin—in one detail—the patent-medicine detail—making itself the protector of that perilous business, collecting money out of it, and appointing no committee of experts to examine the medicines and forbid them when extra dangerous. Really, when a man can prove that he is not a jackass, I think he is in the way to prove that he is no legitimate member of the race. (*Letters/Paine*, 2:689–92)

7

THE AUTOPSY

"Dissection by the Doctors!"

Dental surgeons suggested doctors, doctors suggested death...

—Mark Twain, *A Tramp Abroad*

As much as Jane Clemens tried to protect her young son from measles, scarlet fever, and cholera, she could not isolate him from the reality of death. He witnessed the deaths of his own young siblings. He saw the terrifying and brutal deaths of strangers. From an early age, Samuel Clemens came to learn that death was omnipresent, death could come with little warning, and sometimes death could be frighteningly violent. Clemens's early childhood experiences exposed him to death in many of its most disturbing variations, and these encounters created horrifying memories that he could never entirely get out of his head.

"It is hard to forget repulsive things" (*Inn. Abroad*, 175), Clemens proclaimed in *The Innocents Abroad*, as he recounted an upsetting childhood incident in which he encountered a corpse in his father's office. In September 1843, before he was even eight years old, Sam Clemens sneaked through the window of his father's office late at night, in the hope of avoiding punishment after he had skipped school. He soon sensed that he was not alone in the dark, and he came to discover that he was sharing the room with a dead man. James McFarland had been stabbed near John Clemens's office earlier that afternoon and died within an hour of being carried into the office for medical care.[1] Years later, Clemens still recalled his emotions when he first found a pale hand on the floor and then discovered that "the pallid face of a man was there, with the corners of the mouth drawn down, the eyes fixed and glassy in death!" He watched in fright as the moonlight slowly crept down the man's bare chest until it eventually displayed the "ghastly stab" that was the cause of death. Sam Clemens then rushed out through the window, eager to take any punishment that might await him at home rather than stay one more minute with the dead man. From that moment on, death was a reality that Samuel Clemens could never escape. "I have slept in the same room with him often, since then—in my dreams" (*Inn. Abroad*, 177).

Violent death visited young Sam Clemens again in 1845, when Hannibal merchant William Perry Owsley shot a local farmer, Sam Smarr, after Smarr accused Owsley of stealing a large sum of money from a friend. The shooting took place at the corner of Hill and Main Streets, not far from Clemens's boyhood home. After the shooting, Smarr was carried into the nearby drugstore owned by Dr. Orville R. Grant, where he was placed on the floor with the bullet hole in his chest exposed. His death, half an hour later, was observed by nine-year-old Sam Clemens. The details of the episode were reinforced in the boy's mind as his father, as justice of the peace, took depositions from twenty-nine witnesses. The killing was used as the model for a shooting in chapter 21 of *Adventures of Huckleberry Finn*, in which Clemens changed the identity of the shooting victim from Sam Smarr to a harmless drunk that he identified as "old Boggs." This death had a profound impact on Clemens. Fifty-five years after the shooting, in 1900, he wrote: "I can't ever forget Boggs, because I saw him die, with a family Bible spread open on his breast."[2]

In 1846, John Clemens's financial problems caused him to move his family from their home on Hill Street into the upstairs of the same Grant's Drug Store where Sam Clemens had watched the death of Sam Smarr a year earlier. In 1847, John Clemens contracted pneumonia after riding his horse in a sleet storm to the county seat in Palmyra, Missouri, and he died in one of the upstairs rooms in Grant's Drug Store. Even though Samuel Clemens's relationship with his father had always been cool and strained, that fact did nothing to blunt the eleven-year-old boy's emotional trauma at the death of his father.

As though the youngster's distress at the death of his father would not have been enough to deal with, the pain and shock intensified profoundly after Samuel Clemens surreptitiously observed his own father's autopsy by the family's physician, Dr. Hugh Meredith. Due to the secretive and psychologically traumatic nature of this bizarre experience in the life of a young boy, the details surrounding this event are fragmented and even a bit circumstantial, but fairly clear. In "Villagers of 1840–3," a collection of notes Clemens wrote in 1897 to recall the most significant people and events from his Hannibal childhood, the entry on his father is followed by a terse note: "The autopsy" (*Inds.*, 105). He revisited the subject in his notebook entry for October 10, 1903: "1847. Witnessed post mortem of my uncle through the keyhole."[3] In truth, there was no uncle who died in 1847; instead it was John Marshall Clemens who died on March 24, 1847. Orion Clemens apparently alluded to this ghoulish event in an autobiography that is no longer extant, and William Dean Howells admonished Sam Clemens to be certain that the passages about the autopsy were never printed.

The reason for the autopsy is uncertain. In *Sam Clemens of Hannibal,* a biography of Clemens's youth, Dixon Wecter has suggested that Dr. Meredith was intrigued by the "mysterious maladies" of John Clemens, which included "the excruciating attacks every spring that he had called 'sunpain,' his nervous exhaustion and the weak lungs that had sent him in early manhood to the Cumberland Mountains, and the later years of self-dosage" with Cooke's pills. Meredith settled his curiosity, Wecter speculated, by seeking Jane Clemens's permission to perform the autopsy "in days when dissection of the human cadaver was still a rare and often clandestine privilege." Regardless of the reason for the autopsy, it was Wecter's opinion that its psychological impact on Sam Clemens was substantial. "Whatever macabre glimpses young Sam's gaze of fascination and horror may have caught as he peered through the keyhole of that death chamber—later unburdening his secret, no doubt, to his elder brother—their effect can well be imagined upon this sensitive child, so long intimidated by the stern man upon whose corpse this last indignity had fallen."[4]

Even many years later, the image of postmortem dissection persisted in the imagination of Samuel Clemens, as he related in a May 1869 letter that he wrote to his wife-to-be, Livy Langdon, in the hope of getting some sympathy from her. "I used to think of sickness with dread—for I always had visions of dreary hospitals—solitude—shut out from friends & the great world—dragging, uneventful minutes, hours, weeks—hated faces of hired nurses and harsh physicians—& then an unmourned death, a dog's burial, and—dissection by the doctors!" (*Ltrs-3*, 239).

Clemens encountered a new version of death in 1853, five years after John Clemens's death. The victim was a stranger, but Clemens felt a personal responsibility for the death, a new dimension that had not been a part of any other death that had touched his life up until that time. It was a cold January night, and "a poor stranger, a harmless, whisky-sodden tramp" by the name of Dennis McDermid was being harassed by a roving gang of Hannibal boys. McDermid asked for matches to light his pipe. Sam Clemens, in an act of kindness, gave the drunken man the matches he requested. Later that night, the tramp was thrown into the local jailhouse after he terrified a local family with an ax.[5] Before the night was over, McDermid had ignited the straw bedding and dry timbers of his cell, and he burned to death while trapped in the jail. A helpless group of onlookers that included Sam Clemens watched. Clemens recognized the man's face, pleading through the bars, and then he could watch no more. The memory remained with him as one more distressing image of death, as he reported thirty years later in *Life on the Mississippi*.

> I saw that face, so situated, every night for a long time afterward; and I believed myself as guilty of the man's death as if I had given him the matches purposely that he might burn himself up with them. I had not a doubt that I should be hanged if my connection with this tragedy were found out. The happenings and the impressions of that time are burned into my memory, and the study of them entertains me as much now as they themselves distressed me then. (*Life on Miss.*, 549)

In 1858, Clemens once again experienced a harsh reminder of the fragility and uncertainty of life when his brother Henry died from the complications of severe burns sustained in a steamboat explosion. Clemens, who was very close to Henry, not only felt great remorse but even considered himself to be responsible for his younger brother's death, for it was he who had found a job for Henry on the ill-fated *Pennsylvania*. Clemens was steadfastly at Henry's bedside for the week that his brother lingered prior to his death. There does not seem to be much doubt that Henry's fate was sealed from the beginning due to the severity of his burns. A Memphis newspaper reporter was present when Clemens first visited Henry in the makeshift hospital that had been set up for victims of the explosion. There was no question in the reporter's mind that Henry was "dangerously ill from the injuries received by the explosion," and this seemed equally obvious to Clemens; as Clemens approached Henry's bedside for the first time, "his feelings so much overcame him, at the scalded and emaciated form before him, that he sunk to the floor overpowered."[6]

In his autobiographical dictation from January 1906, Clemens concluded that his personal responsibility was twofold. His actions not only put Henry on the doomed steamboat, but in addition he was personally responsible for the ultimate cause of Henry's death from overmedication. According to Clemens's revised version of Henry's demise, Memphis physician Dr. Thomas J. Peyton ("a fine and large-hearted old physician of great reputation in the community" [*Autob/NAR*, 148]) had worked diligently to bring Henry out of danger. Dr. Peyton gave Sam Clemens the responsibility of asking the medical student on watch to give Henry a small dose of morphine, if needed, to assure that Henry slept peacefully. During the night, Henry awoke in pain, and Clemens requested the dose of morphine that was needed to overcome the pain.[7] Henry died later during the night, and Clemens came to the conclusion that the death of his brother was directly attributable to an overdose of morphine that had been administered as a result of his request. "The physicians on watch were young fellows hardly out of the medical college, and they made a mistake—they had no way of measuring the eighth of a grain of morphine, so they guessed at it and gave him a vast quantity heaped on the end of a knife blade, and the fatal effects were soon apparent. I think he died about dawn" (*Autob/NAR*, 148).

Henry's death had parallels to the death of the tramp in Hannibal's jailhouse—both deaths were by burning, and Clemens considered himself to be the responsible party in each case. Life was difficult enough when he learned as a small child that death could strike so quickly and so arbitrarily. It became far more complicated when he learned as a young man that the death of another human being could occur as a result of his own well-intentioned actions, such as giving a match to a cold tramp or asking for morphine to alleviate the pain of a scalded brother. Even before he was married and responsible for his own family, Samuel Clemens was probably beginning to understand his mother's motivation for trying to take control of her family's medical care. It was not logical to sit back and do nothing when people were sick; they had a way of dying if their fate was left to Nature. At the same time, health was too important a responsibility to leave in the hands of the inept.

As much as Clemens's childhood experiences sensitized him to the never-ending threats of disease and death, he was increasingly influenced by another observation that repeated itself through his adult life. *Doctors did not appear to be of much help to those who were seriously sick.* They did not prevent his young siblings Margaret and Benjamin from dying shortly after the onset of acute illnesses. Physicians could not stop James McFarland from dying after his stabbing. They did not help Sam Smarr recover from his bullet wound. Doctors did not save his father from death by pneumonia, but instead they heaped on further insult by dissecting his body. Doctors did not prevent Henry from dying from his terrible burns (and, if anything, the doctors may have even hastened his death through their misuse of their own therapies). The doctors he knew throughout his life were like the doctors he wrote about in his story "Two Little Tales": "The Emperor commanded the physicians of greatest renown to appear before him for a consultation, for he was profoundly disturbed. He was very severe with them, and called them to account for letting his soldiers die; and asked them if they knew their trade, or didn't; and were they properly healers, or merely assassins?" (*CT-2*, 499).

Clemens explored the concept of "death by doctor" further in *Which Was It?* by lampooning the excesses of allopathic medical therapy. When Dr. Bradshaw is called upon to treat the ailing George Harrison, he treats Harrison with traditional allopathic treatments that include bloodletting, purging, and the prescription of vile medications. Harrison had been visited earlier by the ghostly premonition of his own death ("Deathshead"), but Dug Hapgood suggests that Dr. Bradshaw himself poses an even more ominous threat to Harrison's survival than the Deathshead: "Good-bye, George! I said good-*bye*,—understand? Better to have him than Deathshead—hey? *Quicker*, you know—and certainer; I said *certainer*—get it?" Hapgood elaborates on the risks of being treated by a medical doctor such as Bradshaw:

> "Say, George, you didn't need them both; I said you didn't need them *both*. Get it? Deathshead and the doctor, you know. Either'll do, though of course if there was a bet on, I'd put my money on the doctor. Deathshead's good—I ain't meaning to disparage Deathshead, George—but he's only an amature, when all's said and done, whereas old Bradshaw's been in the business since creation, I reckon; and besides he's got *science* back of him, and it makes an awful difference George, don't you know." (*WWD&OSW*, 286–87)

In 1905, Clemens expanded on the concept that doctors were killers. He expressed the opinion that physicians may be deadlier than the most efficient army, based on the experiences of the Spanish-American War, and he suggested that the military could become an even more efficient killing machine if its soldiers were to be replaced by doctors.

> [T]he lessons of the Cuban War were not lost upon the Government. Immediately after that conflict it reorganized its military system and greatly improved it. It discarded soldiers, and enlisted doctors only.

These it sends against the enemy, unencumbered by muskets and ar-
tillery, and carrying 30 days' ammunition in their saddlebags. No other
impediments. The saving in expense is quite extraordinary. Where
whole armies were required before, a single regiment is sufficient now.
In the Cuban War it took 142,000 Spanish soldiers five months to kill
268 of our defenders, whereas in the same five months our 141 doctors
killed 3,849 of our said defenders, and could have killed the rest but
they ran out of ammunition. Under our new system we replace 70,000
soldiers with 69 doctors. As a result we have the smallest army on our
planet, and quite the most effective. (*WWD&OSW*, 539–40)

As the years went by, it seemed that Clemens could come to one logical conclusion about the effectiveness of medical treatment. *Doctors do
not appear to be very well trained, and they are unlikely to be helpful when people
need them the most. Doctors may be more likely to harm than to help.* Clemens
shared his conclusion with his friend Henry Rogers in a letter he wrote
in September 1902. "It seems a stupid idea to keep a student 4 years in a
medical college to merely learn how to guess—and guess wrong. If ever
I am deadly ill I hope you will stand by me and bar out the doctors and
let me die a natural death" (*Ltrs-Rogers*, 506).

It is noteworthy that Clemens was concerned not only about the ability of physicians but also about the quality of their medical school training. Perhaps this is related to the fact that a medical student's mistake
may have played a role in Henry's death. Samuel Clemens probably
knew more about medical schools than did most Americans of his day.
The first medical school west of the Mississippi had been started in St.
Louis during his adolescence, a short distance downstream from his hometown of Hannibal. Its founder, Dr. Joseph McDowell, was a brilliant
lunatic whose peculiarities caused him to become well known to the citi-
zenry of Hannibal. McDowell was a superb medical educator and a
skilled surgeon who had an obsession with death that drove him to purchase the local cave in Hannibal (a popular recreational site for Samuel
Clemens and his boyhood comrades) in order to conduct some odd
experiments. Dr. McDowell was one of the leading physicians of his day,
and he had a major influence on Samuel Clemens's understanding of
medicine, medical education, and medical care. What Clemens learned
from McDowell was far more ghoulish than appealing, and would have
done little to increase Clemens's confidence in orthodox medicine.

8

THE GREAT DR. JOSEPH MCDOWELL

Truth is stranger than fiction, but it is because Fiction is obliged to stick to possibilities; Truth isn't.

—Mark Twain, *Following the Equator*

At the southern end of Hannibal is a cave that was discovered in 1819 by hunter Jack Simms. The cave was first called Simms's Cave or Saltpeter Cave after the discovery that saltpeter could be produced from its deposits of bat guano. The cave was purchased by Dr. Joseph Nash McDowell (1805–1868) of St. Louis during Samuel Clemens's boyhood and subsequently became known as McDowell's Cave. Clemens played in the cave as a boy, and in *The Adventures of Tom Sawyer* he changed its name to McDougal's Cave and used it as a place for Tom Sawyer and Becky Thatcher to get lost and for Injun Joe to die. In his *Autobiography*, Clemens described a macabre feature of McDowell's Cave and its unusual owner:

> The cave was an uncanny place, for it contained a corpse—the corpse of a young girl of fourteen. It was in a glass cylinder inclosed in a copper one which was suspended from a rail which bridged a narrow passage. The body was preserved in alcohol and it was said that loafers and rowdies used to drag it up by the hair and look at the dead face. The girl was the daughter of a St. Louis surgeon of extraordinary ability

and wide celebrity. He was an eccentric man and did many strange things. He put the poor thing in that forlorn place himself. (*Autob/ MTA*, 9)

The highly peculiar Dr. McDowell was a medical legend and a larger-than-life presence in the St. Louis–Hannibal area during Clemens's growing-up years. In *A History of Medicine in Missouri*, E. J. Goodwin declares, "Dr. Joseph Nash McDowell was probably one of the best known physicians who ever practiced in Missouri. . . . Dr. McDowell was a man of many eccentricities, but possessed great ability. He was a skillful surgeon, a polished orator, a brilliant teacher."[1]

McDowell was a highly respected doctor who was elected vice president of the American Medical Association in 1860.[2] A man of extremes, he was kind to the poor, attentive to his family, but unrelentingly ferocious in his attacks on his enemies. He was an excellent surgeon and a remarkable teacher who "had a story to go with every bone, vein, and muscle in the body," and his students admired his ability to "make the dry bones talk."[3] At times they hated him for his vicious sarcasm and condescending attitude, but they also took pleasure in his invectiveness. The students played tricks on him that took advantage of his fears, loaned him money when he needed it, helped him find his way home when he was drunk, and willingly accompanied him on his graveyard raids to obtain cadavers for his medical school. He was a modern-day Pied Piper who organized his students as his personal army, with Don Quixote visions of marching westward to capture northern California for the United States.

McDowell's influence is seen throughout Clemens's writings. For example, his prominence as a medical authority in the Mississippi River valley is evident from a testimonial given by the name-dropping and self-promoting Colonel Eschol Sellers in *The Gilded Age*:

I've been down to St. Louis, and I happened to run across old Dr. McDowells—thinks the world of me, does the doctor. He's a man that keeps himself to himself, and well he may, for he knows that he's got a reputation that covers the whole earth—he won't condescend to open himself out to many people, but, Lord bless you, he and I are just like brothers. . . . Well, the other day he let me into a little secret, strictly on the quiet, about this matter of the plague. (*Gilded Age*, 111–12)

McDowell was a peculiar genius who has been described as a "mixture of commendable attributes and most detestable traits." His enemies

Joseph Nash McDowell. Courtesy of Becker Medical Library, Washington University School of Medicine, St. Louis, Missouri.

feared his never-ending onslaught of epithets and verbal abuse; his colleague Samuel D. Gross said that "no man ever wagged a fouler tongue." Gross continued, "His conduct ... was that of a madman rather than that of a sane person." Henry Clay thought that McDowell "had the greatest mind on earth except for its eccentricities."[4] Those eccentricities, however, were far from trifling things—Max Goldstein of the *St. Louis Star* said that McDowell "was eccentric to a point approximating insanity."[5]

McDowell himself was a tall and imposing man whose gaunt features made him appear almost cadaverous. His passions were both medical and military. On every Fourth of July he would parade about with patriotic zeal, bedecked in a three-cornered Revolutionary War hat with a rooster feather and wearing a large sword under his brass-buttoned blue swallowtail coat as he directed his medical students to fire the cannon he had made by melting down the college bell. He was a superstitious man who refused to give lectures on Fridays. He was so frightened of thunderstorms that he would hide under a bed when one approached. When an armed mob entered the medical school building in pursuit of him after he robbed the grave of a young girl, McDowell claimed he saw the spirit of his deceased mother standing near an embalming table and that he used the light from her halo to help him escape his attackers.[6] He could talk extemporaneously for hours about the evils of alcohol as he took swigs from a pitcher of gin at his side. Dr. Robert Schlueter of St. Louis described McDowell as "a loveable man in his calmer moods, devoted to his family and friends," but also as a man who "never hesitated to talk of his grievances, heaping abuse and epithets upon those who had aroused his ire."[7]

Born in Lexington, Kentucky, on April 1, 1805, McDowell came from a medical family, and he obtained his medical degree at Transylvania University in Kentucky in 1827.[8] He was a superb anatomist and became chair of anatomy at Transylvania for one year, and then he spent another year at Jefferson Medical College in Philadelphia for further anatomic studies.

McDowell returned to Kentucky to join the practice of his uncle, Dr. Ephraim McDowell, who was famous for performing the first abdominal operation in 1809 to remove a large ovarian tumor. McDowell later had a falling out with his legendary uncle and spent considerable energy through the rest of his life in his efforts to destroy Ephraim's reputation.

In 1835, McDowell moved to Cincinnati, where the Medical Department of Cincinnati College had been founded by Dr. Daniel Drake, the brother of McDowell's wife, Amanda, and previously one of McDowell's professors at Transylvania. McDowell served on the faculty as adjunct professor of anatomy and physiology from 1835 until the school's failure in 1839. Increasingly famous for his bombastic outbursts, he adorned his gaunt facial features with a large walrus mustache in an effort to look even more ferocious. He became wrapped up in the battle of extermination between his medical school and the competing Medical College of Ohio, escalating the level of animosity between the schools by hurling abuse and obscenities at faculty and publicly cursing the competing school: "Give me one year's time and I'll blow the damned Ohio College to hell!"[9]

McDowell moved to St. Louis in 1839, after the school in Cincinnati failed, and in 1840 he promptly founded the first medical school west of the Mississippi River. His medical school initially functioned as the Medical Department of Kemper College, a struggling literary institution supported by the Episcopal Church. In 1847 the school became an independent organization known as Missouri Medical College, but it was usually referred to as "McDowell's Medical College." By the mid-nineteenth century, for-profit proprietary medical schools such as McDowell's Medical College had come to dominate and replace the earlier system of apprentice training. Once the medical school movement got started, it took off quickly. Only three American medical schools existed in 1800, but twenty-six new ones were founded between 1810 and 1840, and even more were created in the following years. Entrance requirements for the nineteenth century's medical schools were virtually nonexistent. Literacy was not a requirement, and the majority of medical students had no more than an elementary school education. The course of education was very brief and far from rigorous—each term lasted sixteen weeks during the winter, and after a student completed two identical terms the M.D. degree was awarded automatically. The education was almost entirely didactic, and students often received a degree without ever examining a patient. The demonstration of academic ability was no more of a requirement for graduation than it had been for admission.[10]

The building that Joseph McDowell erected for his school in 1847 symbolized both the impressive success of McDowell's Medical College and the nature of the man who built it. McDowell, a staunch proslavery advocate and a bitter secessionist, designed his building at the corner of Eighth and Gratiot Streets to have a fortresslike appearance. The structure has been described as "a pretentious stone building of octagonal design, with all conveniences for the accommodation of the school," "a strange-looking graystone building that consisted of a three-story octagonal tower and two wings."[11] Its foundations were six feet thick, and it had portholes in its thick walls, with an interior that had a medieval and dungeonlike character. McDowell hoped to eventually extend the structure to eight stories and surround the top with ramparts to round out its appearance as a fortress. He also planned to have a large column extend from the basement to the roof, containing niches for copper vases that would hold the remains of himself and his family members, or perhaps faculty members, but this amenity never came to pass.[12]

McDowell purchased 1,400 discarded muskets from the U.S. Arsenal, and he made several cannons from scrap brass during the political unrest of the 1850s, with the alleged intention of helping Texas preserve its independence. McDowell stored the arms in the medical school building's cupola until the outbreak of the Civil War. (After the Civil War started, he gave the Confederacy a gift of "several brass cannon that had been used on the campus of the McDowell College for salutes.")[13] Passersby often claimed they could see the muzzles of the cannons sticking out from the portholes around the top of the college's tower. In 1851, a mob gathered to throw rocks at McDowell's fortress following rumors that he had lured a German woman into the medical school and murdered her for dissection purposes. The crowd prepared to assault the building, but then fled in all directions after McDowell and some students loaded a cannon and aimed it at them.[14]

Religious paranoia may have been a factor in the design of McDowell's Medical School and in his accumulation of firearms.[15] When a new medical school affiliated with St. Louis University, a Jesuit institution, opened one year after the launching of McDowell's school, McDowell concluded that the Jesuits were out to get him (even though plans to start such a school had been discussed by members of the St. Louis medical society five years earlier), and he gave a two-hour speech in which he harangued against Catholics, Jesuits, and the competing medical school. The dean of the St. Louis University Medical School was Dr. Charles Pope, and McDowell took great pleasure in ranting about "Pope's College" without indicating whether his primary target was the Pope in St. Louis or the Pope in Rome. Fearful of attacks from Catholic enemies, he took to regularly wearing a brass breastplate. The presence of mounted cannons in the copper-covered cupola of the school has also been attributed to McDowell's anxiety about Catholic attackers. (Ironically, but in keeping with his unpredictable nature, McDowell repented and converted to the Catholic faith on his deathbed, with the blessing of Father Pierre J. De Smet, the famous explorer and Indian missionary.)

McDowell's carrying on against "Pope's College" gave medical students such delight that students from both St. Louis medical schools would attend his valedictory speeches. On one such occasion, he told his audience to "sit straight and face the music," and he proceeded to play his violin for several minutes before launching into his speech. He then predicted a poignant and touching scene in which a grateful student would return in future years to pay his respects at McDowell's gravesite, in a field of "rank weeds and seedless grass." McDowell's speech went on to describe the emotional picture of the student honoring his old professor at the "simple marble slab" that would commemorate McDowell's final resting place: "As he stands there contemplating the rare virtues and eccentricities of this old man, suddenly, gentlemen, the spirit of Dr. McDowell will arise upon ethereal wings and bless him. Yes, thrice bless him. Then it will take a swoop, and when it passes this building it will drop a parting tear, but gentlemen, when it gets to Pope's College, it will expectorate upon it."[16]

Not everyone was amused with McDowell's public style. Dr. William Beaumont, president of the Medical Society of Missouri, criticized the

> vain, vindictive itinerants and egotistical characters called Professors of a self-generated, ill-begotten Semi-vital institution yclept "medical school" somewhere in the vicinity, which alike regardless of the common courtesy of Medical communities and destitute of professional decency and etiquette obtruded itself into public notice like a swarm of ephemeral insects by the disgusting noise of its own creation in its sudden transit to decay and nothingness, and of whom we know little, but hear much of senseless vaunting and self-indited plaudits and fraternal adulation in newspapers and pamphlets, and personal gasconading garrulity in community.[17]

McDowell's career as a medical educator was interrupted by the Civil War. It was no secret that McDowell was a rabid gun-toting Southern sympathizer, and home guards stormed his medical college on May 10, 1861, after the attack on Camp Jackson in St. Louis. McDowell fled to Memphis and served as a surgeon in the Confederate army. Because of McDowell's allegiance to the South, the medical school building was seized as contraband to the United States and was converted into a federal military prison (the Gratiot Street Prison). Three wagon loads of human bones were removed from the basement of the medical school, and the medical dissection room was converted into a dining room. Ironically, the building that had been constructed to house McDowell's Medical College became the site of epidemics of smallpox and terrible outbreaks of measles, pneumonia, chronic diarrhea, erysipelas, and vermin infestations. The Gratiot Street Prison suffered from the typical problems of Civil War prisons—severe overcrowding, inadequate ventilation, and poor sanitation. Inmates included Confederate prisoners of war, Southern sympathizers, spies, mail runners, and Union deserters. Nearly all of the prisoners' quarters were reconditioned classrooms, and the fact of the building's earlier function as a medical school was not lost on the im- prisoned—inmates referred to one another as "student," and those who were exchanged or transferred to another prison were said to have "graduated from medical school."[18]

After the war, McDowell returned to St. Louis and reestablished his medical school, and he continued to practice until his death in 1868. His medical school went on successfully and was the predecessor of today's Washington University School of Medicine.

How much did Samuel Clemens know about Dr. Joseph Nash McDowell? Clemens biographer Dixon Wecter states, "Whether in Han- nibal or St. Louis young Sam Clemens probably met the noted doctor."[19] Although there is no documentation that this is so, there is no question that the doctor was well known by name in Hannibal as the owner of McDowell's Cave, a location very familiar to Samuel Clemens. After McDowell purchased the cave, he promptly called attention to himself by first enlarging the original entrance and then sealing it with a stone wall. In the wall, he placed either a gate of iron or a door of thick wood (in *The Adventures of Tom Sawyer*, the cave had a "massive oaken door"), barring the citizens of Hannibal from getting into the cave.[20]

What did McDowell want with the cave? He had a long-lasting inter- est in caves, dating back to his medical school days at Transylvania Uni- versity, where Dr. Samuel Brown was the professor of chemistry. Brown was an expert on saltpeter and the saltpeter mines of Kentucky and prob- ably introduced McDowell to Mammoth Cave in Kentucky, famous as a source of saltpeter. Saltpeter was used for the manufacture of gun- powder and was also thought to have unusual preservative capabilities. In the early nineteenth century, several mummified bodies of American Indians had been discovered in the saltpeter caves in the vicinity of Mammoth Cave, and scientific reports described the excellent state of their preservation.[21] Simms's Cave, also known as "Saltpeter Cave," and soon to become McDowell's Cave, would be attractive to anyone inter- ested in munitions or the preservation of bodies. McDowell was in- terested in both, and the cave was close enough to St. Louis to be readily accessible by boat.

Wecter's biography of Samuel Clemens advises us that Dr. McDowell used his cave as an arsenal for the storage of his weaponry. It is not clear whether McDowell's major military goal was to annex northern California, defend Texan freedom by invading Mexico, fight the Catholic Church, or support the Southern cause (and it seems likely the man changed his military target fairly regularly). If McDowell ever did plan to use the cave to store any of the 1,400 muskets he had purchased, he seems to have changed his mind in favor of keeping the weapons closer at hand in his medical school building.

McDowell *did* store something in his cave more grotesque than firearms—the vat containing the cadaver of a little girl, believed to be his own fourteen-year-old daughter. It has been suggested that the placement of the body in the cave was simply an experiment by McDowell to see whether the limestone cavern would "petrify" a body. Questions and concerns about death had weighed on his mind for a long time. Following the death of one of his children, McDowell placed the body in a copper-lined coffin, which was then filled with alcohol and buried in an orchard. He had the coffin exhumed a year later and removed the body, which he placed in a copper vase shaped like a diploma case, which was filled with alcohol and hermetically sealed. After he purchased the cave in Hannibal, McDowell took the vase containing the girl's body and suspended it from the roof of the cave by means of hooks.[22]

The citizens of Hannibal interfered with McDowell's experiment. The unexplained closure of the cave's mouth generated the predictable curiosity. Local boys found alternative openings into the cave along the hillside, and their explorations led to discovery of the body. Adults broke down the door. Clemens gave an account of the events in *Life on the Mississippi*.

> There is an interesting cave a mile or two below Hannibal, among the bluffs. I would have liked to revisit it, but had not time. In my time the person who then owned it turned it into a mausoleum for his daughter, aged fourteen. The body of this poor child was put into a copper cylinder filled with alcohol, and this was suspended in one of the dismal avenues of the cave. The top of the cylinder was removable; and it was said to be a common thing for the baser order of tourists to drag the dead face into view and examine it and comment upon it. (*Life on Miss.*, 547)

Because of the vandalism by curiosity seekers, McDowell had little choice except to remove the body after it had been in the cave for two years, and he returned it to the family vault in St. Louis.[23]

Later, when McDowell himself was seriously ill and convinced he was going to die, he asked his partner, Dr. C. W. Stevens, and his oldest son, Dr. Drake McDowell, to promise that they would place his own body in a copper receptacle filled with alcohol and suspend it from the roof of Mammoth Cave. He insisted vehemently that he had already received permission for doing so.[24] Of note, McDowell's signature can be found in Mammoth Cave, scratched into a large rock called the Giant's Coffin, with the date of 1839,[25] the year he moved from Cincinnati to St. Louis.

Even before McDowell was blocking off the entryway to his cave in Hannibal, a close relative of Samuel Clemens's was a medical student at McDowell's Medical College. James Andrew Hays (Jim) Lampton, the half brother of Samuel Clemens's mother, was only eleven years older than Clemens. He had lived next door to the Clemenses' Hill Street home in Hannibal in 1845 or 1846, before attending Joseph McDowell's medical school during the 1847–1848 academic year. Jim Lampton moved to New London (ten miles south of Hannibal) in 1849 and visited the Clemens family in Hannibal in 1850 (*HH&T*, 330, 356).[26] By that time, all of Hannibal would have been abuzz with rumors and speculation about the happenings at Dr. McDowell's cave. The *Hannibal Gazette* had described McDowell's activities in the cave on two separate occasions in 1847, mentioning not only the storage of firearms but also the presence of his daughter's body.[27] Cave Hollow, the valley at the cave's entrance, was a popular recreational site for the community. There can be no doubt that the inquisitive Sam Clemens would have pumped Jim Lampton for every bit of information he could get about McDowell and the activities at the strange doctor's medical school in St. Louis.[28]

What bits of information would Samuel Clemens have gained from his young uncle? Clemens's writings show surprising familiarity with the role of anatomic study in medical education—skeletons, cadavers, and autopsies recur throughout his work. His awareness of anatomic issues probably reflects his knowledge of the instructional course at McDowell's Medical College—if medical schools of the era had any focus of excellence, it would be anatomy, and there is no question that McDowell's was a leader in this subject.

In nineteenth-century medical schools, anatomic study occurred in the dissecting rooms where the cadavers were stored. In an episode in the original manuscript of *Adventures of Huckleberry Finn* that was deleted before publication, Clemens portrayed these rooms as ghoulish and frightening places. In this segment, Jim tells Huck Finn the story of a terrifying event that had occurred years earlier, when Jim had been working in a medical college. In the words of Victor Doyno, "the episode presents a relatively rare look at early medical school conditions."[29] The fictional medical school building described by Jim ("a powerful big brick build-

Missouri Medical College, 1847–1870, better known as "McDowell's Medical College." Courtesy of Becker Medical Library, Washington University School of Medicine, St. Louis, Missouri.

ing, three stories high . . . a great big old ramblin' bildin'")[30] could easily have been McDowell's citadel on Gratiot Street. The deleted episode describes Jim's frightening experience in the dissecting room when a cadaver slid off the rollers and perched itself on his neck. This incident may well have been taken from a real medical school experience of Samuel Clemens's uncle, as hinted at in a short entry made by Clemens in his 1866 notebook: "Jim Lampton & the dead man in Dr. McDowell's College" (*N&J-1*, 136).

Samuel Clemens would also have learned from Jim Lampton that the procurement of cadavers, so essential for anatomic study, was a difficult issue for medical schools of the nineteenth century. This high demand created a market for grave robbers, known as "resurrectionists." McDowell was famous for his own grave-robbing activities, and Samuel Clemens used McDowell's nocturnal cemetery excursions as the model for the robbery of Hoss Williams's fresh grave by Muff Potter, Injun Joe, and Dr. Robinson in *The Adventures of Tom Sawyer*.

Clemens's admiration for McDowell is evident in his unpublished notes, in which McDowell is characterized in just a few words: "great

surgeon—contempt for human race—rough, but at bottom kind."[31] In
his *Autobiography,* Clemens speaks of "the lamented Dr. McDowell, whose
name was so great and honored in the Mississippi Valley a decade before the Civil War" (*Autob/MTA,* 10). Dr. Joseph McDowell shared many
of the characteristics of the brusque and highly opinionated physician in
Clemens's short story "Was It Heaven? Or Hell?":

> He was a good doctor and a good man, and he had a good heart, but
> one had to know him a year to get over hating him, two years to learn
> to endure him, three to learn to like him, and four or five to learn to
> love him. It was a slow and trying education, but it paid. He was of
> great stature; he had a leonine head, a leonine face, a rough voice, and
> an eye which was sometimes a pirate's and sometimes a woman's,
> according to the mood. He knew nothing about etiquette, and cared
> nothing about it; in speech, manner, carriage, and conduct he was the
> reverse of conventional. He was frank, to the limit; he had opinions on
> all subjects; they were always on tap and ready for delivery, and he
> cared not a farthing whether his listener liked them or didn't. Whom
> he loved he loved, and manifested it; whom he didn't love he hated,
> and published it from the housetops. (*$30k Bequest,* 71–72)

A large part of Clemens's interest in McDowell was undoubtedly related to the physician's quirky, erratic, and outrageous demeanor. However, there was also no one in the medical profession of the mid-nineteenth
century who had better credentials than McDowell—he was head of
surgery for St. Louis's first two hospitals, a successful medical educator,
a skilled and highly regarded surgeon, and vice president of the American Medical Association. In his *Autobiography,* Clemens gave a fascinating portrait of McDowell's professional style.

> Dr. McDowell—the great Dr. McDowell of St. Louis—was a physi-
> cian as well as a surgeon; and sometimes in cases where medicines
> failed to save he developed other resources. He fell out once with a
> family whose physician he was and after that they ceased to employ
> him. But a time came when he was once more called. The lady of the
> house was very ill and had been given up by her doctors. He came into
> the room and stopped and stood still and looked around upon the
> scene; he had his great slouch hat on and a quarter of an acre of gin-
> gerbread under his arm and while he looked meditatively about he
> broke hunks from his cake, munched them, and let the crumbs dribble
> down his breast to the floor. The lady laid pale and still, with her eyes
> closed; about the bed, in the solemn hush, were grouped the family

softly sobbing, some standing, some kneeling. Presently the doctor began to take up the medicine bottles and sniff at them contemptuously and throw them out of the window. When they were all gone he ranged up to the bed, laid his slab of gingerbread on the dying woman's breast and said roughly:

"What are the idiots sniveling about? There's nothing the matter with this humbug. Put out your tongue!"

The sobbings stopped and the angry mourners changed their attitudes and began to upbraid the doctor for his cruel behavior in this chamber of death; but he interrupted them with an explosion of profane abuse and said:

"A pack of snuffling fat-wits! Do you think you can teach me my business? I tell you there is nothing the matter with the woman—nothing the matter but laziness. What she wants is a beefsteak and a washtub. With her damned society training, she—"

Then the dying woman rose up in bed and the light of battle was in her eye. She poured out upon the doctor her whole insulted mind— just a volcanic irruption, accompanied by thunder and lightning, whirlwinds and earthquakes, pumice stone and ashes. It brought the reaction which he was after and she got well. (*Autob/MTA*, 9–10)

In this vignette, McDowell is portrayed as a crude, insensitive lunatic with a coarse bedside manner. He is the very antithesis of the model of the "perfect" physician in possession of personal warmth, sensitivity, and compassion. This description of McDowell is useful in a historical context, as it confirms that Samuel Clemens was familiar with McDowell and his reputation, whether or not they had actually met. However, far more important than Clemens's description of McDowell is Clemens's recognition that the patient benefited from McDowell's nontraditional approach. Clemens saw that McDowell had an insight into his patient's condition that other physicians did not, and in his unique understanding was hidden the key to her recovery. Dr. McDowell's outrageous behavior provoked his patient to overcome her illness.

In later years, Samuel Clemens would come to learn about another case in which a similarly odd medical approach was used with equally impressive success. The second case, however, struck much closer to home for him—it was the story of how his wife-to-be, Olivia Langdon, had been bedridden in a state of paralysis. She had been resistant to traditional medical treatment, but she was eventually cured by a traveling quack. The afflictions of Livy Langdon, like those of Dr. McDowell's bedridden woman of society, seemed to be different in nature from the acute, devastating, and life-threatening illnesses Clemens knew from his childhood. In his youth, he had learned more than he cared to know about the diseases that traveled as epidemics and put so many people into an early grave. As he grew older, he started to discover another type of malady. The newer ailments were debilitating, but rarely fatal. They seemed to require a significantly different type of treatment.

Section II

I DON'T LIKE MEDICINES

I don't like medicines—and moreover I have but a pale and feeble confidence in them. There's an old Denver pox-patient here who is loaded to the eyes with mercury, and is a poisoned hulk. As between mercury and pox, which would you prefer?

—Mark Twain, letter to Henry Rogers, August 3, 1899

Samuel Clemens's childhood experiences with disease taught him about the toxicities of allopathic medicine. His mother's use of patent medicines showed him that her system was no better. Like other citizens of his era, however, he had many other alternatives, and at one time or another he pursued most of them. His quest for other medical options was learned from Jane Clemens, who was never hesitant about trying new treatment systems. She obviously had no qualms about subjecting her family to the unpleasant and overpriced patent medicines of her day, high in alcohol content and laden with undefined additives. However, she was also willing to explore other therapeutic choices, and she eventually experimented with a form of medical treatment that was much different from patent medicine. The new system used a therapeutic agent that was clean, clear, cheap, and unadulterated. This treatment was hydrotherapy, the "water cure," a benign nontherapy that derived from the concept that water was medicine. Hydropathic medicine was minimalist medicine, a sophisticated system of doing nothing. Philosophically, it was the direct opposite of allopathic medicine (the sanctioned approach of aggressive and excessive treatment) and patent medicine (with its secret and unshared remedies). After all, water was the basis of life; nothing could be less toxic; nothing was more universally available. It was not surprising that hydrotherapy impressed Jane Clemens as a superb alternative to allopathy.

After his introduction to the "water cure," Samuel Clemens went on to explore the potential healing powers of other nontraditional systems such as electrotherapy, "rest cure," and osteopathic medicine. His initial enthusiasm for each new system evolved into disappointment and frustration. Even so, each medical experience was important in adding to Clemens's understanding about the nature of health, disease, illness, and medical care.

9

Hydropathic Medicine

The Flush Times

I began to take the baths and found them most enjoyable; so enjoyable that if I hadn't had a disease I would have borrowed one, just to have a pretext for going on.

—Mark Twain, "Aix-les-Bains"

In a 1901 speech to the New York General Assembly, Clemens suggested that his mother introduced him to hydropathic medicine in 1844.

I can remember when the cold water cure was first talked about. I was then about nine years old, and I remember how my mother used to stand me up naked in the back yard every morning and throw buckets of cold water on me, just to see what effect it would have. Personally, I had no curiosity upon the subject. And then, when the dousing was over, she would wrap me up in a sheet wet with ice water and then wrap blankets around that and put me into bed. I never realized that the treatment was doing me any particular good physically. But it purified me spiritually. For pretty soon after I was put into bed I would get up a perspiration that was something worth seeing. (*MT Speaking*, 386–87)

Hydrotherapy or hydropathic medicine, also known as "water cure," arose in the nineteenth century as an alternative medical care system based on the presumed therapeutic properties of water. In its many variations, hydrotherapy encompassed prolonged bathing in spas, intensive water drinking, and induction of intense perspiration. As with the other sects of medical practice that became popular in the nineteenth century, a major attraction of hydropathic medicine was its apparently benign nature, which set it apart from the excesses of allopathic medicine.

By the time of hydrotherapy's peak in appeal, it had expanded its domain to become more than a method of medical therapy—it incorporated concepts of "healthy" living with an emphasis on dietary and hygienic principles, and it became as much a social movement as it was a healing ideology. The presumption that water was a source of health can be traced back to the Roman baths, but the modern system of hydropathy was developed by a Silesian peasant, Vincenz Priessnitz, around 1829.[1] The hydropathic movement quickly spread throughout Europe. American medical journals began to publish information about hydrotherapy, mainly derived from European medical journals, in the 1830s. The system of Priessnitz became popular in the United States in the 1840s and spread quickly.

Clemens's recollection of his introduction by his mother to "the water cure" in 1844, if accurate, was a strong testimonial to his mother's ability to keep up with the newest trends in medical care. In 1844, when Sam Clemens was nine years old, there would have been nothing newer than the hydropathic movement. Realistically, Jane Clemens would not have been able to utilize hydropathic treatments on her son much later than 1844. By 1848, Sam Clemens had become a fairly independent and high-spirited printer's apprentice and an unlikely candidate for yielding to his mother's whims by standing naked in the backyard as she doused him with frigid water. If he truly subjected himself to such treatment at all, the age of nine years would have been close to the upper limit at which his mother could have managed to enlist his cooperation. In any case, Jane Clemens's enthusiasm for applying hydrotherapy treatments to her son became part of the family folklore; Clemens's niece, Annie Moffett Webster, recalled, "Sam was a seven months' baby and very delicate until he was about six years old. Grandma was strong for the water cure, and he claimed she was always dousing him and giving him cold-packs" (*MTBM*, 45).

The specifics of hydropathic treatment varied. Water could be applied directly to the eye, foot, head, or other affected part of the body through a number of techniques. Most water cures followed the techniques of Dr. Joel Shew of New York, who found that water worked best when it was administered gradually through the skin. Most treatments involved the "wet sheet method," in which a sheet of cotton or linen was dipped in cold water and spread on thick woolen blankets. The sheet and blankets were wound around the patient and fastened with large pins and tape. A feather bed was then thrown on top, where it stayed anywhere from twenty-five minutes to several hours. After the patient developed profuse perspiration, he was unwrapped. Next, cold water was poured over him, or he was immersed in a cold bath, and then he was rubbed vigorously until dry.[2]

The hydrotherapist's underlying principle was very much the same as that of the allopath's scarification methods (although water cure's methodology was certainly much gentler). Just as the creation of a skin wound by the allopath's cupping and blistering would lead to drainage of pus, the sweating created by the hydropath's wet sheet pack provided an obvious and "natural" pathway by which disease-producing internal evils could be removed from the body. By the time Samuel Clemens was first finding out about hydrotherapy, the English poet Alfred Lord Tennyson had become a strong proponent of the advantages of hydropathic medicine over traditional allopathic therapies, stating in 1844 that "much poison has come out of me, which no physic ever would have brought to light."[3] Clemens described the process in detail in *The Adventures of Tom Sawyer* and with tongue in cheek suggested that hydrotherapy might do more than remove disease from within Tom's physical body—it might even be capable of drawing out moral imperfections from the depths of Tom's soul:

> The water treatment was new, now, and Tom's low condition was a windfall to [Aunt Polly]. She had him out at daylight every morning, stood him up in the wood-shed and drowned him with a deluge of cold water; then she scrubbed him down with a towel like a file, and so brought him to; then she rolled him up in a wet sheet and put him away under blankets till she sweated his soul clean and "the yellow stains of it came through his pores"—as Tom said. (*Tom Sawyer*, 108)

Other common techniques of hydropathic medicine involved the use of baths of various types, including the pouring bath and the plunge bath. The most popular was the sitz bath, which required the patient to sit in a washtub roughly one-third full of water, with the feet extended outside the tub. Showers were also used commonly. One type of shower, the douche, consisted of a strong stream of cold water that fell from a height of five to twenty feet as it was directed to the afflicted part of the body. With the shower bath, water was sprayed on the patient from overhead. Clemens was familiar with all of the techniques of hydrotherapy, and he described how Aunt Polly eagerly applied most of them in her effort to raise Tom's sinking spirits: "Yet notwithstanding all this, the boy grew more and more melancholy and pale and dejected. She added hot baths, sitz baths, shower baths, and plunges. The boy remained as dismal as a hearse" (*Tom Sawyer*, 108–9).

Although hydropathic therapy is traditionally viewed as having originated in Europe and become most strongly established on the eastern seaboard of the United States, there is no doubt that American allopathic physicians of the early nineteenth century applied hydropathic principles even before the official arrival of the hydropathic movement. At least one component of hydrotherapy, the promotion of sweating, was particularly popular with allopathic physicians. Profuse sweating was the aqueous analog of the purging and bleeding used by allopathic doctors for the evacuation of disease processes from their patients, and allopaths were not above using hydropathic interventions as a means of flushing disease out of their patients. When Dr. William M. McPheeters of St. Louis described his personal experiences in treating the 1849 cholera epidemic, he made it clear that hydropathic measures were an important part of his arsenal (thus confirming that hydrotherapy had arrived in the Mississippi River valley by the 1840s): "The warm bath, the cold douse were also severely tried . . . blankets wrung in hot water, etc., etc."[4]

The "water cure" occupied an interesting position in the spectrum of medical therapies used by individuals such as Jane Clemens. It was a treatment that was accessible to the common citizen. Although a new wave of nineteenth-century physicians trained in medical schools that taught only hydropathic medicine, hydrotherapy could easily be self-administered, so there was no real need for consultation with a trained practitioner. In this regard, it shared the same attraction for Jane Clemens as did patent medicine. On the other hand, hydropathic medicine adhered to one of the most basic principles of allopathic medicine—the need to remove disease forcibly from the body of the patient. However, unlike allopathy, which exulted in its efforts to puke, purge, bleed, flush, or sweat disease out of the afflicted, hydrotherapy limited itself to using the gentlest of the potential routes of bodily evacuation.

Although hydropathic medicine superficially resembled the allopathic medicine of the era, hydropathic medicine moved American medicine beyond the stagnation of allopathic medicine in several ways. In its basic underlying philosophies, hydropathy was very much anti-allopathic. Hydrotherapists took advantage of every opportunity to contrast their own methods to the intensity and unpleasantness of the treatments of the orthodox physician, the toxicity of his potent drugs, and the dreadful and repulsive nature of his treatments of bleeding, purging, and blistering. Hydrotherapy replaced abhorrent chemicals with soothing water, substituted unquestioned physician authoritarianism with educated patient self-determinism, and rearranged the doctor-dominated system of allopathy into a structure of doctor-patient equality and partnership. Allopathy's scorch-and-burn approach to the war on disease was replaced with the soothing and gentler attitude of hygienic self-improvement through healthier living that was championed by water cure practitioners. The water cure movement began to have great appeal to some of the nation's best educated and most affluent citizens, which included the family of Samuel Clemens's future wife, Olivia Langdon. It also created a new paradigm of looking at health and disease, as hydropathic medicine evolved until it was as much a liberal social movement as it was a system of medical care.

In spite of Clemens's declaration of his annoyance with the backyard hosing-down hydrotherapeutic efforts of his mother in the 1840s, he was far from finished with the methods of hydropathic medicine when he left the home of his childhood. In fact, he purposefully submitted himself to hydrotherapy treatments in the 1860s, and (at least for the public record) he claimed to be convinced of the benefit of the water cure. Clemens had earlier achieved his childhood dream of becoming a steamboat pilot until the Civil War shut down most of the steamboat traffic on the Mississippi River. Essentially unemployed, Clemens took advantage of an opportunity to move west to the Nevada Territory with his brother Orion, and he started working as a reporter for the *Virginia City Territorial Enterprise*. He developed a severe cold in July 1863, which he used as an excuse for taking some time off from his duties. He spent two weeks recuperating at Lake Tahoe, and then he went to Steamboat Springs in Washoe County for another week. The springs had been discovered in 1860 and, by the time of Clemens's 1863 visit, the grounds contained a hotel in addition to a hospital and a bathhouse that were owned by Dr. Joseph I. Ellis (*ET&S-1*, 270–71). Clemens sent a letter to the *San Francisco Morning Call* that gushed about the medical benefits of the establishment with all of the enthusiasm of an advertiser for a patent medicine. He claimed that the steam baths could "restore to health, or at least afford relief, to all classes of patients but consumptives.... Erysipelas, rheumatism, and most other human distempers, have been successfully treated here for three years. Scarcely a case has been lost, the majority are sent home entirely cured, and none go away without having derived some benefit" (*ET&S-1*, 282).

It is not certain whether this comment truly reflected his level of confidence in the healing power of the springs; an alternative interpretation is that Clemens was providing some free advertising for the facility as payment for his interval of vacation there.[5] He described the facilities in further detail in his letter to the *Virginia City Territorial Enterprise* of August 23, 1863, where he noted that "the fame of the baths rests chiefly upon the miracles performed." He described a therapeutic sequence that took him from a cold shower bath to a hot steam bath (where profuse sweating was induced), followed by a visit back to the cold shower bath, and then concluded with a vigorous scrubbing with coarse towels. This letter was burlesque in its tone, and his desire to play to the amusement of his cronies back home in Virginia City was obvious. "More than two-thirds of the people who come here are afflicted with venereal diseases. . . . I know lots of poor, feeble wretches in Virginia [City] who could get a new lease of life by soaking their shadows in Steamboat Springs for a week or two." Clemens also took advantage of the opportunity to take a shot at the methods of traditional physicians by noting that "all ordinary ailments can be quickly and pleasantly cured here without a resort to deadly physic" (*ET&S-1*, 273–74).

In spite of Clemens's enthusiasm for the benefits to be derived from hydrotherapy, the water cure at Steamboat Springs was apparently not as successful in helping him with his own medical complaints. The severe cold and bronchitis that drove him to the springs lingered for more than a month. This lengthy illness gave him an opportunity to write a sketch, "Curing a Cold," that was a parody of the numerous ineffective therapies he pursued. The piece was published in the *San Francisco Golden Era* on September 20, 1863, and it became a standby for Clemens; he revised, reworked, and republished it on several occasions until its final appearance in *Sketches, New and Old* in 1875. The litany of unsuccessful interventions that he subjected himself to included a cold shower bath, ingestion of a quart of warm saltwater, and his trip to the steam baths of Steamboat Springs. Notably, the sketch includes a description of a classic hydrotherapy treatment with a "sheet-bath" in which a sheet soaked in ice water was wound around his bare trunk. The sheet-bath treatment that Clemens described in "Curing a Cold" was similar to the wet-sheet therapy purportedly administered by his mother in Hannibal nineteen years earlier.

"Curing a Cold" is the lead-in illustration for the story by the same name in which Clemens describes his numerous unsuccessful attempts to rid himself of a cold. This drawing by artist True Williams demonstrates the hydropathic method known as a "sheet-bath." Williams often used caricatures of Clemens for the illustrations in Clemens's books; in this drawing, Samuel Clemens is the patient. From *Sketches New and Old* (Hartford: American Publishing Company, 1875), 300. Courtesy of Kent Rasmussen.

Clemens's experience at Steamboat Springs presaged many future encounters with other systems of health care. He readily accepted the claims of validity for essentially every new approach to medical therapy that came his way, and he publicly proclaimed the great benefit to be derived from the treatments (even as his personal experience argued for the opposite conclusion). This willingness to believe in the tenets of every medical care sect that came along, and to embrace them with unrelenting enthusiasm (coupled with his stubborn unwillingness to let an unsuccessful system go, even after its shortcomings had been demonstrated repeatedly), was a mark of the man.[6]

Clemens was not finished with hydropathic medicine when his vacation at Steamboat Springs came to an end. In fact, his introduction to hydropathic medicine through his mother's experimentations and his later encounters with hydrotherapy at Steamboat Springs were only the beginning of his water cure experiences. In spite of the many reasons for him to be cynical about the claims of water cure, his attitude eventually changed from sarcastic to enthusiastic. This change was driven by the influence of the family of his eventual wife, Olivia Langdon. No other person in Clemens's adult life was as influential as Livy Langdon. In his courting days, Clemens's desire to impress Livy and her parents had no limits. The Langdon family lived in Elmira, New York, the epicenter of the water cure movement. The Langdons had been enthusiastic proponents of "water cure" since approximately 1841,[7] and Clemens realized that he needed to accept the ideology of hydropathic medicine if he wanted to be accepted by the Langdon family.

The Elmira Water Cure, located on the road between Elmira and Quarry Farm,[8] was founded in 1852. It was among the first and longest-lived of the two hundred or more American hydropathic facilities that were in operation at the movement's peak. The introduction of the Water Cure to the Elmira area was the beginning of a new era of health care reform. Hydrotherapy's doctrines went beyond a focus on the role of water as a therapeutic agent, and its commitment to temperance and women's reform made it attractive to socially liberal families such as the Langdons. The prominent clientele of the Elmira Water Cure included the likes of Susan B. Anthony, Vice-President Schuyler Colfax, and the mother of Emily Dickinson. Its founder, Dr. Silas O. Gleason, had received his medical degree in 1844 from Castleton Medical College in Vermont, and he had practiced at three other water cures (the Cuba Water Cure, Glen Haven Health Resort, and the Forest City Water Cure) prior to opening the Elmira Water Cure. Gleason was an established and highly regarded leader in the hydropathic movement, and he was elected a vice president when the American Hydropathic Society was organized in New York City in 1849.

The pleasant contrast of the hydropathic treatment program to the harshness of the allopathic therapies led to its rapid rise in popularity.

Elmira Water Cure, ca. 1870s. Photographer unknown. Courtesy of Chemung County Historical Society, Elmira, New York.

The Jamestown Water-Cure at Chautauqua was described as having "an abundance of water of dewey softness and crystal transparency, to cleanse, renovate, and rejuvenate the disease-worn and dilapidated system."[9] Testimonies of miraculous results from water cure were widespread. The benefits of hydrotherapy were extolled as the risks of competing allopathic medicine were condemned. The comment of a patient who was treated in Biloxi reflects the feelings of patients who were converted from allopathy to hydropathy: "It is a happy change indeed from poisonous drugs to pure cold water. Would to heaven, I had come here when I was first taken sick; instead of being butchered by Pill givers. How many hours of pain and anguish I might have been spared."[10]

Hydrotherapy emphasized the sharing of knowledge between the doctor and the patient, and in promoting its own accessibility and availability it deemphasized the importance of university training. The patient's active involvement was believed to be essential to the success of the water cure treatment program, and the expectation was that expertise would be shared between the practitioner and the patient; self-treatment at home was one of hydrotherapy's basic doctrines. Ideally, each patient of hydrotherapy should also be his or her own doctor of hydrotherapy, utilizing hygienic living principles at home and instructing others in the creed.

Hydrotherapy's approach of putting the patient on equal footing with the physician was a dramatic shift in medical mind-set. This set the stage for hydropathy to evolve into an egalitarian political movement with a liberal reformist and emancipationist agenda (a water cure establishment in Massachusetts, owned by Dr. George Hoyt, doubled as a station on the Underground Railroad). Livy's father, Jervis, who had become wealthy in the coal industry, was not only a friend of Frederick Douglass but was also a well-known abolitionist who helped found the antislavery Park Congregational Church in Elmira.[11]

Water cure was also the women's health movement of its age; it viewed puberty, childbearing, and menopause as normal physiological processes rather than as devastating pathological events. Its commitment to the physiology and health of women spilled over to issues of personal and social importance. The leadership of the hydrotherapy movement actively encouraged the participation of female physicians. Hydropathy was a springboard for involvement in issues of dress reform and anti-slavery activities, and those who were already active in social movements seemed particularly attracted to its tenets. Harriet Beecher Stowe and Clara Barton were among those who sought therapy and respite at water cures. For women in the nineteenth century, "hydrotherapy offered an all-encompassing, accessible, and empowering medical and social ideology that valued them for their 'innate' characteristics, for their abilities as individuals, and for the central importance in the campaign for reform of American health and living habits."[12]

The water cure was more than treatment with water. Hygienic principles were emphasized. Dietary modification was an important adjunct to hydrotherapy and included the avoidance of hot or spicy foods. Abstention from alcohol and smoking was a tenet of the system, and most treatment plans included an aggressive course of water drinking. Large amounts of exercise were also prescribed, and many spas provided a variety of recreational activities.

If Clemens had any problem with convincing Livy of his sincere commitment to the tenets of hydropathic medicine, it came from the matter of his smoking. Clemens, who claimed that he started smoking at the age of eight, long believed that no harm could come from the habit, and he even suspected that smoking might be health-promoting in its own way (or so he tried to convince Livy in a letter he wrote in January 1870): "Now there are *no* arguments that can convince me that *moderate* smoking is deleterious to me. . . . I have smoked habitually for 26 of my 34 years, & I am the only healthy member our family has. . . . My health is wholly faultless—& has been ever since I was 8 years old. My physical structure—lungs, kidneys, heart, brain—is without blemish. The life insurance doctor pronounced me free from all disease & *remarkably* sound" (*Ltrs-4*, 21).

Regardless of any benefit or harm from smoking, Clemens was certain it would not be difficult for him to stop whenever he *really* wanted to quit. "You seem to think it will be a Herculean task for me to suddenly cast out a loved habit of 26 years, Livy dear. Either you do not know me, or I do not know myself. I think differently about it. Speak the words, Livy dear—unaccompanied by any of the hated arguments or theories—& you shall see that I love you well enough to follow your desires, even in *this* matter" (*Ltrs-4*, 22).

Clemens never did made a serious attempt to stop, and his love of smoking became part of the classic image of Mark Twain of the later years—white-suited, white-maned, with tousled hair, bushy mustache, and cigar in hand. Clemens's public position was consistent through the years; he was convinced that smoking was not harmful, and actually was a healthful habit, in spite of its detractors. By 1909, while he was suffering from the severe angina that plagued him at the end of his life, he was finally willing to privately admit that his smoking was a major contributor to the cardiac disease that eventually led to his death.

> It is decided that I have what is technically termed a "tobacco" heart. This will move even the wise to laugh at me, for in my vanity I have often bragged that tobacco couldn't hurt me. Privately & between you & me, I am well aware that I ought to laugh at *myself*—& would if I were a really honest person.
>   However the victory over me is not much of a victory after all, for it has taken 63 years to build this disease. I was immune *that* long, anyway.[13]

Nor did Clemens ever show commitment to another major component of the hydropathic system—maintaining fitness through a regular routine of physical activity. He wrote disparagingly about the very concept of regimented exercise for the purpose of improving health after he visited the Marienbad spa in 1891.

> You are strictly required to be out airing and exercising whenever the sun is shining, so I hate to see the sun shining because I hate air and exercise—duty air and duty exercise taken for medicine. It seems ungenuine, out of season, degraded to sordid utilities, a subtle spiritual something gone from it which one can't describe in words, but—don't you understand? With that gone what is left but canned air, canned exercise, and you don't want it. (*Complete Essays*, 103)

In 1905, he gave a speech at his seventieth birthday dinner in which he made clear his dislike of exercise. "I have never taken any exercise, except sleeping and resting, and I never intend to take any. Exercise is loathsome. And it cannot be any benefit when you are tired; and I was always tired" (*CT-2*, 716).

In addition to its focus on health and lifestyle, the hydropathic movement was committed to issues of women's reform, and many hydropathic physicians advocated dress reform both for the improvement of health and for women's advancement. As far as they were concerned, the use of heavy layers of voluminous amounts of fabric with overlying shawls and undergirding tight corsets, all held together with confining lacing and stays, might be fashionable in the eyes of some but could not possibly be natural or healthy. If anything, such restrictive clothing was only one more outward symbol of the confinement of women of Victorian America. Far healthier was the wet dress that was popularized by

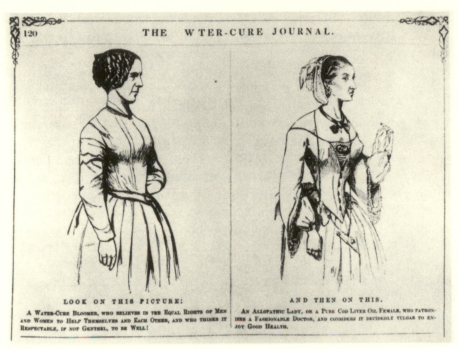

Illustration from the *Water-Cure Journal* (16:120, November 1853). The woman on the left is "A Water-Cure Bloomer, who believes in the Equal Rights of Men and Women to Help Themselves and Each Other, and who thinks it Respectable, if not Genteel, to be Well!" In contrast, the woman on the right is "An Allopathic Lady, or a Pure Cod Liver Oil Female, who patronizes a Fashionable Doctor, and considers it decidedly vulgar to enjoy Good Health."

water cure enthusiasts. Also known as the "Bloomer costume," the dress was a gown with very wide sleeves that was worn during water cure treatments as a convenient alternative to the standard "wet sheet." This loose-fitting dress or coat, similar to Turkish trousers, could be gathered at the ankles above house slippers or fitted into boots. The users of this garment also tended to cut their hair short for ease in drying. Through their departure from traditional women's dress, women of the hydropathic movement declared that they were no longer slaves to the stifling fashions of the day; instead, they had been "emancipated from the bondage of trailing skirts, petticoat, corsets, and corkscrew curls."[14] The suffrage movement adopted the loose and free hydropathic uniform, and the dress became an emblem of female radicalism.

Shortly after Priessnitz's system reached the United States, several water cure journals began publication, and medical schools of hydropathy opened.[15] Natural mineral springs became popular sites, and by the mid-1850s there were twenty-seven hydropathic sanatoriums in the United States, predominantly in rural areas, where water quality was presumably superior. As the "water cure" movement emigrated from Europe, it became most strongly established in the Northeast. Places such as Saratoga became desirable destinations, especially for the wealthy. *The Water-Cure Journal,* published by the well-known phrenologists Orson and Lorenzo Fowler, had more than a hundred thousand subscribers at its peak. Bearing the slogan "Wash and Be Healed," its contents included testimonials to the benefits of hydrotherapy as well as attacks against the negative features of traditional medicine. It published poems and anecdotes describing the benefits of a healthy, hygienic lifestyle. It gave advice on nutrition, warned about the adverse effects of tobacco and liquor, and had regular features on dress reform. As hydropathic medicine decreased in popularity toward the end of the nineteenth century, the water cure movement placed less and less emphasis on hydrotherapy and directed more attention toward hygiene and nutrition, to the extent that the journal eventually felt obligated to revise its name accordingly—in its last years it was simply titled *Health.*

Samuel Clemens continued to be ambivalent in his attitude toward this particular approach to medical care. In public discussion, he showed his doubts that hydropathic medicine was anything better than a second-class rival to allopathic and homeopathic medicine. In an 1867 letter to the *New York Sunday Mercury* ("Official Physic"), Clemens protested the fact that the governing bodies of New York state were taking away the public's medical freedom of choice through their exclusive assignment of specific public health duties to either allopaths or homeopaths. He sarcastically suggested that the state government should feel obligated to make at least a token effort to give some of the other medical sects a share in the duties, with the recommendation that "the hydropathists might be pacified by being allowed a share in public hygienics." In the same letter, in terms that were less than laudatory, he characterized hydrotherapy advocates as individuals "who like to be washed into eternity, or soaked like over-salt mackerel before they were placed on purgatorial gridirons" (CT-1, 228–30).

For the private consumption of the Langdons, however, Clemens deemed it more advisable to portray himself as an unwavering advocate of hydropathic medicine. In a letter written in November 1869, Clemens apparently forgot about the cynical commentary he had made to the *Sunday Mercury* two years earlier as he told Livy about his own personal success with hydrotherapy: "I cured my cold with two long & severe Turkish baths taken in immediate succession, with cold shower baths between—next morning I was entirely well" (*Ltrs-3*, 397).

Even so, he could not restrain himself entirely from lampooning the readers of *Health* and the followers of hydrotherapy methods as he wrote *The Adventures of Tom Sawyer*. The burlesque was gentle and lighthearted, however—probably because Aunt Polly was modeled after his own mother, and because members of his wife's family were such dedicated hydrotherapy followers.

> [Aunt Polly] was a subscriber for all the "Health" periodicals and phrenological frauds; and the solemn ignorance they were inflated with was breath to her nostrils. All the "rot" they contained about ventilation, and how to go to bed, and how to get up, and what to eat, and what to drink, and how much exercise to take, and what frame of mind to keep one's self in, and what sort of clothing to wear, was all gospel to her, and she never observed that her health-journals of the current month customarily upset everything they had recommended the month before. (*Tom Sawyer*, 108)

The water cure movement brought with it a novelty in the world of American medical care—the concept that a woman could be a physician. Hydropathic medicine's policy of progressiveness in women's issues opened opportunities for women in the practice of medicine that had not been available through traditional allopathic medicine. Between 20 and 30 percent of hydropathic physicians were women. Silas Gleason's wife and partner at the Elmira Water Cure, Dr. Rachel Brooks Gleason (1820–1905), had studied medicine privately with her husband prior to entering Central Medical College in Rochester, and in 1851 she became the fourth woman to receive a medical degree in the United States. She specialized in the diagnosis and treatment of the medical problems of women, was heavily involved in dress reform activities and other women's issues, and was an author and lecturer on topics of women's health.

The ready availability of a woman doctor held great appeal for the Langdon family. Livy had a history of medical problems that can be dated back to at least 1860, when, at the age of fourteen, she was treated for gynecological problems by Dr. Rachel Gleason for five months at the Elmira Water Cure. She was treated again at the cure just prior to her sixteenth birthday for menstrual pain.[16] Livy's confidence in Rachel Gleason as her physician was obvious. Dr. Gleason was Olivia Langdon

Dr. Rachel Brooks Gleason and Dr. Silas Gleason. Photograph by McFarlain and Speck's Photographic Studio, October 1892. Courtesy Chemung County Historical Society, Elmira, New York.

Clemens's lifelong physician, and she delivered all three of the Clemens's daughters. Family correspondence indicates that Clemens considered the Gleasons to be the best physicians in Elmira.[17] In 1871, when Livy became sick from typhoid fever, Clemens fired the family physician (a homeopathic physician) and brought Dr. Rachel Gleason from Elmira to Buffalo in order to care for his wife.

After he married Livy in 1870, Clemens gave the impression of being a solid believer in the precepts of hydrotherapy. His writings from that era reflected his knowledge of hydropathic techniques, and he devoted particular attention to the topic in "A Boy's Manuscript" (a short story written in 1868, while he was courting Livy) and in *The Adventures of Tom Sawyer* (which he wrote between 1872 and 1875).[18] He and other family members were treated at the Elmira Water Cure. Hydrotherapy was "the cure-all of the nineteenth century," and in an 1872 letter to sister-in-law Mollie Clemens, Livy wrote that her husband insisted she have hydropathic treatments for her backache and for the depression that occurred after the death of her son Langdon in 1872: "Mr Clemens is determined that I shall bath. . . . Mr Clemens is going to make me take sitz baths.... My back is troubling me so this is the reason that Mr C. is taking these vigorous measures."[19]

Even so, there was always doubt in Clemens's mind about how effective hydropathic medicine *really* was. Part of him wanted to have full confidence in it. Having faith in the utility of hydrotherapy would enable him to maintain harmony with the beliefs of Livy and her family and would also help rationalize his avoidance of the aggressive but ineffective treatments of allopathic doctors. In 1871, his older sister Pamela spent a considerable amount of time at the Elmira Water Cure, and Clemens initially appeared to believe that her time was well spent, as evidenced by his statement that "Pamela has been here some time at the Water Cure, for her health is very bad" (*Ltrs-4*, 451). However, Clemens was troubled by the apparent discrepancy between the claims of the hydropathists and what he could observe with his own eyes. He was not convinced that the water cure was really helping his sister in any obvious way, as he confessed in an earlier letter written to his mother on June 11, 1871. "I saw Pamela yesterday, & she seemed to me about the same she has been all the time since she came here. I cannot discover that she improves any great deal, though I believe they contend that she is really improving, & very steadily, too" (*Ltrs-4*, 403).

As hydrotherapy shifted from its emphasis on "water cure" to an increasing focus on hygienic principles, the sect ultimately weakened its image as a unique form of medical therapy. Its open acceptance of self-trained practitioners created a loose system that became increasingly vague in its definition and unclear in its image. Its open-minded philosophy drove hydrotherapists to reject any consideration of standards, as they hoped to avoid the appearance of the elitism and exclusivity that damaged the public's perceptions of the allopaths. This liberal approach to its own definition may have been very costly to hydropathy in the long term, particularly when the AMA tightened up allopathic medicine's image further through its increasing insistence on uniform credentialing and standardization of education. As a result, orthodox medicine strengthened its own position as the icon of scientific medical practice while weakening the position of "nonscientific" practitioners such as the hydropathists. This loosening of strict adherence to hydropathy's initial principles by its practitioners, followed by the eventual breakdown of the hydropathic movement, appears to be a pattern that is repeated with most medical sects: "Movements such as osteopathy, homeopathy, and eclecticism generally have a natural life cycle. They are conceived by a crisis in medical care; their youth is marked by a broadening of their ideas; and their decline occurs when whatever distinctive notions they have as to patient management are allowed to wither. At this point, no longer having a compelling reason for existence, they die."[20]

In addition to allowing erosion of its earlier standards as a medical care system, hydrotherapy also started to soften its stance on reform issues—its leaders refused to take a strong position in the Civil War for fear of alienating the Southern states. Society was changing too, and the American attitude of the Gilded Age became the antithesis of hydrotherapeutic principles. "Self-denial and self-control . . . gradually gave way to a far more ostentatious, self-indulgent, pleasure-seeking, consumer-oriented vision of the good life. . . . Personal happiness and success came increasingly to be correlated with conspicuous wealth, leisure-time distractions, and escape from drudgery."[21]

The dilution of hydrotherapy's principles was not only reflected in the simplification of the title of the *Water-Cure Journal* to the less definitive *Health* but was also accompanied by the transition of many "water cure establishments" into "resorts." As the water cures became spas, they became vacation destinations for the well-to-do in search of pampering. These individuals composed a clientele whose worries about their health far exceeded their problems with their health.

In contrast to the decreasing influence of hydrotherapy in the United States, the hydropathic movement in Europe flourished into the late nineteenth century, and even through the twentieth. In his 1880 travel book *A Tramp Abroad*, Clemens mentioned his experiences in the baths of Baden-Baden, a resort town in southwestern Germany. His main reason for traveling through Europe at the time was to write a travel book, and not because any medical issues were heavy on his mind. As a result, he could afford to be a bit flippant in his comments.

> It is an inane town, filled with sham, and petty fraud, and snobbery, but the baths are good. I spoke with many people, and they were all agreed in that. I had had twinges of rheumatism unceasingly during three years, but the last one departed after a fortnight's bathing there, and I have never had one since. I fully believe I left my rheumatism in Baden-Baden. Baden-Baden is welcome to it. It was little, but it was all I had to give. I would have preferred to leave something that was catching, but it was not in my power. (*Tramp Abroad*, 200)

A decade later, Clemens's situation had changed considerably, and he purposefully sought treatment at the popular European spas and baths as he looked for solutions to the various family ailments that were coming to a head in the 1890s. Livy's health was deteriorating, and perhaps Clemens believed she would find some of the same benefits from hydropathic medicine that she had received years earlier at the Elmira Water Cure.

In the European model of hydrotherapy, the water in each location was specific for particular maladies, and it was felt to be important to match each disease with the appropriate water. In a May 20, 1891, letter to William Dean Howells, Clemens's tone was more that of desperation than of confidence. "For her health's sake Mrs. Clemens *must* try some baths somewhere, & this it is that has determined us to go to Europe. The water required seems to be provided at a little obscure & little-visited nook up in the hills back of the Rhine somewhere" (*Ltrs-Howells Sel.*, 299).

In August 1891 Clemens and his family spent most of their time at two spas, Marianske Lazne (Marienbad) and Frantiskovy Lazne (Franzensbad), in an area that in 1918 became part of Czechoslovakia.[22] These spas claimed to provide a large range of curative capabilities, as Clemens described in "Marienbad, a Health Factory," written in 1891: "Marienbad—Mary's bath. The Mary is the Virgin. She is the patroness of these curative springs. They try to cure everything—gout, rheumatism, leanness, fatness, dyspepsia, and all the rest" (*Complete Essays*, 101). Clemens gave further details about his European hydrotherapy experience in "Aix-les-Bains," written the same year:

> The bathhouse is a huge and massive pile of white marble masonry, and looks more like a temple than anything else. It has several floors and each is full of bath cabinets. There is every kind of bath—for the nose, the ears, the throat, vapor baths, swimming baths, and all people's favorite, the douche.... The "course" is usually fifteen douche baths and five tub baths. You take the douche three days in succession, then knock off and take a tub. You keep the distribution through the course. If one course does not cure you, you take another one after an interval. You seek a local physician and he examines your case and prescribes the kind of bath required for it, with various other particulars. (*CT-2*, 9)

Seven years later, in the summer of 1898, Clemens and his family again found themselves in a rural hydrotherapy resort, this time near Vienna. Due to concern about Livy's ongoing medical problems, his daughter Jean's recurrent problems with epilepsy, and his own chronic aches and pains, Clemens sought medical advice in Vienna, which was recognized as a center of medical knowledge and sophistication. Always eclectic in his medical pursuits, Clemens sought opinions from specialists of every type, and he did not restrict himself to allopathic physicians. Homeopaths, naturopaths, and osteopathic physicians were also consulted. Eminent physicians who were involved in the evaluations included the neuro-pathologist Heinrich Obersteiner, the psychiatrist Richard von Krafft-Ebing, several colleagues of Sigmund Freud at the University of Vienna, and the pediatrician Alexander von Huettenbrenner. Clemens did not find encouragement from any of his prominent consultants, and he and his family eventually found themselves at the "Austrian cold water cure" at Kaltenleutgeben. Founded by Dr. Wilhelm Winternitz (1834–1917), this spa was alleged to be particularly effective for problems with circulation, rheumatism, and nervous disorders.[23] It attracted the likes of Otto von Bismarck and other members of the upper tier of European society and politics. Because of the presumed specificity of the various spas, Winternitz examined Livy, Jean, and Clara in March 1898 to determine whether the unique waters at Kaltenleutgeben would "suit the complexion of their ailments."[24]

Needless to say, Winternitz found that Kaltenleutgeben could provide exactly what Samuel Clemens's family needed. In "At the Appetite Cure," written in 1898, Clemens commented on the claim of specificity of each spa's water for particular medical problems: "My subject is health resorts. All unhealthy people ought to domicile themselves in Vienna, and use that as a base, making flights from time to time to the outlying resorts, according to need. A flight to Marienbad to get rid of fat; a flight to Carlsbad to get rid of rheumatism; a flight to Kaltenleutgeben to take the water cure and get rid of the rest of the diseases. It is all so handy" (*Hadleyburg*, 148). Livy and Jean were prescribed a program of cold water plunges, calisthenics, and naturopathic medicines derived from the roots of various plants. In a letter to his friend and benefactor Henry Rogers on June 10, 1898, Clemens made clear his optimism about the help he anticipated from Kaltenleutgeben: "It just occurs to me: this place is a cold-water-cure, and has an immense reputation. Come over, bring Mrs. Rogers, and try it. You can't do a better thing. It will set you up, sound as a drum, for ten years" (*Ltrs-Rogers*, 351).

When the treatment program at Kaltenleutgeben had been completed, though, Clemens was not impressed that any good had come from the experience. He decided that the claims of the water cure establishments were greatly exaggerated, as he explained to the public through the words of one of the enthusiasts he claimed to have met there.

It's great, these baths. I didn't come here for my health; I only came to find out if there was anything the matter with me. . . . The doctor said I was a grand proof of what these baths could do; said I had come here as innocent of disease as a grindstone, and inside of three weeks these baths had sluiced out of me every important ailment known to medical science, along with considerable more that were entirely new and patentable. Why, he wanted to exhibit me in his bay window! (*CT-2*, 10)

From a personal perspective, however, Clemens saw that the failure of the baths was nothing to laugh about. Livy was not any healthier, and there was no apparent improvement in the frequency of Jean's seizures. In the absence of any apparent benefit, Clemens was unable to maintain his rekindled faith in hydrotherapy for very long, and on July 10, 1898 (one month after he wrote his enthusiastic letter to Rogers), he privately expressed his disappointment in the treatment. "I am not happy about the water-cure. I expected it to do great things for Mrs. Clemens, but I think she is not as strong as she was when she began. It may be that the benefit comes after the course. I hope so" (*Ltrs-Rogers*, 352).

In his disappointment from seeing no benefit for his family, Clemens became convinced that hydropathic medicine was just another type of quackery. Following his experiences in 1898, he finally lost all faith in the methods of the water cure. In a sense, the fact that he had even given hydrotherapy another try at that time is remarkable, and perhaps emblematic of his wishful thinking regarding his hope of finding the perfect medical system, inasmuch as he had characterized water cure practitioners as incompetents in an 1894 letter to Henry Rogers.

Susy still has the fever this morning—and here we are, a thousand miles from a doctor. For a bath-village doctor is necessarily a doctor who can't make his living anywhere else and would starve anywhere else. This one here said Susy had no fever. I went and got a thermometer and took her temperature—102°. Then I went to him and he ciphered with his pencil and showed me that 102° Fahrenheit was only 28 3/4 centigrade—[as] if that affected the matter in any way. Mrs. Clemens administers medicines of her own, now, and I throw the doctor's out of the window. *His* are for constipation; he gives nothing for the fever, contending that there *isn't* any. (*Ltrs-Rogers*, 70).

By the end of the nineteenth century, hydrotherapy's time had come and gone, not only for Samuel Clemens's family but also for the rest of

America. It did not fail to leave its mark, however. As with most alterna-tive health care approaches that survive for any significant interval, it had some attractive and redeeming qualities, and it contributed new perspectives that ultimately became incorporated into mainstream med-icine. Its very existence and its transient success pushed regular medi-cine ever so slightly toward a more holistic and humanistic orientation. The downfall of hydrotherapy occurred when it became obvious that water alone will cure very little. Its most important contribution may have been the appreciation that hygiene, good diet, stress reduction, and thoughtful attention to the general well-being of the individual are essen-tial components of the care for virtually all human ailments (the same sentiment that was articulated by Dr. Francis Peabody in 1927 in his widely quoted comment, "The secret of the care of the patient is in caring for the patient"). The "water cure" was a protest against the impersonal, reductionistic, disease-targeted style of the nineteenth century's allopathic medicine, and this may have been the main reason Samuel Clemens kept coming back to it, in spite of his recurring moments of doubt.

The considerable success of the hydropathic movement can be attrib-uted to the appeal of its basic principles to the educated, liberal, and affluent segment of the population that was represented by Livy Lang-don's family. Water cure physicians were of the opinion that two types of imbalance could cause health problems: poor hygiene,[25] or the intrinsic lack of nervous energy, a condition that came to be known as "neuras-thenia." Neurasthenia appeared to be an epidemic condition among the intelligent, the delicate, the sensitive, and the sophisticated, and many medical practitioners of the era considered neurasthenia to be the origin of most illness. The Langdons' wealth could not protect them from this cause of illness (and, if anything, the medical paradigm of the times was that their good fortune and prominent position in society made them even more susceptible to neurasthenia than the average citizen).

During Samuel Clemens's early years on America's frontier, his mother taught him that measles, smallpox, and cholera were among the greatest threats to his health and survival. Throughout his adult life, he learned from his wife and her family that "neurasthenia" could be as virulent (and, in some ways, as devastating) as any infection he had ever encoun-tered in the West. Neurasthenia defined the health of nineteenth-century America as no other illness has ever defined any other era, and the con-cept of neurasthenia is central to an understanding of health, illness, and the medicine of the times.

10

NEURASTHENIA

The American Disease

"These mumps is different. It's a new kind, Miss Mary Jane said."

"How's it a new kind?"

"Because it's mixed up with other things."

"What other things?"

"Well, measles, and whooping cough, and erysiplas, and consumption, and yaller janders, and brain fever, and I don't know what all."

"My land! And they call it the *mumps?*"

"That's what Miss Mary Jane said."

"Well, what in the nation do they call it the *mumps* for?"

"Why, because it *is* the mumps. That's what it starts with."

"Well, ther' ain't no sense in it. A body might stump his toe, and take pison, and fall down the well, and break his neck, and bust his brains out, and somebody come along and ask what killed him, and some numskull up and say, 'Why, he stumped his *toe.*' Would ther' be any sense in that? *No.* And ther' ain't no sense in *this*, nuther."

—Mark Twain, *Adventures of Huckleberry Finn*

Although the Victorian period in the United States is usually defined by its attitudes, fashions, and architecture, Americans of the Victorian era should also be given credit for the creation of their own disease. The times were changing quickly. America was increasingly urbanized, upbeat, and sophisticated, the economy was booming along, and times were golden (or at least gilded, as Samuel Clemens was the first to point out). It appeared that life just could not be any better, and yet for unknown reasons it seemed that some folks were not thriving with the times. They suffered from weakness, fatigue, generalized malaise, dyspepsia, depression, and insomnia. The times were dynamic, exciting, and energetic; if life did not always glitter for everyone who lived in the Gilded Age, there had to be a medical reason. An earlier generation had focused on dysfunction of the liver with its attendant "biliousness" as the basis of most illness, but this concept was no longer in vogue with the fashionable set; instead, the "elites of late 19th century focused on their nerves."[1] Those who could not keep up with the fast pace of the times had "nervous exhaustion," "nervousness," "nerve weakness," or "neuralgia" (all of which became recognized as variations of "neurasthenia").

Neurasthenia was not anything to be ashamed of—after all, it was the "American disease," and the afflicted could suffer with patriotic pride. The cardinal features of neurasthenia were generalized weakness and prostration, various aches and pains, irritability, moodiness, sluggish or impaired cognitive function, "morbid fears" (including a feeling of impending death), and melancholia. The disorder was first described by Dr. George Beard in his 1869 book, *A Practical Treatise on Nervous Exhaustion (Neurasthenia): Its Symptoms, Nature, Sequence, and Treatment*. Beard noted that *neurasthenia* could be translated literally from the Greek as "lack of nerve strength." He wrote more and more on the disease as he learned more about it, and he was able to list more than seventy-five symptoms of the syndrome by the time he came out with his similarly titled 1880 book, *A Treatise on Nervous Exhaustion, (Neurasthenia): Its Symptoms, Nature, Sequences, Treatment*. Beard suggested that previously used designations that covered a vast expanse of medical territory, including "general debility," "nervous prostration," "spinal weakness," "spinal irritation," and "nervous dyspepsia," could all be classified under the general and inclusive category of neurasthenia. Afflicted individuals might have "sick headaches," impaired ability to concentrate, and lightheadedness, and it was not unusual for them to "fret and worry and become irascible over trifles."[2] Other symptoms included muscle spasms, sensitivity to changes in weather, back pain, or sexual dysfunction, not to mention stomach upsets and digestive problems.

What caused all of this? Some type of conflict seemed likely to those who were involved in the description of the disorder. Perhaps the disease was the result of a collision between the dramatic changes of nineteenth-

George M. Beard. Courtesy of the National Library of Medicine (B2556).

century society and the limited physiological adaptability of each individual. Maybe the "good times" were *too* good (at least too boisterous and too raucous) for the genteel and refined; perhaps the whole world was changing too fast for those of delicate and sensitive makeup. Beard had worked with Thomas Edison and knew a few things about electricity; he knew the electric lights would dim when the dynamo was overworked, and this seemed to be an excellent analogy for neurasthenia. The most susceptible individual would be a person "with a nervous tendency driven to think, to work, to strive for success," the sort of person who "presses himself and his life force to the limit, straining his circuits like an overloaded battery.... The sufferer's electrical system crashes down, spewing sparks and symptoms and giving rise to neurasthenia."[3]

With scientific precocity, Beard even devised a molecular explanation for the apparent hereditary predisposition to neurasthenia in susceptible individuals—in vulnerable people, he suggested in terminology nicely biochemical, the excessive stimulation in the physical and intellectual environment caused the nervous system to become "dephosphoralized."[4] The higher classes of society were predisposed to neurasthenia because they had a more highly evolved (and thus more sensitive) nervous system, as Beard's reasoning went (and certainly no neurasthenic would ever see any reason to argue the point). In her 1989 review of neurasthenia, Dona Davis puts this attitude in perspective: "Among the neurasthenic set the very name of the disease connoted elite status. The neurasthenic was viewed as a cultured, sensitive genius, tortured by worry, and world wear—a brainworker."[5]

Samuel Clemens understood the concept well. He was very much aware that anyone who attempted to be a creative writer was at risk for developing the debility of the nervous system that arose from intellectual overwork; even though his words were somewhat tongue in cheek, he effectively utilized the imagery of nervous exhaustion in a passage in *Roughing It.* "Nobody, except he has tried it, knows what it is to be an editor... fancy how you would feel if you had to pump your brains dry every day in the week, fifty-two weeks in the year.... How editors can continue this tremendous labor, this exhausting consumption of brain fibre (for their work is creative, and not a mere mechanical laying-up of facts, like reporting), day after day and year after year, is incomprehensible" (*Rough. It*, 400–401).

Neurasthenia was "a condition that was thought to afflict the best and the brightest"; the American disease was one of the "Fashionable Diseases," a veritable badge of distinction for the sufferer.[6] William James, Jane Addams, and Theodore Roosevelt were among the well-recognized and creative individuals of the Victorian era who were diagnosed as having neurasthenia. Beard differentiated the traditional definitions of nervousness (which related to emotion and temper) from the debility of the nervous system that was the basis of neurasthenia, and there was no doubt that this was a *physical* disorder and *not* an emotional problem— in the words of Dona Davis, "nerves, the experience of nerves, and the theory of nerves flourished during the late 19th century." To be neurasthenic was to have status and respectability. By the end of the century neurasthenia had permeated every aspect of society. It was virtually a badge of distinction, and those afflicted with it became "role models for people with anxiety, depression and other psychological conditions."[7]

Environmental factors such as exhausting business activities or fatiguing intellectual work were viewed as contributors to neurasthenia, but intrinsic weakness of the constitutional "nerve force" was ultimately the root of the clinical presentation of the neurasthenic. Accidents and other emotional stresses could induce neurasthenia, according to many physicians. Another possibility was that the body produced toxic agents that damaged the nervous system, in which case a healthy diet might provide a cure.

Women were especially vulnerable to neurasthenia, according to Beard and his contemporaries. Nerve force was a finite entity that needed to be zealously protected. It seemed to make good biological sense that women were intrinsically endowed with less nerve force than men (just as they had less muscle mass), and thus it was easier for them to be drained of these vital energy forces. The uterus was an obvious cause of an excessive energy drain that taxed the limited reserve of the nerves; the era was also the "Age of the Womb" (and gender conflicts between women and their male physicians have been blamed as contributors to illnesses such as anorexia, hysteria, and neurasthenia). Women from the upper classes were particularly at risk due to their refinement, advanced intellect, and emotional nature. Female physicians such as Dr. Margaret Cleaves, herself a neurasthenic (and author of the anonymous *The Autobiography of a Neurasthene, As Told by One of Them and Recorded by Margaret A. Cleaves*, published in 1910), shared the belief that women were especially susceptible to developing neurasthenia. The existence of neurasthenia as a disease process played a major role in the success of hydropathic medicine, which had a strong focus on nutrition and a commitment to women's health.

Neurasthenia was also targeted by the patent medicine industry. Ayers' Sarsaparilla was a cure for all of the symptoms that were synonymous with neurasthenia, including "Weakness, General Debility, Nervousness, Nerve Exhaustion, Nervous Prostration" (at least in the opinion of Dr. Ayers). Lydia Pinkham, the most important businesswoman of her day, founded her lucrative patent medicine career on the premise that neurasthenia was a rampant condition and on the promise that she as a woman could understand female troubles far better than could any male physician. In 1876 she developed Lydia Pinkham's Vegetable Compound, composed of the plant derivative black cohosh (a stimulant and cathartic). The fact that the cohosh was dissolved in a solvent of alcohol was a nice additional touch. Mrs. Pinkham's remedy cured "Nervous

Prostration, General Debility, Sleeplessness, Depression and Indigestion," and thus would seem to be as good an antineurasthenic agent as Dr. Ayers's product.[8]

Pinkham was not only a giant of the patent medicine industry, but she was also a participant in abolition and social reform movements and a major feminist of her time. Through her own success, she seemed to promote the success of all women; paradoxically, this success was based on her contribution to the perception of the female as the weaker gender—as she brought the American disease of neurasthenia to the less educated, rural, and working-class woman, she promoted the concept that nerve weakness was a universal attribute of *all* women, not just the delicate and sensitive. George Beard has been viewed by some critics as a misogynist because of his "invention" of neurasthenia (a criticism that seems exceptionally harsh, considering that Beard placed himself among the ranks of the neurasthenics), but it was Lydia Pinkham who profited most as she promulgated the image of Everywoman as Neurasthene.

The Pinkham patent medicine enterprise, which was still selling its products as late as 1979, was actually started by Lydia's sons but found its greatest success only after she became the spokesperson and image of the company. In many ways her beliefs were similar to those of the individuals involved in the hydrotherapy movement (including Clemens's in-laws and Livy's longtime personal physician Dr. Rachel Gleason)—her passions included woman suffrage, the temperance and antislavery movements, and spiritualism. Like the hydrotherapists, Pinkham was influential in the promotion of women's health issues and hygiene. She reached out to larger populations than the relatively elite group who were advocates of water cure. Her advertisements were classical neurasthenia fare (titles included "I'm Simply Worn Out," "Women Who Have the Blues," and "I'm not Well Enough to Work"), and they invited women to consult with Lydia for their female problems—which they could not discuss comfortably with a male physician. She responded personally to each letter (a service that continued long after her death, as her daughter-in-law and thirty professional writers answered in the name of "Mrs. Pinkham").

Pinkham was not as precise as Beard in emphasizing the physical nature of nerve weakness, and she tended to blur the distinction between emotions and the physical dysfunction of the nervous system's electrical activity. Her focus was on the reproductive tract, and in her 1901 "Treatise on the Diseases of Women" she described how problems in the

pelvis might irritate surrounding nerves and cause widespread problems. She, too, picked up the imagery of impaired nerve force; as nerves
became a "fashionable disease" in the late nineteenth century, the image
of gentility combined with "snob appeal" allowed Pinkham to introduce
"nerves" to her audience, and emotional weakness replaced the womb as
the source of female infirmity. Dona Davis has explained how Lydia
Pinkham followed George Beard's lead in promoting the concept of
neurasthenia to the American public: "Pinkham copy came to sound
more and more like Beard. The image of Pinkham women became both
morbid and genteel; they were worn out, nervous, irritable, and so
sickly they could not work or bear children."[9]

Samuel Clemens knew all about neurasthenia. He married a neurasthenic. When Clemens was a young man courting his wife-to-be, he
learned about her frailty as a young woman, and he heard about how
she was bedridden for two years from the age of sixteen to eighteen.
Clemens described Livy's ailment in his *Autobiography:* "She became an
invalid at sixteen through a partial paralysis caused by falling on the ice
and she was never strong again while her life lasted. After that fall she
was not able to leave her bed during two years, nor was she able to lie in
any position except upon her back. All the great physicians were brought
to Elmira one after another during that time, but there was no helpful
result" (*Autob/MTA*, 183–84).

In current medical terminology, Livy's paralysis might be characterized as a "conversion reaction." In the era in which her paralysis occurred,
however, the suitable diagnosis would have been "neurasthenia," and a
total loss of "nerve force" would readily account for her symptoms. During this interval of bedridden paralysis, according to her biographer Resa
Willis, Livy Langdon "was living in the self-centered, sheltered world of
the nineteenth-century Angelic, Beautiful Invalid. . . . The disease of frailty
has always been with us, but it became a high art in Victorian times that
saw women as weak, childlike, to be lifted onto a pedestal."[10] There is
no doubt Clemens had the same vision of his future spouse, as he used
the language of neurasthenia to describe her most striking characteristics: "She was slender and beautiful and girlish—and she was both girl
and woman. She remained both girl and woman to the last day of her
life. Under a grave and gentle exterior burned inextinguishable fires of
sympathy, energy, devotion, enthusiasm and absolutely limitless affec-
tion. She was *always* frail in body and she lived upon her spirit, whose
hopefulness and courage were indestructible" (*Autob/MTA*, 183).

Other biographers of Livy Langdon have argued that she suffered a physical disorder, suggesting that the term *neurasthenic* was just another synonym for "neurotic" or "hysterical" in the vocabulary of nineteenth-century male clinicians with antifeminist inclinations.[11] To the contrary, however, neurasthenia was a *physical* disorder in the nineteenth century's paradigm of illness, and to be neurasthenic was *anything but* a derogatory designation for the sufferer. Neurasthenia was the new disease of Clemens's Gilded Age, and the diagnosis gave legitimacy to the symptoms of its victims. Livy Clemens had features consistent with neurasthenia, but so did Samuel Clemens. According to the concepts of the time, women appeared to have increased susceptibility to neurasthenia, and both sociological and biological explanations were offered. The role of women was rapidly changing in a new industrial society. A woman's world had expanded far beyond the traditional home and hearth, and women had new opportunities to obtain higher education and to find new roles in business and in the professions. Conflicts in roles abounded. The achievement of personal success through financial and intellectual accomplishments clashed with the traditional model of being a self-sacrificing wife and mother. The roles for women were being freshly defined, but many times the ambivalence of society itself greatly hindered and frustrated the educated "new woman" in her efforts to fulfill her newly found aspirations, ambitions, and potential.[12]

In a letter of November 30, 1878, Livy Clemens discussed the intense demands that were made on the women of her day:

> I told Mr. Clemens the other day that in this day women must be everything. They must keep up with all the current literature, they must know all about art, they must help in one or two benevolent societies, they must be perfect mothers, they must be perfect housekeepers and graceful gracious hostesses, they must go and visit all the people in the town where they live, they must always be ready to receive their acquaintances, they must dress themselves and their children becomingly and above all they must make their homes charming and so on without end—then if they are not studying something their case is a hopeless one.[13]

A number of highly educated and very successful women, including Charlotte Perkins Gilman and Jane Addams, who wrote directly about their personal experiences provide support for this argument. Gilman, who was treated for neurasthenia by Dr. S. Weir Mitchell (a disciple of George Beard), attributed her own ailment to her personal unhappiness with her role as wife and mother. Even after leaving her husband (whose presence seemed to trigger her symptoms) to pursue her career as a writer and lecturer, she had further periods of severe fatigue and lassitude. Jane Addams, founder of Hull House and a pioneer social worker, was also treated by Mitchell. She similarly blamed her symptoms on the conflicts that arose between her education and goals and the social restraints of her era. Alice James, the "talented, protected, and always mysteriously ill" sister of novelist Henry James and psychologist William James, was haunted by similar discord, and efforts to recharge her "nerve force" with electrical therapy were of little benefit.[14] Edith Wharton and Virginia Woolf were also among the many women for whom intellectual pursuits were declared to be the cause of ailments that included pain, moodiness, listlessness, and despair.

Men were also afflicted, and their sufferings with neurasthenia (which had been conceived from the beginning as a gender-neutral disorder) promoted its credibility and acceptability while steering the disease's image away from being labeled as a variant of "hysteria." Having the disease became evidence of overwork related to an extreme commitment to obligation (a condition described in the twentieth century as being "burnt out"), and neurasthenia became an acceptable and even a desirable illness for men. Beard and Mitchell were themselves neurasthenia victims and were eager to make the diagnosis a respectable one. Beard reported that more than 10 percent of his patients were male physicians. The disease provided evidence of high intelligence, sensitivity, and social accomplishment as it gave justification for failures of achievement. There was value to the victim in keeping the symptoms lumped under the heading of a physical, organic ailment, allowing the sufferer to avoid the negative implications of having a psychosomatic or hypochondriacal ailment. Robert Martensen has described neurasthenia in the context of its times in a 1994 article in the *Journal of the American Medical Association.*

Neurasthenia was one of those wonderful 19th-century diagnostic entities that promised something for almost everyone involved. A disease with loads of symptoms and little—well, finally, no—organic pathology, it satisfied a number of the conditions any nosologic category must meet if it is to be broadly applied. During its heyday, which lasted from the 1870s to the turn of the century, the diagnosis of neurasthenia provided patients with a scientifically (and, hence, I would argue, socially) legitimate explanation for their inability to perform their expected roles. Furthermore, the patients, who tended to be in their 20s and 30s and from the urban middle classes, mostly recovered.[15]

Livy's own physician, Dr. Rachel Brooks Gleason, used the vernacular of neurasthenia when she declared that the hurried and hectic lifestyle of America had a tendency to "wear upon the nervous system of all, especially that of sensitive, impressible women. Those who are brilliant and fascinating early become frail, freaky, fidgety—a condition difficult to cure, but which could be prevented by leading a quiet life, with more of simple, useful work, of which this world furnishes an abundance."[16]

In truth, Livy Langdon had a history of personal frailty that preceded her fall on the ice by at least two years. When she was treated at the Elmira Water Cure in 1860 at the age of fourteen, Livy was already "in very delicate health," according to family friend Isabella Hooker (who was Livy's roommate at the Water Cure). Hooker used typical neurasthenia terminology to report that Livy "has been living on her nerves instead of her muscles all her life so far—and will not have *any thing* left to live upon pretty soon."[17] In 1861 Livy was back at the Water Cure for further treatment by Dr. Gleason, possibly for dysmenorrhea.

Livy's fall on the ice occurred during the winter of 1861–1862. After receiving treatment in a sanatorium in Washington, D.C., in March 1862, she was taken to the Institute of Swedish Movement Cure in New York City from June 1862 until mid-1864, under the supervision of Drs. George and Charles Taylor. The Taylors' eclectic backgrounds included the use of hydropathic principles to treat gynecological problems. They later became recognized as orthopedic specialists whose treatments were centered around a system of physical therapy described as "kinesipathy," and their treatment strategies included the use of braces and immobilization.[18]

Livy returned to Elmira in June 1864, apparently no better than when she had left, despite her lengthy stay away from home. All available treatments had failed her. She was in need of a medical miracle.

11

Dr. Newton, the Quack

No one doubts—certainly not I—that the mind exercises a powerful influence over the body. From the beginning of time, the sorcerer, the interpreter of dreams, the fortune-teller, the charlatan, the quack, the wild medicine-man, the educated physician, the mesmerist, and the hypnotist have made use of the client's imagination to help them in their work. They have all recognized the potency and availability of that force.

—Mark Twain, *Christian Science*

Out of desperation to help the bedridden Livy, the affluent Langdon family (having exhausted every other available option) decided to resort to the services of a famous charlatan, as reported by Clemens in his *Autobiography*.

In those days both worlds were well acquainted with the name of Doctor Newton, a man who was regarded in both worlds as a quack. He moved through the land in state; in magnificence, like a potentate; like a circus. Notice of his coming was spread upon the dead walls in vast colored posters, along with his formidable portrait, several weeks beforehand.

One day Andrew Langdon, a relative of the Langdon family, came to the house and said: "You have tried everybody else; now try Doctor Newton, the quack. He is downtown at the Rathbun House, practicing upon the well-to-do at war prices and upon the poor for nothing. *I saw him* wave his hands over Jake Brown's head and take his crutches away from him and send him about his business as good as new. *I saw him* do the like with some other cripples. *They* may have been 'temporaries' instituted for advertising purposes, and not genuine. But Jake is genuine. Send for Newton." (*Autob/MTA*, 184)

The family followed Andrew Langdon's recommendation and sent for the faith healer Dr. James Rogers Newton. Newton was a successful businessman with little, if any, medical training, according to a collection of tributes to his clinical achievements that was published in 1879 as *The Modern Bethesda, or The Gift of Healing Restored*. The book gave examples of Newton's ability to cure paralysis in bedridden young women such as Elizabeth Southwick, who had been restricted to bed or a wheelchair for twenty months until a fifteen-minute treatment by Newton enabled her to descend a flight of stairs and go for a two-mile walk.[1] On November 30, 1864, Newton enacted a similar "miracle" for the Langdons, and it was not long until Livy was walking again. Clemens described the scene in his autobiography.

Newton came. He found the young girl upon her back. Over her was suspended a tackle from the ceiling. It had been there a long time but unused. It was put there in the hope that by its steady motion she might be lifted to a sitting posture, at intervals, for rest. But it proved a failure. Any attempt to raise her brought nausea and exhaustion and had to be relinquished. Newton opened the windows—long darkened—and delivered a short fervent prayer; then he put an arm behind her shoulders and said, "Now we will sit up, my child."

The family were alarmed and tried to stop him, but he was not disturbed, and raised her up. She sat several minutes without nausea or discomfort. Then Newton said, "Now we will walk a few steps, my child." He took her out of bed and supported her while she walked several steps; then he said: "I have reached the limit of my art. She is not cured. It is not likely that she will *ever* be cured. She will never be able to walk far, but after a little daily practice she will be able to walk one or two hundred yards, and she can depend on being able to do *that* for the rest of her life."

His charge was fifteen thousand dollars and it was easily worth a hundred thousand. For from the day that she was eighteen until she was fifty-six she was always able to walk a couple of hundred yards without stopping to rest; and more than once I saw her walk a quarter of a mile without serious fatigue. (*Autob/MTA*, 184)

J. R. Newton. Frontispiece in A. E. Newton, *The Modern Bethesda, or the Gift of Healing Restored.*

Austin Hall, Newton's secretary, wrote about the cure of Livy Langdon in *The Modern Bethesda*. According to Hall, Newton went to Elmira "to treat Miss Libbie [*sic*] Langdon, whom he cured, and she has since married the author known as 'Mark Twain.' Dr. N. found her suffering with spinal disease; could not be raised to a sitting posture in her bed for over four years. She was almost like death itself. With one characteristic treatment he made her to cross the room with assistance, and in a few days the cure was complete."[2] Clemens described the event not only in his dictated *Autobiography* but also in a footnote in his book *Christian Science*: "January, 1903. I have personal and intimate knowledge of the 'miraculous' cure of a case of paralysis which had kept the patient helpless in bed during two years, in spite of all that the best medical science of New York could do. The travelling 'quack' (that is what they called him), came on two successive mornings and lifted the patient out of bed and said 'Walk!' and the patient walked. That was the end of it. It was forty-one years ago. The patient has walked ever since" (*Christian Sci.*, 36).

Livy's "cure" by Newton was not as dramatic as Clemens reported— Newton's touch may have been able to get her up and walking, but her mother's diary indicates that Livy's period of convalescence and recuperation involved three additional years of gradually improving strength and function. This is not surprising; after two years of restriction to her bed, the already frail eighteen-year-old Livy would have had significant deconditioning of her muscles, and her recovery would undoubtedly have required a slow and prolonged course of physical therapy. There is other evidence that her recovery was not instantaneous. Dr. Newton revisited her on June 3, 1865, and she even returned to New York in October 1866 for further treatment from Dr. Charles Taylor, by that time at the New York Orthopedic Dispensary, where she stayed three months and participated in "movement cure" treatment.

The course of Livy's illness and gradual recovery argues strongly against serious organic disease—to be paralyzed by a physical injury to the spinal cord for two years is to be paralyzed forever. In an effort to find a "physical" explanation for her illness, it has been suggested that Livy's paralysis may have come from Pott's disease (tuberculosis of the spine). This consideration was triggered by the observation that she was treated by Dr. Charles Taylor, who had a professional interest in treating Pott's disease. In addition, pictures of Livy from that interval show evidence of weight loss, which can also be a feature of tuberculosis. However, the overall medical history of Livy Langdon is inconsistent with such a hypothesis. On the other hand, the suggestion of a psychophysiological basis for Olivia's symptomatology would seem to be fully compatible with her clinical course, as Laura Skandera-Trombley observed in *Mark Twain in the Company of Women:* "no miraculous cure had occurred here. What Dr. Newton presumably did was to convince Olivia to shake off the malaise which still lingered from her prolonged bed rest and instill in her the confidence to again become active."[3]

According to the concepts of hydropathic medicine, there was nothing unusual about Livy's illness. Livy Langdon grew up in a household of believers in the concept of neurasthenia and in the benefits of hydropathic medicine. The underlying principles of hydropathy were based on the belief that disease was caused by the interactions of an inescapably unhealthy environment (poor "hygiene") with individuals who were susceptible to such conditions (neurasthenics). The water cure was a system of improving the hygiene (which included nutritional status and general environment) for those who easily contracted illness as a result of their deficient "nerve-force."

When Samuel Clemens married into the Langdon family, he also had to marry into their medical "religion" of hydropathy. When he and Livy had children of their own, it became one of his parental responsibilities to educate his own children in the ways of the family's health-care theology. On July 19, 1877, he presented his two oldest daughters with gifts of dolls and bathtubs that were used as props to explain the basic tenets of hydrotherapy. In his letter to Clara, who was then age three, he explained the use of water cure for those who are of "delicate" health. "I have bought two bath tubs & two dolls . . . for you and Susie. One of the dolls is named Hosannah Maria & is in quite delicate health. She belongs to you.—She was out driving & got rained on, & caught a very severe cold. It settled on her mind. When she had partially recovered, she caught a new cold, which paralyzed the sounding-board of her ears & the wobbling nerve of her tongue. She has never heard or spoken since. I have consulted the best physicians. They say constant & complicated bathing will fetch her." He wrote a similar letter to his daughter Susie,[4] who was five years old at the time. "Your doll is named Hallelujah Jennings. She early suffered a stroke of some sort, & since that day all efforts of the best physicians have failed to take the stiffening out of her legs.—They say incessant bathing is the only thing that can give her eventual relief" (*Ltrs-Love*, 202).

In these letters, Clemens invented the names of his daughters' new dolls, but he also created something of even greater significance—he borrowed from the medical history of his wife to establish a medical history for the dolls.[5] In so doing, he actively promoted the system of hydropathic medicine that was embraced by the Langdon family. Both letters described how "the best physicians" had been consulted to treat the dolls' infirmities, using terminology that is reminiscent of the description in Clemens's *Autobiography* of how "all the great physicians" had been called upon to treat Livy's paralysis. The stiffened legs of "Hallelujah Jennings" are conspicuously suggestive of Livy's own paralytic episode.

However, the content of the letters did not fully follow the historical record. Clemens did not propose to his daughters that the cure for the dolls would require the skills of a faith healer, as had been the case for Livy. To the contrary, he advised his daughters to apply "constant and complicated bathing" and "incessant bathing" for the therapy of their dolls, an obvious reference to the benefits of the hydrotherapy that was so heartily embraced by Livy and the Langdon family. What was the motive behind the letters? Susie and Clara were too young to read their father's letters themselves, and it is quite possible the letters were written primarily for the benefit of Livy. There was a good chance that, as they grew older, the Clemens children would hear stories about their mother's paralysis and her wonderful recovery. The letters may have been prepared to anticipate such a possibility by creating a revisionist version of the family record. If the girls understood from an early age that their mother's recovery from the paralysis of her youth came from hydropathic treatments, their parents might be able to avoid the awkwardness of trying to explain how Livy was cured by a faith healer.

12

ELECTROTHERAPY

Taking Charge with the Current Fad

Pretty soon, various kinds of bugs and ants and worms and things began to flock in out of the wet and crawl down inside my armor to get warm. . . . Even after I was frozen solid I could still distinguish that tickling, just as a corpse does when he is taking electric treatment.

—Mark Twain, *A Connecticut Yankee in King Arthur's Court*

Samuel Clemens was a victim of severe, recurrent, and debilitating attacks of gout, an arthritic condition that results from the deposition of crystals of uric acid into the joint spaces. Joints in the feet and ankles, and especially the big toes, are most commonly involved. The crystallization of uric acid in the joints provokes an inflammatory response that causes horrendous and excruciating pain. The miserable sufferer will eventually turn to any treatment that promises relief—even treatments that are unproven. Clemens's first attack of gout in 1894 was typical of the disease:

I got knocked flat on my back with gout. It was in my starboard ankle-bone. It took very little while to disable me. I supposed it was some new kind of super-devilish rheumatism, and imagined it would stop hurting presently. But it didn't. It made me so tired that I went to sleep at midnight slept till 3. Then followed 5 or 6 hours wherein the gout was the only presence present, Mrs. Twain and I counting for nothing

135

at all. This is one of the oldest pains known to medical science, and is perhaps the most competent. (*Ltrs-Rogers*, 95–96)

A week later, Clemens's gout had not relented, and it continued to be a source of immense nuisance and intense pain.

> I have had the gout a couple of weeks; it struck me hard and without warning, and kept us all at the hotel a day or two longer than necessary. But I was finally bundled into a close carriage, and brought to this house and this room, and this bed, whence I have not stirred since. Yesterday I was comfortable at last, and supposed I was going to be soon well; but last night I was hit hard in the other ankle by the gout, and now I am disabled in both legs. (*Ltrs-Rogers*, 97)

After another bedridden week, Clemens was improved, but by then he was completely disheartened. "I am out of bed at last, and seem to have got the best of the gout. I don't know how long I have been in bed, but it seems several years; the fog is thick, the daylight is black, and I feel defeated and in a state of surrender to fate" (*Ltrs-Rogers*, 98). As weeks passed, it seemed increasingly likely that the gouty attack had retreated, and his spirits rose again, as reflected in his comment to Henry Rogers in December 1894: "The gout seems to be entirely gone and I am as well and strong as I ever was. The profound weakness disappeared all of a sudden a week ago" (*Ltrs-Rogers*, 106). His recovery was short, however, and he was afflicted with another attack within several months, as he reported to Rogers in April 1895: "I've got a new touch of the gout" (*Ltrs-Rogers*, 142).

Considering the severity of the symptoms, the disabling nature of the disease, and the frustrations of its recurrences, it is not surprising that Clemens would turn to any treatment for gout that offered even a small hope of relief. His circumstances were precisely the ones that tend to spawn a patient's interest in "alternative" medical therapy—he had an annoying and disabling problem that was chronic in nature, and he had found no relief from traditional medical treatments. He desperately pursued almost every conceivable remedy that offered any promise of relieving his gout, but without benefit. Finally, in April 1895, he decided to try a treatment known as electrotherapy. At the time, electrotherapy was becoming a popular (if not outright faddish) treatment for a multitude of medical conditions. Its proponents claimed that it was of particular benefit for chronic rheumatic problems, especially those associated with gout. Given the degree of suffering experienced by Clemens, and the failure of other interventions to influence the course of his disease, a trial of electrotherapy seemed to be a reasonable choice for him.

The treatment of gout by electrical stimulation can be traced to the first century A.D., when Nero's freed slave Anthero accidentally stepped on a live electric ray, or "torpedo fish," while he was strolling on a beach. As the story goes, the electrical shock eliminated Anthero's chronic pain from gout. Claudius Galen, who lived in the second century A.D. (and who was, for many, the ultimate medical authority, even into the nineteenth century), reported that headaches could also be cured by applying a live torpedo fish to the sufferer.[1] The torpedo fish continued to be recommended for treatment of headaches and arthritic pain through the Middle Ages. As the nature of electricity became better understood in the eighteenth century, the torpedo fish was studied by the anatomist and physiologist John Hunter. It even became a party game prop (the challenge was to see how many people could hold hands in a circuit and transmit the current from a single fish).

As scientific knowledge increased in the eighteenth century, electricity's use as medical therapy (especially for pain treatment) expanded.[2] Benjamin Franklin used an electrical apparatus (consisting of an electrostatic generator with a Leyden jar to produce and store an electric charge) to give low-grade shock treatments to patients with a variety of maladies. Franklin himself had some doubts about the effectiveness of his spark and shock treatments, and he came to suspect that the patients may have benefited as much from the walk to his house as they did from their electrification. This form of electrotherapy became known as Franklinism despite the skepticism of its namesake. John Wesley, the founder of Methodism, became a practitioner of Franklinism. A man of faith in more ways than one, Wesley appeared to have a greater belief in Franklinism than even Franklin himself could muster. In *Primitive Physic,* one of his 417 books, Wesley claimed that the proper use of electricity could cure problems ranging from blindness and deafness to headache and, of course, gout. In 1760 he advocated the use of electrical treatment for pain relief in *The Desideratum: or, Electricity Made Plain and Useful,* and he reported specific cases to support the usefulness of this treatment— Anthero may have been the first recorded case of an electrical gout cure, but he certainly was far from the last: "Slight Attacks of the *Gout* are suddenly and effectually removed, by drawing Sparks from the Part affected…Mr. *Joshua W* of *Pershore,* was troubled for seven or eight Years with a Pain in his second Toe. Tho' nothing was to be seen it was as tender as a Boil, and the Pain was so great, particularly in walking, that he at length determined to have it cut off. By drawing Sparks he was cured in an Hour."[3]

It was not long before electrical medicine became far more sophisticated than the simple static electricity treatments used by Franklin and Wesley. In 1800, Allesandro Volta created an electrical current by alternating silver coins and zinc discs separated by pieces of water-soaked cards. In so doing, he not only invented the original battery, but he also created a new technology that provided even more therapeutic options for those who saw electricity as a means of cure. The invention of these voltaic piles meant that patients could be treated with serious shocks of electricity, and not just buzzed with a little static. The static electricity of Franklinism became old-fashioned and outdated and gave way to trendier replacements that employed free electricity moving in a current. The modern and stylish "science" of Galvanism used battery-initiated currents to treat everything from visual problems (by applying an electrode to the eye socket) to the pains of rheumatism. Galvanism itself was destined to be replaced. When Michael Faraday invented the first transformer in 1831, he opened the door to the development of even more "advanced" modes of electrical therapy, complete with suitably impressive nomenclature.

Dr. George Beard, the father of neurasthenia, was also a leading advocate of electrotherapy. If neurasthenia was caused by the loss of "nerve force," it followed that replenishment of that nerve force by electrical currents would be the most logical therapy. Beard and his medical partner Dr. Alphonse D. Rockwell were strongly devoted to the study, use, and promotion of electrotherapy. Their book *A Practical Treatise on the Medical and Surgical Uses of Electricity* was published in 1871. Even though the New York Medical Society refused Rockwell the right to present his work, arguing that only quacks would use electrotherapy, Beard aggressively championed its use for neurasthenia. Working from the belief that neurasthenia was simply a deficiency of "nerve-force," Beard used electric therapy to restore this lacking vital force in much the same way that an anemic patient today would receive a blood transfusion to replenish red blood cells. The reputations of Beard and Rockwell were enhanced through their association with Dr. S. Weir Mitchell, who in addition to being Beard's disciple was a highly respected neurologist, physiologist, pharmacologist, and pioneer in the study of nerve injuries. Mitchell's 1877 book, *Fat and Blood,* recommended the use of electricity as a method of providing muscular exercise for patients at rest.

Beard helped popularize treatment with a more sophisticated type of electrotherapy, which he referred to as "Faradization" to indicate that his system was even more advanced that Franklinism and Galvanism. To be treated, patients were required to be partially undressed while seated with their bare feet placed on a copper sheet. The copper sheet was then connected to one pole of a generator; the other electrode was composed of either a wet sponge or the hand of the operator, which was then placed on the afflicted body part. One version of this was the "electric bath," a form of treatment in which the patient was placed into a bath containing a positive electrode, and the negative electrode was attached to a body part such as the sternum.[4] This was judged to be particularly effective in treating subacute and chronic gout.

Electrotherapy was a perfect fit for the last half of the nineteenth century. The Gilded Age was noted for its fads and schemes and deceptions. Its very name suggested an enthusiasm for metals, magnetism, and money making, and the times were ripe for the concept of electricity as a plausible (and profitable) medical intervention. Clemens's Gilded Age was also the Golden Age of Electrotherapy.[5] Electromedicine banked on the name recognition of the leading electricity scientists of the era to legitimize its therapeutic schemes, and each ruse quickly overpowered its predecessor as the course of science (and pseudoscience) charged ahead.[6] Anyone who was anyone in the world of electricity got on the electrotherapy bandwagon—a communication read at the International Congress in Berlin in 1890 described Thomas A. Edison's report of the use of an electric bath to successfully treat several cases of gout.[7]

It comes as no surprise that Samuel Clemens (a great believer in the wonders of technology and a chronic sufferer from devastating attacks of gout) would eventually come to seek the benefits of treatment by electrical currents. After all, gout had been successfully treated by electricity for the preceding 1,800 years, whether it was administered from a torpedo fish, by electric bath, or by electro-puncture (a method that combined acupuncture with electrotherapy). Nero's Anthero, Methodism's John Wesley, and the venerated inventor Thomas Edison all marched in the same electrical parade, and Samuel Clemens (undoubtedly unwilling to repeat the weeks of suffering of the prior year) was about to join this diverse group. And, as is frequently the case for seekers of cure, his initial experience suggested he had indeed found the answer he was seeking, as he told Henry H. Rogers one day after his new "touch of gout" had appeared: "Most of my gout is gone, and have been on my

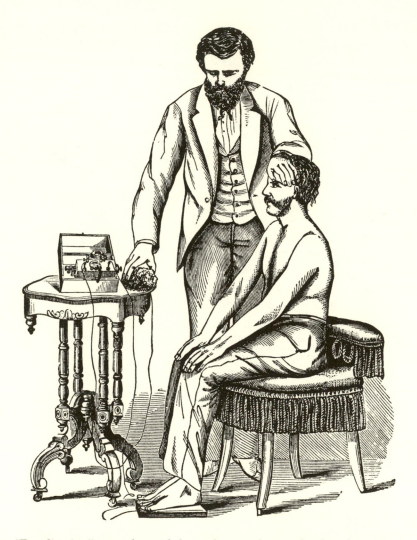

"Faradization" was a form of electrotherapy that used induced currents.
The illustration is from *Medical and Surgical Electricity,* a standard textbook of electrotherapy by George Beard and Alphonse Rockwell.

feet all day without discomfort," he reported with enthusiasm. And there
was no doubt in his mind about the source of his cure: "Electricity did
it" (*Ltrs-Rogers,* 144).

Except for this brief spark of success, however, there is no evidence
Clemens found lasting or recurring relief from his gout with electrotherapy. Instead, he continued in a never-ending search for the gouty Holy

Grail, trying one therapy after another without success. In a letter from Vienna written in 1897, two years after his positive result from the electric treatment, electricity was no longer given even a passing mention, even though his gout was still flaring.

> We have been here nine days and I have spent seven of them in bed—with gout. I am up and around, yesterday and to-day, but the rainy and snowy weather keeps all of us except Mrs. Twain in the house—colds, cough, and gout-possibilities the reason.... All the gouty people in Austria and Germany write me and tell me what is good for gout, and some of the remedies are good. I mean to try the whole lot the next time I get the disease. They can't all fail. (*Ltrs-Rogers*, 302)

Clemens's frustration and aggravation relating to his impairment and disability from gout, not to mention the empty hopes of cure, can be traced over many years. After his first episode in 1894, he continued to suffer from attacks of gout into the final decade of his life, as he complained to Henry Rogers's wife, Emilie, in April 1901: "I am bedridden again." In May 1901, he told Rudyard Kipling: "Between Jan. 3 and May 1 I had 3 gout attacks and spent among them 21 days in bed" (*Ltrs-Rogers*, 459). He let Rogers know about another attack in November 1903: "I was knocked down with gout and needed mental reinforcement. I am over the attack, now, and shall get up before night" (*Ltrs-Rogers*, 543).

Clemens wrote again about his frustrations with gout in three separate letters to Rogers in August 1905. On August 7, he reported that he was miserable in general. "I am having a time. Nothing agrees with me. If I drink coffee it gives me dispepsia; if I drink wine it gives me the gout; if I go to church it gives me dysentery. A vacation seems necessary" (*Ltrs-Rogers*, 595). His letter of August 14 carried a tone of desperation: "I am stranded here with gout. Pray for me" (*Ltrs-Rogers*, 596). By August 21, his gout had disabled him again. "For a little while I thought the gout had retired ... but next day I was bedridden again" (*Ltrs-Rogers*, 597). And, in November 1906, he told Emilie Rogers about his fear of having a recurrent attack and his proposal for a novel form of therapy: "the weather was not auspicious for gout, and I am threatened with that, these days. The billiards will knock it out" (*Ltrs-Rogers*, 620).[8]

What was Clemens thinking in 1895 when he subjected himself to electrotherapy for his gout? Electricity had been used for treatment of medical problems on and off for nearly two millennia, but its use was based on an underlying biological premise that seemed highly questionable, and most of its support came from testimonials that were far from convincing.

It should have been apparent to Clemens that electrotherapy was just another version of patent medicine and water cure, perhaps more updated in its terminology but every bit as useless in its effectiveness. Electrotherapy had been used by Galen, and it was Samuel Clemens, after all, who had criticized Missouri doctors (in *Those Extraordinary Twins*, published a year earlier, in 1894) for their unquestioned use of Galen's antiquated and unproven treatments. He was vicious in his attacks on Galen's prescriptions.

> It was one of Galen's; in fact, it was Galen's favorite, and had been slaying people for sixteen thousand years. Galen used it for everything, applied it to everything, said it would remove everything, from warts all the way through to lungs—and it generally did. Galen was still the only medical authority recognized in Missouri; his practice was the only practice known to the Missouri doctors, and his prescriptions were the only ammunition they carried when they went out for game. (*PW&TET*, 410–11)

Clemens had also heaped derision on Galen's obsolete therapies in his 1890 article "A Majestic Literary Fossil": "[I]f Galen should appear among us to-day, he could not stand anybody's watch; he would inspire no awe; he would be told he was a back number, and it would surprise him to see that that fact counted against him instead of in his favor. He wouldn't know our medicines; he wouldn't know our practice; and the first time he tried to introduce his own we would hang him" (*£1m Banknote*, 243).

Now, after publishing two attacks on Galen's old-fashioned treatments in the preceding five years, Clemens was poised to use one of Galen's own remedies himself. Why did Clemens change his attitude? In truth, it is unlikely Clemens knew the long history of electrotherapy's use for gout, and it is even less likely he knew of Galen's recommendation of treating headache pain with the electrical current of a torpedo fish. More likely, it was a matter of electrotherapy being available and fairly convenient (at the time, he was in Paris, where Livy was receiving electrotherapy for her own medical problems with apparent success). But availability and convenience alone would not have been sufficient to encourage Clemens to pursue electrotherapy. Like other patients who are driven to pursue alternative medical therapies, he was driven by the feelings of desperation that had accumulated through the years he unsuccessfully sought relief. Most of all, he needed to be sustained by a sense of *hope,* and he invested his emotional energy in the hope that electrotherapy would be the magical treatment that would solve the gout problem for him as no other therapy had done.

The reason for going to Paris in the first place had been to determine whether electrotherapy treatments might help Livy. In the context of the times, this seemed to make a great deal of sense. Intelligent, well-educated, "sensitive," and troubled young women—in other words, women with backgrounds similar to Livy's—were the most common targets for electrotherapy. As mentioned previously, Alice James, the sister of psychologist William James and novelist Henry James, was treated with electrotherapy for chronic and poorly defined medical problems attributed to neurasthenia.[9] Livy Clemens seemed to be an excellent candidate for electrotherapy as her health deteriorated in the late nineteenth century. Suffering from heart failure, she was once more chronically ill, unresponsive to traditional medical interventions, and again in need of another miracle. With her history of weakness, listlessness, and malaise dating back to her youth, Livy had the typical characteristics of a neurasthenic— she was a frail, delicate being who had not been endowed with sufficient "nerve force" to withstand the rigors of daily living. When medical scientists started to apply electrical currents to the afflicted individuals in an effort to restore their depleted stores of nervous energy, it seemed to be the perfect solution to Livy's chronic weakness. Samuel Clemens, ever the optimist when new technology was involved, was hopeful for a good result. It had been many years since Livy's recovery from the paralysis of her youth, but Clemens could never have forgotten the explanation that had been given by the "quack" Dr. Newton for how he had performed his miracle in overcoming the paralysis of the bedridden young Livy Langdon. "I met Newton once, in after years, and asked him what his secret was. He said he didn't know but thought perhaps some subtle form of electricity proceeded from his body and wrought the cures" (*Autob/MTA*, 185). Newton told others the same thing—electrical activity seemed to be involved in his cures, whether they were accomplished through the work of an intermediary ("I will, through you, give him a pleasant shock as from an electric battery, and with it his disease will depart") or by direct application (Newton suggested that he emitted a shock "just as much and as powerful as that from a galvanic battery").[10]

In fact, Livy's initial treatments with electrotherapy seemed to restore some of her lost vitality, and for a while it appeared as though electrotherapy would be the solution to the major medical concerns of the Clemens family. The human electricity of Dr. Newton had provided the cure of Livy's youth, and perhaps the advanced technology of the nineteenth century might contribute another jolt of electricity to give her the miracle she so desperately needed as an adult. Livy was in Paris in February 1894, and Clemens wrote to her to endorse her pursuit of electrotherapy: "I am so glad Susie has gone on that trip and that you are trying the electric. May you both prosper" (*Ltrs/Paine*, 2:611). It did not take long for him to be impressed that the therapy was beneficial, as he stated the next month in a letter to Henry Rogers: "Mrs. Clemens... wants to go home for the summer but the doctor forbids. She is improving decidedly now under the electrical treatment" (*Ltrs-Rogers*, 51). Perhaps technology really could provide the answers to every human problem.

Clemens reported to Rogers that Livy was "in great spirits on account of the benefit which she has received from the electrical treatment in Paris" and that she was eager "to take it up again and continue it all the winter" (*Ltrs-Rogers*, 71). Clemens continued to be pleased with the effectiveness of electrotherapy into late November of the same year. Buoyed by the hope that his wife would be healthy enough to return to the United States in the spring of 1895, he wrote to Rogers and predicted ongoing success with electromedicine. "By that time Mrs. C.'s electric treatment here will have carried its health-restoring work a long way toward completion. Her doctor is very proud of the progress he has made" (*Ltrs-Rogers*, 100). However, despite Livy's promising initial response to electrotherapy, her improvement did not last; continuing experience with the electrical treatments showed that electrotherapy was as futile as all the other methods that had been tried for restoring her health.

As might be expected, Sam and Livy Clemens's experiences with electrotherapy were not unique. There was little evidence that electrotherapy was of any long-standing benefit to anyone. As was the case for the purveyors of patent medicines and the champions of hydrotherapy, the electrotherapy charlatans had more success in creating feasible explanations for why their treatment *should* work than they did in showing that any of it *did* work.

Even so, electrotherapists found that it was easy enough to develop theories that could link the body's electricity to any conceivable disease, and the potential applications of electrotherapy seemed unlimited. The work of physicists such as Volta, Hertz, Faraday, and others permitted the development of a pseudoscientific movement that incorporated the contemporary theories and terminology of physics to legitimize its treatments and instruments. The transient popularity of electrotherapy illustrates an important principle that is essential to the success of any therapeutic system. There must be a credible explanation for how a treatment alters a disease process before the treatment can gain popular support. Regardless of the era or the intervention, the public will accept a treatment system as legitimate only if that system is able to utilize the scientific concepts (or, at least, the scientific jargon) of the day. Patients will not accept any system of medical treatment (nor will they have a response to treatment) unless the nature of the treatment is congruent with the character of the disease. Electrotherapy worked best when neurasthenia was a well-accepted disease. When neurasthenia became extinct, electrotherapy lost its niche in the medical ecosystem.

Samuel Clemens's experimentation with electrotherapy demonstrated the critical factors that drive the pursuit of all nontraditional methods. Dissatisfaction with the failures of traditional medical therapy is necessary, but, paradoxically, those who switch to alternative therapy rarely require the new treatment system to provide any proof of its own effectiveness. The patient must be able to perceive that there is an underlying "science" that can give an aura of credibility to the upstart methodology, but the patient rarely demands any hard proof that the newer treatment plan will actually be any better than the old one. Ultimately, the long-term survival of unproven "alternative medicine" systems is based on an innocent faith that, somewhere, somehow, there must be an answer that is not being provided by the traditional approaches.

Like Samuel Clemens, most seekers of cure by alternative medical systems meet one disappointment after another. Time is taken, money is spent, energy and emotion are invested, yet the maladies continue. At some point the law of diminishing returns might suggest that some medical illnesses are just not amenable to medical therapy and, perhaps, the best option might be to leave well enough alone. This rarely happens. Instead, the feeling that *some* type of medical intervention *must* be employed seems to be almost universal, at least in Western societies. In medical matters, there has always been a belief that doing *something*, even something that is obviously futile, is always better than doing nothing. When in doubt, an error of commission usually seems preferable to an error of omission (even though the history of medical practice repetitively demonstrates the fallacy in this philosophy). Dr. Eugene Robin has criticized the use of unproven technology in the intensive care setting, and in so doing he has taken the medical profession to task for adhering to the dogma that almost any intervention can be justified when patients are very sick. In rejecting the common wisdom that lighting a single candle is preferable to cursing the darkness, Robin cites the observations of Dr. W. A. Silverman that doctors *can* make things worse; when the darkness is encountered inside a fireworks factory, it is far preferable "to curse the darkness than to light the wrong candle."[11] The greatest wisdom of all comes from having the restraint to sit quietly in the darkness of the fireworks factory. Few of us have such self-control, and Clemens certainly did not.

Clemens eventually did realize that electrotherapy was not giving him any relief from his gout. He also came to see that it was not going to help Livy recover from her chronic downhill course with her failing heart. Until this became clear to him, however, he and Livy continued to be treated by electrotherapy, and electrotherapy gave them both something that was of immense value. Electrotherapy gave them *hope*—the hope of returning to the lives that had been stolen from them by disease. Even when there was no feasible cure in sight, the hope they received from electrotherapy was far better than having nothing at all. This gift of hope would not have been available to Clemens and Livy if they had chosen to follow the more prudent course of abstaining from any therapy that was not of proven effectiveness (for them, this would have meant avoidance of all therapies). As with all frustrated chronic sufferers, Clemens's memories of his previous miseries were so intense that he was willing to subject himself to the unpleasantness of electrical shock treatments in the hope of relief. For a while, electrotherapy seemed as likely to help as anything else that was available to him. As it turned out, though, the claims of electrotherapy were just more empty promises. Clemens continued to suffer from his attacks of gout because the application of electrical currents did not prevent the deposition of uric acid crystals into his joints. Livy spiraled further downward to her death from congestive heart failure because her problems came from the weakened heart muscle of a patient with cardiac disease, and not from the depleted "nerve force" of a neurasthenic.[12]

Clemens came to realize that electrotherapy was just one more illusion, and it joined the ranks of allopathic medicine, patent medicine, and hydropathic medicine on his lengthening list of medical disappointments.

13

The Rest Cure

Then that old family doctor arrived and went at the matter in an educated and practical way—that is to say, he started a search expedition for contusions and humps and bumps and announced that there were none. He said that if I would go to bed and forget my adventure I would be all right in the morning—which was not so. I was *not* all right in the morning. I didn't intend to be all right and I was far from being all right. But I said I only needed rest and I didn't need that doctor any more.

—Mark Twain, *The Autobiography of Mark Twain*

In the Age of Neurasthenia, the failure of electrotherapy to restore vitality to those who suffered from depleted nerve force created an opening for other methods that might be able to recharge the failing physiological batteries of the chronically ill. "Rest cure" seemed to be an option with considerable promise. If the direct application of electrical current was incapable of replenishing the body's waning energy, perhaps the best strategy was to limit the intense demands that caused the depletion of energy in the first place. The rest cure, aided by special diets and medications, was designed to allow the body to gradually restore its own energy through avoidance of stress. The neurasthenia specialist Dr. S. Weir Mitchell explained the basis of rest cure in his 1871 book *Wear and Tear.* He pointed out that the body has an innate system of protection

Silas Weir Mitchell.
Courtesy of the
National Library of
Medicine (B19384).

that prevents the muscles from being overused—anyone who exercises vigorously will eventually be forced to stop and rest due to muscle fatigue. In contrast, the mind can be worked just as vigorously as muscle, but it does not have a similar means of self-protection and is therefore at risk of becoming worn out unless it can be given intervals of rest.

Mitchell suggested a neuroanatomic basis for neurasthenia in which stress weakened fragile neural functions and caused nervous exhaustion severe enough to disrupt the nervous system's normal processes. Since the brain was unable to protect itself from wearing out, Mitchell developed a systematic program that forced the overworked brain to slow down for a mandatory rest period. Mitchell's goal was to replace the weak neuroanatomic pathways that created the predisposition to neurasthenia with newer, healthier, and stronger circuits.[1] His program included improved nutrition and lectures on self-control, in addition to periods of forced rest. The rest had to be absolute, with the patient required to stay in bed for several weeks. Mitchell was confident that disrupted pathways could regain their normal function with adequate rest. However, it was essential to isolate the patient not only from stress but also from the excessive sympathy of concerned relatives; as Mitchell saw it, the nerve pathways that supported the patient's selfish emotions could be created and reinforced by such misguided sympathy. Mitchell took complete control of his patient's environment by isolating her in a quiet room and forbidding reading material, visitors, or contact with any component of her former life "until we have broken up the whole daily drama of the sickroom, with its little selfishness and its craving for sympathy and indulgence."[2] Samuel Clemens did not see the situation in the same light as Mitchell, at least when *he* was the one who was sick. In February 1868, Clemens suggested to his friend Mary Fairbanks that he personally could do without sympathy when he was sick, but he could not get along without the indulgences. "One should not bring sympathy to a sick man. It is always kindly meant, & of course it has to be taken—but it isn't much of an improvement on castor oil. One who has a sick man's true interest at heart will forbear spoken sympathy, & bring him surreptitiously soup, & fried oysters & other trifles that the doctor has tabooed" (*Ltrs-2*, 190).

The rest cure became very popular in the United States, and a number of private sanatoriums offered programs centered around rest and good nutrition. The rest cure movement shared clientele with the water cure movement, and both were generally targeted toward the weak and fatigued of middle- and upper-class origins. Treatment by rest cure was not restricted to the world of spa-goers, however, and the rest cure approach gained a high level of acceptance throughout the traditional medical community in the last two decades of the nineteenth century. Even the voice of mainstream medicine, the *Journal of the American Medical Association*, borrowed from the vocabulary of neurasthenia in 1896 as it promoted the use of America's hospitals as effective rest cure sites for standard medical and surgical patients.

The benefit, it appears, lies chiefly in being removed from the everyday, familiar scenes, where every object is apt to remind the invalid of some duty undone or some mountain ahead. It is a species of the "rest cure." There seems to be a dreamy drowsy atmosphere about a hospital patient's existence which is very soothing to invalid nerves . . . there are many pleasant memories connected with a few week's [sic] stay. There comes a time when the pains and aches are a thing of the past, and then the patient relapses into the delightful, dreamy, dolce far niente existence called getting one's strength back . . . the only effort demanded of one is to select a small list of delicacies for the next meal.[3]

Rest cure inventor Weir Mitchell shared a friend in common with Samuel Clemens—author William Dean Howells. Howells (1837–1920), one of Clemens's most trusted friends, was a major literary figure of his day, an author and the editor of *Atlantic Monthly*. Howells advised Clemens throughout his career, corrected Clemens's manuscripts, and promoted Clemens's works in his book reviews. Their admiration was mutual; it was Howells who characterized Mark Twain as "the Lincoln of our literature." Clemens came to learn of the benefits of rest cure through his relationship with Howells. Howells's seventeen-year-old daughter Winifred was treated with "rest cure" in 1881–1882 after she suffered a "nervous breakdown." Winny Howells was said to have pre-cocious literary gifts and suffered periodic exacerbations of "nervous exhaustion." In August 1881, Howells told Clemens that "our dear girl has to lie *abed* now all the time—rest cure" (*Ltrs-Howells Sel.*, 173). Ulti-mately, this approach turned out to be a tragic failure. The rest cure did not seem to help the young woman's condition, and Howells became concerned that the rest had been too restrictive for his daughter's health. On September 11, 1881, Howells wrote to Clemens: "Winny is still trying the rest cure; but we are going to get her up as soon as the doctor comes home. If she could have been allowed to read, I think the experiment might have succeeded; but I think the privation has thrown her thoughts back upon her, and made her morbid and hypochondriacal" (*Ltrs-Howells Sel.*, 178). Winifred Howells died on March 3, 1889, in a country rest home, after a regimen of forced feeding and treatment for "hysteria" under the care of Dr. Mitchell (*Ltrs-Howells Sel.*, 281).

A few weeks after he first heard about Winny's rest cure, and while Howells still had great hope for its success, Clemens imposed a rest cure on himself so that he could recuperate from the mental exhaustion that came from the intense intellectual effort he was expending by writing a play. Clemens described his own distress in terms of the typical symp-toms of neurasthenia. As he envisioned it, his brilliant and creative mind was on the brink of burning itself out if he did not force himself, virtu-ally against his own will, to rest quietly in bed (Mark Twain expert Hal Holbrook has described Clemens as "a man whose nerve fibers must have been burning all the time").[4]

What I call my mind, has been in a state of fierce irruption during three successive days. The consequence is, I am on my back, burnt out, devastated, & merely smouldering....I've done the first & second Acts; but this was too much work for three days; so I am in bed. But I am in bed really as a precaution, only; it is to guard against wandering up to the study; I should go to work, sure—& I have had some rough lessons in the matter of over-work. (*Ltrs-Howells Sel.*, 174–75)

Clemens's self-application of rest cure reflects his understanding of the basis of neurasthenia. He was aware that men could be afflicted with neurasthenia as easily as women, particularly if they were hardworking, intelligent, and sensitive. Thus, when Clemens's nephew by marriage, Charles Webster, failed to live up to expectations in managing Clemens's publishing company, his shortcomings were not of his own making, according to Clemens's biographer Paine. "Webster was ambitious, nervous, and not robust. He had overworked and was paying the penalty. His trouble was neurasthenia, and he was presently obliged to retire altogether from the business" (*Ltrs/Paine*, 2:489). Clemens was well aware of Webster's neurasthenia, and in February 1887 he advised his harried publisher that "a moment's rest from work is good medicine for neuralgia" (*MTBM*, 376). In a July 12, 1887, letter to his sister Pamela (Webster's mother-in-law), Clemens not only expressed his acceptance of Webster's neurasthenia as an explanation for his inadequacies as a businessman, but he also indicated his commitment to the value of rest cure as therapy. "I had no idea that Charley's case was so serious. I knew it was bad, and persistent, but I was not aware of the full size of the matter... he must take the required rest, whether the business can stand it or not."[5]

Years later, Clemens's daughter Clara utilized the rest cure when she developed significant emotional problems following her mother's death in 1904 (Clara suffered from what Clemens described as "two-thirds of a nervous breakdown," and her bothersome behavior included an attempt to jump into her mother's open grave). Clemens himself added to her distress by giving Clara an exaggerated description of a minor injury that had befallen her sister Jean. Because Clemens's own behavior was blamed as a factor in Clara's difficulties, he was banned by her doctors from contacting his own daughter. In August 1904, Clemens leased a house on Long Island to provide Clara with a suitable location for her rest cure. "It is the quietest place I could find; and Clara is going to need the quietest kind of quiet for many months to come, I think. She is not perceptibly better or stronger than she was when we arrived...she is thinner than her mother was" (*Ltrs-Rogers*, 579). Clara remained bedridden and distraught for more than seven months. Separated from her family for more than a year in order to limit the stress on her fragile system, Clara moved from one rest cure to another, and Clemens wrote in March 1905, "[Clara] will go from the rest-cure in this city to the rest-cure in Norfolk Conn. and we shall not see her before autumn" (*Ltrs/Paine*, 2:772). The family had not seen her since the middle of October 1904, and it was not until November 1905 that she was allowed to rejoin her father in his New York City home. In the meantime, however, her rest cure had become less restrictive and Clemens was permitted to regain his visiting privileges. Even so, the privilege of visiting his daughter did not come without a price. Clemens became severely exhausted after traveling in hot weather to see Clara, and as he wrote in September 1905, he had to undergo another rest cure himself in order to recover from his energy-depleted condition. "I am still doing the rest-cure in bed—nearly ever since the journey to Clara in the hot weather broke me down. . . . The journey from here to Boston in hot weather is murderous, and I *expected* it to knock me out, and it did" (*Ltrs-Rogers*, 598).

Even though Samuel Clemens employed rest cure for more than two decades, he never seemed to have much enthusiasm for it. Rest cure may have been too passive and too tame to suit him. It might have provided a good excuse for getting some relaxation or for taking a temporary escape from the stresses of life, but it did not seem to be the kind of treatment that was really going to *fix* anything. It was at best a temporizing therapy that allowed the exhausted sufferer an opportunity to restore some depleted nerve force.

Clemens wanted something better. Ever the seeker, he felt compelled to look for something more active and more dynamic than rest cure. For a time, he thought he might have found the answer when he discovered a new system of therapy that directed its attention to the physical body. The revolutionary treatment that was to become Clemens's newest panacea was known as osteopathic medicine.

14

OSTEOPATHY

The Medicine of Manipulation

I like osteopathy. It is quicker and you don't have to take any medicine.

—Mark Twain, "Remarks on Osteopathy"

As Samuel Clemens sought cures for the increasing number of medical problems that afflicted his family, he eventually discovered a new system that impressed him more than any he had encountered before—osteopathic medicine. Clemens was angered by the atrocities of allopathy and frustrated with the impotence of the competing therapeutic systems. He was willing to try anything that might help his family. The system of osteopathic medicine had been born in Clemens's home state on the American frontier, but Clemens had to travel to Europe in order to discover it for himself. He was immensely impressed with the effectiveness of the newly developed field, and he became an outspoken and enthusiastic advocate of its therapeutic benefits. He aggressively challenged the traditional medical establishment as he became a fierce proponent for the legal approval of osteopathic medicine.

Osteopathic medicine arose in the nineteenth century as one of the many sects that challenged the tenets of the allopaths. Osteopathy did not subscribe to the belief that a patient had to be drugged, bled, flushed out, hosed down, or electrified in order to get better. Instead, the osteopathic approach involved physical manipulation of the body (particularly the spine); this manipulative management was believed to get to

Andrew Taylor Still.
Courtesy of the
National Library of
Medicine (B8539).

the root of disease by correcting the disruptions of vital forces caused by abnormalities of skeletal structure.

Andrew Taylor Still (1828–1917), credited with being osteopathy's founder, was born in Virginia. His father, Abram, was a self-taught physician and a circuit-riding Methodist Episcopal minister. When Abram was assigned to do missionary work in Missouri, he moved his family to the western frontier, propelled by the same pioneering spirit that drove John Marshall Clemens to settle in Missouri. There is no evidence that Abram's son Andrew actually had any formal medical training. Andrew learned the medicine he knew from his father and his father's books, supplementing his knowledge of anatomy by digging up bodies from an Indian burial ground and gaining further experience as a hospital steward during the Civil War.[1]

Not unlike their religious counterparts, originators of medical sects often claim a moment of epiphany, and it was no different for Andrew Still, who dated his discovery of osteopathic principles to an event that occurred when he was ten years old. While he was playing on a rope swing, a severe headache disappeared as he inadvertently applied pressure to the back of his neck. Years later, after gaining a better knowledge of anatomy, he speculated that the cure had come about because the pressure of the rope had "suspended the action of the great occipital nerve, and given harmony to the flow of the arterial blood to and through the veins." Fifty years later he reported that this momentous episode was the first event that allowed him to be "fully established in the belief that the artery is the father of the rivers of life, health and ease, and its muddy or impure water is first in all disease."[2]

The "discovery" of a new medical therapy, no matter how dramatic, is never sufficient in its own right to spawn an alternative medical care movement. There must also be dissatisfaction with the established mainstream system. For Still, who had himself entered regular medical practice in Kansas in the 1850s, the defining moment of dissatisfaction with the traditional medical system came from the death of his three children from an epidemic of meningitis in 1864. He watched in frustration as the various physicians he called upon argued about therapy and ineffectually changed drugs and doses, and he became convinced that the therapy of the "regular" physicians was not scientifically based. (Samuel Clemens was destined to have similar frustration with allopathy's shortcomings after his daughter Susy died of meningitis in 1896.) Even so, Still continued to practice orthodox medicine in Kansas for another ten years as he developed the details of osteopathic therapy.

Other factors played a role in Still's development of his osteopathic system. His Methodist background convinced him that alcohol was a poison, and he saw no difference between liquor and many of the alcohol-based medications used by traditional doctors. He opposed the dosing of drugs; in place of medication, it is said, he liberally substituted "a healthy dose of moralism."[3] He looked into a number of drugless sects, including hydrotherapy, but he became most impressed with the concepts of "magnetic healing." Franz Mesmer (1734–1815), a leader among the magnetic healers, believed that a universal magnetic fluid flows throughout the body, and that disease is caused when there is an inadequate flow of this substance to specific parts of the body (a concept that is consistent with the imagery of "neurasthenia"). Mesmer proposed that the flow of this force could be redirected by making "passes" over the affected body parts, either with magnets or with the healer's own hands. Still was able to combine the theoretical aspects of Mesmer's magnetic healing with his own manipulative skills in the folk healing art of bonesetting. According to his viewpoint, the displacement of bones (especially the spine) caused disease by obstructing vital blood flow. Blood was Still's essential fluid, in contrast to the magnetic fluid that was envisioned by Mesmer and the "nerve force" of Beard. As Andrew Still saw it, the readjustment of displaced bones into their proper position would allow the body to heal itself by improving blood flow.

Still officially cut his ties to traditional medicine when he formally introduced his new system in 1874. He renounced regular medical practice, and in newspaper advertisements he declared himself to be a "Magnetic Healer." His initial hope had been to teach the principles of osteopathy in Baldwin, Kansas, but his new ideas were harshly rejected there, for reasons that seem quite understandable, based on the claims he made at the time: "when I said I could twist a man one way and cure the flu, fever, colds and the diseases of the climate; shake up a child and stop scarlet fever, croup, diphtheria, and cure whooping cough in three days by a wring of its neck, and so on, all my good character was at once gone."[4]

Still moved to Kirksville, Missouri, by May 1875. He established a practice as an itinerant healer, and he practiced from an office in Clemens's hometown of Hannibal for several months in 1889.[5] He continued his personal studies in anatomy, physiology, and chemistry. After years of harassment, Still eventually established the first college of osteopathy in November 1892 in Kirksville. (Earlier, Still had been petitioned by a delegation from Hannibal to consider opening the school there, and he was offered land in the town for that purpose.)

Despite his own Missouri origins, Samuel Clemens was not aware of osteopathy's development in the midwestern United States. By the late nineteenth century he had long been an easterner and a citizen of the world, and he discovered American osteopathy only after encountering a European version in 1899, while searching for a cure for the seizure disorder of his daughter Jean. Jean's epilepsy was a recurring frustration. Her first seizure occurred in school in 1895, but she had experienced personality changes several years before. Jean's situation was disturbing to the family. Unsure about how to deal with it, the Clemenses kept the nature of Jean's problem a secret, even from closest friends, until February 1900, when Clemens told his confidant Henry Rogers about the situation.

Jean's head got a bad knock when she [was] 8 or 9, by a fall. Seven years ago she showed capricious changes of disposition which we could not account for; and four years ago the New York experts pronounced her case *epilepsy*. This we learned when we got back from around the world. We put her into the hands of the world's head expert in Vienna, who said that in some cases this disease had been outgrown, but that he knew of no authentic instance of its cure by physicians. (*Ltrs-Rogers*, 430)

As time went by, Jean's momentary lapses of awareness (petit mal seizures, also known as "absence" seizures) increased in frequency, occurring up to twenty times a day. To Clemens's immense frustration, Jean had received no help in three years from doctors, drugs, or baths; there had been no benefit from the consultations with specialists in Vienna, the "City of Doctors."[6] She had been taking bromide up to three times daily in an attempt to help what Clemens and Livy euphemistically referred to as her "absent-mindedness."

In their ongoing quest for an effective treatment for Jean's epilepsy, Clemens and his family left Vienna in May 1899 and settled in London, following a lead provided by the American journalist Poultney Bigelow. Based on his own positive experience, Bigelow suggested to the Clemenses that they might find help from Dr. Jonas Henrik Kellgren and his Swedish Movement Cure at the Swedish Institution in London. Bigelow had been bedridden for seven months with dysentery and had not responded to traditional medical therapy, but he was out of bed in one day after treatment by Kellgren, without use of medication.

Kellgren had a fashionable practice in London's Belgravia district and an even more successful sanatorium in his native Sweden. Of importance to the case of Jean Clemens, his treatments were reported to be effective in cases of "non-hereditary" epilepsy. The Clemenses arrived in London on June 3, 1899, and by the end of the month they had been persuaded to spend the summer at Kellgren's sanatorium by the lake in the Swedish village of Sanna. Clemens initially had some skepticism about Kellgren's claims: "If I can believe these patients here, they get cured of all sorts of devilish diseases without the use of medicines. . . . They claim to cure any disease that is not cancer or other incurable malady" (*Ltrs-Rogers*, 404). Any doubts were short-lived, and by September 1899 Clemens told Joseph Twichell he had seen evidence that Kellgren's methods were successful: "The people actually do several of the great things the Christian Scientists pretend to do" (*Ltrs/Paine*, 2:683).

Because of the apparent benefit Jean derived from treatment, the entire family eventually "took the cure" for its various medical problems from July through October. Clemens soon came to view osteopathy as the panacea he had been seeking for such a long time, as he told Henry Rogers. "I have a very good time here experimenting with the system in my own person and watching the patients. I wish you were here and had about a hundred diseases to experiment on, so that I could keep the record. They would knock them out of you as fast as you could call game" (*Ltrs-Rogers*, 408). Clemens made a similarly passionate observation in a letter to William James: "It is my conviction that Kellgren can modify any ailment, & can cure any that is curable. In typhoid, scarlet fever, influenza, & all such things, he is a master hand."[7] Clemens's exuberant enthusiasm for the osteopathic system is also evident in a letter he wrote to Richard Watson Gilder in July 1899: "Damn all the other cures, including the baths and Christian Science and the doctors of the several schools—*this* is the satisfactory one! Every day, in 15 minutes it takes all the old age out of you and sends you forth feeling like a bottle of champagne that's just been uncorked" (*Ltrs-Rogers*, 407).

Clemens was not only pleased with Jean's improvement, which was his major purpose in pursuing osteopathy, but he also believed that Kellgren's method had a remarkable effect on his own bronchitis. "I got them a chance to see what they could do with one of my old long-lasting bronchial coughs. They relieve it in ten minutes every morning. . . . I am obliged to confess that no medicine has ever given me a week of anything approaching such comfort" (*Ltrs-Rogers*, 405). Livy joined in and underwent manipulation treatment for a painful rheumatic hip that kept her awake at night. Clemens was so impressed by the benefits of osteopathy that eventually all the family became involved and took massage treatments for twenty minutes each morning. "We decided to come here to the summer establishment and take the treatment 3 months. Jean and her mother and I have been at it 3 weeks, now and are quite reconciled to continue. I like it. It is vigorous exercise, and *other people do it for you.* Isn't that nice?" (*Ltrs-Rogers*, 404). Of greatest importance to Clemens, however, Jean's epilepsy improved. Even though she stopped taking the bromides, her spells of "absentmindedness" decreased to two daily; despite the improvements, Kellgren wisely covered all his bases by warning that it was still possible for the bad attacks to return at any time. For more than a month, Jean had no more than slight losses of awareness lasting a minute or two in the morning, and she had no grand mal seizures.

The family continued her treatment in a branch of Kellgren's office in London in the fall of 1899.

Due to the apparent success of Kellgren's treatments, Clemens was reluctant to do anything that might disrupt his daughter's therapy, even though he was eager to return to America after the long interval abroad. After Clemens described the success of Kellgren's system to his sister Pamela, he was surprised to learn that Pamela herself had been receiving similar treatment in the United States. As a result of this unanticipated piece of promising information, he was hopeful that Jean might be able to continue with the successful treatments at home. "By the accident of writing my sister and describing to her the remarkable cures made by Kellgren with his hands and without drugs, I brought upon myself a quite stunning surprise; for she wrote to me that she had been taking this very treatment in Buffalo—and that it was an American invention" (*Ltrs/Paine*, 2:689).

Clemens was initially concerned that the European and American versions of osteopathy might be dissimilar enough to thwart his plans to return to the United States. However, as he began to research the nature of osteopathy in the United States, he became convinced that Andrew Still's American osteopathy was the same as Kellgren's treatments.

> My temper is under a heavy strain this morning, for I find that the Kellgren system (under the new name of "Osteopathy,") is being practiced all over America! . . . We are here only to have the Kellgren treatment for Jean, yet we could get it in several places in New York; and now we are tied here till April or May, because we have taken the flat for 7 1/2 months and have paid half of the rent in advance.
>
> I happened to write my nephew about the treatment and now I find that his mother has been taking it several months in Buffalo. She sends me circulars and pamphlets which show that Osteopathy is exactly the Kellgren treatment. (*Ltrs-Rogers*, 414)

Clemens was never willing to accept the idea that simple coincidence could account for the simultaneous occurrence of the same idea, invention, or event in two different places. Instead, he believed that the concurrent development of osteopathy on two different continents was due to some type of "mental telegraphy" between Still and Kellgren. Even so, it was essential for him to be convinced that the two methods were absolutely identical, and not just similar. Before he returned to America with

Jean, Clemens wanted to be certain that Jean could continue to get the same helpful therapy she had been receiving in Europe.

> Kellgren has treated Jean 7 1/2 months. She has made great improvement. Her natural disposition—lost during 7 years—has returned. Her physical condition is good. Her mind is sound and capable.... We are obliged to believe that in time (indefinite,) Kellgren can accomplish the cure. Nobody else can do it, except, possibly, an osteopathist. If the osteopathists can do it, we can go home; otherwise we must stay here, and stick it out. (*Ltrs-Rogers*, 430)

Because Clemens was loath to desert the only medical treatment that had been helpful for his daughter, he asked his friend Joseph Twichell to confirm that osteopathy in the United States was comparable to the treatments used by Kellgren. However, Twichell failed to pursue the investigation in the manner Clemens had requested. Clemens wanted a detailed description of the methods of American osteopathy so that he might compare them to the techniques used in Kellgren's European system. However, instead of going to American osteopaths to get the necessary facts, Twichell simply asked "regular" physicians for their personal opinions about osteopathy's efficacy. Clemens thought that his friend's approach to resolving the question was absurd, and he was not reluctant to let Twichell know of his annoyance. "You wish to advise with a *physician* about it? Certainly. There is no objection. He knows next to something about his own trade, but that will not embarrass him in framing a verdict about this one. I respect your superstitions—we all have them" (*Ltrs/Paine*, 2:683).

As Clemens complained about Twichell's failure to obtain the information he so desperately wanted, he noted with disdain that the assessment of osteopathy by allopathic physicians was predictably negative and of absolutely no use to him in his effort to determine the utility of American osteopathy: "Maybe I managed to make myself misunderstood, as to the Osteopathists. I wanted to know how the men impress you. As to their art, I know fairly well about that, and should not value Hartford's opinion of it; nor a physician's; nor that of another who proposed to enlighten me out of his ignorance. Opinions based upon theory, superstition and ignorance are not very precious" (*Ltrs/Paine*, 2:695). Clemens was not only annoyed at Twichell's incompetence as an information gatherer, but he was further irritated by the apparent collusion among traditional physicians who automatically rejected nontraditional methods. He ventilated his frustrations in a letter to Henry Rogers: "those friends did not go to osteopathists for information, but to physicians! It was as sane as going to Satan to find out about the Christian religion. By consequence I am rich in knowledge of what the doctors think of osteopathy, but poorer than poverty in any valuable information concerning that art" (*Ltrs-Rogers*, 430–31).

Clemens eventually recruited his nephew Samuel Moffett to be his agent of inquiry, and he sent Moffett with a list of questions to a New York osteopath, Dr. George J. Helmer. Until he could find out the facts about osteopathy in the United States, Clemens decided to keep his family in London through the summer. As he learned more about American osteopathy, Clemens gushed to Rogers about its benefits, encouraging him to seek out osteopathic treatments in New York for his own ailments.

> There are establishments at 156 Fifth avenue; 107 East 23d; and 136 Madison avenue, corner 31st street. I beg you to go in at one of those places and take the treatment for a month, whether there is anything the matter with you or not. It will set you up and make you gay. I wish you would take it *two* months. It will cost you but a trifle of time—15 or 20 minutes two or three times a week—3 times is best.
>
> And when there *is* anything the matter with you, send for those people. You can't possibly regret it.... They will take the lassitude and fatigue out of you and enable you to work double tides if you want to.
>
> I took the treatment daily during 2 months. I began again 3 days ago because I was not sleeping well and was seedy and needed freshening up for work. I am all right again, now. (*Ltrs-Rogers*, 414–15)

Clemens finally brought his family back to the United States in October 1900, but only after he was convinced that Jean could get effective osteopathic therapy in New York. Although Clemens had been introduced to osteopathy by Kellgren, he came to see osteopathy as an American invention, and he criticized Europe for its relative ignorance of this greatest of all medical systems. He wrote a letter to Dr. Andrew Still in February 1900, petitioning to enroll one of Kellgren's students in Still's Kirksville school: "The young man is a Swede; is of fine character and capacities; has studied and worked four years with Kellgren; and (*under* Kellgren) is now head of the establishment. While the principles underlying your system and Kellgren's are the same, there are differences in the application of them: Wherefore this gentleman wishes to take your course and acquire your diploma as his purpose is to practice in America."[8]

Clemens's enthusiasm for osteopathy as a great American institution had almost a patriotic zeal. American allopathic medicine in the nineteenth century had been significantly redefined by the influence of French and German medical systems (which were felt to be better than the American ones),[9] and his increasing distrust of allopathic medicine may have been reflected in his anti-European attitude. For Clemens, both Europe and allopathy were stagnant and outdated, and America was the land of osteopathy and progress.

> Yes, I was greatly surprised to find that my mare's nest was much in arrears: that this new science was well known in America under the name of Osteopathy. Since then, I find that in the past 3 years it has got itself legalized in 14 States in spite of the opposition of the physicians; that it has established 20 Osteopathic schools and colleges; that among its students are 75 allopathic physicians; that there is a school in Boston and another in Philadelphia, that there are about 700 students in the parent college (Dr. Still's at Kirksville, Missouri,) and that there are about 2,000 graduates practicing in America. Dear me, there are not 30 in Europe. Europe is so sunk in superstitions and prejudices that it is an almost impossible thing to get her to do anything but scoff at a new thing—*unless it come from abroad;* as witness the telegraph, dentistry, &c.
>
> Presently the Osteopath will come over here from America and will soon make himself a power that must be recognized and reckoned with; and then, 25 years from now, England will begin to claim the invention and tell all about its origin, in the Cyclopedia B- as in the case of the telegraph, applied anaesthetics and the other benefactions which she heaped her abuse upon when her inventors first offered them to her. (*Ltrs/Paine,* 2:690)

Clemens became convinced that osteopathy was the only legitimate, honest, and effective medical system. In his opinion, all other approaches to medical care, and particularly allopathic medicine, were nothing more than variations of quackery.

> Fifteen years ago I had a deep reverence for the physician and the surgeon. But 6 months of closely watching the Kellgren business has revolutionized all that, and now I have neither reverence nor respect for the physician's trade, and scarcely any for the surgeon's. I am convinced that of all the quackeries, the physician's is the grotesquest and the silliest. And they know they are shams and humbugs. They have taken the place of those augurs who couldn't look each other in the face without laughing. (*Ltrs/Paine,* 2:691)

Clemens's great confidence in the abilities of osteopathy persisted for a number of years, and he continued to be an outspoken advocate of osteopathic medicine into the twentieth century. New York osteopath Dr. George J. Helmer, who had been a helpful source of information when Clemens was comparing Kellgren's techniques to American osteopathy, became Clemens's personal osteopath. Clemens had unquestioning confidence in Helmer's techniques. "I worked without a fire, yesterday afternoon, and caught a very severe cold, and that means a bronchial attack to-morrow, unless Helmer stops it to-day, which I don't doubt he will do. He stopped the last one with a single treatment when it had had 5 days' start" (*Ltrs-Rogers*, 524). Clemens recommended Helmer to Rogers with enthusiasm, and he made it clear he considered osteopathic medicine far superior to allopathic medicine. "Why did you send Mr. Randel to Georgia? There was no use in it. You should have sent him to Dr. Helmer, corner of 36th and Madison avenue—osteopath. Can't I beat it into your head that physicians are only useful up to a certain point? There their art fails, and then one osteopath is worth two of them" (*Ltrs-Rogers*, 441).

Everyone in Clemens's family seemed to benefit from osteopathic therapy at one time or another. Clemens, Livy, and Jean had all experienced favorable responses to Kellgren's treatments, and the range of illnesses that seemed to respond to osteopathy was a wide one. In January 1901 Clemens reported, "Clara is in the hands of the osteopath, getting the bronchitis pulled and hauled out of her" (*Ltrs/Paine*, 2:706). Clemens eventually came to believe that osteopathy would have saved the life of his oldest daughter, Susy, who died from meningitis in 1896, three years before his discovery of Kellgren's treatment system. Susy's tragic death had been one of the greatest emotional blows of his life, and he never fully recovered from it. His dissatisfaction with allopathic medicine rose to a level of anger and disdain for traditional medical therapy as he struggled to come to terms with his profound loss. Clemens not only convinced himself that Susy died as the result of the ignorance of orthodox physicians,[10] but he became equally certain that osteopathy would have had the solution to her illness.

> Kellgren would have cured her without any difficulty. The menengitis manifested itself on a Friday at noon; her doctors immediately told her friends that the case was now hopeless, and they made no further effort—which was quite right, for they could only have done damage,

which is their main trade. She lived until noon the following Tuesday. I have seen Kellgren's performances daily for six months, and I know that what he cannot do for a patient, those licensed quacks need not attempt. It is my conviction that outside of certain rather restricted limitations they are all quacks without an exception. (*Ltrs-Rogers*, 426)

Clemens became so confident in the osteopathic approach (and so distrustful of traditional medical therapy) that he advised Livy against calling for an allopathic doctor when she had a respiratory illness. He was convinced that the osteopathic approach was the only meaningful way to treat illness: "I only said we knew no good doctor, and it could not be good policy to choose at hazard; so she allowed me to send for Kellgren. To-day she is up and around—cured" (*Ltrs/Paine*, 2:692).

As osteopathic medicine gained in popularity, its practitioners sought official recognition. Recognizing the value of having a well-known spokesman, the osteopaths recruited Clemens to speak in their favor. In 1901, he appeared before the Assembly Committee in New York to speak in behalf of the Seymour bill, which proposed the legalization of osteopathy in New York. Clemens's decision to take this public stance was undoubtedly influenced by his belief in the effectiveness of osteopathy, although his annoyance at the ineffective treatments of the allopathic physicians also contributed to his support of osteopathy. "One of the gentlemen who spoke referred to my having acquired such knowledge of osteopathy as I had in Sweden. That is true. About a year and a half ago in London I met Mr. Kellgren, who I believe is the most noted practitioner of this kind abroad. He calls himself Mr. because he has not acquired the privilege of giving a certificate when a patient dies on his hands" (*MT Speaking*, 385). Clemens's devotion to supporting an underdog was undoubtedly another significant factor in his decision to put himself in the public spotlight of medical politics: "I don't know as I cared much about these osteopaths until I heard you were going to drive them out of the state, but since I heard that I haven't been able to sleep" (*MT Speaking*, 386).

In publicly supporting the osteopathic movement, Clemens was in opposition to the New York County Medical Society's delegation of prominent physicians and the New York Society of Masseurs. According to the *New York Times* of February 28, 1899, Clemens sat by quietly as he was caustically attacked by Dr. Frank Van Fleet: "One of the reasons which are given why this should be passed is that Mark Twain favors it. Mark Twain is a very funny man. He writes humorous books. People read them and roll over on the floor with laughter. But no one ever takes Mark Twain seriously."[11] Dr. Robert T. Morris added further criticism of Clemens's role in the debate by accusing him of being a foil of the osteopaths.

> Mark Twain may come to you with jokes, but we are here dealing with life and death. It is a part of the game which these people play to get noted men to indorse their practice. When a patent medicine man wants to advertise his medicine he goes to a clergyman. They are used to taking things of faith. These osteopaths and others go to the great men in public life, who give their indorsement to get their pictures in the papers or to get rid of the preying solicitor. When the physician wants to try a new remedy he first tries it on the dog. He does not fool with precious human life. I notice that a lot of the indorsements of these osteopaths come from Vermont. Well, Vermont has such lax laws with regard to medical practice that it is now the garbage ground of the profession.[12]

During the proceedings, Dr. Morris unwrapped a bundle that contained the spinal column of a child. Morris was critical of osteopathy's claim that a neurological condition (locomotor ataxia) could be treated by rubbing the spinal cord to adjust the bones that were out of position. He challenged any osteopath "to move a part of that bone the fraction of an inch," but no one responded to the dare. When it was his turn to speak, Clemens defended the osteopaths with an evasive tongue-in-cheek comment.

> Now, gentlemen of the committee, when I came here, I came with a purpose of some kind, but it is difficult for me to find out now just what it was. These debaters have knocked it all out of my head. They have put my mind in a sort of maze with their scientific terms. I must say that I was both touched and distressed when they brought out that part of a child. I suppose the object of it was to prove that you cannot take a child apart in that way, and I suppose we must concede that they have proved that. (MT Speaking, 384)

Clemens never appeared to have any definite concepts about how osteopathy actually worked. In an October 1908 letter to Emilie Rogers, he reverted to the imagery of neurasthenia's impaired nerve function to explain the actions of osteopathy: "the Arnold electric vibrating machine...stops headaches for Miss Lyon and cures and limbers lame and stiff backs for me. It claims to ease all sorts of pains, and I judge it can do it, for it stirs up the circulation quite competently and tones up the nerves—and that is really the essential function of osteopathy and kindred treatments" (*Ltrs-Rogers*, 655). Some osteopaths, including Andrew Still, were of the opinion that 90 percent of the benefit of osteopathy came from simply getting patients to abandon their allopathic treatments.[13] Proponents of osteopathic therapy shared the same viewpoint with practitioners of virtually every other nontraditional sect—the "regular" physicians temporarily improved symptoms but failed to influence the underlying disease.

Even as Samuel Clemens supported osteopathy in its legal battles against traditional medicine, he learned that it was not the cure-all he had once envisioned. Ultimately, he came to find that osteopathic therapy was no more effective for Jean's seizures than any of the other treatments that had been tried. Despite her apparent improvements from osteopathic treatments in 1900, Jean's difficulties with seizures became more severe after her mother's death in 1904. Jean was institutionalized for most of the next five years. She tried to kill housekeeper Kate Leary on two occasions in 1905 and 1906, with the homicidal behavior attributed to her epilepsy.[14] Jean spent eight years in and out of sanatoriums and rest homes as her seizures came and went, interspersed with severe bouts of depression and violent behavior. She was found dead in her bathtub on Christmas Eve 1909, apparently drowned after a seizure, one of the many tragedies of Clemens's later years.

In the final analysis, the osteopaths had been no more successful in controlling Jean's epilepsy than the despised allopaths had been in treating Susy's meningitis. And Sam Clemens's wonderful discovery of osteopathy, the definitive therapy for all human ailments, appeared to be as much a sham as every other medical system he had encountered.

Section III

ANY MUMMERY WILL CURE

Any mummery will cure, if the patient's faith is strong in it.

—Mark Twain, *A Connecticut Yankee in King Arthur's Court*

Allopathic medicine is orthodox medicine. It has always had its opponents, and homeopathic medicine was allopathic medicine's major competitor throughout most of the nineteenth century. If it is true that every action triggers an opposite and equal reaction, it was homeopathy that arose as the ultimate antithesis of allopathic medicine's aggressive attacks on illness. Homeopathic medicine was a very elaborate way of doing nothing, and it served as the fundamental model for what is now recognized as the placebo effect. Homeopathy was benign, and it appeared that it might even be effective. The apparent success of homeopathic medicine generated profound questions about the legitimacy of allopathic practices (and, in so doing, homeopathy became the prototype for all of the other "alternative" medical practices).

Few people in the world knew more about the competition among medical systems than Samuel Clemens. Due to the experiences of his own family members and his own medical explorations, he was familiar with the efficacy and toxicity of allopathic medicine, patent medicines, hydrotherapy, electrotherapy, and osteopathy. His observations of the battles that raged between practitioners of allopathy and homeopathy gave him even more insight into the nature of the healing process. Clemens reached a new level of understanding as he came to realize that the faith of the patient was a critical factor in the process of recovering from illness. This discovery created profound dilemmas when he tried to apply it to his own situation. Even as Clemens experienced improvements in his health as he applied "mind cure," he also saw that the benefits were only transient. He became antagonistic toward the application of Christian Science as a system for healing, and he doubted the integrity of Christian Science founder Mary Baker Eddy. He had significant ambivalence about the role of the "faith cure" that had appeared to be so helpful to his mother and his wife.

Through his own experiences and observations, Clemens came to understand the reasons for the popularity of medical treatments that are now designated as nontraditional, "alternative," or "complementary." He came to realize that most alternative care approaches were essentially very elaborate ways of doing nothing. In the era of heroic medicine's toxicity and excesses, such approaches were often the most reasonable methods a patient could pursue.

"Doing nothing" is exceptionally safe. Even when "doing nothing" does not help a patient, it will also not make the patient any worse. "Doing nothing" should be the standard of safety against which all untested therapies are measured. "Doing nothing" may also be the most appropriate therapy for patients who have serious, advanced, or terminal illnesses, particularly if there are no established effective treatments. "Doing nothing" is more than just safe. It may be the most effective therapy for illnesses that are self-limited, poorly defined, or nonexistent. In 1897, when Clemens suffered from another attack of the gout that had been bringing him episodes of misery for the preceding three years, he recognized that all prior attempts at medical therapy had been useless, and he also remembered that each episode of gout eventually cleared up on its own: "I am down with the gout again; but this time I haven't any doctor at all. This is the very Past-Mastership of wisdom" (Ltr-Pötzel). It is particularly important for nontraditional health care approaches that the category of self-limited maladies encompasses by far the greatest number of illnesses.

For the patient who has a self-limiting illness that may respond to nontraditional approaches, the patient's confidence in his treatment can have a profound influence on its effectiveness. Even when the treatment consists of doing nothing at all, patients often benefit from nontherapy that they believe in. Samuel Clemens came to understand that any mummery can cure. He also made another crucial discovery about healing—the name of the mummery might not be very important, but the patient's faith in the mummery is essential to its success.

15

THE PLASMON CURE

Mrs. Clemens detests plasmon, yet she has to live on it, as far as keeping up her strength goes.

—Mark Twain, letter to Henry Rogers, September 11, 1902

Traditional medicine failed Samuel Clemens time and again, but so did the alternatives of water cure, electrotherapy, and osteopathy. Out of desperation, he invented his own treatment program for Livy as he saw her health and her life slipping away. He did not start out purposely to do so; his initial goal had been to find an investment that would help him overcome his indebtedness. He hoped that the investment would prove to his financial mentor Henry H. Rogers that he, Samuel Langhorne Clemens (the notorious champion of money-losing causes), had finally come to financial maturity and joined Rogers's ranks as a tycoon. It was the dawn of the twentieth century, and Samuel Clemens led the way down a path many others would follow—he had discovered the health food business. His personal version was known as "the Plasmon Cure."[1]

While Clemens was living in Vienna in 1899, American ambassador Charlemagne Tower told him about a health food made from dried, powdered skim milk. The product was initially called "Vienna albumen" but was later given the trade name *Plasmon*. A company in Berlin intended to form a British syndicate to market Plasmon internationally. Clemens took some Plasmon himself and, with his usual unquestioning enthusiasm for anything new and possibly profitable, convinced himself it might be

169

an effective treatment for virtually all ailments. It was cheap to produce and seemed to have potential for dealing with famine. In April 1900, he tried to interest Rogers in investing in this new panacea: "Plasmon is pure albumen, extracted at an expense of sixpence a pound, out of the waste milk of the dairies—the milk that is usually given to the pigs. The pound of powder contains the nutriment of 16 pounds of the best beef, and will do the same nourishing that the 16 pounds would do, besides being no trouble to digest. The pound of Plasmon retails at 62 1/2 cents. It has neither taste nor smell." The testimonials in support of Plasmon were impressive, as Clemens explained: "All the great physicians and the hospitals nourish their sick upon it, for it is not only pure albumen but it dissolves without the aid of an alkali, and 99.4 per cent of it digests" (*Ltrs-Rogers*, 439).

Clemens was convinced he was getting into an outstanding investment opportunity at the ground level. He explained to Rogers that the product was not going to be advertised until the English company was set up and funded, but in the meantime Plasmon was being developed under contract to a supplier who initially could furnish a thousand pounds a week, with the intention of increasing productivity as rapidly as possible. Based on the success of the company in Berlin, Clemens anticipated immense success for the English company as soon as an independent source could be developed. The potential market seemed endless. "The Berlin Co can only let us have a ton a week at present, and the doctors already require more than that; for when their patients get well they go on putting Plasmon into their food and the food of their families, because they find that it is not only very nourishing but drives out indigestion and keeps it out" (*Ltrs-Rogers*, 439–40). As usual, Clemens was much influenced by the testimonials of the experts, and he hoped their words would buttress his own support for Plasmon.

> I must send you some pamphlets containing the reports on Plasmon made to the German government by their official experts, the two greatest authorities in Europe, Virchow and Hoffman. Virchow has spent half his life seeking a cheap food for the people.[2] Bovril and Leibig are only stimulants, not *food*, and are very expensive. Bovril costs six shillings a pound, retail. Virchow says "Plasmon is not only more digestible than all other albumen preparations, but also *more than meat*, (and in the experiment the best fillet steak was used"). (*Ltrs-Rogers*, 440)

Clemens went to London and received a share of the American rights to Plasmon. The American Plasmon Company, like most of Clemens's investments, would ultimately lose money for him (although Clemens gained some profit when the British Plasmon Syndicate, in which he had also invested, was sold). In his great enthusiasm for Plasmon, Clemens began to use the product himself. Plasmon was not palatable unless it was dissolved in boiling water, but Clemens was such a believer in its benefits that he started simply to eat it as a dry powder. "I used to take it in my coffee, but it settled to the bottom in the form of mud, and I had to eat it with a spoon; so I dropped the custom and took my 2 teaspoonfuls in cold milk after breakfast. If we were out of milk I shoveled the dry powder into my mouth and washed it down with water. The only essential is to get it down, the method is not important" (Ltrs/Paine, 2:704).

For Clemens, Plasmon became more than a dietary supplement. It was not just a form of albumen. It was the "Plasmon cure," a medical care program that joined the "water cure" and osteopathy as a method for promoting health and well-being. Livy Clemens doubted that the powdered form was as palatable as her husband claimed, and he acceded to her request that he tone down his zeal about its ease of administration. "Mrs. Clemens is greatly troubled about that Plasmon-cure, and wants me to write you and tell you to boil it before using," he confessed to Rogers. Clemens used this opportunity to put in another plug on behalf of Plasmon, telling Rogers that two months of treatment with Plasmon had cured his "fiendish dyspepsia of 8 years' standing" and was still keeping him "sound" three years later (Ltrs-Rogers, 441).

For Clemens, Plasmon was a winner in every way. It was a source of profit that made him feel like a dazzlingly intelligent businessman, on a par with his financial savior and idol Rogers. Even after clearing a huge profit, the British syndicate still had two tons of surplus that it could philanthropically give to the war department of the British government for use in the hospitals of South Africa, where "the sick soldiers prefer it to the other food." Clemens enhanced his own family's health through his great medical discovery and gained the admiration of prominent physicians for this boon to humanity. "In this family we eat very little meat—Jean has tasted none for several weeks. Plasmon takes the place of it, and is no trouble to digest. Among us we eat about a quarter of a pound of it per day—the equivalent of 4 pounds of steak. The result is improved health. All the big doctors boom plasmon outspokenly" (Ltrs-Rogers, 445).

Clemens's enthusiasm for Plasmon was also driven by his frustrations with the shortcomings of traditional medicine. His short attention span for medical methodologies drove him to flit from one alternative system to another—but, when he finally committed himself to a new approach, he would pursue it unrelentingly. His impatience with the status quo and his eagerness to try newer methods reached a fever pitch whenever the health of his immediate family was involved. His wife's declining health and her failure to respond to traditional treatments coincided with his heavy involvement in the entrepreneurial promotion of Plasmon, and his newfound enthusiasm drove him to argue for a trial of Plasmon for her. His conviction in the benefits of Plasmon was as obvious as his frustration with the bumbling efforts of Livy's traditional physicians.

> I wonder she is alive at all. It has been one continued guess, guess, guess, change, change, change, from one incompetent drug to another, and from one indigestible food to another. . . . We have had three doctors, and I implored them all to feed the madam solely on plasmon for three days; but only two-thirds of a day would they ever stand—then they got scared and went to guessing again and raised some more hell. At last, having tried everything else and failed, this one consented yesterday to a 24-hour trial; the time is up, now, and the results are so good that the madam is herself almost convinced, and is willing to chance another 24. The only strength she has she got from the plasmon that was mixed with the failures—as the doctor has to admit. (*Ltrs-Rogers*, 506)

Samuel Clemens's Plasmon, of course, would turn out to be no more of a cure than any of the doctors' incompetent drugs and indigestible foods. But, at least for a while, Plasmon was extremely important to him. It may have been important because he had "discovered" it himself (just as he had "discovered" osteopathy for Jean's seizures). More likely, Plasmon was important because it offered hope when traditional medicine was failing his dying wife, and just as osteopathy offered him hope when traditional medicine was unable to control Jean's seizures. Livy was terminally ill, refractory to every therapy, and Clemens was at his wit's end. He wondered that Livy was alive at all. He needed to find for himself the hope that no one else was able to give him. For a while, at least, Plasmon *was* his hope. All of his previous hopes had failed him—hydrotherapy, osteopathy, and allopathy among them—and, when his Livy was involved, his need for hope was insatiable.

16

Lies That Help and Lies That Hurt

An injurious truth has no merit over an injurious lie.

—Mark Twain, "On the Decay of the Art of Lying"

Honesty is the foundation of modern medical ethics. Patients trust their physicians to be dependable truth tellers. Patients cannot be effective and active participants in the medical decision-making process if honesty on the part of the doctor is lacking. Patients are unable to maintain their autonomy if they doubt the integrity of their physicians. Perhaps more than any other expectation, patients rely on the openness and honesty of their doctors. The idea that a physician serves a patient's best interests by withholding bad news is generally viewed as antiquated, paternalistic, and dishonest.[1]

The practice of medicine is based on far more than honesty, however. In addition to the obligation to be truthful to his patient, the physician is bound by an ancient professional oath to "do no harm." For Hippocrates, there was no doubt about the primacy of this specific responsibility to the patient—*first of all*, he stated, *do no harm*.

With every interaction between a doctor and a patient, no matter what else may transpire, the patient should have unquestioning trust that the doctor will unfailingly adhere to these two constant guiding principles: (1) to always be truthful to the patient, and (2) to never harm the patient. Little else can be guaranteed in a relationship between a doctor and a patient, but these two expectations (one derived from contemporary medical ethics, the other dating back to the era of Hippocrates) are of unquestioned magnitude. The success of the patient-doctor relationship is based on the unspoken contract between doctor and patient that these guidelines are inviolate.

Yet, somehow, these two guiding principles, so perfect in their conceptualization, often contradict each other in their application. The competing directives—"always tell the truth" and "never do harm"—have the potential to create conflicts that defy apparent resolution. At times, it seems, truth has the power to *cause* harm. Too much truth in the wrong context or at the wrong time may worsen a patient's medical prognosis. Truth can take away hope, and there is evidence that hope itself can improve a patient's prognosis. The rituals of Native American healers are designed to help their patients visualize their future; no healing can occur unless the patient is able to do so, since, as one such healer notes, "you must envision [a future] before you can have one."[2] Some patients with advanced malignancies tend to overestimate the survival odds for their disease, but for some reason the overly optimistic patients actually *do* live longer.[3] Among patients with unexplained symptoms that defy diagnosis, 64 percent will get better when their physician misleadingly indicates that he understands their condition, but only 39 percent will recover if no explanation of any kind is offered for their unexplainable symptoms.[4] When patients with terminal illnesses such as AIDS have unrealistically positive beliefs about their prognosis, they also have longer survival durations and an improved quality of life when compared to those who have a more realistic perspective. Such patients may not have received the unvarnished truth, but they *did* benefit from receiving "truth in the most optimistic way."[5] They were not harmed by the deception, but instead they were helped by it.

In following the principle of steadfast truth telling, a physician often runs the risk of violating the principle of doing the patient no harm. The clash between the two guiding principles creates the dilemma of choosing which of the inviolable rules should be violated in order to adhere to the other. Doctors can find themselves in a miserable quandary. How much "truth" should physicians communicate to seriously ill patients if they suspect that absolute honesty will rob quality and meaning from their patients' lives and leave behind a sense of desolation and hopelessness? The responsibilities of telling the truth and preserving hope commonly clash, and physicians are not always able to serve these two masters simultaneously. The issue has been stated clearly by John Lantos in a recent discussion of medical ethics: "A certain amount of lying, or at least of hypocrisy, seems to be part of every child's moral education, a part of what it means to be a civilized human being, and certainly a part of what it means to be a doctor."[6]

Adopting the style used by Samuel Clemens in writing *Letters From the Earth*,[7] Dr. Michael LaCombe has addressed the emotional distress a doctor experiences in trying to be simultaneously honest and compassionate. In Clemens's work, Satan is forced out of heaven and visits Earth, whence he writes a series of letters to his fellow archangels Gabriel and Michael focusing on the foibles, hypocrisies, and inconsistencies of human beliefs and behaviors. In LaCombe's medical variation, a letter written from the point of view of Evil gives instructions on the best ways to produce misery in the lives of physicians.

> Truth is always a good place to insert the knife. Doctors glorify themselves with their honesty....
>
> Truth for them becomes a part of their nature. To say what is so is for them as natural as prevarication is for the rest. Keep your doctors always seeking some vague virtue they call Truth. Remind them of this; help them to make it their god....
>
> All doctors pride themselves on their honesty with their patients. Very well. Allow them to be blunt with their honesty. "The truth hurts," remind them. That sort of thing. Then deliver your masterful stroke. Permit your physicians to see—devoid of any empathy—the trembling anxiety they have caused with their honesty....
>
> Permit them a brief, condescending Kindness, which they immediately see in themselves and for which they are quietly and humbly proud. Now insert a brilliant change in their thinking.... Whereas before they have been blunt, even cruel, with their honesty for the sake of Truth, now you will have them deceive for the sake of Kindness. In their Kindness, they will hide the truth, manipulate, evade, even lie, "for the good of the patient." How Mephistophelean![8]

The dissonance created by this conflict between truth and hope is the basis for the existence of alternative health care systems. No single system can comfortably and effectively deliver both truth and hope in a blend that fully meets the emotional and psychological needs of every patient. Some patients want unadulterated truth only, while others are looking for a diluted version of truth made more palatable by being sweetened with a heavy dose of hope. Traditional medicine markets itself as the medicine of truth, while alternative medicine promotes hope over reality. The separations between traditional and alternative medicine in this regard are distinct but not absolute, and either faction will cross the boundary into the other's turf if such an excursion will strengthen its position without violating its primary purpose. Orthodox medical practice centers itself on scientific truth but is often willing to provide small measures of hope to the hopeless (hope that is frequently given grudgingly as a means of compensating for the acknowledged limitations in its understanding of absolute truth). This attitude may vary from one medical specialty to another, and the ground rules can be redefined based on the level of comfort and insight of the individual physician. Thus, an experienced and caring oncologist has suggested that a physician's duty to a patient with an incurable illness should transcend medicine's traditional goals of telling the truth and avoiding harm. Instead, in his opinion, "the physician's task is to tell the truth, and to preserve hope . . . [n]ot to prevent death, which is not possible, but to prevent death with despair."[9]

Alternative medicine works toward the center from the opposite pole by emphasizing hope above everything else, while doing its best to avoid any appearance that it might be shortchanging the truth. These efforts are made easier by the tendency of each alternative medical system to define its own version of truth as it goes along, while traditional medicine is stuck with the more rigid truths that are determined by the less malleable laws of nature. The dissension on whether truth or hope has primacy is at the root of the antagonism between traditional and nontraditional medicine. No practitioner can simultaneously serve his two masters, truth and hope, equally well, and ultimately one has to be favored over the other.

Samuel Clemens defined his viewpoint on the tension between truth and hope in the December 1902 issue of *Harper's Weekly*. In his story "Was It Heaven? or Hell?" Clemens addressed the question of whether the morality of truth telling should dominate over the morality of easing a patient's suffering by the telling of lies. His fictional account is centered on a woman who is restricted to her sickroom as she is dying of typhoid fever.[10] When her daughter tells an innocent lie, the woman's overly righteous aunts force the girl to confess her moral transgression face-to-face to her mother, in spite of the family physician's order that the mother must be kept in isolation. The doctor is angered when he finds out that the girl was unnecessarily exposed to the mother's infection for such a trifling reason, and he is further enraged when the aunts rationalize their action through their rigid advocacy of truth telling at all costs.[11] In the physician's retort to the aunts, Clemens makes clear his own position that

an unwavering commitment to the absolute truth is not always compatible with the role of the physician as healer: "The doctor glowered upon
the woman a moment, and seemed to be trying to work up in his mind an
understanding of a wholly incomprehensible proposition; then he stormed
out: 'She told a lie! *Did* she? God bless my soul! I tell a million a day!
And so does every doctor'" (*$30k Bequest*, 78). The aunts remain stead-
fast in their belief that all lies are sinful, even as the physician argues
that purposeful lying may be anything but a sin. In fact, in his opinion,
telling a lie may be the *only* moral action that can be taken under some
circumstances.

As a result of her unnecessary exposure to her mother's typhoid fever,
the girl dies after she herself contracts the illness. Initially, the woman's
aunts feel compelled to maintain their commitment to the truth, and they
fully intend to tell the dying woman that her daughter has preceded her
in death. When they realize that this truth will bring profound despair to
the dying woman, the aunts find themselves reversing their own strongly
held moral position, and they proceed to invent a series of lies to spare
the girl's mother from learning of the girl's death. As a result of their
compassionate decision, the woman goes to her grave believing that her
beloved daughter is still alive and well. Samuel Clemens ends the story
with the rhetorical question that he posed in its title—"Was it Heaven?
or Hell?"—but there is no doubt about his personal verdict.[12]

In order to write this story, Clemens required a disease that was very
contagious, but also a disease that usually ran a prolonged course and
was associated with a fairly high death rate. Typhoid fever was the perfect disease for the story, and Livy Clemens's severe illness with typhoid
fever in 1871 had made Sam Clemens painfully familiar with the details
of the infection. The Clemens household had initially been exposed to
the disease in 1870. Emma Nye, an old school friend of Livy's, visited
the Clemens family in Buffalo while on her way from her home in South
Carolina to a teaching job in Detroit. Livy's father, Jervis Langdon, had
died on August 6, 1870, and it was hoped that Nye's visit would cheer
Livy. Nye came down with typhoid fever during the visit, however, and
was nursed through her prolonged illness by Sam and Livy Clemens until
her death on September 29. Livy Clemens, pregnant with her first child
at the time and severely exhausted, was confined to bed in October. She
gave birth to the Clemens's son, Langdon, on November 7, but continued
to suffer from listlessness and fatigue. In February 1871, Livy herself developed high fever and "rose spots" on her abdomen and was diagnosed
with typhoid fever. She required around-the-clock nursing, and it was

not until mid-March that she was even able to get out of bed and walk with assistance.[13]

Coming on the heels of Emma Nye's death from typhoid in the Clemenses' own bedroom, Livy's infection with typhoid created severe anxiety in the household. The Clemenses had become all too familiar with the devastating illness as they watched Nye's gradual and miserable death. They had observed every terrible feature of the infection with their own eyes. In a letter written in September 1870, Clemens lamented, "Poor little Emma Nye lies in our bed-chamber fighting wordy battles with the phantoms of delirium. . . . The disease is a consuming fever—of a typhoid type . . . the poor girl is dangerously ill" (*Ltrs-4*, 191). Months later, even as Livy appeared to be recovering from her own battle with typhoid, Clemens's worry remained intense, in spite of his guarded optimism: "Livy is *very, very* slowly & slightly improving, but it is not possible to say whether she is out of danger or not—but we all consider that she is *not*" (*Ltrs-4*, 334–35). The weariness created by the prolonged illness pushed Clemens to his emotional limits, and his writing came to a standstill: "I am still nursing Livy night & day & *cannot* write anything. I am nearly worn out . . . I have been through 30 days' terrific siege" (*Ltrs-4*, 341). As soon as it appeared that Livy was on the road to recovery, Sam Clemens began making plans to leave Buffalo: "At last my wife is clear out of danger & mending tolerably fast. . . . We are selling our dwelling & everything here & are going to spend the summer in Elmira while we build a house in Hartford. Eight months' sickness & death in one place is *enough*" (*Ltrs-4*, 346–47).

Thirty-one years following Livy's infection with typhoid fever in 1871, her unforgettably severe sickness provided Clemens with the knowledge he needed to create the ethical dilemma at the heart of "Was It Heaven? or Hell?" Then, through bizarre coincidence, Livy became seriously ill again, shortly after "Was It Heaven? or Hell?" was published in 1902. The ethical dilemma that Clemens posed in the story turned from a theoretical question into a personal reality. Livy appeared to be terminally ill with advanced heart disease, and the severity of her disease forced Clemens to agonize over the same conflicts between truth telling and hope giving that were the focus of his story. In this sharply painful episode of his life in which his beloved Livy was cast in the role of the dying woman, Clemens stood firm and did not budge from the stance he had advocated in the fictional "Was It Heaven? or Hell?" For Clemens, the real challenge was not in deciding whether or not he should tell a lie in order to protect Livy's health, for there was never any doubt that the truth was far less important to him than his wife's well-being. Clemens had made clear his position on this very point in his essay "On the Decay of the Art of Lying": "Lying is universal—we *all* do it; we all *must* do it. Therefore, the wise thing is for us diligently to train ourselves to lie thoughtfully, judiciously; to lie with a good object, and not an evil one; to lie for others' advantage, and not our own; to lie healingly, charitably, humanely" (*SWE*, 224). Samuel Clemens's major struggle had nothing to do with the decision of whether or not to lie to Livy. Instead, his real challenge came from the difficulties in orchestrating the falsehoods so that Livy would not find any glaring inconsistencies in the chain of deceptions.

Although Livy Clemens had suffered in her youth from the lassitude and malaise that occurred in patients who carried the diagnosis of "neurasthenia," the full spectrum of the symptoms of her later years leaves no doubt that she had organic disease. She had typical features of congestive heart failure, and she probably suffered from hyperthyroid heart disease.[14] As her condition became more fragile, her physicians restricted her to her room in order to protect her from excessive stimulation and stress. The family dynamics became increasingly complicated on Christmas Eve 1902, when Clemens's daughter Jean developed pneumonia. The family was fearful that Livy's condition would deteriorate if she found out about Jean's illness. To protect against any worsening of Livy's health, the decision was made to hide Jean's condition from her. Jean's sister Clara (who was responsible for running the household) was given the duty of creating an elaborate web of deception to hide from Livy the fact that Jean was ill. Clemens visited Livy's sickroom regularly, and he had to be extremely cautious in his conversations with her in order not to contradict any of Clara's reports about Jean's well-being.

Hiding the truth from Livy became the family's chief occupation during this time. Telling lies became a way of life, and Clemens became convinced that Livy's life was saved by the conspiracy to lie to her. There was no doubt in his mind that the most useful lies came from Clara, due to the great trust Livy had in her daughter's integrity. Clemens wrote to Henry Rogers on Christmas Day 1902 that "Clara is lying to her with an expertness and ability born of sick-room practice, and making her believe Jean is having pleasant times out-doors; if she knew Jean's temperature of yesterday (103 2/5) and to-day (103 4/5) and that the doctor cannot determine what the disease is, she would go out of her mind" (*Ltr-Rogers*, 513). Lies provided by the nurse and the doctor also helped add credibility to the fraud.

The burly English butler carried Mrs. Clemens upstairs to her bed and left her there with the trained nurse. When he closed that bedroom door he shut the truth out from that bedchamber forever. The physician, Dr. Moffat, came once or twice a day and remained a few minutes. If any doctor-lies were needed he faithfully furnished them. When the trained nurse was on duty she furnished such lies as were needful. Clara stood a daily watch of three or four hours, and hers was a hard office indeed. Daily she sealed up in her heart a dozen dangerous truths and thus saved her mother's life and hope and happiness with holy lies. She had never told her mother a lie in her whole life before, and I may almost say that she never told her a truth afterward. It was fortunate for us all that Clara's reputation for truthfulness was so well established in her mother's mind. It was our daily protection from disaster. The mother never doubted Clara's word. Clara could tell her large improbabilities without exciting any suspicion, whereas if I had tried to market even a small and simple one the case would have been different. I was never able to get a reputation like Clara's. It would have been useful to me now, but it was too late to begin the labor of securing it, and I furnished no information to the bedchamber. But my protection lay in the fact that I was allowed in the bedchamber only once a day, then for only two minutes. The nurse stood at the door with her watch in her hand and turned me out when the time was up. (*Autob/MTA*, 331–32)

Jean recovered from her pneumonia, but the never-ending effort to deceive Livy continued month after month. Even letters had to be screened as part of the effort to shelter Livy from any type of distressing news, as Clemens told his friend Joseph Twichell in a letter written in May 1904: "You've done a wonder, Joe: you've written a letter that can be sent in to Livy. . . . You *did* whirl in a P.S. that wouldn't do, but . . . I was able to clip off the margin clear across both pages. . . . It was about Aldrich's son. . . . That son died on the 5th of March. . . . On the 18th Livy asked after that patient, and I was prepared, and able to give her a grateful surprise by telling her 'the Aldriches are no longer uneasy about him'" (*Ltrs/Paine*, 2:754). For Samuel Clemens, statements that would have been considered lies under any other circumstance were euphemistically referred to as "sick-room veracity."[15]

Clara spells the trained nurse afternoons; I am allowed to see Mrs. Clemens 20 minutes twice a day and write her two letters a day provided I put no news in them. No other person ever sees her except the physician and now and then a nerve-specialist from New York. She saw there was something the matter that morning, but she got no facts out of me. But that is nothing—she hasn't had anything but lies for 8 months. A fact would give her a relapse. (*Ltrs/Paine*, 2:735)

In Samuel Clemens's opinion, Livy's life was prolonged because of the concerted effort made to shield her from any knowledge that might be stressful to her. As he saw it, lies are not all created equal. A lie that will benefit another human being is preferable to a lie that can cause pain and injury; a helpful lie is far superior to a hurtful truth. Sam Clemens's own perspective was identical to that of his fictional doctor who chastised the truth-obsessed aunts in "Was It Heaven? or Hell?": "Well, upon my word, I never heard such nonsense! Haven't you got sense enough to discriminate between lies? Don't you know the difference between a lie that helps and a lie that hurts?" (*$30k Bequest*, 78).

Patient autonomy is commonly regarded as the highest principle of medical ethics.[16] Patients cannot be autonomous unless they know the truth, but neither can they be autonomous if they are robbed of all hope. The bioethicist William Ruddick holds that it may be appropriate for a doctor to withhold devastating news if it is the kind of news that would destroy the meaning of a patient's life. Such "deceptive hope-giving" can be justified when it helps the patient maintain a level of autonomy that would have been eliminated by the truth.[17]

In the final analysis, the purpose of medicine is to help the patient. Ethical considerations might suggest that lies should never be a part of medicine, but Samuel Clemens realized that lies were a part of every facet of life, and he knew it would be profoundly naive to think that lies did not have a role in medical practice. He accepted that fact without difficulty and became a champion of the "lie that helps."[18] In a letter to Livy's physician, written in 1904, Clemens entreated Dr. Wilberforce W. Baldwin to deceive his patient.

I hope that you will come with your mind and conscience all prepared to commit a lofty and righteous deception—if need be—to save Mrs. Clemens' life. Tell her that you want to make a more thorough examination by the light of the last few days' regime, and then tell her there is nothing the matter with her heart that need alarm her.... You can lift the patient up again where she was before and I want to see you come and conspire with you to drive her fatal imaginings out of her head.[19]

This letter to Dr. Baldwin is of immense importance in showing how far Sam Clemens had come in his understanding of the healing process.

There is no doubt about his acceptance of the value of "lofty and right-eous deception" in medical care. He had come to understand that recovery from illness is significantly influenced by the patient's belief system and, thus, come to know the secret of the placebo effect. He realized that a great deal of human suffering is the result of "fatal imaginings," and any ruse that could overcome such suffering was far more than a cynical fraud; it was a valuable and important form of therapy. The "lofty and righteous deception" that is known as the placebo effect often makes a substantial contribution to the successes of orthodox medicine, but it plays an even greater role in nontraditional medicine. And even though every medical system has discovered the utility of employing the principles of the placebo effect to some extent, none ever relied on the placebo response more than homeopathic medicine.

17

HOMEOPATHIC MEDICINE

Dilutions of Grandeur

Physicians cure many patients with a bread pill; they know that where the disease is only a fancy, the patient's confidence in the doctor will make the bread pill effective.

—Mark Twain, *Christian Science*

Throughout Samuel Clemens's lifetime, homeopathic medicine was allopathic medicine's greatest competitor. Clemens began employing homeopathic physicians to care for his family in the early 1870s. While living in Buffalo in 1870 and 1871, his family was treated by Dr. Andrew R. Wright (1825–1900), who had trained at the Cleveland Homeopathic College. Wright apparently delivered Clemens's son Langdon and cared for him until at least mid-March 1871. Clemens initially had great trust in Wright's abilities, as he wrote in September 1870: "Ours is an excellent physician, & we have full confidence in him" (*Ltrs-4*, 191). However, the always sickly Langdon took a turn for the worse, and by March 1871 Clemens had begun to doubt Wright's competence. "The cubbie is not well, & Livy thinks Dr. Wright will help us lose him if he can get ten days more to do it in. I wish we were in Elmira, for I think a good deal as Livy does. It will be hard, *very* hard to go & discharge Wright & take another physician, & yet we have got to do it if the baby gets really sick" (*Ltrs-4*, 191). Clemens finally decided to dismiss Wright. In early 1871, hydrotherapist Dr. Rachel Gleason (Livy's physician from her days at the Elmira Water Cure) was called to Buffalo from Elmira to replace Wright as physician to Livy, who was ill at that time with typhoid fever.

The Clemens family moved to Hartford later in 1871 and experienced further emotional trauma when the eighteen-month-old Langdon became ill with diphtheria and died on June 2, 1872. Clemens considered himself responsible for Langdon's death, as the child's illness developed after Clemens took him on a carriage ride that exposed the child to cold, damp weather. At that time, the death rate from diphtheria in Connecticut was about 100 per 100,000 population, and fatalities from the disease occurred predominately in children younger than five years of age.[1] Clemens's personal sense of guilt over the death of his only son became one more stimulus to his pursuit of any medical system that might keep his family alive and well.

Once the Clemenses were settled in Hartford, their medical care was provided by a series of homeopathic doctors. The first of these, Dr. Cincinnatus A. Taft (1822–1884), was considered to be Hartford's leading doctor. Taft had received his medical degree in 1846, and he had trained as an allopathic physician before he took over his brother's large homeopathic practice in Hartford in 1847.[2] Taft was flexible in his medical ideology, however, and his obituary in the *Hartford Courant* noted that "he exercised a certain eclectic independence, which looked rather to cure than to creed, and was not entirely within the limitations of any one 'school'" (*Ltrs-4*, 333). When Clemens heard that Taft was ill, he wrote a letter to Mrs. Taft expressing his great respect for the doctor: "And to my mind, first of all the good physician is *our* good physician; and to him I and mine send homage and greeting and the highest best hopes and the broadest and deepest and warmest good wishes that can be spoken."[3]

After Taft's death in 1884, the role of family doctor was granted to another homeopathic physician, Dr. Edward W. Kellogg (1840–1921). Kellogg had practiced homeopathic medicine in Southington, Connecticut, for four years before moving to Hartford. There may have been other physicians between Taft and Kellogg who did not live up to Livy's standards, according to a letter from Clemens: "Livy has been at sea and unsatisfied and unrestful as to physicians from the day that Dr. Taft died until now. But, all that is past. She is thoroughly satisfied with Dr. Kellogg and will want no substitute for him nor accept of any."[4] It is likely that it was not only Livy who was unhappy with some of the Hartford physicians who came after Taft. A conflict between Clemens and Dr. Edward K. Root is suggested by an entry in Clemens's notebook for 1883–1884 in which he noted Root's name and address, followed by the

Cincinnatus A. Taft. Courtesy of the Mark Twain House, Hartford, Connecticut.

statement, "Ich habe mich verbannt; ich komme nicht wieder bis Ihr verdammtes Haus in Brand gesteckt wird" ([N&J-3, 51]; the phrase can be translated as "I've exiled myself; I won't come back until your damned house is set on fire").

Beyond the knowledge of homeopathy that Clemens gained directly from his Hartford physicians, he undoubtedly gained further insight through his relationship with Dr. Daniel St. John Bennett Roosa. Roosa was an eye and ear specialist who taught at both the University of the City of New York and the University of Vermont. Clemens's journal for 1885 contained a reminder, in German, to see "Dr. Roosa about my thumb and my ear" (N&J-3, 202) and contained instructions (probably from Roosa) for preparing a salt solution for use in soaking his thumb. The journal indicates that Clemens consulted with Roosa again in 1887 and

1889 (*N&J-3*, 295, 470). Roosa was not only Samuel Clemens's personal physician in the 1880s, but he was also a close social acquaintance who sought (and gained) Clemens's support after Roosa founded the New York Post Graduate Medical School. In his 1909 speech upon receiving his honorary degree from the school, Clemens gave it high praise as one of "the two greatest institutions in the country": "This school, in bringing its twenty thousand physicians from all parts of the country, bringing them up to date, and sending them back with renewed confidence, has surely saved hundreds of thousands of lives which otherwise would have been lost" (*MT Speaking*, 632).[5]

Although Roosa was an allopathic physician, he strongly advocated cooperation between the competing allopaths and homeopaths. He aggressively opposed the policies of the American Medical Association that were aimed at destroying homeopathic medicine. In particular, the AMA's code of ethics contained a "consultation clause" that forbade an orthodox doctor from consulting with a homeopath, and this clause intensified the longstanding antagonism between allopathic and homeopathic doctors. The difficulties associated with this policy were profound.[6] In 1881 and 1882, Roosa and other members of the Medical Society of the State of New York tried to invalidate the consultation clause that stood in the way of their professional interactions with their homeopathic brethren. Roosa, who "was noted for a dominant personality, a 'sonorous' voice, and a forceful expression, qualities which made him a formidable opponent," was of the opinion that there was no reason for *any* formal code of ethics. As he saw the issue, the spirit of the code of ethics could be distilled into a simple statement that would define ethical violations as "acts unworthy [of] a physician and a gentleman." New York eventually adopted a new code that allowed allopathic-homeopathic consultation, but the actions of the New York society caused it to be condemned at the 1882 national AMA meeting. As he battled with his allopathic colleagues in the AMA, Dr. Roosa argued emphatically in his own defense that the New Yorkers were not seeking "the privilege of 'affiliating with quacks'" but instead desired only the liberty of "giving our advice wherever it is asked for, whether by Homeopath or Eclectic, Zulu or Modoc."[7]

As the political voice of allopathic medicine, the AMA had every reason to oppose the homeopaths. Homeopathic practice was based on the philosophy that the least therapy is the best therapy, and homeopathy's minimalist approach made it a significant threat to "regular" medicine as no other "irregular" sect had been. At homeopathy's peak of popular-

Daniel St. John
Bennett Roosa.
Courtesy of the
National Library of
Medicine (B11781).

ity around 1880, fourteen American homeopathic medical schools were
in operation, and more than 10 percent of all U.S. medical practitioners
were homeopathic doctors. Homeopathy's success was related not only
to the sharp contrast between the benign nature of its therapies and the
harshness of allopathy but also to the prominence of its influential clientele, which included John D. Rockefeller and President James Garfield.
Homeopathy's practitioners also gave the sect a very positive image—
they were generally well-educated, prosperous, and open-mindedly
flexible in their approach to the care of their patients. Clemens's selection of homeopathic physicians Dr. Andrew Wright, Dr. Cincinnatus
Taft, and Dr. Edward Kellogg to care for his young family in Buffalo and
in Hartford was not surprising given Livy's liberal medical upbringing
in the hydropathic movement and Clemens's own eclectic medical belief
system.

Samuel Christian Hahnemann. Courtesy of the National Library
of Medicine (B29268).

Homeopathic medicine was the invention of the German physician
Samuel Christian Hahnemann (1755–1843).[8] Frustrated by the shortcomings of traditional medicine of the late eighteenth century, Hahnemann
gave up his medical practice and began working as a translator of classical works into German. While translating William Cullen's *Materia Medica* in 1790, Hahnemann became intrigued by the actions of quinine
(cinchona, or "Jesuits' bark"), which was used in the treatment of "intermittent fevers" (malaria). He was skeptical of the explanation that the
drug's bitter taste was the basis for its effectiveness. Out of curiosity, he
took large amounts of quinine for several days. This caused him to develop fever and chills (the same symptoms that occur in malaria), and
the experience led him to postulate that the drug was effective in curing
malaria because it produced a milder, artificial form of the disease that
displaced the more severe natural one. This observation led him to propose his "law of similars," the first law of homeopathy. According to this

principle of "like cures like," a substance that causes symptoms of a particular disease when given in large amounts to a healthy individual can cure a patient who is suffering from that disease when it is administered in small amounts. Although his methodology was dramatically different from that of the allopathic doctors, Hahnemann's image of disease was no more sophisticated than the model used by the traditional physicians of the era—for both allopath and homeopath, disease was nothing more than an aggregate of symptoms, and the goal of medical treatment was to neutralize the symptoms.

As intriguing as his first law was, Hahnemann gained his greatest notoriety when he developed the highly controversial and counterintuitive second rule of homeopathy, the "law of infinitesimals." According to this law, which is the antithesis of the classic dose-response relationship that is the foundation of traditional pharmacology, drugs become increasingly effective as their dosages *decrease*. In Hahnemann's system, the highest dilutions of drug were paradoxically referred to as "high potencies." He added further controversy by proclaiming that homeopathic drugs required a specific technique of preparation to make the dilutions effective—as sequential dilutions of a drug were made, it was necessary to "succuss" the vial containing the drug by striking it against a leather pad. Hahnemann believed that the medicinal actions of drugs were latent until they were excited by the succussion process. When his critics showed through mathematical calculations that his highly diluted homeopathic doses did not contain a single molecule of their presumably "active" agent,[9] Hahnemann explained that the molecules of water continued to be therapeutically active because they could "remember" the drug that had been there earlier; this memory was the result of the succussion that was used in their preparation.

Clemens was fascinated by the imagery of the infinitesimally small homeopathic dose. In "Captain Stormfield's Visit to Heaven," he observed that there is only one white angel in heaven for every hundred million angels who are "copper-colored," and to see a white person in heaven was about as unlikely as "scattering a ten-cent box of homeopathic pills over the Great Sahara and expecting to find them again. You don't expect us to amount to anything in heaven, and we don't."[10] In *Roughing It*, he described a tiny pistol as "a pitiful little Smith & Wesson's seven shooter" that "carried a ball like a homeopathic pill, and it took the seven to make a dose for an adult" (*Rough. It*, 23). Clemens found homeopathy's imagery to be useful in describing certain kinds of weather when he wrote a burlesque of Victor Hugo: "Snow never falls otherwise than in flakes. When it falls in icy pellets it is hail—in homeopathic pills, it is sleet—in globules of water, it is rain."[11] In *Life on the Mississippi*, when Clemens wanted to make it clear that a boat was maximally loaded and had absolutely no further space for accommodation of even the smallest conceivable item, he explained that "she wouldn't enter a dose of homeopathic pills on her manifest after that" (*Life on Miss.*, 198). Clemens, who was susceptible to feelings of guilt that made his life absolutely miserable, had a suspicion that his life would be more enjoyable if he could decrease the size of his conscience, and in the sketch "The Facts Concerning the Recent Carnival of Crime in Connecticut" he wished that his conscience could be reduced to "the size of a homeopathic pill.... That is about the style of conscience *I* am pining for... shrunk down to a homeopathic pill" (*SWE*, 124).

Homeopathic medicine grew rapidly after it was introduced to the United States in the 1820s. Because homeopathic "drugs" consisted of only a diluent of water or alcohol, but contained no active substance, they could cause no harm. Patients of homeopaths commonly fared far better than the allopathic patients who were aggressively treated by bleeding, emesis, and catharsis. The reputation of homeopathy was enhanced when outbreaks of illness such as the cholera epidemic in 1849 (the same one that stimulated Jane Clemens to administer Perry Davis's Pain-Killer to her son Sam as a preventative) gave homeopaths the opportunity to publish statistics showing outcomes that were impressively better than those achieved by traditional physicians. The homeopathic claims are debatable, and the patients of homeopathic doctors may not have actually benefited from their treatments as much as the homeopaths claimed. Even so, at the very least, the homeopathic results raised the possibility that doctors *can* do worse things for patients than not treating them (or treating them with placebo, as the case may be). Hahnemann staked out homeopathy's position as being far safer than allopathy by describing traditional medicine as a "non-healing art... which shortened the lives of ten times as many human beings as the most destructive wars and rendered many millions of patients more diseased and wretched than they were originally." Oliver Wendell Holmes (a poet, physician, medical educator, and Sam Clemens's friend) responded on behalf of orthodox medicine by describing homeopathy as "a mingled mass of perverse ingenuity, of tinsel erudition, of imbecile credulity, and of artful misrepresentation."[12]

Clemens himself was skeptical of the conflicting claims of the battling medical factions, and in his 1867 letter to the *New York Sunday Mercury*

("Official Physic") he expressed his lack of confidence in both allopathy and homeopathy.

> [T]here was a war of lancets, and many hard pills to swallow were administered by the rival homeopaths and allopaths. Among other arguments used were those founded on the questionable statistics of the number of patients who recovered while being treated by the rival systems. Some sarcastic people, justified by the saying of the well-known Oliver Wendell Holmes, may be of the opinion that more people get well in spite of the doctors than by their help, and that a doctor is as likely to be famous from the number that he kills as from that which he cures. (*CT-1*, 228–29)

The battle between allopathy and homeopathy intensified through the years. Allopaths used their political power to block homeopaths from working in a number of municipal hospitals. This move was countered with the establishment of homeopathic hospitals, typically funded by the wealthy and influential patients who were attracted to the practices of the leading homeopathic physicians. Homeopathic medical colleges were started in most major cities, and by the 1880s the ranks of homeopathic schools included the Boston University College of Medicine, the New York College of Medicine, Hahnemann Medical College in Philadelphia, and the University of Michigan (where both allopaths and homeopaths were educated simultaneously, allopaths by allopaths and homeopaths by homeopaths).[13]

The give-and-take between allopathy and homeopathy forced both sides to alter their therapeutic philosophies through the years. In the 1860s and 1870s, the allopathic enthusiasm for the "depletive" principles of bleeding and purging waned, and allopaths placed increasing reliance on kinder and gentler pharmaceutical treatments (such as the use of quinine for fever and of alcohol as a "tonic"). In order to keep up his business, the orthodox physician was forced by the homeopath to apply therapies that were milder and less debilitating than the traditional allopathic treatments; regular physicians actually followed the Hippocratic precept of *primum non nocere* ("first, do no harm") for the first time in centuries, and as they did so it became more evident than ever before that most ailments had a natural tendency toward recovery regardless of the intervention. Similarly, homeopathy was also on the move toward the therapeutic middle ground as Hahnemann's original ideas were questioned and challenged. Many homeopaths were especially bothered by the ridicule aimed at their infinitesimal-dose concept. In *The Devil's*

Dictionary, Ambrose Bierce defined a homeopath as "the humorist of the medical profession."[14] A verse in an 1848 article in the *United States Magazine, and Democratic Review* expressed a similar sentiment.

> The homeopathic system, sir, just suits me to a tittle
> It proves of physic, anyhow, you cannot take too little;
> If it be good in all complaints to take a dose so small,
> It surely must be better still, to take no dose at all.[15]

In response to this kind of derision, homeopaths loosened their strict adherence to the dogma of the infinitesimal, and some even adopted allopathic techniques such as bloodletting and the use of emetics and purgatives. Eventually, homeopathy became a medical system that was divided against itself. A few practitioners remained pure homeopaths of the old school, but the majority practiced an eclectic form of homeopathy that was less rigid about the optimal degrees of dilution and even questioned whether the law of similarities was valid. By 1880 the majority of homeopaths were prescribing allopathic treatments in nonhomeopathic doses in addition to using the traditional homeopathic therapies.

As medical politics raged, the public came to view allopathy and homeopathy as near equivalents. There was an increasing perception that there were no meaningful differences between the two types of physicians. Political pressures forced the arbitrary division of professional responsibilities between the two factions, and medical gerrymandering was rampant. Medical positions were won and lost through lobbying of the appropriate authorities. The commissioners of charities and correction in New York City assigned the treatment of patients in Ward's Island Hospital to the county homeopathic society in 1875, after the organization petitioned for the right to treat patients with mental illness in public hospitals. Samuel Clemens was infuriated when the distribution of medical care responsibilities became just one more item to be bartered among the Gilded Age politicians in exchange for political favors and pork-barrel considerations. He was outraged by the politically motivated assignment of clinical duties between allopathic and homeopathic physicians, and he was caustic in his attacks on the medical boards that made such illogical (if not downright cynical) decisions.

> [I]mmediately after the appointment of the allopath to that Board which will authoritatively recommend the kind of physic good for the

public bowels in the event of the spread of an epidemic ... the Governor paid the high but rather sarcastic compliment to homeopathy of appointing one of its disciples to a place on the Board of Commissioners for the new State Lunatic Asylum to be located at Poughkeepsie. No doubt, the Governor thought that people divested of reason could offer no reasons against the appointment; and that if the lunatics were not improved by sugar pills, they would at least die sweetly—a lunatic more or less being of little account. (CT-1, 229)

As the evolving homeopathic movement began to blend itself into mainstream allopathic medicine, the AMA put further pressure on homeopathy through its sponsorship of *Medical Education in the United States and Canada,* better known as the Flexner report of 1910.[16] Six years earlier, the Council on Medical Education of the AMA had performed an inspection of the 162 medical schools in the United States, and it prepared a report that was never published. The council then asked the Carnegie Foundation for the Advancement of Teaching to conduct a similar study, which resulted in the famous report of Abraham Flexner. Flexner based his assessment of medical education on the premise that medicine was a discipline grounded in scientific knowledge. In his opinion, the scientific method was as applicable to clinical practice as it was to research, and any system of treatment that was driven by fixed protocol was probably bad medicine. Recognizing that the quality of the existing medical schools ranged from superb to abysmal, he targeted the weakest commercial schools as the ones that should be the first to be closed down, characterizing them as "mercenary concerns that trade on ignorance and disease." The Flexner report, described as a "classic piece of muckraking journalism," recommended a draconian decrease in medical schools in Canada and the United States to only thirty-one, with the survivors being the university schools committed to academic pursuits and research. The fact that such a move would result in a dramatic decrease in production of medical manpower was not an issue of importance to Flexner. The United States already had an excessive number of poorly trained doctors, and in Flexner's opinion the country would presumably be better off with fewer doctors that were of higher quality.[17]

Even though Flexner's report did not formally distinguish between orthodox and alternative medical colleges, few of the homeopathic colleges (which peaked in number at twenty-two in 1900) could meet the standards defined by Flexner. Even before the Flexner report, the AMA had been trying to squeeze out allopathy's competition by exerting more and more pressures on the educational and licensing regulations that were the underpinnings of the medical system.[18] From its start, the AMA advocated educational reforms that tended to promote its own type of medical practice as the only legitimate one. Its members were a relatively select group; they were frequently from wealthy families, and they commonly gained appointments at the better medical schools and universities. This background gave them the financial ability to promote the allopathic agenda by becoming involved with issues of licensure, educational reform, and medical politics. With the advent of new licensing laws in the 1890s, AMA members (with their backgrounds as educators and researchers) readily gained seats on the licensing boards. The state licensing examinations began to favor allopathy over homeopathy by emphasizing basic sciences (which were essential to the principles of allopathy) over therapeutics and materia medica (which were the foundations of homeopathy). Although the constituency of the AMA was small (less than 7 percent of U.S. medical practitioners were AMA members in 1900), its membership included a disproportionate number of well-educated physicians with a background of postgraduate training in Europe, and many of them were affiliated with hospitals as researchers and educators. In their public relations efforts, allopathic physicians began to refer to their type of practice as "scientific medicine" in order to further distinguish themselves from the competing "quacks."

The AMA's control over the licensing boards effectively denied licensure to graduates of unapproved schools and essentially brought the pluralistic system of American medical care to an end.[19] Homeopathy's death knell rang in 1935 when the AMA declared that no institution of "sectarian medicine" would be included on the approved list of schools and hospitals, at which time the two remaining homeopathic medical schools dropped their (by then) only nominal homeopathic identification.[20]

In spite of his employment of homeopathic physicians to care for his family, Clemens never expressed significant enthusiasm for the "do nothing" nature of homeopathy. He did recognize, however, that it was a medical care approach of considerable importance because (against all logic) it *did* seem to be of benefit to some patients, and thus it opened up all sorts of critical questions about the nature of illness and the basis of the healing process. In Clemens's opinion, the greatest accomplishment of homeopathic medicine was its profound influence in dampening the enthusiasm of allopathic physicians for their most toxic, nauseating, and debilitating drugs.

When you reflect that your own father had to take such medicines . . . and that you would be taking them to-day yourself but for the introduction of homeopathy, which forced the old-school doctor to stir around and learn something of a rational nature about his business, you may honestly feel grateful that homeopathy survived the attempts of the allopathists to destroy it, even though you may never employ any physician but an allopathist while you live. (*£1m Bank-note*, 260)

Although allopathic physicians generally viewed the methods of homeopathic medicine as irrational, some allopaths (in agreement with Clemens) were willing to concede that orthodox medical practice had been improved by its need to react to the influence of the homeopathic movement. Dr. George B. Wood, president of the AMA in 1856, credited homeopathy with forcing allopaths to reassess their methods and eliminate ineffective or harmful treatments. The greatest contribution of Hahnemann's nontherapy, according to Wood, was in proving to all that "diseases often get well of themselves, if left alone." Dr. H. C. Wood (editor of the *Philadelphia Medical Times*) praised the homeopathic movement in the 1880s for dissuading allopathic doctors from "letting blood with reckless abandon, applying leeches, and administering massive doses of calomel." He emphasized, however, that homeopathy's role in creating a great revolution in orthodox medicine was not because of any "truths contained in the theories of the German dreamer," but only because Hahnemann's high-order dilutions were much safer than the bloodletting and purging of the allopaths.[21]

Allopathy and homeopathy had staked out the two ends of the therapeutic spectrum of the nineteenth century, and each was able to attract a large portion of the American population. In many ways, it seems surprising that the patients of allopathic physicians fared as well as they did after they were exposed to the toxic and unpleasant treatments of traditional medicine. An even more intriguing question, however, is why so many people seemed to benefit from the nothingness of homeopathic treatment.

18

PLACEBO EFFECT

Curing Warts with Spunk-Water

"[H]e's the wartiest boy in this town; and he wouldn't have a wart on him if he'd knowed how to work spunk-water. I've took off thousands of warts off of my hands that way, Huck."

—Mark Twain, *The Adventures of Tom Sawyer*

The apparent success of homeopathic medicine created a serious dilemma for anyone who hoped to understand the process by which the human body recovers from illness. The popularity of homeopathy was understandable, due to the advantage it had over all of its competitors by virtue of its lack of toxicity. On top of that, homeopathic therapy appeared to be at least as effective as any competing medical system. The intellectual stumbling block arose with the realization that therapy by homeopathy was the same thing as *no* treatment at all.

Oliver Wendell Holmes presented the classic attack on homeopathic medicine in two lectures in 1842 that were later published as *Homeopathy, and Its Kindred Delusions.* Holmes ridiculed the principle of dilutions, noting that patients did not receive any active substance after all of the repetitive dilutions of Hahnemann's therapy. As Holmes saw it, any benefit to the patient must have come from the power of suggestion rather than through any pharmacological process. Holmes observed that it was difficult to evaluate the benefits of homeopathy, or any of its "kindred delusions," because the vast majority of patients will recover from their maladies under *any* system of treatment. He asserted that 90 percent of the illnesses commonly seen by a physician would get better "provided nothing were done to interfere seriously with the efforts of nature." According to Holmes, *any* system of therapeutics or *any* placebo should have a "cure" rate of 90 percent. Dr. Worthington Hooker, a Connecticut physician, continued Holmes's attack on homeopathy into the 1850s by using mathematics to point out the absurdity of the theory of infinitesimals. He was unimpressed by the claim that many homeopaths were converts from the ranks of allopathy; he suspected that some of them had been bad allopaths, and that fact alone would account for the better outcomes they achieved by switching to the inert treatments of homeopathy. In Hooker's opinion, the results of the reformed allopaths did not provide real proof that homeopathy was any good, but showed only that homeopathy was "better than *bad* allopathy."[1]

In truth, there have been essentially no effective treatments for most medical problems throughout most of the history of mankind; until very recently, "the history of medicine could be considered the history of the placebo effect." The effective use of placebo has always been an important component of medical practice. "One of the most successful physicians I have ever known," reported Thomas Jefferson, "has assured me, that he used more bread pills, drops of coloured water, and powders of hickory ashes, than of all other medicines put together." Nineteenth-century physician Richard Cabot observed that he was trained "as I suppose every physician is, to use placebos, bread pills, water subcutaneously and other devices acting upon a patient's symptoms through his mind." Cabot was opposed to the use of placebo, which he saw as a dishonest approach to patient care that injured the physician's integrity: "it is only when we act like quacks that our placebos work."[2] More often than not, however, placebo has not been used for the purposeful deception of the patient; instead, both physician and patient have believed in the utility of therapies that, in reality, were no more than placebo.

The effect of placebo is real. "Placebo effect" is not the result of any pharmacologic or physiologic actions of a treatment but instead is the change in a patient's status that results from the symbolic effects of an intervention. Placebo therapy is associated with measurable and clinically meaningful improvement in 30 to 50 percent of patients who suffer from depression. The inherently high response to placebo in patients with depression has led experts in the treatment of mood disorders to conclude that it is not only ethical but absolutely essential to utilize a placebo-treated group for comparison before declaring that any new treatment is effective. Treatment with placebo can improve the symptoms of 30 to 80 percent of patients who have chronic stable angina. The placebo effect not only results in the improvement of subjective outcomes such as the diminution of the severity of chest pain but is also correlated with objective changes such as a decrease in nitroglycerine usage, improvement in the electrocardiogram, and improved exercise tolerance. Placebos are effective in about 35 percent of cases of pain, cough, headache, and the common cold, and in up to 70 percent of cases of asthma and duodenal ulcer. Similarly impressive statistics have been reported in a study of the controversial treatment known as chelation therapy, which is typically administered in private clinics by doctors who generally consider themselves to be practitioners of "alternative medicine." A 1994 study showed that chelation can improve walking distance in 60 percent of patients who suffer from intermittent claudication, a condition in which poor blood flow creates leg pain during exercise. For a 60 percent chance of improving their functional status, many patients may be willing to try intravenous infusions of chelation treatment, in spite of the expense and the accompanying risk of kidney damage. However, a sufferer from claudication might look at the situation differently after hearing the rest of the story—the same degree of improvement was experienced by 59 percent of the patients who received a placebo.[3]

The effect of placebo is woven into every form of medical therapy. The practice of homeopathic medicine represents placebo effect in its purest form, but the placebo effect carries significant implications for all medical care systems. There is no doubt that placebos really do "work." A famous medical study of the drug clofibrate, which was administered to decrease the risk factors for coronary artery disease, reported a five-year mortality rate of 15 percent in the subjects who reliably took the medication, compared to a mortality rate of 25 percent for those who did not. At first glance, this would seem to be a testimony to the benefit of taking the medication. However, an entirely different conclusion is reached when the group of subjects who were assigned to take placebo is taken into account—the mortality rate was also 15 percent in those who took the placebo consistently, compared to a mortality of 29 percent in those who did not adhere to the prescribed use of placebo! The trial was seen as an indictment of the utility of clofibrate, but it should also be seen as a testimony to the effect of the placebo. Of greater significance, it suggests that the simple act of reliably following a treatment plan (even a plan that is a formalized form of "no therapy") can create *something* of value (at least for the patients who have a physiology—or perhaps a philosophy—that enables them to faithfully adhere to a prescribed treatment protocol).[4]

Samuel Clemens pursued a lifelong medical journey to determine the types of therapy that would work best for him and his family. On this quest, he encountered therapeutic sects that included faith healing, hydropathy, electrotherapy, osteopathy, homeopathy, and allopathy. At times he was convinced of the benefits to be derived from each of these approaches; on other occasions he was frustrated by each method's futility and ineffectiveness. The alternatives were almost too numerous to count; in 1864, Dr. Thomas L. Nichols described the challenge Clemens would have faced in trying to determine the optimal form of medical care: "There are allopaths of every class in allopathy; homoeopaths of high and low dilutions; hydropaths mild and heroic; chrono-thermalists, Thompsonians, spiritualists with healing gifts, and I know not what besides. What is worse, perhaps, is the fact that there is no standard—no real science of medicine—no absolute or acknowledged authority."[5]

Clemens's difficulty in judging the utility of a medical intervention was not unique to him and his era but continues to be a universal problem for anyone who wishes to determine the best available treatment for a medical condition. Many medical disorders will improve even when no treatment has been administered. Symptoms such as pain or dizziness may clear up on their own, and visible physical abnormalities such as rashes or warts often go away without any kind of treatment. Thus, a study that showed improvement in 69 percent of warts by chemical cauterization with silver nitrate also revealed that 25 percent of warts improved in the control group where the warts were simply marked with black ink. Local heating can cure 86 percent of hand warts, but placebo treatment causes resolution of 41 percent of the warts in the control group. A review of the medical literature identified seventeen studies on the treatment of common skin warts that had a placebo group; after an average treatment interval of ten weeks, the average cure rate for placebo therapy was 30 percent.[6] Such statistics emphasize the importance of including a control group in trials of treatment. For an advocate of homeopathy who was unaware that warts commonly respond to placebo, a demonstration that homeopathic therapy will cure plantar warts in 20 percent of afflicted patients could reasonably be seen as a testimony to the effectiveness of homeopathic treatment. There is certainly no reason to doubt that the subjects who were rendered wart-free will become strong believers in the homeopathic treatment of warts (after all, they have seen the results with their own eyes). The enthusiasm for homeopathic treatment of plantar warts will be substantially blunted, however, when the homeopathy enthusiast discovers that placebo alone will cause plantar warts to disappear in 24 percent of the patients.[7]

The fact that homeopathic treatments and placebo are of similar benefit in the removal of warts should not be interpreted as an indictment of homeopathy. Instead, the valid conclusion should be that some patients will improve when treated with a placebo, and that homeopathy is one type of placebo. Because homeopathy is a version of placebo, it is not surprising that homeopathy might work *as well as* placebo. The critical realization, however, is that homeopathy can never be *better than* placebo. The traditional method for defining the efficacy of any medical treatment is to set up formal studies that compare the effectiveness of the treatment in question to the effectiveness of placebo treatment. In the case of homeopathy, studies to compare homeopathic treatments to placebo are counterintuitive and scientifically implausible. Any placebo-controlled study of a homeopathic treatment is only a test of "the absurd idea that placebo can be better than itself, or that water can remember what was once in it." The dilemma of homeopathy is that "the 'infinite dilutions' of the agents used cannot possibly produce any effect. A randomised trial of 'solvent only' versus 'infinite dilutions' is a game of chance between two placebos." Indeed, a meta-analysis of placebo-controlled trials of homeopathy was unable to identify any single clinical condition for which homeopathy is clearly efficacious.[8] Curiously, the only evidence that supports the benefit of homeopathic medicine is the evidence that placebo treatment is effective.[9]

This raises a number of important questions regarding the response to a placebo. Does any particular placebo work better than another one? Does the placebo have to be elaborate and intricate, such as the tiresome system of multiple dilutions that was advocated by Hahnemann's homeopathy? Or, for example, is there any reason to think that something as simple as a dead cat could be used effectively as a placebo?

Samuel Clemens was familiar with many of the folk remedies of his day. In general, most folk treatments can be looked upon as regional variations of homeopathy/placebo. Clemens described a number of folk cures in the books that sprang from his Hannibal childhood. In *The Adventures of Tom Sawyer*, Tom and Huck discuss the use of a dead cat as a wart remover.

"Say—what is dead cats good for, Huck?"
"Good for? Cure warts with." ...

"But say—how do you cure 'em with dead cats?"

"Why, you take your cat and go and get in the graveyard 'long about midnight when somebody that was wicked has been buried; and when it's midnight a devil will come, or maybe two or three, but you can't see 'em, you can only hear something like the wind, or maybe hear 'em talk; and when they're taking that feller away, you heave your cat after 'em and say, 'Devil follow corpse, cat follow devil, warts follow cat, I'm done with ye!' That'll fetch any wart." (*Tom Sawyer*, 65–66)

As with most medical treatments that rely on the placebo effect, folk remedies required a specific pattern of ritual for the therapy to be successful. Whenever the underlying condition improved, the patient was pleased to give credit to the therapeutic program for the success and was likely to recommend it to others. If the treatment did not work, the patient was rarely in a position to doubt the effectiveness of the plan; because of the elaborate nature of the prescribed process, he was much more likely to suspect that he had not followed each step to the letter. *Tom Sawyer* contains descriptions of other wart-removing folk remedies that were popular during Clemens's youth. Huck explains to Tom:

"You take and split the bean, and cut the wart so as to get some blood, and then you put the blood on one piece of the bean and take and dig a hole and bury it 'bout midnight at the crossroads in the dark of the moon, and then you burn up the rest of the bean. You see that piece that's got the blood on it will keep drawing and drawing, trying to fetch the other piece to it, and so that helps the blood to draw the wart, and pretty soon off she comes."

"Yes, that's it, Huck—that's it; though when you're burying it if you say 'Down bean; off wart; come no more to bother me!' it's better." (*Tom Sawyer*, 66)

Because of the tendency of warts to go away on their own, it is not surprising that many methods of getting rid of them were in use, and there was no lack of individuals willing to testify to the success of a favorite treatment. Undoubtedly more than one person could have claimed that he had seen his warts disappear after sticking his hands in "spunk-water," the fetid water that accumulates in a rotten stump. It was guaranteed to be as effective as placebo. Spunk-water was not difficult to find for the citizens who lived in the woodlands of the Mississippi River valley, so there were also going to be stories of failed therapy. As Tom explained to Huck, however, the treatment cannot be blamed if the appropriate rites are not followed in consummate detail.

"Shucks! Now you tell me how Bob Tanner done it, Huck."

"Why, he took and dipped his hand in a rotten stump where the rain water was."

"In the daytime?"

"Certainly."

"With his face to the stump?"

"Yes. Least I reckon so."

"Did he say anything?"

"I don't reckon he did. I don't know."

"Aha! Talk about trying to cure warts with spunk-water such a blame fool way as that! Why, that ain't a-going to do any good. You got to go all by yourself, to the middle of the woods, where you know there's a spunk-water stump, and just as it's midnight you back up against the stump and jam your hand in and say:

'Barley-corn, Barley-corn, injun-meal shorts,
Spunk-water, spunk-water, swaller these warts.'

and then walk away quick, eleven steps, with your eyes shut, and then turn around three times and walk home without speaking to anybody. Because if you speak the charm's busted." (*Tom Sawyer*, 65)

As with most alternative medicine approaches, it was essential to follow the prescribed technique to the letter. If accepted treatments such as spunk-water were unsuccessful, the lack of efficacy could be blamed on the poor methods of the practitioner (or a lack of faith on the part of the patient) rather than any shortcoming of the treatment regimen itself.

The successes achieved by the followers of homeopathy and other users of placebo therapies are no different from the successes accomplished by the folk medicine remedies for curing warts. Both are based on the three factors that underlie every placebo response: (1) positive expectations of the patient; (2) positive expectations of the health care provider; and (3) a good relationship between the patient and doctor.

The placebo response has been viewed as the explanation for much of the success of alternative medical practices, but it is also an important component of the therapies of traditional physicians. Dr. Howard Spiro, who has written about "the power of hope," has described the importance of the placebo effect in the recruitment of the patient's expectations and as an aid in the healing process: "In clinical practice, what someone thinks may happen can happen, and that is why more than a few experienced physicians do not stint on the reassurance of rhetoric."[10]

Regardless of the medical system employed, there is no doubt that the patient's degree of belief in the validity of the treatment will influence its efficacy. Five treatments for angina pectoris that are now known to be useless (the use of xanthines, khellin, vitamin E, ligation of the internal mammary artery, and implantation of the internal mammary artery) were 70 to 90 percent effective in relieving angina when there was a consensus that they were effective treatments. When further studies demonstrated that these treatments had no benefit over placebo, their effectiveness fell to 30 to 40 percent. In a comparison of the efficacy of acupuncture and massage for treatment of back pain, patients were more likely to receive benefit if they had a high expectation of improvement. Those who expected a better result with acupuncture did indeed have greater benefit from acupuncture, while those who predicted that massage was the better treatment achieved more improvement with the use of massage.[11]

A patient's trust in a medical therapy is influenced by the rituals that accompany the therapy. The rituals of medicine go a long way in helping the patient expect success. Rituals are commonly associated with the ceremonies of Native American healers, but rituals are also employed by young boys who want to get rid of their warts, as well as by regular physicians who understand the healing process. Dr. Lewis Mehl-Madrona has explained this phenomenon in his book on Native American healing, *Coyote Medicine:* "People need ceremony. It's not enough just to think about life or healing. Ceremony creates the magic that allows healing to happen. It doesn't much matter which ceremony, as long as both the healer and the supplicants believe in it." This undoubtedly accounted for much of the success of J. R. Newton, the faith healer who successfully treated Livy Langdon's paralysis after all the traditional doctors had failed. Newton admitted that he was not always successful in his endeavors, but he was aware of what was required for him to be successful: "I do not claim to effect a cure in all cases thus presented to me, nor are all cures completed in one treatment. The causes of failure however, rest oftener with the patient than with myself. The power is strong with me; I impart it to the patient. If he, from lack of faith or other cases, is unreceptive, the effects may in a measure be lost; but if he puts himself in an attitude, mentally and spiritually, to receive it, physical benefit must result." Traditional medical practice is steeped in rituals, and so is nontraditional medicine. It is likely that such rituals enhance the placebo effect of unconventional therapies, creating outcomes that seem particularly dramatic and compelling from the perspective of the patient.[12]

As important as ceremony may be, the specific rituals and treatment techniques of any particular medical sect (including those of traditional medicine) are not the most important constituents of the therapeutic

process. Far more critical to the outcome is the physician's skill in interacting with the patient in a positive manner. An effective clinician is able
to use the power of the relationship to modify the patient's perceptions
of illness in a way that helps the patient feel better. The best physicians
have a "therapeutic personality," and their unique professional charisma
may be the most effective form of placebo available. More than simply
a good "bedside manner," a physician's personality and style can be a
powerful therapeutic agent.[13] Through his own experiences, Samuel
Clemens came to realize that the presence of a therapeutic personality
was the secret behind every successful faith healer, hydrotherapist, elec-
trotherapist, homeopathic physician, osteopath, and allopathic doctor
he had encountered. A letter he wrote to the wife of the ailing Dr.
Cincinnatus Taft on August 14, 1883, indicates his opinion on the power
of the personal attributes of the individual physician.

> I must not add a hair's weight—not even the weight of a friendly &
> solicitous letter—to the sick man's burdens; so we come to you, Mrs.
> Clemens & I, to say we are troubled by these newspaper reports; we
> cannot *have* him helpless who has been everybody's help, we cannot
> have him "weak" who has been everybody's strength, we cannot have
> him tottering from mountain to sea, seeking health, who all these years
> has been health's own chosen messenger to waiting thousands. Rest?—
> *yes;* let him rest, for he has earned it, wasting his impaired forces in un-
> timely night journeys to such as us, that we might live & be strong
> again: but let it stop with resting; do not tell us he shall not be himself
> again, nor that he must withdraw & clothe another in the semblance
> of his art & skill & send him in his place—for what is Sir Kay in Sir
> Launcelot's armor, but only Sir Kay after all, & not Sir Launcelot? (*Ltrs-
> Microfilm-2,* vol. 2, #2821)

The healing personality that engenders the faith and trust of the patient
might be a placebo, but it is an essential and effective placebo,[14] as
Clemens noted in *Christian Science.*

> *Faith in the doctor.* Perhaps that is the entire thing. It seems to look like
> it. In old times the King cured the king's evil by the touch of the royal
> hand.[15] He frequently made extraordinary cures. Could his footman
> have done it? No—not in his own clothes. Disguised as the King, could
> he have done it? I think we may not doubt it. I think we may feel sure
> that it was not the King's touch that made the cure in any instance, but
> the patient's faith in the efficacy of a King's touch. Genuine and remark-
> able cures have been achieved through contact with the relics of a

saint. Is it not likely that any other bones would have done as well if the substitution had been concealed from the patient? (*Christian Science*, 34–35)

Through his interactions with all of the major medical sects of the nineteenth century, Clemens was finally able to understand why all of them had their moments of success, in spite of the striking disparities in their methods and principles. Clemens had seen an improvement in his gout from electrotherapy, a lessening of Jean's seizures from osteopathic therapy, and the restoration of Livy's health from the water cure. There was no question that his gout *did* go into remission; Jean's seizures *did* decrease in frequency; Livy's stamina *did* improve.[16] He had seen the improvement with his own eyes. In every case, however, he was later disappointed by the temporary nature of these "cures" and the ultimate failure of the treatments that had initially seemed so certain.

Clemens learned two major lessons from all of these medical experiences. The first lesson was that medical problems tend to wax and wane, and the variations in the disease pattern may have nothing at all to do with the therapy that is administered. If treatment is started when the disease is very active and bothersome (which is when a patient is most likely to seek relief), the treatment will be given credit for the subsequent improvement, even though the improvement represents simply the natural fluctuation in disease activity.

The other thing Clemens learned was the power of the placebo effect. The concept of "placebo effect" had not yet been fully developed, but Clemens came to understand its guiding principle: the patient's faith in a treatment can go a long way in influencing how much benefit the patient will get from the treatment. Hope is a powerful force, and the strength of the placebo springs from its ability to provide hope. Patients with cancer usually rely on three coping mechanisms—faith, hope, and charity—in order to maintain a meaningful existence: their faith is focused on their doctor's ability to benefit them, their hope is aimed toward their life in the future, and their charity is directed to others who are more needy than they themselves. Whether it is defined as faith or hope or trust, placebo provides the essential first step in any healing process, as explained by Mehl-Madrona: "To be healed, we need to believe in the possibility of healing."[17]

For Samuel Clemens, this raised the question of whether inordinate attention was being paid to the details of the specific treatments of the competing medical sects. There did not appear to be a single medical system that could really heal the body; it seemed more likely that the body had to heal itself. *Any* medical system might help the healing go faster if the patient had faith in the system. In the mind-body duality, it appeared the mind might be the dominant force in healing the body. It eventually occurred to Clemens that, perhaps, health care should not be so fixated on therapies directed toward the physical body. Instead, he reasoned, the answer to health might come from utilizing the healing abilities of the mind.

19

ANYTHING...EXCEPT CHRISTIAN SCIENCE

The patients tell such wonderful things that you half believe you have wandered into an asylum of Christian Science idiots.

—Mark Twain, letter to Henry Rogers, August 3, 1899

Samuel Clemens's observations and experiences gave him remarkable insight into the complex interactions of the social, physical, and emotional factors that contribute to health and disease, and he had little use for "those dull people who think that nothing but medicines and doctors can cure the sick" (*Hadleyburg*, 108–9). Always the entrepreneur, Clemens even came to develop his own personal system for maintaining physical health, based on an observation he made in 1866. He had been in Honolulu when fifteen survivors of the burning of the clipper ship *Hornet* arrived in port. The sailors were all in surprisingly good condition, considering that they had survived a forty-three-day journey in an open boat that held only a ten-day supply of food. This led Clemens to speculate that self-deprivation might be an effective means of purification that would eliminate disease. In his account of the sailors' voyage ("My Début as a Literary Person"), Clemens credited their forced starvation for their unexpectedly good health, despite the duress and deprivations of the voyage: "Twenty-five days of pitiless starvation ... will weaken the men physically, but if there are any diseases of an ordinary sort left in them they will disappear" (*Hadleyburg*, 109–10).

As the result of this observation, Clemens came to believe that many diseases could be cured by "starving" them. Starvation was self-sacrificial, a religious-like form of self-cleansing that borrowed from the dogma of the hydrotherapists. He put his theory to the test by "starving" his own colds and found great success. "A little starvation can really do more for the average sick man than can the best medicines and the best doctors. I do not mean a restricted diet; I mean *total abstention from food for one or two days*. I speak from experience; starvation has been my cold and fever doctor for fifteen years, and has accomplished a cure in all instances" (*Hadleyburg*, 109).

Clemens had complete confidence in the value of starvation as a treatment for his own colds, as he described to Henry Rogers in February 1896. At the time, Clemens was on a critical around-the-world speaking tour. The tour had been arranged so that he could earn enough money to get himself out of bankruptcy, and it was essential for him to appear at each of his scheduled lectures. He found that he could rely upon starvation to fend off any disease that threatened to interfere with his speaking schedule. "[M]y first 2 days in Calcutta I am spending in bed with a cold, and hoping [I] shan't develop a cough for the platform here next week. However, yesterday I dropped back onto my long-neglected remedy for cold in the head—starving; and now, after 24 hours of starving the cold is entirely gone" (*Ltrs-Rogers*, 193).

Clemens confidently recommended the starvation treatment to others. In a letter written in March 1885 to his brother Orion and sister-in-law Mollie, Clemens's confidence in his method is obvious.

> Orion's cracker diet is—well let us not characterize it. If he will stop eating—utterly, completely, uncompromisingly—for two or three days, his cold will disappear, no matter *how* strong or old a cold it is.... I have exposed myself in every sort of way this winter, & recklessly & without fear, as long as my stomach was right—& when it wasn't, I skipped from one to four meals, & *put* it right. Result—I passed the months of October, Nov. Dec. Jan & Feb. without a cold. (*MTBM*, 305)

For Samuel Clemens, starvation was an ideal medical therapy. The concept of abstaining from food was a simple one. He did not need professional guidance or instruction in how to starve himself. He made the decision to starve himself when he believed it would be beneficial, and he decided how long his fast would go on. "When you have any ordinary ailment, particularly of a feverish sort, eat nothing at all during twenty-four hours. That will cure it. It will cure the stubbornest cold in the head, too. No cold in the head can survive twenty-four hours on modified starvation" (*Hadleyburg*, 166).

In years to follow, others joined the "fasting for health" crusade. In 1911, Upton Sinclair's book *The Fasting Cure* outdid Clemens's enthusiasm for starvation, proclaiming that not only was starving good for the common cold, but it was also effective for treating diseases such as cancer, tuberculosis, syphilis, and asthma. In *Book of Life*, Sinclair proclaimed that he "would not like to guess just what percentage of dying people in our hospitals might be saved if the doctors would withdraw all food from them."[1]

Starvation was a program of self-treatment that did not require the intervention of any other person. There was no reason to consult a physician in order to derive the benefits of a treatment that could be carried out as an individual. Clemens's approach to starvation as therapy reflected the pioneering spirit that arose in the era of Jacksonian democracy, when the dominant political sentiment was that every person had the right to make his own decisions without interference. This attitude was a significant contributor to the success and popularity of the many medical sects that flourished throughout the nineteenth century, and to a large extent created the mind-set that drove Clemens's ongoing explorations of one medical sect after another.[2]

Samuel Clemens, who extolled the independent attitude that characterized the American people, clearly believed in an independent and personalized approach to medical care. He criticized the European health spas for charging people for doing things they could easily do for themselves. In May 1898, Clemens completed a parody, "At the Appetite Cure," in which he suggested that the effectiveness of the Austrian health spas was the direct result of the various forms of abstinence (including starvation) that were incorporated into their regimen.[3] Samuel Clemens the entrepreneur may have been intrigued by the concept that even starvation itself could be marketed as therapeutic, and that there was a profit to be made by promoting fasting to the rich and famous.[4]

> ". . . Do you know the tricks that the health-resort doctors play?"
> "What is it?"
> "My system disguised—covert starvation. Grape-cure, bath-cure, mud-cure—it is all the same. The grape and the bath and the mud make a show and do a trifle of the work—the real work is done by the surreptitious starvation. . . . Six weeks of this régime—think of it. It starves a man out and puts him in splendid condition. It would have the same effect in London, New York, Jericho—anywhere." (*Hadleyburg*, 162–63)

In *Following the Equator,* Clemens tells of being bedridden from a backache ("lumbago"). His smoking, dietary excesses, and consumption of caffeine and alcohol interfered with the effectiveness of his physician's therapy. In response to his doctor's recommendations to change his habits, Clemens stopped smoking and drinking alcohol for two days and nights. He "cut off all kinds of food, too, and all drinks except water," and as a result of his abstinence "the lumbago was discouraged and left me" (*Foll. Equat.,* 31). The conclusion to be drawn by the thoughtful reader, presumably, is that bad habits should be avoided in order to maintain optimal health. Clemens, however, promoted a different interpretation and argued that his experience was a testimony in favor of *maintaining* deleterious personal habits so that they might be discarded later as a form of ballast—but only when it becomes absolutely necessary to do so in order to promote recovery from an illness.

> It seemed a valuable medical course, and I recommended it to a lady. She had run down and down and down, and had at last reached a point where medicines no longer had any helpful effect upon her. I said I knew I could put her upon her feet in a week. It brightened her up, it filled her with hope, and she said she would do everything I told her to do. So I said she must stop swearing and drinking and smoking and eating for four days, and then she would be all right again. And it would have happened just so, I know it; but she said she could not stop swearing and smoking and drinking, because she had never done those things. So there it was. She had neglected her habits, and hadn't any. Now that they would have come good, there were none in stock. She had nothing to fall back on. She was a sinking vessel, with no freight in her to throw overboard and lighten ship withal. Why, even one or two little bad habits could have saved her, but she was just a moral pauper. When she could have acquired them she was dissuaded by her parents, who were ignorant people though reared in the best society, and it was too late to begin now. It seemed such a pity; but there was no help for it. These things ought to be attended to while a person is young; otherwise, when age and disease come, there is nothing effectual to fight them with. (*Foll. Equat.,* 31–32)

As devoted as he was to the idea that starvation is therapeutic, Clemens had a dramatic change in his conceptualization of how starvation actually worked after his family was introduced to "mind cure" by Lilly Gillette Foote (1860–1932); Miss Foote was a relative of Clemens's neighbors the Gillettes and the Hookers, and she became the governess for the Clemens children in 1880. After he came to understand the principles of mind cure, he reasoned that his repetitively proclaimed cures by starvation had nothing at all to do with the act of starvation. Instead, he reasoned, the benefits he obtained were actually the results of his *belief* that starvation was an effective form of treatment. It is not clear whether this insight came to him as an epiphany when he first learned about mind cure, or whether the introduction of mind cure into his vocabulary allowed him to formulate ideas that had been brewing for many years.

"Mind cure," the belief that people could overcome their ailments through mental effort, arose as a self-help approach to health in the 1890s. The driving force behind mind cure was the concept of "mind over matter," and it was an especially appealing approach for overcoming physical ailments without being subjected to the unpleasant features of traditional medicine. In contrast to the allopathic model of disease, with its increasing attention to the inner workings of the physical body, most alternative care systems of the late nineteenth century minimized the significance of the physical body. Instead, they emphasized the crucial role of the mind in determining an individual's health. This viewpoint resulted in the strong conviction that the cause for most illness is found within the patient, linked to the corollary belief that the cure for disease must also be found internally.

Clemens was personally familiar with "mental science" in several of its versions. As a child, he had seen the effectiveness of a faith healer firsthand.

> When I was a boy a farmer's wife who lived five miles from our village had great fame as a faith-doctor—that was what she called herself. Sufferers came to her from all around, and she laid her hand upon them and said, "Have faith—it is all that is necessary," and they went away well of their ailments. She was not a religious woman, and pretended to no occult powers. She said that the patient's faith in her did the work. Several times I saw her make immediate cures of severe toothaches. My mother was the patient. (*Christian Sci.*, 35)

Clemens was quite impressed with these cures by the "faith doctor," whose name was Mrs. Utterback. In his *Autobiography*, he recalled clearly the two occasions when he accompanied his mother on a horseback ride to the Utterback farm, where he saw the prompt cure of Jane Clemens's toothaches after Mrs. Utterback laid her hand on his mother's jaw and said "Believe!" (*Autob/NAR*, 119).

Mrs. Utterback may have been the first faith healer Clemens knew about, but she would not be the last. Although her ability to cure Jane

Clemens's toothache was certainly an impressive feat, it did not begin to compare with the miracle performed when the faith healer Dr. Newton rescued Livy Langdon from her state of paralysis. The great success of faith healing in helping the two most influential people in his life created a sharp contrast to Clemens's own experiences with the orthodox medical system that was so quick to dismiss the utility of nontraditional therapies. His wife and children had not fared well under the care of traditional physicians, and restoring their health became an elusive dream that took the Clemens family all over the world. He was interested in results more than in dogma and was willing to explore any medical care system that might represent the panacea he sought.

Miss Holden, the mind cure advocate of Hartford, convinced Livy that the mind cure was so effective that even nearsightedness could be corrected by it. Susy and Livy tried mind cure to improve their vision, and they were able to convince themselves it had been successful. Clemens himself became interested enough in the potential of mind cure that he stopped using his own eyeglasses for a while. The level of his interest in mind cure is apparent in the biography of Clemens written by Susy at the age of fourteen. She first discussed the subject in her entry for March 14, 1886.

> Papa has been very much interested of late, in the "Mind Cure" theory. And in fact so have we all. A young lady in town has worked wonders, by using the "Mind Cure" upon people; she is constantly busy now curing peoples deseases in this way—and curing her own even, which to me seems the most remarkable of all.
>
> A little while past, papa was delighted with the knowledge of what he thought the best way of curing a cold, which was by starving it. This starving did work beautifully, and freed him from a great many severe colds. Now he says it wasn't the starving that helped his colds, but the trust in the starving, the mind cure connected with the starving.
>
> I shouldn't wonder if we finally became firm believers in Mind Cure. The next time papa has a cold, I haven't a doubt, he will send for Miss H. the young lady who is doctoring in the "Mind Cure" theory, to cure him of it.
>
> Mamma was over at Mrs. George Warners to lunch the other day, and Miss H. was there too. Mamma asked if anything as natural as near sightedness could be cured she said oh yes just as well as other deseases.
>
> When mamma came home, she took me into her room, and told me that perhaps my near-sightedness could be cured by the "Mind Cure" and that she was going to have me try the treatment any way, there

could be no harm in it, and there might be great good. If her plan suc-
ceeds there certainly will be a great deal in "Mind Cure" to my oppin-
ion, for I am *very* near sighted and so is mamma, and I never expected
there could be any more cure for it than for blindness, but now I dont
know but what theres a cure for *that*. (*Autob/NAR*, 167–68)

Susy gave a progress report in her entry for April 19, 1886.

> Yes, the "mind cure" does seem to be working wonderfully. Papa, who
> has been using glasses now for more than a year, has laid them off en-
> tirely. And my nearsightedness is really getting better. It seems mar-
> velous. When Jean has stomack-ache Clara and I have tried to divert
> her by telling her to lie on her side and try "mind cure." The novelty of
> it has made her willing to try it, and then Clara and I would exclaim
> about how wonderful it was she was getting better. And she would
> think it realy was finally, and stop crying, to our delight.
>   The other day mama went into the library and found her lying on
> the sofa with her back toward the door. She said, "Why, Jean, what's
> the matter? Don't you feel well?" Jean said that she had a little stomack-
> ache, and so thought she would lie down. Mama said, "Why don't
> you try 'mind cure'?" "I am," Jean answered.[5]

The thought that "mind-cure" might deliver his loved ones from their
physical ailments was enticing. However, Samuel Clemens's experiences
with mind cure were no different from his experiences with the other
health care systems he had pursued with hope and energy. At first, when
he had great confidence in a new system, the results were exceptionally
positive. Clemens was able to discontinue wearing his eyeglasses because
of the benefits of mind cure, and Susy's nearsightedness was getting better through the power of her own belief. The initial enthusiasm waned,
however, as it became increasingly apparent that the power of mind cure
was *not* improving the family's visual problems. No matter how much
they wished and hoped to the contrary, the mind cure had no effect on
their visual acuity, and they reverted to using their eyeglasses. The family *did* continue to use mind cure for episodes of abdominal pain and
headaches, for which it seemed helpful.[6]

After he developed bronchitis and a cough in December 1893, Clemens
sought treatment from a Madison Avenue mind cure specialist, Dr. Whipple. Dr. Whipple treated his patient by the somewhat unusual technique
of sitting in a corner and silently staring at the wall while Clemens walked
around the room, smoking and talking. The cough seemed to get better.
Clemens could not rule out the possibility that homeopathic powders he

received from a friend might have also had an influence but was willing to entertain the possibility that his mind cure doctor was responsible for the improvement: "Mr. Rogers has been buying homeopathic powders & feeding them to me.... They kept the cough down & moderated it, but didn't remove it. I tried the mind-cure out of curiosity. That was yesterday. I have coughed only two or three times since. Maybe it was the mind-cure, maybe it was the powders" (*Ltrs-Love*, 285).

Clemens's letters at this time, especially the ones he wrote to Livy, often spoke about mind cure and mind curists. He displayed his usual enthusiasm for a new discovery in a letter written in December 1894. "George says Dr. Whipple's cures of Mrs. Edward Perkins & of her son (heart disease & given up by the doctors) have all the aspect of miracles" (*Ltrs-Love*, 285). Around the same time, Clemens made the following entry in his notebook: "*Mind-Curist* Mrs. E.R. de Wolf 1418 Broadway. Cured Mrs. Howells, Dora Wheeler and Rosina Emmet" (*Ltrs-Howells Sel.*, 307). Mrs. Howells was Eleanor Howells, the wife of William Dean Howells. In spite of the Howellses' earlier negative experiences with the "rest cure," they were not opposed to trying new therapies, and Eleanor Howells appeared to have had a dramatic improvement from a serious illness through the application of mind cure. This event appeared to have a dramatic influence on Clemens, and he became convinced that mind cure was the new answer to some of the chronic health problems that had plagued his family. In a letter to Livy in January 1894, Clemens recalled an earlier conversation with William Dean Howells about the impressive benefit that Eleanor Howells had derived from mind cure.

> First, H & I had a chat together. I asked about Mrs. H. He said she was fine, still steadily improving, & nearly back to her old best health. I asked (as if I didn't know):
> "What do you attribute this strange miracle to?"
> "Mind-cure—simply mind-cure."
> "Lord, what a conversion! You were a scoffer three months ago."
> "I? I wasn't."
> "You were. You made elaborate fun of it to me in this very room."
> "I did not, Clemens."
> "Its a lie, Howells, you did." ...
> At last he gave in—he said he remembered that talk, but had now been a mind-curist so long it was difficult for him to realize that he had ever been anything else.
> Mrs. H. came skipping in, presently, the very person, to a dot, that she used to be, so many years ago. (*Ltrs-Howells Sel.*, 306–7)

At this point, according to Clemens, Eleanor Howells joined the conversation to express her opinion that mind cure was simply another form of hypnotism. After hearing about the benefits of mind cure from the Howellses, Clemens (who was in New York) encouraged Livy to seek mind cure treatment for Susy in Paris (where Livy and Susy were living at the time).

> [Eleanor Howells] convinced me, before she got through, that she and William James are right—hypnotism and mind-cure are the same thing; no difference between them. Very well; the very source, the very centre of hypnotism is Paris. Dr. Charcot's pupils & disciples are right there & ready to your hand without fetching poor dear old Susy across the stormy sea. Let Mrs. Mackay... tell you whom to go to to learn all you need to learn & how to proceed. Do, do it, honey. Don't lose a minute. (*Ltrs-Howells Sel.*, 306–7)[7]

Clemens's expression of urgency reflected his ongoing concern about Susy's health. Clemens's oldest daughter was extremely intelligent, but she had grown from a child with charming precocity into a young woman who was becoming increasingly morose and fragile. She has been characterized as "[v]olatile, charming, impractical about time and money, averse to routine and steady habits." Going away to college only seemed to make her worse, and biographer Dixon Wecter suggested that Susy "pined under the first separation from her family as a freshman at Bryn Mawr, and developed thenceforth a state of poor health" (*Ltrs-Love*, 315). Although Clemens blamed much of Susy's difficulties on her college experience and the associated homesickness, he may have also been displeased with the intensity of a friendship that had developed between Susy and another student, Louise Brownell. In any case, Clemens believed Susy's symptoms were psychosomatic, and he hoped to interest her in mental healing.

Four months after his letter imploring Livy to seek hypnotic therapy for Susy in Paris, Clemens wrote a letter to Livy in May 1884 confirming that he continued in search of a solution for Susy's chronic medical problems. At the time, he was crossing the Atlantic Ocean from New York to France and had heard of the successes of Dr. William S. Playfair in the treatment of neurasthenia.[8] Playfair was the author of a chapter on the treatment of neurasthenia in the 1892 *Dictionary of Psychological Medicine* (in which he advocated the benefits of absolute bed rest for several weeks).[9] In May 1894, Clemens wrote a letter to Livy describing Playfair's success in treating neurasthenia, and he raised the question of whether Susy would benefit from the same approach. "Mrs. P. T. Barnum is on board. She was an invalid 8 years, with nervous and other troubles, & spent most of the time in hospitals. She said her case was apparently hopeless, but she fell into Dr. Playfair's hands in London & in 5 months he has made a well woman of her. She thinks Susy ought to go to him" (*Ltrs-Love*, 302–3).

Susy did not pursue mind cure while she was in Europe, but she became very interested in the method after she returned to the United States. Susy's malaise seemed to worsen when she was separated from her family, and the winter of 1895–1896 may have been particularly difficult for her—she was at home in Hartford as her parents and younger sister Clara traveled around the world. In a letter written from India in February 1896, Clemens seemed to be concerned about Susy's well-being, and he encouraged her to actively pursue her interest in mind cure (although his tone was somewhat condescending and carried a hint of insincerity).

> Mamma is busy with my pen, declining invitations. And all because we haven't you or Miss Foote or Miss Davis here to argue some of our stupid foolishnesses out of us and replace them with healthy thoughts— and by consequence physical soundness. I caught cold last night, coming from Benares, and am shut up in the hotel starving it out; and so, instead of river parties and dinners and things, all three of us must decline and stay at home. It is too bad—yes, and too ridiculous. I am perfectly certain that the exasperating colds and the carbuncles came from a diseased mind, and that your mental science could drive them away, if we only had one of you three here to properly apply it. I have no language to say how glad and grateful I am that you are a convert to that rational and noble philosophy. Stick to it; don't let anybody talk you out of it. Of all earthly fortune it is the best, and most enriches the possessor. I always believed, in Paris, that if you could only get back to America and examine that system with your clear intellect you would see its truth and be saved—permanently saved from the ills which persecute life and make it a burden. Do convey my deep gratitude to Miss Davis and Miss Foote—I owe them a debt which would beggar my vocabulary in the expression and still leave the debt nine-tenth unpaid. (*Ltrs-Love*, 316)

Even though Clemens had great enthusiasm for the possibilities of mind cure, he had doubts about the motivations of those who claimed to be mind cure practitioners; his skepticism is evident in the manner in which he introduced Colonel Sellers in *The American Claimant*. "By the door-post were several modest tin signs. 'Col. Mulberry Sellers, Attorney at Law and Claim Agent,' was the principal one. One learned from the others that the Colonel was a Materializer, a Hypnotizer, a Mind-Cure Dabbler, and so on. For he was a man who could always find things to do" (*Amer. Claim.*, 28).

Although Clemens dabbled in mind cure himself, and initially hoped it would be of benefit to him and his family, he was an outspoken critic of the popular mind cure derivative known as Christian Science. Because he was inclined to accept the concept that physical disease can be eliminated if the will is strong enough, Clemens was initially intrigued by the reports of healing by Christian Science. Even though the Christian Science movement had been created as a religion, its therapeutic aspects were what caught public attention and attracted converts to the church. Samuel Clemens, who had been able to see some benefit in virtually every alternative medical care system he encountered, was nonetheless unable to accept the tenets of Christian Science as a rational approach to medical care. His skepticism began as he studied the writings of the religion's founder, Mary Baker Eddy (1821–1910), and he vehemently attacked both Eddy and Christian Science. Clemens believed that Eddy was fixated on power and money, and he wrote satirical accounts of Christian Science healing for magazines between 1899 and 1903 and in a book, *Christian Science*, published in 1907.

The history of the Christian Science movement was the history of Mary Baker Eddy. Eddy had suffered numerous illnesses throughout her youth, ranging from colds to liver ailments to backache and depression and "nervousness." Her lifelong mission was to find remedies for disease, and she experimented with most of the available "alternative" medical systems of the nineteenth century. In the 1830s, she tried the approach championed by Sylvester Graham of "Graham cracker" fame of a healthy and simple diet (consisting of vegetarian dishes, pure water, and coarse whole wheat bread).[10] Eddy became familiar with "mesmerism" ("animal magnetism") during the 1840s. Her approach was homeopathic during the 1850s as she studied the principles of similia and minima and treated herself and her acquaintances with homeopathic therapies. When her patients recovered after they were treated with dilute homeopathic solutions that contained no active substance, she concluded that the cure could not have come from the medicine but was the result of the patients' *faith* in the medicine, and it was her opinion that homeopathy itself was a type of mind cure.

By 1862, Eddy was consulting with the famous mental healer Phineas Parkhurst Quimby (1802–1866) for treatment of her own persistent maladies. Quimby had studied magnetic healing since 1838, and he concluded that its cures were effected by a patient's trust in the healer. His approach included an effort to establish rapport with his patients through experiencing their symptoms, massaging the head or extremities, and offering words of encouragement. Quimby "cured" Eddy's complaints (although only temporarily), and she continued to consult him for treatment and lessons in mental healing as she became a proponent of Quimbyism. Shortly after Quimby's death in 1866, Eddy slipped on an icy street and lost consciousness. She suffered from pain in her head, neck, and back, but she found no relief from her treatment by a homeopathic physician. She turned to her Bible for solace and read the account of the healings of Jesus. This led her to discover the "healing Truth" of Christian Science, and she had a spontaneous recovery from her suffering. In summer of 1868 she began to advertise herself in a spiritualist journal as a healer. Following Quimby's approach, she vicariously acquired her patients' symptoms, which then caused her to suffer from recurrences of her own medical complaints. She wrote a pamphlet, *The Science of Man, By Which the Sick Are Healed,* in 1870, and after several attempts to come up with a suitable name for her approach she finally settled on "Christian Science."

Eddy had competition from the large number of other "mind healers" who appeared in the 1880s. These spiritualists shared the belief that the mind can resolve all the difficulties of humanity, and they created the movements of "mind cure," "mental cure," and "metaphysical healing." Eddy attempted to distinguish her Christian Science from the competing systems of the "New Thought" movement by emphasizing the unique Christian heritage of her own sect, which had been revealed directly to her by God. As her detractors accused her of "selling religion like patent medicine,"[11] she advocated a healthy lifestyle, and she shared Graham's opposition to alcohol, tobacco, coffee, and tea. Eddy attempted to legitimize her activities by obtaining a charter for the Massachusetts Metaphysical College in 1881. She took on an academic title of Professor of Obstetrics, Metaphysics, and Christian Science. Her curriculum included instruction in Christian Science dogma and the healing techniques required to start a practice. The movement spread westward from Boston;

sixteen similar institutes were founded in Illinois and Iowa in the 1880s and 1890s.

As was the case with hydropathic medicine, Christian Science became a way for women to overcome the cultural and social restrictions of the mid-nineteenth century that had prevented them from getting out of the home, obtaining an education, and serving a professional role. Eddy's discipline was female-friendly; the 1881 edition of *Science and Health* referred to God by feminine pronouns, and women outnumbered men as Christian Science practitioners by a ratio of five to one by the 1890s.

In sharp contrast to traditional medical practice in which the physician is expected to take a thorough history in order to accurately define and understand the patient's disease process, the Christian Science practitioner was careful to avoid any meticulous review of the patient's symptoms. The underlying principle of Christian Science was that nothing existed except God, and God is good. God, being good, would not make pain (or evil, or illness); therefore, sickness, sin, and suffering could only be imaginary states. Any focus by the healer on the patient's physical complaints would only reinforce the patient's misconceptions that his symptoms might have a physical basis. Instead, the Christian Scientist wanted to get a general idea of the patient's imagined distress in order to be more effective in eliminating it. Once the patient's general concerns were determined, the therapy consisted of an "argument" by the practitioner to convince the patient that he was intrinsically healthy. Clemens lampooned this approach in *Christian Science* by creating a conversation between a man who had fallen off a mountainside (and who had become "an incoherent series of compound fractures extending from [his] scalp-lock to [his] heels" [*Christian Sci.*, 5]) and a Christian Science healer who happened to be in the area.

> ... Then I thought I would tell her my symptoms and how I felt, so that she would understand the case; but that was another inconsequence, she did not need to know those things; moreover, my remark about how I felt was an abuse of language, a misapplication of terms.
>
> "One does not *feel*," she explained; "there is no such thing as feeling: therefore, to speak of a non-existent thing as existent is a contradiction. Matter has no existence; nothing exists but mind; the mind cannot feel pain, it can only imagine it."
>
> "But if it hurts, just the same—"
>
> "It doesn't. A thing which is unreal cannot exercise the functions of reality. Pain is unreal; hence, pain cannot hurt."

In making a sweeping gesture to indicate the act of shooing the illusion of pain out of the mind, she raked her hand on a pin in her dress,
said "Ouch!" and went tranquilly on with her talk. (*Christian Sci.*, 9–10)

Eddy cleverly developed the philosophy of Christian Science treatment
so that it could never be a failure. The effectiveness of Christian Science
depended solely on the ability of the patient to believe in Christian Science. If a patient did not recover, it was not the fault of Christian Science.
Instead, all failures represented the failure of the patient to develop a
full and accepting faith in the Christian Science dogma.

Christian Science was based on the premise that there is no substance,
no disease, and no death in the universe; there is "no Life, Substance, or
Intelligence . . . all is mind and there is no matter."[12] Clemens carried
Eddy's philosophy to its ultimate extreme in his manuscript *No. 44, The
Mysterious Stranger.* Eddy proclaimed that nothing existed except God,
but Clemens (through the words of the Stranger) went a step further to
propose that there was not even a reason to think that God existed.

> *"Life itself is only a vision, a dream."*
> It was electrical. By God I had had that very thought a thousand
> times in my musings!
> "*Nothing* exists; all is a dream. God—man—the world,—the sun,
> the moon, the wilderness of stars: a dream, all a dream, they have no
> existence. *Nothing exists save empty space—and you!*"
> "I!"
> "And you are not you—you have no body, no blood, no bones, you
> are but a *thought.* . . .
> ". . . there is no God, no universe, no human race, no earthly life, no
> heaven, no hell. It is all a Dream, a grotesque and foolish dream. Noth-
> ing exists but You. And You are but a *Thought*—a vagrant Thought, a
> useless Thought, a homeless Thought wandering forlorn among the
> empty eternities!" (*Mys. Stranger Mss.*, 404–5)

In spite of Clemens's personal hostility toward the sect, Christian Science was attractive to several members of his immediate family. His sister
Pamela treated Clemens's arthritis with Christian Science "in absence"
(by long distance), and in a letter written in March 1892 he grudgingly
allowed that she may have had some success in doing so. His tone indicates that he was not entirely convinced, however (and, considering the
sarcasm he heaped on the concept of long-distance healing in his book
Christian Science, his report of the alleged benefit may have been little
more than an attempt to humor Pamela).[13]

Your letter has come, & finds me with a cold in the head which makes me want to swear, & rheumatic threatenings which make me afraid to. These are the first rheumatic suggestions which I have had since last Christmas (to amount to much), & I reckon maybe they are due to your Christian Science. I couldn't make out what was the trouble before. Still, I am obliged to allow that possibly you have staved off the bulk of the attack & allowed only the remnant of it to get at me. (*MTBM*, 397)

Susy Clemens, previously attracted to "mind cure" as an adolescent in 1886, developed an interest in Christian Science due to the influence of her Hartford neighbors. Her interest in the religion may have persuaded her to refuse consultation with a traditional physician when she developed her fatal episode of spinal meningitis in 1896.[14] Clemens excluded Christian Science from even being an option for Jean, who had tried a variety of therapies for her epilepsy with little success. Open-minded about almost every type of alternative medicine, Clemens made his opposition to Mary Baker Eddy's creation very clear when he indicated that he was willing to let Jean "try anything . . . except Christian Science" (*Ltrs-Rogers*, 403). In spite of Clemens's intense animosity toward Christian Science, his daughter Clara became a Christian Scientist after his death.[15]

Eddy eventually retreated from many of her initial positions due to political and legal pressures. Christian Science practitioners increasingly faced charges of breaking vaccination laws, practicing medicine without a license, or endangering their patients' lives. Concerns about lawsuits "drove Scientists from the school of medicine to the sanctuary of religion."[16] In 1901, Eddy decreed that obstetrics was no longer part of Christian Science. She advised parents to obey the laws regarding compulsory vaccination of their children. Eddy's personal comfort also seemed to influence her policies; after she required morphine to control the severe pain of a kidney stone (a pain that was apparently anything *but* imaginary), the 1905 edition of *Science and Health* was revised to permit the use of analgesics. Even though present-day Christian Science has come to focus more on religious concerns than on medical issues, it was the original Christian Science of Mary Baker Eddy that irritated Samuel Clemens so much that he could not refrain from making derogatory comments about anyone who believed that Christian Science was a legitimate method of health care.

I cannot help feeling rather inordinately proud of America for the gay and hearty way in which she takes hold of any new thing that comes along and gives it a first rate trial. Many an ass in America is getting a deal of benefit out of X-Science's new exploitation of an age-old healing principle—*faith*, combined with the patient's imagination—let it boom along! I have no objection. Let them call it by what name they choose, so long as it does helpful work among the class which is numerically vastly the largest bulk of the human race, i.e. the fools, the idiots, the pudd'nheads. (*Ltrs/Paine*, 2:690)

Sam Clemens's hatred of Christian Science was intense, and he felt obligated to write at length to point out its inherent absurdities. In doing so, he also grudgingly acknowledged that, illogically, Christian Science *did* appear to be helpful to some people. He was finally able to resolve this apparent paradox by coming to the conclusion that the benefits derived had nothing to do specifically with Mary Baker Eddy or Christian Science. Instead, he determined, every beneficial outcome was a manifestation of the healing that was created by the faith of the patient in the healer and in the system of healing.

20

FAITH

Believing What You Know Ain't So

On the inquest it was shown that Buck Fanshaw, in the delirium of a wasting typhoid fever, had taken arsenic, shot himself through the body, cut his throat, and jumped out of a four-story window and broken his neck—and after due deliberation, the jury, sad and tearful, but with intelligence unblinded by its sorrow, brought in a verdict of death "by the visitation of God."

—Mark Twain, *Roughing It*

The history of Christian Science is but one instance of the complex interactions between religious faith and medical care that have occurred through the ages. Religion and medicine have been closely intertwined throughout history, and it has not been unusual for medical and spiritual care to be delivered by the same person. Religious figures are often viewed as healers; medical practitioners frequently attribute their successes to the intervention of God. Sam Clemens recognized the relationship of religion to medicine; even as he argued with the particulars of the Christian Science philosophy, he was willing to concede that "it is a fine thought, too—marrying religion to medicine, instead of medicine to the undertaker in the old way; for religion and medicine properly belong together, they being the basis of all spiritual and physical health" (*Christian Sci.*, 20).

A 1996 *USA Today* poll concluded that 79 percent of adult American respondents believed that spiritual faith can help people recover from disease, and a *Time* magazine national survey the same year found that 82 percent of Americans believed in the healing power of prayer.[1] Clemens described an example of healing by prayer in *A Connecticut Yankee in King Arthur's Court*, a satire set in sixth-century England that attacks the beliefs and institutions of both medieval and modern times.

> Up by Astolat there was a chapel where the Virgin had once appeared to a girl who used to herd geese around there—the girl said so herself—and they built the chapel upon that spot and hung a picture in it representing the occurrence—a picture which you would think it dangerous for a sick person to approach; whereas, on the contrary, thousands of the lame and the sick came and prayed before it every year and went away whole and sound, and even the well could look upon it and live. Of course when I was told these things I did not believe them; but when I went there and saw them I had to succumb. I saw the cures effected myself, and they were real cures and not questionable. I saw cripples whom I had seen around Camelot for years on crutches, arrive and pray before that picture, and put down their crutches and walk off without a limp. There were piles of crutches there which had been left by such people as a testimony. (*Conn. Yankee*, 337–38)

A recent study of unconventional medical therapies showed that prayer is used by 25 percent of Americans who employ alternative treatment methods. The belief in prayer is not limited to the lay public. A survey in 1996 at a meeting of the American Academy of Family Physicians revealed that 99 percent of the doctors surveyed believed that religious beliefs can heal, and 75 percent thought that a patient's recovery could be speeded through the prayers of others.[2]

Dr. Dale Matthews, author of *The Faith Factor*, has explored the topic in depth, and he attributes some of the benefit of faith to the same factor that underlies the benefit of other approaches to healing—the placebo effect.

> Our religious traditions teach us to expect great things from God, thus setting in motion the health-boosting effect of positive expectancy— hope. In medicine this dynamic is known as the placebo effect, a well-known phenomenon in which patients get better simply because they believe they will. . . . We evoke the power of the placebo effect when we connect to a transcendent realm where our present worries pale in comparison to the wonder of God's ultimate promises.[3]

Although "spirituality" is a somewhat amorphous concept, a "spiritual" individual can be recognized not only by his belief in a higher power but also by his gratitude for life as a "gift" and through his ability to find meaning in suffering.[4] Religious beliefs are often used by patients with cancer to sustain their level of "hope," which can be viewed as a "trust in the future." These spiritual values provide an active philosophical perspective from which such patients can sort through and deal with the implications of their illness.[5] Faith healing or prayer cannot reverse the course of underlying pathological processes, but religious healing *can* alter what an illness means to the sufferer. Faith healing becomes more understandable if healing is not defined as the elimination of disease but instead as a "form of persuasion that alters a person's 'assumptive world.'"[6] Through his description of Native American healing rituals, Mehl-Madrona explains the differences in attitude and expectation between traditional physicians and nontraditional healers.

> [A] healing is a spiritual journey. As most people intuitively grasp (except maybe doctors, who are trained to disbelieve the idea), what happens to the body reflects what is happening in the mind and the spirit. People *can* get well. But before a person can do so, he or she must often undergo a transformation—of lifestyle, emotions, and spirit—besides making the necessary shift in the physical body.
>
> Healing and doctoring are distinct pursuits.... It is no exaggeration to say that healers and doctors inhabit different worlds.[7]

In standard medical therapy, physicians direct their attention to the biomedical aspects of the treatment. Allopathic doctors do not expect their patients to make any contribution to the healing effort beyond a reasonable level of cooperation. Their therapy is, after all, a matter of "science." No objection is made if some patients wish to insert their own faith into the process, but the physician will usually see a patient's faith as a nicety that is somewhat superfluous to the real treatment. In reality, the patient's belief in the doctor, the treatment, and even the possibility of recovery can be an important contributor to the patient's ability to get better. The faith of the patient becomes even more important if the therapist is a nontraditional healer—to a large extent, alternative practitioners view themselves less as healers than as facilitators of patient self-healing, and self-healing depends on the patient's trust in the process. The benefits achieved by devotees of nontraditional (alternative) health-care systems lie more in the sense of self-empowerment that is given to each patient than in any specific therapeutic regimen. Although traditional practitioners often fail to understand why it happens, patients find that the sense of control over destiny they gain from their faith is of greatest benefit when their doctor is an orthodox medical practitioner whose own mechanistic view of disease does not require the insertion of factors of faith into the therapeutic process.

Introducing a role for spiritual factors in the healing process can be a mixed blessing. On the positive side, the premise that the source of recovery lies within the mind and spirit of the patient can create an important sense of autonomy, an "empowerment through faith" that may permit the patient to cope with large amounts of adversity. There is, however, a negative side to the insertion of religious-based healing (whether it is as mind cure, Christian Science, or any other system based on prayer or belief) into health care: through their underlying tenets, any healing approach that calls on the patient's faith can create a "responsibility paradox" that may be injurious to a patient's emotional well-being.[8] In any situation where faith is considered the primary healer, rather than merely the chief comforter, the failure of a patient to get well can easily be blamed on the limitations of his or her personal belief. A patient with a self-limited illness that will always improve on its own has little risk of being seen as a failure in faith; it is even possible that the recovery from such an illness may be hastened through the positive consequences of the patient's belief. However, recovery is not a realistic expectation for patients who happen to be afflicted with a more severe disease in which the underlying pathological processes are profound, advanced, and irreversible. In a faith-oriented healing system, the failure of a disease to improve cannot be attributed to the inadequacy of an antibiotic or the limitations of a surgical procedure, nor can it be explained away as the unrelenting natural course of a serious illness; in a faith-driven system of healing, a failure to improve is the fault of the patient. In such a system, the harm to psyche and spirit can be severe.

Interestingly, therapeutic failures are seldom reported in alternative care systems, where the deck has been stacked in favor of the dealer. When the patient gets better, the system gets the credit. When the patient fails to recover, it is the patient's fault. When the patient's own faith is the prerequisite for a positive outcome, "the system does not fail; patients do."[9] When parents sued the Christian Science Church for malpractice following the death of their child from bacterial meningitis after the Christian Science practitioners had discouraged medical consultation, the president of the church testified that "whenever Christian Science is *properly applied*, it heals." In his opinion, the real fault resided not in the Church, but in the parents who "were much more intent on physical healing than in spiritual growth and regeneration." Samuel Clemens had no respect for those who used any type of religious blackmail as a prerequisite for healing; in this regard he found the nonjudgmental attitudes of traditional medical care to be superior to the restrictive exclusivity that is often demanded by religious healing. He made this clear in a letter he wrote on August 14, 1883, to Ellen Taft, the wife of Dr. Cincinnatus Taft: "To my poor mind, the first of holy callings is the physician's; & he should walk before Pope, & Cardinal, & all the priestly tribe, for he heals all that fall in his way, not merely the chance sufferer here & there who is willing to say, first, 'Good Galilean, I subscribe to the conditions'" (Ltrs-Microfilm-2, vol. 2, #2821).

Thus, the employment of faith in the healing process can become a double-edged sword. To simultaneously apply traditional medicine and religious faith in dealing with the same illness suggests that the patient may be hedging his bets due to his doubts about both the quality of his medical care and the power of his faith. When any failure to cure is interpreted as a deficiency in the patient's faith, a circular argument is created in which it becomes impossible to assess faith's ability to cure.[10] In fact, a comprehensive review of the subject of religion and healing, published in the Lancet in 1999, found little reason to conclude that faith alone can cure disease and suggested that patients can be done a serious disservice if their state of health is used as a barometer for the integrity of their spiritual being. "Even in the best studies, the evidence of an association between religion, spirituality and health is weak and inconsistent. . . . No-one can object to respectful support for patients who draw upon religious faith in times of illness. However . . . suggestions that religious activity will promote health, that illness is the result of insufficient faith, are unwarranted."[11]

In the real world of medical care, of course, the choice between traditional medicine and faith healing is never a simple "either-or" proposition. Even when the straightest party-line practitioner employs the most orthodox and "scientific" version of traditional medicine, each patient's belief system introduces a component of "contamination" into the pristine science, and the unpredictable nature of the impurity blurs the boundaries between science and religion. The scientific physician believes that his cures arise from his science rather than from within himself; his non-scientific patient may not understand the science, but always brings his faith in the doctor into the mix. And even faith itself is rarely absolute, and at times can be very shaky, as Clemens knew so very well: "There are those who scoff at the schoolboy, calling him frivolous and shallow. Yet it was the schoolboy who said, 'Faith is believing what you know ain't so'" (*Foll. Equat.*, 132). The emotionally based faith of the patient is an unpredictable input that can disrupt the chemistry between doctor and patient if the physician has difficulty incorporating it into the equation of therapy. More often, it has a great potential to enhance the effectiveness of the doctor-patient relationship, particularly when the doctor is open-minded to it (and if the science and the faith have the correct proportions to create a strong alloy). Mehl-Madrona, trained in both allopathic medicine and Native American healing, encourages physicians to make use of their patients' belief systems: "If we truly want to be healers, we must be willing to use anything that works, regardless of our theoretical positions. Because if it works, it's good medicine."[12]

While traveling in the Middle East as an "innocent abroad," a young Sam Clemens observed firsthand the religious nature of medical practice as he watched one of the physicians in his party stop to treat the strangers encountered on the journey. Clemens was impressed not only by the religious-like faith of the patients, but also by the ritualistic behavior of the physician as he prepared his therapeutic formulation. Clemens realized that both the faith of the patient and the ritual of the doctor were critical to successful treatment.

> The little children were in a pitiable condition—they all had sore eyes, and were otherwise afflicted in various ways. They say that hardly a native child in all the East is free from sore eyes, and that thousands of them go blind of one eye or both every year. I think this must be so, for I see plenty of blind people every day, and I do not remember seeing any children that hadn't sore eyes....
> As soon as the tribe found out that we had a doctor in our party, they began to flock in from all quarters. Dr. B., in the charity of his nature, had taken a child from a woman who sat near by, and put some sort of a wash upon its diseased eyes. That woman went off and started a whole nation, and it was a sight to see them swarm! The lame, the halt, the blind, the leprous—all the distempers that are bred of indolence, dirt, and iniquity—were represented in the congress in ten minutes, and still they came! Every woman that had a sick baby brought it along, and every woman that hadn't, borrowed one. What reverent and what worshiping looks they bent upon that dread, mysterious power, the Doctor! They watched him take his vials out; they watched him measure the particles of white powder; they watched him add drops of one precious liquid, and drops of another; they lost not the slightest

movement; their eyes were riveted upon him with a fascination that nothing could distract. I believe they thought he was gifted like a god. When each individual got his portion of medicine, his eyes were radiant with joy—notwithstanding by nature they are a thankless and impassive race—and upon his face was written the unquestioning faith that nothing on earth could prevent the patient from getting well now. (*Inn. Abroad*, 473–74)[13]

Dr. B. was Dr. George Bright Birch (1822?-1873?) of Hannibal.[14] The opportunity to observe his interactions with his patients gave Samuel Clemens one of the most significant insights that he gained on the trip. He learned that the process of healing is not impeded by barriers of culture, language, economics, and education, as long as two essential conditions are met. The doctor has to care about the patient. And the patient must have faith in the doctor.

Ultimately, Samuels Clemens came to understand that, for many maladies, the patient's faith is the essential factor in the process of recovery. This power called "faith" was not easily defined, as it seemed to come in so many different versions. For some people, the faith that promoted healing arose from an abiding and constant trust in the healing powers of an all-powerful and merciful God. For others, the object of faith might be something far less divine—Clemens had seen that trust in a human healer such as Mrs. Utterback or Dr. Newton could lead to a cure, and so too could belief in the methods of electrotherapy or water cure. For that matter, having faith in the healing properties of stump water or in the restorative actions of starvation also seemed to lead to recovery from sickness. Collectively, all of these treatments were forms of "mind cure," and Clemens had seen that every single one of them could have beneficial results.

All of contemporary medicine, whether it is labeled "traditional" or "alternative," continues to rely on this power of "mind cure," the mysterious force that arises from the patient's faith in *something* (or perhaps *anything*) that might have a positive influence on health. In reality, it is not the patient's health (as defined in biological terms) that is changed by the numerous versions of mind cure; instead, it is the patient's *perception* of well-being. However, it is this perception that is often the most important contributor to the nebulous condition that is referred to as "health." Even now, there is little understanding of how these variations of "mind cure" really work, and there is ongoing debate in the medical world as to whether it is even possible to better define the role of faith in the healing process through research and scientific scrutiny.[15] Some researchers have suggested that the important conclusion may be that human beings are "more connected" and "more responsible to each other" than has generally been believed, even though it may never be possible to determine whether the benefits are mediated through "the agency of God, consciousness, love, electrons, or a combination."[16] Terminology has changed through the years, but the patient's belief is as important as ever. Physicians no longer speak of "mind cure," but they are all familiar with the identical process that goes by the designation of "placebo effect."

21

Any Mummery Will Cure, if the Patient's Faith Is Strong in It

Doctor and osteopath have failed with me, but I am curing myself by a scheme of my own invention. Maybe it won't succeed, but I know one thing, for sure: it will either cure me or kill me.

—Mark Twain, letter to Emilie Rogers, April 28, 1903

In the final analysis, the story of Samuel Clemens and medicine is largely the story of Clemens's progressive insights into the role of placebo in medical therapeutics. The story's most fascinating component may be the fact that, unlike most individuals who have found success with placebo therapies, Clemens developed a remarkable understanding of what the placebo effect really meant. His lifelong pursuit of alternative care systems, which became the basis for his knowledge about placebo, was a result of his profound dissatisfaction with traditional medical therapy. Through his personal experiences, Clemens had become convinced that the allopathic medicine of the nineteenth century was not only worthless (which also might be said of most of its competitors) but also dangerous to the patient (which was less likely to be the case with its competition).[1] In a letter he wrote to Joseph Twichell in January 1900, Clemens poked fun at Livy for seeking care from a regular physician:

See what a powerful hold our ancient superstitions have upon us: two weeks ago, when Livy committed an incredible imprudence and by consequence was promptly stricken down with a heavy triple attack—influenza, bronchitis, and a lung affected—she recognized the gravity of the situation and her old superstitions rose: she thought she ought to send for a doctor—Think of it—the last man in the world I should want around at such a time. Of course I did not say *no*—not that I was indisposed to take the responsibility, for I was not, my notion of a dangerous responsibility being quite the other way—but because it is unsafe to distress a sick person; I only said we knew no good doctor, and it could not be good policy to choose at hazard. (*Ltrs/Paine*, 2:691–92)

Clemens was not the only person to be critical of allopathic medical regimens during the days of aggressive treatment. The first effective protest against heroic medicine occurred in 1835 when Jacob Bigelow, in his paper "On Self-Limited Diseases," suggested that a patient's recovery from illness is more dependent on nature than on the dosing of drugs. Dr. Samuel Jackson in 1840 also questioned the value of the medical treatments of the age. Patients voiced their concerns as well. William Maclay, U.S. senator from Pennsylvania, complained about the treatment he received in 1789 for rheumatism. His two physician consultants recommended a full course of antimonials to cleanse his stomach, he remarked with incredulity, even though his pain was in his knee! One of the highlights of his therapeutic program took place on September 8, he recorded in his journal, because his doctors did "not call to-day, and it seems like delivering me from half of my misery."[2] Oliver Wendell Holmes, who left the practice of medicine in the mid-nineteenth century to become a full-time author and lecturer, was heavily criticized by the rest of the medical profession for his infamous statement, "I firmly believe that if the whole materia medica, as now used, could be sunk to the bottom of the sea, it would be all the better for mankind, and all the worse for the fishes."[3]

In *Those Extraordinary Twins*, Clemens shared the sentiment expressed by Holmes that the natural history of an illness might well be preferable to the treatments offered by the medical profession: "During Monday, Tuesday and Wednesday the twins grew steadily worse; but then the doctor was summoned south to attend his mother's funeral and they got well in forty-eight hours" (*PW&TET*, 425).

In *Which Was It?* Clemens followed up on the concept by lampooning the excesses of allopathy in his account of a doctor's elaborate prescription: "It took him fifteen minutes to do it. It contained a bushel of assorted and chaotic ingredients; among them all the forest weeds and herbs in the neighborhood, along with cloves, lunar caustic, castor oil, cinnamon, horse-dung, aqua fortis, sugar, dried lizards, turpentine, blue vitriol, molasses, and so on" (*WWD&OSW*, 286).[4] The concoction shared some of the more notable features of Perry Davis's Pain-Killer—it was another variety of "hellfire." After Dug Hapgood took a dose that had been intended for George Harrison, he told Harrison, "I risked my life to save yourn," and he described the distressing effect the medicine had on him—"it was like I had my bowels full of cats" (*WWD&OSW*, 292).

In spite of the few voices in the wilderness, however, the use of noxious drugs, bloodletting, and associated heroic measures remained the standard treatment for virtually all illnesses from the 1790s until the 1860s and 1870s. In 1807, prominent American surgeon Philip Syng Physick prescribed leeches and general bleeding for inflamed eyes. Physick also found bleeding of benefit for dislocated joints; Benjamin Rush suggested that the unconsciousness resulting from the blood loss made manipulation easier for the physician. In the 1833 edition of William P. Dewees's *Practice of Physic*, the author observed that bloodletting was so widely accepted it had "almost become a domestic remedy."[5] Clemens suggested that if Galen himself had come to administer medical care when Clemens was a boy, he would have found little difference between the medical treatments of Missouri in the early nineteenth century and the type of medicine he himself had practiced centuries earlier.

> He would have examined me, and run across only one disappointment—I was already salivated; I would have him there; for I was always salivated, calomel was so cheap. He would get out his lancet then; but I would have him again; our family doctor didn't allow blood to accumulate in the system. However, he could take dipper and ladle, and freight me up with old familiar doses that had come down from Adam to his time and mine; and he could go out with a wheelbarrow and gather weeds and offal, and build some more, while those others were getting in their work. (*£1m Bank-note*, 243)

Medical practices finally started to become more moderate in the 1840s, particularly in the South, where quinine began to replace calomel as the mainstay of treatment (with some apparent benefit).[6] The balance between the benefits and the risks of medical therapy still leaned strongly in the direction of the harmful, however. In 1849 the editor of the *United States Magazine, and Democratic Review* suggested that doctors "have been, to no inconsiderable extent, accessory both to the reduction of disease, and—of life itself."[7] Clemens himself made the same observation in *Pudd'nhead Wilson:* "Percy Northumberland Driscoll . . . was a married man, and had had children around his hearthstone; but they were attacked in detail by measles, croup and scarlet fever, and this had given the doctor a chance with his antediluvian methods; so the cradles were empty" (*PW&TET,* 22). In *Which Was It?* Clemens burlesqued the atrocities of allopathic medicine in a description of Dr. Bradshaw's treatment of George Harrison, who was suffering from "suppressed itch."[8]

> Bridget held the bowl, and he bled the patient in the foot and arm; cupped him in the back; hung a fringe of leeches on his temples; ordered a raiment of mustard-plasters for him; gave him a purge and a vomit, timed to go off together; then devised a soothing draught which Bridget was to compound on the premises, boil down, distil, concentrate to a "compromise with hell-fire" as Dug Hapgood afterward described it, and wake him up and give him a shovelful every three-quarters of an hour until he got better or died. (*WWD&OSW,* 286)

Although alternative care movements are based on their successful application of the placebo effect, traditional medical practice has been equally reliant on the patient's response to placebo therapies through most of its history. In 1938, Dr. W. B. Houston suggested that all of the medicines that had been used up to his time had been placebos. The medications had not done anything useful in their own right, in his view, but they worked by reinforcing the encouragement, comfort, and hope that was offered by the physician. Houston recognized that there were some very successful doctors who were acclaimed for their skill in healing, but he doubted that their success had anything to do with their knowledge of anatomy, biochemistry, physiology, or pharmacology. Instead, according to Houston, the most effective clinicians achieved their accomplishments in healing through the application of an essential personal skill: "Their skill was a skill in dealing with the emotions of men. They themselves were the therapeutic agents by which cures were effected. . . . The history of medicine is a history of the dynamic power of the relationship between doctor and patient."[9]

Sixty years later, Dr. Howard Spiro wrote in support of Houston's concept that the interaction of the healer with the patient is the most important component of the healing process. Placebos are effective, he noted, but placebos alone cannot heal. Spiro recognized that the power of the placebo comes from the patient's trust in it (or, perhaps more specifically, from the patient's trust in the physician who prescribes it), and he was able to explain the success of the placebo in simple terms: "Inert and inactive, the placebo has no power; the miracle comes in one person helping another. The patient does the work while the doctor or the placebo takes the credit."[10]

The insights offered by Houston and Spiro explain the great success of the placebo-based treatment programs that collectively are referred to as "alternative medicine." Traditional medicine has tried very hard to debunk alternative medical factions through repetitively demonstrating the inconsistencies in the principles and methods of the numerous competing approaches. Intellectually, the methods of homeopathic medicine and mind cure just do not make any sense. Even so, this is a debate that the traditionalists can never win, because orthodox medicine is not fighting the same battle as its challengers. The proponents of each nontraditional system are not interested in why their particular approaches are illogical and should not work; all they care about is that their methods *do* work, at least for the patients who trust in them. With so many varieties of nontraditional medical care available, based on so many divergent and incompatible philosophies, it initially seems surprising that they would *all* seem to work. In recent years, traditional medicine has had an increasing interest in sorting out which of the alternative care methods might have components that are useful. After some reflection, though, it would appear that the real challenge is not in determining *which* of the alternative methods are effective; instead, the important issue is whether any *one* of them is effective. Once it is established that *one* of the nontraditional methods is beneficial, they will *all* have to be beneficial. No matter how different they may appear in their techniques or styles, all versions of alternative care share one essential component—every one of them is placebo-based. Each one is a form of "mind cure," relying on the faith of the patient for its effectiveness. If any one of these alternative systems is successful, the utility of placebo has been confirmed, and all the others will be successful.

The proof of the utility of the "placebo response," the modern terminology for the "mind cure" of Samuel Clemens's era, comes from homeopathic medicine. Homeopathy is the gold standard of alternative care methods; all of the other alternative care regimens claim that they are doing something to a patient that might deliver a medical benefit through a mysterious mechanism that traditional medicine does not have the sophistication to recognize. This is not so with homeopathy. When a patient has a successful response to treatment with a homeopathic therapy that has been diluted so many times that there is *nothing* in it, the efficacy of therapy with "*nothing*" (that is, placebo) is established. After that is accomplished, all other conceivable variations of "nothing" should be expected to work equally well. And, because patients *do* respond to placebo, it is possible to get better from chiropractic manipulations. Or from wearing copper bracelets around the wrist. Or from placing magnets in shoes. Or from dangling a chunk of quartz from a string around the neck. (Or from being purged by calomel, or having large volumes of blood removed, or undergoing a sham operation to alleviate chest pain.)[11]

The impact of any particular placebo can vary with the expectations of the patient. A placebo for a widely advertised brand of aspirin works better than a placebo for unbranded aspirin in relieving headaches. Since both placebos are equally inactive, the patients who respond better to the "brand name" placebo are influenced by something more than just placebo effect as it is typically defined. Samuel Clemens might have suggested that they were responding to the "mind cure" that came from their faith in the brand name in the same way that his own faith in starvation cured his colds. The benefit that comes from placebo depends on the impact that a treatment has on a patient's belief system, and it may be that a placebo effect is better described as a "meaning response."[12]

Several factors contributed to Clemens's progressive enlightenment about the effectiveness of placebo, but none was more important than his freedom to compare many competing medical systems. These opportunities started with his mother's open-minded explorations of treatment options and were followed by his own lifelong pursuit of the ideal treatment program. Clemens's experiences with diverse treatment philosophies were essential for his medical education; they forced him to think about what was going on in the treatment process and drove him to form his own conclusions.

In "Corn-Pone Opinions," Clemens argued that few people use independent observation and reasoning to define their position on any topic, but instead they simply conform to what is most familiar to them and what they have been brought up to believe in: "Mohammedans are Mohammedans because they are born and reared among that sect, not because they have thought it out and can furnish sound reasons for being Mohammedans" (*CT-2*, 510). He thought the same was true for Catholics, Presbyterians, Baptists, and Mormons, not to mention Republicans and Democrats. He came to learn that the same prejudices applied to the followers of allopathy, homeopathy, osteopathy, and other medical sects. Clemens's advantage was that he was not "born and reared" within the confines of a single medical belief system. His explorations of diverse healing systems helped him to see the limitations of each and gave him the information he needed to map out the fault line that separated the successes from the failures for each medical sect. It was at the fault lines that he discovered the placebo.

Considering the power of the placebo effect, it is not so amazing that Samuel Clemens encountered positive outcomes from every health care system he used, even though the most serious medical conditions were never resolved by placebo therapies. And even as most systems pursued by Clemens seemed to be beneficial to some extent, it became obvious that the benefit derived from any single approach was conditional upon his ability to believe that it *would* work. Clemens recognized that faith and trust and hope were essential to the healing process, and he came to understand that these terms were all synonymous with the placebo effect. He also believed that it was the responsibility of the physician to create the placebo of hope whenever it was absent. Clemens stated his position clearly in 1904 when he asked Dr. Wilberforce Baldwin to lie to Livy about the seriousness of her illness; he believed that such a deception was the placebo that was needed to lift her spirits and possibly to save her life: "Medicine has its office, it does its share and does it well; but without hope back of it, its forces are crippled and only the physician's verdict can create that hope when the facts refuse to create it."[13]

Samuel Clemens was no different from any other human being who is concerned about his own health and the health of his family. The overriding expectation of anyone who is sick is the anticipation that *something* will be done to negate the illness. Nonetheless, patients do not all have the same expectations when they seek medical care, and the differences in their expectations can create differences in outcomes. A patient's outcry for action is not muted by the doctor's advice that there is nothing useful that can be done. A large part of the success of alternative medicine comes from the fact that the purveyors of nontraditional therapy are not in the business of suggesting that the patient has run out of options. There is always *some* type of treatment that they can offer the patient. Most medical problems resolve spontaneously, and any treatment that preceded the recovery is given credit for the cure. As a result, ineffectual treatments do not usually have much trouble in attracting enthusiasts.

Allopathic therapy is equally susceptible to the demands of patients that some intervention be initiated. Through their insistence on receiving the most popular treatments in the allopathic portfolio, patients themselves contributed to the persistence of the excesses of medical care of the age of heroic medicine.[14] The general public tended to share the confidence of the allopathic doctors in the benefits to be derived from treatment with calomel and bleeding, and a physician who was unwilling to prescribe the aggressive therapy expected by a patient ran the risk of having his own qualifications brought into question. This pressure from patients to "do something" has been discussed by Martin Kaufman in his 1971 review of the history of homeopathic medicine in America:

Physicians of every age have found that the most recent medical miracle was always in demand for every and any ailment. If not purged, bled, and sweated, it can be expected that the early nineteenth-century patient would have had little respect for his physician. Whether the cure-all was blood-letting, alcohol, opium, stimulants, or the penicillin and sulfa drugs of the twentieth century, patients have insisted upon it. Woe to the doctor who is unwilling to accede to the demands of his patients.[15]

Sam Clemens made the same observation himself. In the unfinished sketch "Indiantown," he described the widow Wilkerson, who was "ready for any new kind of doctrine, or doctoring, or patent medicine, or any other good and lofty diversion that came along." The widow shared many traits with Jane Clemens and Tom Sawyer's Aunt Polly, including an intense passion for experimenting with anything that was new or different in the line of medical treatment: "She was small and thin, always and inveterately ungracefully dressed, and had drugged herself with deadly medicines till there was not enough blood in her to blush with. She had doctored herself for every disease under the sun and had never had one of them. She was periodically in an eager enthusiasm over some new fatal nostrum and trying to betray her friends into taking chances in it" (*WWD&OSW*, 162).

The survival of unproven, fraudulent, dangerous, or otherwise inappropriate medical care systems can be attributed to the fact that patients will recover from most ailments even if they do not receive any treatment. If a patient's spontaneous recovery happens to follow the application of a specific medical intervention, the inevitable conclusion will be that the treatment was directly responsible for the good outcome. In *Which Was It?* Dr. Bradshaw prescribes a particularly noxious remedy for George Harrison and becomes ecstatic when Harrison has a remarkable recovery. Bradshaw begins to spread the news of his "medical miracle" even though, unbeknownst to him, Harrison never actually took any of the prescribed medicine. At this juncture, Clemens playfully introduces the alternative (and literally correct) opinion of the "Rev. Mr. Bailey" (who is also under the belief that Harrison had taken Bradshaw's medicine, but intends to put in a plug for the ultimate role of divine intervention in the miraculous cure) that the credit for Harrison's recovery belongs "else-where" (*WWD&OSW*, 294). After finally establishing that Harrison's recovery had nothing to do with Dr. Bradshaw's prescribed therapy, Clemens proceeds to attack the toxicity of allopathic medicine by point-ing to the real "glory" of Harrison's cure as it is explained by "Hamfat" Bailey ("Idiot Philosopher" and the brother of Reverend Bailey): "God could have cured him *without* the medicine; indeed, as any sane person can see, the real miracle was that He didn't kill him *with* it—and therein lies the glory. . . . It was ordained from the beginning of time, that this man should commit suicide with that remedy and survive it" (*WWD& OSW*, 294).

Sir William Osler (a contemporary of Samuel Clemens's and the most influential and revered physician of the modern era) shared the view-point expressed so often by Clemens, and he suggested that the time had come for doctors to "appreciate the difference between the giving of medicines and the treatment of disease." In spite of Osler's warning, physicians who withheld traditional and routine treatments were criti-cized for committing "the sin of omission, which not infrequently rises to the dignity of a crime," even in circumstances where the expected treatment was toxic and without proven benefit.[16] In 1892, Osler charac-terized pneumonia as "a self-limited disease" that is "uninfluenced in any way by medicine," and he observed that the typical course of the disease was to "terminate abruptly and naturally, without a dose of med-icine having been administered." Osler used few drugs, recognizing the ability of the body to heal itself; one of his favorite prescriptions was "time, in divided doses." Osler subscribed neither to the use of homeop-athy nor to the polypharmacy that was so prevalent in his day (and has become an increasingly common cause of modern-day iatrogenic illness as pharmaceuticals proliferate). He recognized the challenge to the physi-cian in denying unnecessary medication to expectant patients in a famous aphorism: "The desire to take medicine is one feature which distinguishes man, the animal, from his fellow creatures."[17]

However, treatment of disease has always been an emotionally based as well as an intellectually driven activity, and any doctor who chooses to do nothing (even when doing nothing may well be in the best interest of the patient) is at risk of being identified as a "therapeutic nihilist" (as Osler was labeled by his critics). Because of the likelihood that a patient will recover from most illnesses in the absence of any therapy at all, Dr. Howard Spiro has proposed that the maxim advising "Don't just stand there; do something" deserves a postscript: "Before the patient gets better." When electroconvulsive therapy was new and its potential benefit was yet to be fully defined, the psychiatrist Dr. Harry Stack Sullivan supposedly suggested, "Let's use it while it still works."[18] The perception that a treatment is beneficial is accentuated when recovery comes after a treatment that seems particularly noxious or painfully unpleasant. Any improvement in the patient's condition is interpreted by both the physician and the patient as further evidence that the medical system employed was valid and effective. Each recovery increases the level of faith and acceptance and encourages the patient to undergo future rounds of the same treatment when a similar illness arises. Whether or not the therapy really accomplished anything is not considered as long as a favorable outcome occurs. When Jane Clemens forced her family to take Perry Davis's vile "Pain-Killer" as a preventative during the cholera epidemic of 1849, there is little doubt that the credit for preventing the cholera would have been given to the Pain-Killer (although most of Samuel Clemens's Pain-Killer was poured between the slats in the floor).

The truth of the matter is simple. There is no such thing as alternative medicine. There is only proven medicine, which is supported by scientific evidence, or unproven medicine, which lacks the scientific evidence needed to support its use.[19] Even so, patients can derive some benefit from simply having *something* to believe in, and this may be the greatest contribution of nontraditional medical approaches.

The fact that most of the benefit of alternative systems is derived from placebo effect does not by itself explain the presence, much less the popularity, of alternative medicine. There would be no reason for alternative medical approaches to arise unless there were perceptions of significant shortcomings in the approaches used by mainstream medicine. Conversely, alternative medicine does not have a monopoly on placebos, and the placebo effect can be a significant component of the benefit many patients derive from traditional medicine. Samuel Clemens's experiences with the medical sects of the nineteenth century taught him that allopathic medicine was not intrinsically preferable to hydropathic medicine (or electrotherapy, or osteopathic medicine, or even self-treatment with patent medicine). Even though each of these approaches seemed to be successful some of the time for some of the people, it was always a hit-and-miss type of success. It was possible that some of the patients who seemed to respond to medical treatment would have improved anyway, even in the absence of medical intervention. In general, though, the sickest people always seemed to fare the worst, and sometimes it appeared that medical intervention did nothing except accelerate the pace of their demise.

In many cases, it may be that the predominant role of medical therapy is to distract the patient while waiting for natural forces to play themselves out, and the goal of the patient and the physician should be to choose the least toxic of the distractions available. Through most of Sam Clemens's life, it appeared that this goal was best reached by employing virtually any therapeutic approach *except* allopathic medicine, as Clemens observed in a January 8, 1900, letter to Twichell.

> We do not guess, we know that 9 in 10 of the species are pudd'nheads. We know it by various evidences; and one of them is, that for ages the race has respected (and almost venerated) the physician's grotesque system—the emptying of miscellaneous and harmful drugs into a person's stomach to remove ailments which in many cases the drugs could not reach at all; in many cases could reach and help, but only at cost of damage to some other part of the man; and in the remainder of the cases the drug either retarded the cure, or the disease was cured by nature in spite of the nostrums. The doctor's insane system has not only been permitted to continue its follies for ages, but has been protected by the State and made a close monopoly—an infamous thing, a crime against a free-man's proper right to choose his own assassin or his own method of defending his body against disease and death. (*Ltrs/Paine*, 2:690–91)

Clemens realized that most medical conditions will clear up spontaneously, given enough time. Because of this, it made no sense for a person to be loaded full of toxic chemicals for the sole purpose of self-distraction while nature proceeded to eliminate the disease at its own good speed. On the other hand, if the deception had no toxicity (which, ultimately, is what the "mind cure" of placebo is all about), Clemens had no objection to alternative means of distraction. This perspective is at the root of his own pursuit of therapies such as hydrotherapy, electrotherapy, mind cure, and rest cure, not to mention his own "starvation cure" and "Plasmon cure." For him, it was all largely an issue of personal preference, as he suggested in his letter ("Official Physic") to the *New York Sunday Mercury* of April 21, 1867.

> If a citizen was inclined to take salts by the ton, ipecac by the barrel, mercury by the quart, or quinine by the load, and thus be cured of his

ailment or his sublunary existence by the wholesale, he was at perfect liberty to invite the services of a medicus of the allopathic style; if another citizen preferred to toy with death, and buy health in small parcels, to bribe death with a sugar pill to stay away, or go to the grave with all the original sweetners undrenched out of him, then the individual adopted the "like cures like" system, and called in a homeopath physician as being a pleasant friend of death's.... Then again there were those who saw "good in everything" and who believed that whatever is is right, and these last mixed the allopathic, homeopathic, and hydropathic systems, qualified each with each, and thus passed to their long homes, drenched, pickled, sweetened, and soaked. (*CT-1*, 228)

Samuel Clemens understood that the beliefs and expectations of the individual patient play an essential role in the healing process. He demonstrated the depth of his insight in *A Connecticut Yankee in King Arthur's Court*, where he described the elaborate "king's touch" ceremony that was used to treat scrofula, also known as the "king's evil." The touch of royalty has been thought to be curative, according to popular belief that dates back to biblical and early Roman times; the "royal touch" was used by English monarchs from Edward the Confessor in the eleventh century through Queen Anne in the eighteenth.[20] In Clemens's description of the ritual, the king sat in "a canopy of state," where he was surrounded by "a large body of the clergy in full canonicals." A "hermit of the quack-doctor species" presented the afflicted patients to the king: "Marinel took the patients as they came. He examined the candidate; if he couldn't qualify he was warned off; if he could he was passed along to the king. A priest pronounced the words, 'They shall lay their hands on the sick, and they shall recover.' Then the king stroked the ulcers, while the reading continued.... Would you think that that would cure? It certainly did. Any mummery will cure if the patient's faith is strong in it" (*Conn. Yankee*, 336–37).

Samuel Clemens realized the importance of the patient's trust in the healer. He also recognized the value of pomp and circumstance in creating a sense of the healer's majesty and power. The effectiveness of any treatment can be limited by the absence of suitable ceremony. In the Camelot of Clemens's Connecticut Yankee, it was not a coincidence that magic, medicine, ministry, and majesty overlapped.

Samuel Clemens understood that the magician, the medicine man, the priest, and the king all used the same skills and the same props to achieve their influence and success. He knew that the success of a magician depended upon the distraction of incantations and flourishing capes. He realized that clerics used their robes and their rituals to make their own type of magic work: "In other places people operated on a patient's mind, without saying a word to him, and cured him. In others, experts assembled patients in a room and prayed over them, and appealed to their faith, and those patients went away cured" (*Conn. Yankee*, 338). He understood that the methods of magicians and priests were no different from the ways in which kings utilized the power of their crowns and thrones to create their own authority and majesty: "Wherever you find a king who can't cure the king's-evil you can be sure that the most valuable superstition that supports this throne—the subject's belief in the divine appointment of his sovereign—has passed away. In my youth the monarchs of England had ceased to touch for the evil, but there was no occasion for this diffidence: they could have cured it forty-nine times in fifty" (*Conn. Yankee*, 336–37).

As he finally came to understand the process of healing, Clemens realized that effective physicians were no different from successful ministers, monarchs, or magicians—they too knew how to use the mystique of their rituals and the majesty of their words to create their own magical cures.

22

OLD AGE AND BROKEN HEALTH

Providence is after me with a Gatling.

—Mark Twain, letter to Katharine Harrison, January 12, 1903

As Samuel Clemens chased after nontraditional medical systems, he came to understand the paradox that is implicit within the spirit of the healing profession: truth can clash with hope. When distress is at its peak, and when all reasonable options have been exhausted, the offering of even an inkling of hope can be of immeasurable benefit to the patient. In April 1891, after hearing about the declining health of Joe Goodman, a comrade from his early newspaper days in Nevada,[1] Clemens expressed his concern in a letter to his old friend: "It is dreadful to think of you in ill health—I can't realize it; you are always to me the same that you were in those days when matchless health and glowing spirits and delight in life were commonplaces with us. Lord save us all from old age and broken health and a hope-tree that has lost the faculty of putting out blossoms" (*Ltrs/Paine*, 2:546).

"Lord save us all from old age and broken health." Nowhere does Clemens more clearly state his incentive for seeking medical care than in this letter to Goodman. Clemens's greatest concern, though, was not his dread of aging or his fear of broken health. It was the need to be spared from a deeper and more intense type of pain; more than anything else, he needed to avoid the agony that comes from having "a hope-tree that has lost the faculty of putting out blossoms."

Clemens also discovered the conundrum that is associated with medical hope giving. As important as hope is in sustaining the quality of day-to-day existence, does the temporary benefit of a falsely derived hope outweigh the damage that might be caused if the deception were to be discovered? When a clinical situation appears to be bleak, and the chance of recovery seems slim, to offer hope too readily may smack of dishonesty, and the associated perception of insincerity could weaken the doctor-patient bond at the very time it needs to be at its strongest. On the other hand, if an unwarranted optimism might create a better outcome, can the physician afford *not* to take the chance?

Samuel Clemens spent considerable energy trying to sustain the blossoms on his own hope-tree. His attacks of gout cycled through periods of exacerbation and remission. Each flare of the disease caused misery, but it never threatened his survival; any hope for relief offered by a deception such as electrotherapy was valuable to him. In general, the ministrations of alternative medicine seem to be best suited for illnesses with the same characteristics as Clemens's gout—maladies that lack effective treatments, fluctuate in their severity, and are not life-threatening. Little harm is done when such ailments are treated with therapy whose benefit is questionable; as likely as not, the patient may even gain some relief from the belief that the treatment will help. For more severe medical problems such as Livy Clemens's terminal illness with chronic congestive heart failure, the deception of electrotherapy may seem more troubling ethically, but its use as a source of hope was certainly understandable when it became clear that mainstream medicine had nothing at all to offer (not even the thread of hope).

In the last months of his life, Clemens finally did lose all hope. On Christmas Eve 1909, his daughter Jean died from a seizure in her bathtub. In an attempt to distract himself from his profound pain, Clemens sat down to write, but all he could think of were his cumulative losses:

> I lost Susy thirteen years ago; I lost her mother—her incomparable mother!—five and a half years ago; Clara has gone away to live in Europe; and now I have lost Jean. How poor I am, who was once so rich! Seven months ago Mr. Rogers died—one of the best friends I ever had, and the nearest perfect, as man and gentleman, I have yet met among my race; within the last six weeks Gilder has passed away, and Laffan—old, old friends of mine. Jean lies yonder, I sit here. . . . She lies

there, and I sit here—writing, busying myself to keep my heart from breaking. . . .

Would I bring her back to life if I could do it? I would not. If a word would do it, I would beg for strength to withhold the word. And I would have the strength; I am sure of it. In her loss I am almost bankrupt, and my life is a bitterness, but I am content: for she has been enriched with the most precious of all gifts—that gift which makes all other gifts mean and poor—death. (*Autob/MTA*, 372–75)

Samuel Clemens, disconsolate and devoid of hope, died on April 21, 1910, four months after the death of the last blossom on his hope-tree.

To Clemens, many unpleasant things in life were tolerable, but the one thing he could not live without was hope, the ultimate sustainer of the human spirit. He was willing to deceive his wife, his children, and even himself in order to provide the sense of hopefulness that is required to ameliorate the suffering that comes from illness and injury. He knew that many diseases were untreatable, but he also understood that quality of life was closely linked to the patient's attitude and outlook: "The mind cannot heal broken bones, and doubtless there are other physical ills which it cannot heal, but it can greatly help to modify the severities of them all without exception."[2]

Hope, of course, is not delivered to patients in equal quantities by every practitioner of the healing arts. Mainstream medicine, despite its pride in the sophistication of its scientific prowess, has always been vaguely aware of not offering quite as much hope as it might, especially in comparison to the hope-filled generosity of its competitors. Even so, traditional medicine's best practitioners have always understood the value in serving up a modest dollop of hope when there is nothing else to offer a patient. The physician Francis Trudeau once summarized the goals of medicine as "to cure sometimes; to relieve often; to comfort always." Traditional medicine sometimes gets bogged down in its obsession with accomplishing Trudeau's first objective, the cure, and then has difficulty in moving on to the goals of relief and comfort. Alternative medical sects tend to approach Trudeau's dictum in reverse order; they begin with the provision of comfort and relief and have less concern about the concept of cure. This ploy may be at the heart of the success of alternative medicine.

Orthodox medicine's desire is to provide every patient with a cure; nontraditional medicine's goal is to give every patient a sense of hope. To give a placebo is to give hope. Practitioners of alternative medicine are generous in their use of placebo, which is the center of their therapeutic plan. Many allopathic physicians, as they strive for a cure, would deny that they would ever use placebo therapy in their quest to cure a patient. The loudest denials may come from those who routinely greet every patient with an encouraging pat on the back, a warm smile, and caring words of concern, not realizing that they are using some of the most effective placebos there are. For some doctors, these unacknowledged gestures of caring are a natural part of their professional style; they come automatically and without thought. For others, any attempt to provide comfort comes only as an allopathic afterthought, offered only when the physician realizes that the cure he strives to accomplish is not possible.

Allopathic medicine, with its long tradition of excesses of therapy, somehow feels inhibited from offering up the pure unadulterated hope so freely dispensed by its alternative competitors. Instead, mainstream medicine blends the placebo that is known as hope into its formulations only as a filler, never as the primary active agent. It is clear that the optimal amount of truth, combined with a sufficient amount of hope to create a full therapeutic dose, can become an exceptionally useful treatment. Achieving the right mixture of the two ingredients is always a challenge; a doctor's supplies of truth and hope are rarely stocked in the optimal ratio for any single patient. To overdose a patient with hope unbuffered by a realistic quantity of truth will create just one more version of alternative medicine, even as too much "truth" (unleavened by hope) can produce a despondency that is more toxic than the patient's original disease. "It is the net effect of the health and hope the physician can offer the patient that justifies the special relationship between the two," Dr. W. R. Phillips has noted. In a discussion of the ethics of placebo therapy, Phillips observes, "Nothing but the truth would prove a miserable medicine."[3]

As scientific advances have increased the ability of mainstream medicine to deliver cures, practitioners of allopathic medicine have become, if anything, less skilled in their ability to deliver hope. The antibiotic era created an arrogance of medical invincibility against infection in which cure became the only acceptable outcome. Nature is never static, however, and the emergence of new infections and resistant organisms created a new medical humility that has forced some physicians to rediscover the skills that had been so useful to their predecessors. Dr. Abraham Verghese has sensitively discussed the shift in paradigm that the human immunodeficiency virus (HIV) created for the infectious disease specialists who, up to that time, had been living in the "conceit of cure."

Most of us found out, painfully, that in having no cure to offer, we actually had everything to offer. We discovered what the word "healing" meant and what made the horse-and-buggy doctor of a century ago so effective.... All illness (particularly AIDS) has these two dimensions: a physical deficit and a spiritual violation. And when there is no cure, the one thing we can offer is to really understand the story that is playing out, to aid and abet its satisfactory solution.[4]

This emphasis on the importance of providing care when there is no cure is not a new medical philosophy. It is a concept that permeates the history of medical practice. It is the basis for an old adage of the pre-antibiotic era that recommended "opium and lies" as the optimal therapy for tuberculosis.[5] Curing and caring require different sets of skills and attitudes, and most doctors are more comfortable and skilled in providing one than the other. Dr. Howard Spiro has made the observation that physicians live simultaneously in two conflicting worlds, "the world of science, which provides them with their knowledge of disease, very real advances against those diseases, and current ideals, and the world of people, with instincts, pain, suffering, hope, and joy." The challenge, as Spiro notes, arises from the fact that these two worlds appear to be incompatible: "The first is the universe of physics, the second the realm of the poet."[6] Samuel Clemens was familiar with both of these worlds. He understood that neither the world of hard science nor the world of soft humanitarianism could by itself provide him with every answer for every problem. He realized that it was impossible to find a life of meaning entirely in one world or the other. Each of the worlds brought its unique gifts; each created its own set of problems. The boundaries between science and art are not distinct, and the world of medicine exists at the borders where the universe of physics overlaps with the realm of the poet. When Samuel Clemens could not find what he needed in one of the worlds, he was never reluctant to look in the other. When he sought medical care, his greatest desire was to identify a method of therapy that was based at the interface of science and humanism; his greatest hope was to find a physician who could be effective and comfortable in both worlds.

In the last years of his life, as his overwhelming grief from personal losses seemed never-ending and as illness and death appeared to be the only constants in his family's life, Clemens found great solace in his correspondence with his close friend the Reverend Joseph Twichell. Twichell had the personal qualities that made him a source of comfort and emotional healing, and Clemens recognized that these were the very characteristics that would have made Twichell a superb physician: "You have something divine in you that is not in other men. You have the touch that heals, not lacerates. And you know the secret places of our hearts. You know our life—the outside of it—as the others do—and the inside of it—which they do not. You have seen our whole voyage. You have seen us go to sea, a cloud of sail, and the flag at the peak; and you see us now, chartless, adrift—derelicts; battered, water-logged, our sails a ruck of rags, our pride gone."[7]

Samuel Clemens had come to learn that healing was not to be confused with elusive "cure." Cures were rarely achieved, but healing was always possible at some level. He understood that healing is both a physical and a spiritual process. It has very little to do with the particular details of a specific therapeutic regimen or the underlying philosophy of any single medical system. In the final analysis, as Clemens had come to learn so well, healing is nothing more and nothing less than the product of a positive interaction between two human beings. One of these is a person in need—an individual who has been "adrift" and "battered" and "water-logged," with all pride destroyed. And the other? Someone who, in the words of Sam Clemens, has a "touch that heals," a person who knows "the secret places of our heart" and who possesses the trait that Samuel Clemens described as "something divine"—the ability to care.

Clemens never did find exactly what he was looking for, but he avoided becoming a therapeutic nihilist by embracing a philosophy of therapeutic eclecticism. Although he was recognized for the cynicism of his later years, he maintained a cautious medical optimism. He avoided medical despondency through the hope that there is always *something* that can be done to improve the human condition. He recognized that panacea was a fantasy, but he allowed his medical belief system to evolve to the point that he could envision an eclectic approach in which some benefit might be derived from almost every system. He came to the conclusion that "no art of healing is the best for *all* ills. I should distribute the ailments around: surgery cases to the surgeons; lupus to the actinic-ray specialist; nervous prostration to the Christian Scientist; most ills to the allopath and the homeopath; (in my own particular case) rheumatism, gout and bronchial attacks to the osteopathist" (*Ltrs/Paine*, 2:733–34).

Clemens had many reasons to pursue oddball and offbeat medical therapies. He was very sensitive to the fragility and uncertainty of life. He had seen firsthand that traditional medical approaches were often unsuccessful and frequently dangerous. He had been far too young when he saw so many of his friends and relatives die. With this state of mind,

Clemens had no hesitation in considering alternative approaches. He realized, however, that his mother's nonsystematic approach was not the answer either, and he understood that pure random experimentation could create illness in its own right. Although he had many concerns about allopathic medicine, he did learn from his mother that he could use it as a fallback system while he was looking for a better approach (and, in spite of his criticisms, allopathy *did* seem to be of benefit at times). Even as he was arguing in support of osteopathy to the New York legislators, he was willing to admit that "sometimes my mother's experiments had such an effect upon me that she was obliged to call in 'that ministering angel with the pills' to bring me around. And remembering that, I do not bar allopathy from my experiments now. No, I am willing to take a chance at that for old times' sake. My mother three times tried new remedies on me, and they left me so low that they had to pull me out by means of the family doctor" (*MT Speaking*, 387).

In general, however, his annoyance with his mother's helter-skelter approach to medical care paled before the animosity he directed toward the illogical and dangerous excesses of allopathy's "heroic measures." His mother could be forgiven for being naive and well-intentioned, but the medical establishment's seemingly purposeful and unquestionably dangerous ignorance was unforgivable. Clemens used allopathic medicine's selective use of its most toxic treatments as a metaphor when he attacked organized religion's tendency to prescribe the biblical poisons of hellfire and eternal damnation while it overlooked the ecclesiastical pharmacopeia's stock of mercy, forgiveness, and the milk of human kindness.

> The Christian's Bible is a drugstore. Its contents remain the same; but the medical practice changes. For eighteen hundred years these changes were slight—scarcely noticeable. The practice was allopathic—allopathic in its rudest and crudest form. The dull and ignorant physician day and night, and all the days and all the nights, drenched his patient with vast and hideous doses of the most repulsive drugs to be found in the store's stock; he bled him, cupped him, purged him, puked him, salivated him, never gave his system a chance to rally, nor nature a chance to help. He kept him religion-sick for eighteen centuries, and allowed him not a well day during all that time. The stock in the store was made up of about equal portions of baleful and debilitating poisons, and healing and comforting medicines; but the practice of the time confined the physician to the use of the former; by consequence, he could only damage his patient, and that is what he did.[8]

The medicine of the early nineteenth century was not meaningfully different from the medicine of the preceding two thousand years,[9] and no one was more critically aware of this clinical stagnation than Samuel Clemens.

> [W]hen I was an urchin, nothing was much different from what it had always been in the world. Take a single detail, for example—medicine. Galen could have come into my sick-room at any time during my first seven years... and he could have sat down there and stood my doctor's watch without asking a question. He would have smelt around among the wilderness of cups and bottles and vials on the table and the shelves, and missed not a stench that used to glad him two thousand years before, nor discovered one that was of a later date.... And if our reverend doctor came and found him there, he would be dumb with awe, and would get down and worship him. (*£1m Bank-note*, 242–43)

Samuel Clemens had seen very positive outcomes from extremely bizarre interventions by nontraditional healers. He did not have much confidence in any medical sect, but he carried the hope that, somewhere, he would find a system that was valid. Clemens was also a contrarian at heart. He loved the renegade perspective. He was enthusiastic in his skepticism for the ideas and attitudes and proclamations of the so-called experts. He believed that the majority's viewpoint was likely to be the wrong viewpoint, particularly in scientific and medical issues.

> A consensus consisting of all the medical experts in Great Britain made fun of Jenner and inoculation. A Consensus consisting of all the medical experts in France made fun of the stethoscope. A Consensus of all the medical experts in Germany made fun of that young doctor (his name? forgotten by all but doctors, now, revered now by doctors alone) who discovered and abolished the cause of that awful disease, puerperal fever; made fun of him, reviled him, hunted him, persecuted him, broke his heart, killed him.[10] ...And do look at Pasteur and his majestic honor roll of prodigious benefactions! Damned—each and every one of them in its turn—by frenzied and ferocious Consensuses of medical and chemical experts comprising, for years, every member of the tribe in Europe; damned without even a casual look at what he was doing— and he pathetically imploring them to come and take at least one little look before making the damnation eternal. They shortened his life by their malignities and persecutions; and thus robbed the world of the further and priceless services of a man who—among certain lines and within certain limits—had done more for the human race than any

other one man in all of its long history; a man whom it had taken the Expert brotherhood ten thousand years to produce, and whose mate and match the brotherhood may possibly not be able to bring forth and assassinate in another ten thousand. The preacher has an old and tough reputation for bullheaded and unreasoning hostility to new light; why, he is not "in it" with the doctor! Nor, perhaps with some of the other breeds of Experts that sit around and get up the Consensuses and squelch the new things as fast as they come from the hands of the plodders, the searchers, the inspired dreamers, the Pasteurs that come bearing pearls to scatter in the Consensus sty.

This is warm work! It puts my temperature up to 106 and raises my pulse to the limit. It always works just so when the red rag of a Consensus jumps my fence and starts across my pasture. I have been a Consensus more than once myself, and I know the business—and its vicissitudes. . . .

These sorrows have made me suspicious of Consensuses. Do you know, I tremble and the goose flesh rises on my skin every time I encounter one, now. (*CT-2*, 649–50)

It was obvious to Clemens that Jenner and Pasteur and the "young doctor" Ignaz Semmelweiss were unrecognized geniuses and legitimate medical heroes, and their achievements were magnified further by the ridicule and condemnation they received from their contemporaries. Clemens knew that scientific advancement is never stagnant, and he had no doubt that his own generation was capable of overlooking new medical breakthroughs of equally revolutionary magnitude. It was impossible to predict who would turn out to be the next Jenner, Pasteur, or Semmelweiss.

Clemens knew that allopathy, hydropathic medicine, electrotherapy, osteopathic medicine, and rest cure did not have all the answers to every medical problem. His personal experience taught him that, as different as they were, each of these systems could be beneficial, at least some of the time. Mrs. Utterback was a simple farm woman with no medical training, yet she was able to cure Jane Clemens's toothache because Jane Clemens trusted in her competence. Mrs. Utterback exhorted her patient to "Believe!"; Jane Clemens *did* believe, and her toothache was healed. Dr. Newton may have been a quack, but he was a convincing quack; when no one else could do so, he convinced Livy Langdon to sit up, get out of her bed, and walk. Samuel Clemens believed that starvation could overcome illnesses, and it did; then he understood that it was his *belief* ("mind cure") that was the curative agent, not the starvation. Clemens believed in osteopathy and hydrotherapy, and they helped him the most when he could believe in them the most. He discovered that electrotherapy could cure his gout—when he had faith in it. He was not surprised to learn that, in centuries past, tuberculosis of the lymph glands had seemingly been cured by the touch of a king. It appeared that almost any treatment—any mummery—could cure, if the patient and the healer had a shared faith in it.

Eventually, the theories that explained how the various treatments worked were not of any significance to Clemens. There did not seem to be any perfect way to find out why people got sick or to determine the best way to make them well. None of the popular theories about disease and treatment seemed consistent, and they less frequently seemed logical, but many of the methods were effective anyway. Perhaps Clemens stated his opinion on such theories best through the words of Huckleberry Finn in *Tom Sawyer Abroad*—"theories don't prove nothing, they only give you a place to rest on, a spell, when you are tuckered out butting around and around trying to find out something there ain't no way *to* find out."[11]

As Clemens became "tuckered out" in his quest to find the optimal method for treating every disease and every illness—"something there ain't no way to find out"—he found something that was more valuable to him. He discovered that the success of any therapy was less dependent on its underlying theory than it was on its ability to gain the patient's trust and garner the patient's confidence. He learned that virtually any mummery could work if the patient has sufficient faith in it. And, if it worked, perhaps it was not really mummery after all.

Afterword

HELL IS OF NO CONSEQUENCE TO A PERSON WHO DOESN'T LIVE THERE

Man seems to be a rickety poor sort of a thing, any way you take him; a kind of British Museum of infirmities and inferiorities. He is always undergoing repairs . . . man starts in as a child and lives on disease till the end, as a regular diet. He has mumps, measles, whooping cough, croup, tonsilitis, diphtheria, scarlet fever, almost as a matter of course. Afterward, as he goes along, his life continues to be threatened at every turn: by colds, coughs, asthma, bronchitis, itch, cholera, cancer, consumption, yellow fever, bilious fever, typhus fevers, hay fever, ague, chilblains, piles, inflammation of the entrails, indigestion, toothache, earache, deafness, dumbness, blindness, influenza, chicken pox, cow pox, small pox, liver complaint, constipation, bloody flux, warts, pimples, boils, carbuncles, abscesses, bunions, corns, tumors, fistulas, pneumonia, softening of the brain, melancholia and fifteen other kinds of insanity, dysentery, jaundice, diseases of the heart, the bones, the skin, the scalp, the spleen, the kidneys, the nerves, the brain, the blood; scrofula, paralysis, leprosy, neuralgia, palsy, fits, headache, thirteen kinds of rheumatism, forty-six of gout, and a formidable supply of gross and unprintable disorders of one sort and another. . . . He is but a basket of festering offal provided for the support and entertainment of swarming armies of bacilli,—armies commissioned to rot him and destroy him, and each army equipped with a special detail of the work. The process of waylaying him, persecuting him, rotting him, killing him, begins with his first breath, and there is no mercy, no pity, no truce till he draws his last one.

—Mark Twain, "Man's Place in the Animal World"

It is easy enough to become despondent by dwelling on the over-whelming challenges to survival, and Sam Clemens's encounters with disease and death made him at times about as pessimistic as any human being could be. In 1905, he wrote "Three Thousand Years among the Microbes," narrated from the viewpoint of a cholera germ. The disease-producing bacterium is disgusted with the characteristics of its human host; from the vantage point of the cholera germ, the human body is nothing better than "a sewer, a reek of decay, a charnel house, [that] con-tains swarming nations of all the different kinds of germ-vermin that have been invented" (*WWD&OSW*, 436).

Disease and suffering appeared to be inescapable components of life in the nineteenth century. Sam Clemens pursued most of the medical options that were available to him as he sought ways to neutralize the inexorable march of pathology that often seemed to be directed specifi-cally toward himself and his family. He found great frustration along the way, but his experiences gave him some valuable insights into medical issues that are equally relevant today.

For today's patient, as for Clemens, allopathic medicine is the stan-dard by which other all medical systems are judged. Anyone who is im-pressed with the level of sophistication that has been reached by mod-ern medicine might argue that the educated patients of today would never submit themselves to the toxicities of puking and purging that were the typical approaches used by the allopathic physicians of Clemens's day. However, the experiences of any modern-day patient who has under-gone chemotherapy, or who has had his intestinal tract "cleaned out" in preparation for a colonoscopy, would make a strong argument that many features of medicine have not changed so much from Clemens's day. Today's patients accept such unpleasantness because of the knowledge that there will ultimately be a medical benefit, just as nineteenth-century patients "knew" that purging, blistering, and bloodletting were going to benefit them.

Nor, in general, have the alternatives to allopathy changed much since Clemens's day. Andrew Still's osteopathic medicine has blurred itself into becoming another version of allopathic medicine, far more main-stream than alternative, and no longer recognizable as the distinct and separate medical discipline that had been created by its founder. Chiro-practic "medicine" has become the new "medicine of manipulation" by jumping into the niche that was created as the osteopaths defected into the allopathic world. Homeopathy is still out there, but it is no longer taught in schools that are dedicated to its principles; instead, self-proclaimed experts now dispense their own homeopathic "treatments" to anyone who will believe in their methodology. Patent medicines have not disappeared but have instead evolved into the "nutritional supplements" of the health food store. Electrical treatments can still be found in many versions. Faith healing seems to be as popular as ever. The medicine of the twenty-first century is simply an updated version of the nineteenth-century model, and Sam Clemens's comments on medical care are as valid today as when he first voiced them.

When he was at his most despondent and cynical, Clemens could be absolutely venomous in his criticism of the medical profession. In some ways, he thought, it might be just as well that physicians are so inept, and he wrote a hypothetical scenario describing the important roles played by war and incompetent doctors in controlling the planet's population. "When the population reached five billions the earth was heavily burdened to support it.... Necessarily our true hope did not and could not lie in spasmodic famine and pestilence, whose effects could be only temporary, but in war and the physicians, whose help is constant" (*Ltrs-Earth*, 81–82).

While in this cynical mind-set, Clemens speculated about the problems that would occur if medical practice ever developed to the point of doing more good than harm to the people it treated. The result, he argued, would be calamitous, for then only war would remain as an efficient mechanism for keeping the world's population at a manageable level.

In the past fifty years science has reduced the doctor's effectiveness by half. He uses but one deadly drug now, where formerly he used ten. Improved sanitation has made whole regions healthy which were previously not so. It has been discovered that the majority of the most useful and fatal diseases are caused by microbes of various breeds; very well, they have learned how to render the efforts of those microbes innocuous. As a result, yellow fever, black plague, cholera, diphtheria, and nearly every valuable distemper we had are become but entertainments for the idle hour, and are of no more value to the State than is the stomach-ache. Marvelous advances in surgery have been added to our disasters. They remove a diseased stomach now, and the man gets along better and cheaper than he did before. If a man loses a faculty, they bore into his skull and restore it. They take off his legs and arms, and refurnish him from the mechanical junk-ship, and he is as good as new. They give him a new nose if the needs it; new entrails; new bones; new teeth; glass eyes; silver tubes to swallow through; in a word, they take him to pieces and make him over again, and he can stand twice as much wear and tear as he could before. They do these things by help of antiseptics and anaesthesia, and there is no gangrene and no pain. . . .

What, then, is the grand result of all this microbing and sanitation and surgery? This—which is appalling: the death-rate has been reduced to *1,200 in the million.* And foolish people rejoice at it and boast about it! It is a serious matter. It promises to double the globe's population every twelve months. In time there will not be room in the world for the people to stand, let alone sit down. . . .

Honor to whom honor is due: the physician failed us, war has saved us. Not that the killed and wounded amount to anything as a relief, for they do not; but the poverty and desolation caused by war sweep myriads away and make space for immigrants. War is a rude friend, but a kind one. It keeps us down to sixty billion and saves the hard-grubbing world alive. (*Ltrs-Earth*, 82–83)

Although the major point of this passage is its antiwar message, Clemens has used medicine as a foil to help him drive home his argument. War and medicine can both be terrible and destructive forces, he seems to be saying, but at least there is the hope that medicine will evolve into a more benevolent activity. War will not. By comparing the destructive potential of medicine to the devastation of war, Clemens has made an important observation. As medicine evolves, it will continue to bring about changes that can have either positive or negative results. Some will be predictable and purposeful, but many others will be unintended. However, no matter how much medical science progresses, and regardless of the number of astounding advances and advantages it might create, traditional medicine will never be so dominant as to stand alone; alternative or complementary medical practices will always remain part of the equation. Clemens's experiences demonstrate that alternative medicine is not only ubiquitous but also timeless. Samuel Clemens understood that there is something about human nature that demands alternatives—no matter how many options are available, there is always a desire to have at least one more choice. Clemens believed in a free-market approach to medicine. He thought that any system that wanted to take a chance at succeeding should be allowed to do so. In stating his opposition to governmental intrusion into the regulation of health care, he warned that

the mania for giving the Government power to meddle with the private affairs of cities or citizens is likely to cause endless trouble, through the rivalry of schools and creeds that are anxious to obtain official recognition, and there is great danger that our people will lose that independence of thought and action which is the cause of much of our greatness, and sink into the helplessness of the Frenchman or German who expects his government to feed him when hungry, clothe him when naked, to prescribe when his child may be born and when he may die, and, in fine, to regulate every act of humanity from the cradle to the tomb, including the manner in which he may seek future admission to paradise. (*CT-1*, 230)

In Clemens's day, orthodox medicine had little to offer patients. For the most severe illnesses, such as heart failure or meningitis, no effective treatments existed. Thus, it was not unreasonable for patients of the nineteenth century to choose among the available health care options to find a system that fulfilled their expectations. A patient's likelihood of perishing or surviving was far more dependent on the nature of the disease and the body's ability to rebuff the threat than on the type of treatment. Outcomes were largely unrelated to whether therapy was sought from a physician of the allopathic, hydropathic, osteopathic, or homeopathic persuasion, unless the toxicity of the treatment hastened the patient's demise (which was a real risk of allopathic treatment). For the less severe illnesses in which recovery to full health was the expectation, the specific type of medical care administered was also irrelevant to the final outcome. As a result, there was much to be said for seeking out the practitioner who was willing to give the patient the answers he wanted to hear; this was the approach adopted by Clemens as he suffered from recurring episodes of gout, as he wrote on October 2, 1897: "It was three years ago, in Paris, when I had my first attack of gout. The first physician forbade red wine but allowed whisky; the second forbade whisky but allowed red wine; the third—but by your own experience you see how it ended: by consulting six doctors I achieved permission to drink anything I wanted to—except water. The trouble with less thoughtful people is, that they stop with one doctor" (Ltr-Pötzel).

In the twenty-first century, allopathic medicine will achieve more successes than it did in Clemens's era, but it will create an equivalent toxicity in doing so. And, as always, self-resolving ailments will still improve spontaneously. For some patients, the pursuit of complementary or alternative medical care can be very reassuring, and it can give them a sense of control over their destiny. In so doing, the nontraditional systems will continue to be of great importance to those who subscribe to them.

Today, as was the case in Clemens's lifetime, the popularity of the alternative systems is created by the divergent perspectives of doctors and patients on the meaning of a patient's sickness. Doctors use a vantage point that they call "disease" to help them visualize the basis of a patient's symptoms. A disease is a biomedical process that can be described in a textbook; it has consistent and predictable effects in every person it strikes; it is not influenced by national borders or religious beliefs or the century in which it occurs. When physicians can put a name on a disease, they have "made a diagnosis." Terms such as *diabetes, congestive heart failure, lung cancer,* and *appendicitis* are examples of processes represented by the concept of disease. The terminology of disease is the invention of physicians, but it is accepted as valid by both doctors and patients. Disease is not the same thing as "illness," which is the process that makes a patient feel bad. Illness is a far less concrete concept than disease. Unlike a disease, an illness is not a specific biomedical entity; instead, it is the way a patient *experiences* a sickness. Illness is, at its core, the *suffering* of the individual. It can manifest itself as discomfort or dysfunction. It is a personal experience, but it is also a social experience that is influenced by cultural factors as well as by the patient's educational level, belief systems, and expectations.

Patients often define their illnesses in terms that are not suitable for use by a doctor in making a diagnosis. Patients may report that they have a "sick headache" or a "nervous stomach," or are "worried to death," or sometimes are "just too exhausted to get up in the morning to face another day." These are all legitimate terms in the patient's vocabulary of illness. Unfortunately, they are not easily translated into the doctor's disease-oriented idiom.[1] Thus, when a patient suffers from an illness, the physician is not always able to make a diagnosis, especially when the nature of the patient's suffering does not correspond to any recognizable or established disease. Doctors try to understand illness in the context of a disease, but for many patients there may not be an identifiable disease that can be correlated with the symptoms. For such patients, according to Dr. Frank Davidoff, "illness itself can probably only be understood through metaphor."[2]

Even in the absence of disease, a skilled and experienced physician may still be able to help the patient deal with illness through the use of thoughtful communication, empathy, and compassion. In general, however, scientifically based medicine struggles with recognizing and treating "illness" because of the unfamiliar vocabulary and inconsistent manifestations. The world of textbook-defined "disease" is the more comfortable domain of allopathic medicine, even though many patients have problems that lie outside this domain. It is the failure of traditional medicine to deal effectively with the concept of illness that creates the opportunities for complementary and alternative medical systems to blossom.

When Samuel Clemens suffered his first painful episode of gout, he discovered the tension that can arise between patient and doctor as a result of their differing perceptions about illness and disease; it was clear that Clemens's gout did not carry the same significance for the physician as it did for the patient. Clemens's doctor was interested in gout as a disease, but Clemens himself understood his gout only as a source of profound misery.

> When we got the doctor at last, he said it was only the gout, and an attack of no importance. He seemed to regard it as a pleasure trip. He gave me a hypodermic and appeared to think the business was done— which it wasn't. At the end of ten minutes another. It didn't phaze that pain a bit. So he began to respect it himself, I think. After half an hour he gave me another, and that made me very comfortable. . . . I can bear my foot on the floor this morning. However, I am not kept back by the gout; the gout is no consequence; the doctor says so himself; neither is hell, to a person who doesn't live there. (*Ltrs-Rogers*, 96)

As Clemens's personal experience with the gout demonstrated, physicians are at risk of becoming jaded and insensitive due to their daily exposures to patients who are in distress. Doctors are taught about diseases, and it is easy for them to assume that the illnesses suffered by their patients are no different from the diseases they have learned about. Nothing could be further from the truth. Not only are disease and illness separate entities, but it is possible for illness and suffering to exist even in the absence of any disease. Because of this, a doctor and a patient may have very different perspectives on the source of the patient's suffering, as Samuel Clemens discovered when he was stricken with gout in 1894, and as Dr. Allen Shaughnessy explained in a 1999 letter to the *Annals of Internal Medicine:*

> The goal of orthodox medicine is to prevent, diagnose, treat, and possibly cure disease. Patients have these goals, but only as long as they offer a relief of "suffering." Suffering may be due to pain, bodily symptoms, or any perceived or actual threat that may endanger the intactness of the person. Suffering is not the same as pain and, indeed, may not even be due to a disease process. Treatment may or may not relieve suffering, and improvement of the disease may worsen suffering.[3]

Samuel Clemens understood something about the differences between the viewpoints of doctor and patient when he disputed with his own physician about the severity of an illness: "The doctor says I am on the verge of being a sick man . . . that may be true enough while I am lying abed all day trying to persuade his cantankerous, rebellious medicines to agree with each other . . . I feel as young and healthy as anybody, and as to being on the verge of being a sick man I don't take any stock in that. I have been on the verge of being an angel all my life, but it's never happened yet."[4]

Samuel Clemens's unfinished novel *Which Was It?* contains a masterful study of the differences between illness and disease, with a particularly insightful view of the differing perceptions of doctors and patients. In the story, George Harrison suffers from symptoms related to guilt after he discovers he was responsible for the death of a mill hand by the name of Jake Bleeker. Harrison becomes overwhelmed by a "ghastly sinking at the heart." His suffering is an illness that creates terrible symptoms for him. He does not have a medical disease, but everything that had been meaningful in his life disappears as his sense of guilt escalates. Clemens appears to speak from personal experience as he describes Harrison's remorse at being responsible for the death of another person: "It is an overwhelming moment, the last perfection of human misery, it is death in life; we do not know how to take up our burden again, the world is empty, the zest of existence is gone" (*WWD&OSW*, 242). This passage was autobiographical, for Harrison's symptoms were similar to the anguish and guilt—the "death in life"—that Clemens himself had suffered from his own sense of personal responsibility in the deaths of the tramp Dennis McDermid, his brother Henry, and his son, Langdon.

As the story continues, Harrison becomes increasingly hopeful that his role in Bleeker's death may never be discovered, but he still finds no relief—the apparent success of his deception only increases his misery further, and his dishonesty becomes an illness in its own right. This illness is caused not by a germ but by his deceit. His fraud has become the pathogen that is destroying him: "His ghastly secrets . . . made him sick. He couldn't rid *himself* of them, and that was the main misery. They gangrened the very heart and soul of him" (*WWD&OSW*, 267). As his distress mounts, Harrison is visited by "Deathshead Phillips," a frightening apparition "clothed from skull-cap to stockings in dead and lustreless black," a Grim Reaper with "the face of a ghost; a strenuous white, a ghastly white, dead and lustreless" (*WWD&OSW*, 268). "Deathshead" has come to warn Harrison that his death is imminent. The distress of

Harrison's increasing guilt and self-recrimination sends him to his sick-bed, and the local physician is called in to evaluate a man who is very ill but who has no disease.

> Dr. Bradshaw had been sent for. He arrived now, and made an elaborate examination of the patient and asked a multitude of questions, on a medical basis of a couple of generations earlier, science and the fashions being about that far behind, out West. He questioned Harrison for small-pox; for measles; for phthisis; for liver complaint; for whooping-cough; for cholera morbus; for fits; for "yaller janders," for bots, heaves, scrofula, blind staggers, gravel, hydrophobia—for every ailment mentioned in the books, in fact—and never got a responsive symptom. He was puzzled. Here was a very sick man; he could see that; yet there was nothing the matter with him. Not a thing, so far as he could see. (*WWD&OSW*, 285–86)

Harrison *is* a sick man. Although Dr. Bradshaw may not be particularly up to date in the line of his medical questioning,[5] he is clearly in search of a disease that will explain Harrison's declining condition. Even as Harrison declares "I am a sick man" (*WWD&OSW*, 284), and even as Bradshaw's observations confirm that his patient is "a very sick man" (*WWD&OSW*, 286), Bradshaw is stymied and unable to diagnose Harrison's disease. Bradshaw's problem is the eternal dilemma that haunts every physician. Bradshaw is a doctor, and he is looking for a *disease*—measles, tuberculosis, or rabies. Harrison, his patient, does not have a disease; instead, he has an *illness*. Harrison is infested with the most destructive type of guilt and disgrace. He shows no outward signs of any physical disease, but his psyche is being consumed by a sequestered shame that has "gangreened the very heart and soul of him." It is not very likely that Bradshaw (who is educated in the ways of disease) will be able to help Harrison (who is suffering from an illness of the spirit). Bradshaw would immediately recognize a gangrenous leg that is threatening a patient's life, but the concept of a gangrenous soul is outside the realm of his understanding.

This impasse between the patient and the doctor is a common juncture in medical practice, a point in the relationship where the two often come to a mutually unsatisfactory stalemate. For patients who are suffering from the spectrum of symptoms that compose most illnesses, traditional medical evaluation—no matter how thorough—can never fully satisfy their expectations. Test after test comes back negative, and the disease-seeking physician becomes more and more convinced that he will never identify a serious medical problem, even as the patient becomes more and more convinced that the doctor is inept. Symptoms continue without explanation, with a chronicity that begins to bother the patient more and more, even as it reassures the physician that there is no serious problem. Physicians have their own way of looking at such situations: "Experiencing symptoms is part of normality. Most of these symptoms are not associated with clear-cut biomedical diagnoses, and most do not lead to any use of medical services. The symptoms are then referred to as 'medically unexplained' or 'functional,' the latter term suggesting an alteration of function rather than of structure."[6]

The chronicity of symptoms has the opposite effect on the patient and the doctor. The patient is increasing distressed at the lack of a diagnosis; the doctor is increasingly comforted that the patient cannot be harboring a significant disease. Because the symptoms cannot be correlated with a definitive diagnosis, but the doctor is not able to prove to the patient's satisfaction that there is *not* a disease, the "maybe diseases" have a chance to settle in and take up housekeeping on a permanent basis. The "maybe diseases" become chronic illnesses for these patients, and they continue to cause them suffering long after they have ceased to be a concern of the clinician (who has long since come to accept that the patient's symptoms will never be explained, but is satisfied that they will never cause harm). The allopathic physician has been trained to treat "serious disease," and although he may never know what a patient's "maybe disease" is, he does know one thing for sure—the "maybe disease" is not a "serious disease," and in any case he has no treatment for it. This situation creates most of the market for alternative care; in a survey across medical specialties, between one-third and two-thirds of patients who are evaluated in medical clinics never get a medical explanation for their symptoms. Unexplained symptoms occur more commonly in women and in younger age groups, and these patients are more likely to pursue alternative care therapies than those who have received a biomedical explanation for their symptoms.[7]

In truth, most physicians just do not know how to proceed when they can not identify a textbook-defined disease to explain the misery of a patient. When a patient manifests symptoms that do not correspond to any recognized disease, he has unknowingly violated the doctor's rules of disease, which proclaim that symptoms are permissible only when they can be correlated with a definitive diagnosis. Such a patient may be suspected of being "somatic," or overly focused on his body and trivial symptoms. This conflict often creates an adversarial situation in which "the physician act[s] as a kind of referee . . . a suspicion of somatization [represents] a kind of blowing the whistle on a patient, a determination that he or she is not playing by the rules of sickness."[8]

When a physician questions the validity of a patient's symptoms (a common response when symptoms are not congruent with any known disease process), the doctor's doubt is usually obvious to the patient. The doctor's skepticism frequently has an adverse effect on the course of the patient's illness, and the unexplained symptoms seem to dig their roots ever deeper into the persona of the afflicted patient. When a doctor questions the significance of a patient's symptoms, the resulting tension creates an environment that is not conducive to healing. When a doctor does not understand and is not able to explain the cause of a patient's symptoms, the patient has few options, and getting better is not one of them—for patients who find themselves in such a bind, the "only way to prove the veracity of their distress, in the face of doubt, disbelief, and stigma, is to continue to experience it." When a patient is compelled to expend a great effort to establish the legitimacy of the sick role, there is little energy left for healing: "If you have to prove you are ill, you can't get well," explained Nortin Hadler in a 1996 discussion of the challenges of treating patients with fibromyalgia.[9] This standoff between patient and doctor was the basis for Livy Langdon's continuing paralysis despite the efforts of "all the great physicians" who came to Elmira. When qualified physicians were unable to determine Livy's diagnosis or do anything to help her, an impasse was created—because the doctors could not find a diagnosis, they did not have any therapy to offer, but a spontaneous recovery would raise the possibility that she may have been malingering all along. In this regard, Dr. Newton had a significant advantage over the traditional physicians. His rules of illness were far simpler than theirs. He did not insist on having a diagnosis before he was willing to treat. He did not even require his patient to "prove" she was ill. Livy did not have to prove *anything* to him. By simplifying the rules, Newton gave Livy a chance to get better.

Indeed, much of the popularity of alternative care systems may arise from the fact that nontraditional practitioners do not require their patients to prove they are sick, in contrast to allopathic physicians, who in general are reluctant to treat a patient unless a "disease" has been diagnosed. When Clemens created his fictional Dr. Bradshaw in *Which Was It?* he invented an allopathic physician who was more open-minded than most about such things. Bradshaw had no idea why his patient George Harrison was ill, but he was not hesitant in defining the type of treatment he wanted to pursue: "in such cases there was but one thing to do: so he treated him for suppressed itch."[10] Even though he had not established a diagnosis that would account for Harrison's symptoms, Bradshaw realized it was necessary to treat his patient for *something* if the man was to have any hope of recovering. Bradshaw's approach parallels the one taken by Dr. Newton in helping Livy Langdon recover from her paralysis. Newton may have succeeded where the traditional physicians failed because his only requirement was that she trust him. Dr. S. Weir Mitchell, nineteenth-century neurologist and neurasthenia expert, treated some of the same patients who had supposedly been cured previously by "the charlatan Newton," and it was Mitchell's observation that the type of patient most likely to be responsive to Newton's faith healing would be one "who was merely idea-sick."[11] Whether Livy Langdon was "merely idea-sick" can be debated, but the fact remains that it was the "quack" Dr. Newton who helped her when the allopaths could not.

Although orthodox physicians may not routinely differentiate between the two concepts, alternative medicine practitioners make their living by being keenly aware of the distinctions between disease and illness. Traditional medical practitioners focus on diseases of the physical body, seemingly unaware of the observation of Henry Wheeler Shaw that the "soul has more diseases than the body."[12] The great majority of patients who go to a health care provider are the "worried well" who suffer mainly from anxiety, fear, and worry. It is not unusual for some of the worried well to have clinical findings or laboratory results that hint at the presence of an abnormality. Further evaluation usually shows that such a patient is quite healthy, and the questionable abnormality was only a benign variation of the normal condition. As this is being sorted out, the patient's level of anxiety may escalate further, and the patient will continue to live in a state of "maybe disease" until his concerns are evaluated to his satisfaction. The patient may expect further testing to allay his concerns, even long after the doctor is quite satisfied that the patient has no reason to worry and is comfortable in the belief that additional testing would be unnecessary. At this critical juncture, the quality of a patient's existence may depend far more on the physician's interpersonal skills than on his medical knowledge. "It is more important to know what patient has a disease," advised William Osler, "than to know what disease the patient has."[13] There is no question that some physicians are better suited than others to effectively treat the "worried well"—Charles Dudley Warner, who coauthored *The Gilded Age* with Clemens, astutely observed that "the treatment of disease is a good deal a matter of sympathy" (*Gilded Age*, 283).[14]

The fact remains that up to 80 percent of visits to a doctor are because of symptoms of worry and anxiety that are not related to any disease. This is an extremely important population for anyone who is involved in health care, as Howard Spiro observes: "It is that 80 percent who are eased by complementary approaches, Christian Science, placebos, and other therapies. They compose a very large group, and the help provided by such alternatives is very important."[15] Years earlier, in 1907, Samuel Clemens had come to the same conclusion and used the same statistic, as he wrote in *Christian Science:*

> How much of the pain and disease in the world is created by the imaginations of the sufferers, and then kept alive by those same imaginations? Four-fifths? Not anything short of that, I should think. Can Christian Science banish that four-fifths? I think so. . . . Would this be a new world when that was accomplished? And a pleasanter one—for us well people, as well as for those fussy and fretting sick ones? Would it seem as if there was not as much gloomy weather as there used to be? I think so. (*Christian Sci.*, 53)

Clemens proceeded to expand on the idea that people bring on most of their own illnesses through their unrelenting worries and concerns: "Well, it is the anxiety and fretting about colds, and fevers, and draughts, and getting our feet wet, and about forbidden food eaten in terror of indigestion, that brings on the cold and the fever and the indigestion and the most of our other ailments; and so, if the Science can banish that anxiety from the world I think it can reduce the world's disease and pain about four-fifths" (*Christian Sci.*, 55).

The fact remains that orthodox physicians are trained to treat "real disease," and they tend to feel most comfortable when they are doing so. In contrast, alternative care practitioners have no overwhelming desire to restrict their practices to the 20 percent of the population that suffers from "serious disease" (and, if the truth were to be known, they would just as soon steer clear of such patients). Patients with a high titer of disease have little need for the placebo therapy that is the foundation of complementary and alternative medicine. Instead, such patients require simple truth and traditional medicine—insulin for diabetic ketoacidosis, the cold steel of the surgeon's knife for acute appendicitis, but easy on the smoke and mirrors.

Sam Clemens knew that disease does not respond to placebo in the same way that illness does. Gout, angina, and nearsightedness cannot be cured by mind cure, Christian Science, or chiropractic manipulations, but a headache can be. Alternative care providers recognize the benign nature of the "maybe diseases" that account for 80 percent of visits to doctors, and they are happy to treat them indefinitely. In fact, there is little impetus for them to attack the frustrating "serious diseases" when there is such a large pool of candidates with "maybe diseases." After all, the likelihood of death and a subsequent lawsuit is much greater when patients with serious disease are treated, and, in any case, "there is a nearly bottomless reservoir of people who are well or who have 'maybe disease'" who can provide all the business a nontraditional practitioner could ever desire.[16]

Medical science is always evolving, but it has never been capable of effectively treating every disease that comes its way. Sam Clemens's gout was a disease, and so was Jean Clemens's seizure disorder. Her seizures were caused by inappropriate and chaotic discharges of the brain's electrical energy, and they could have been prevented by medications that alter the threshold for the conduction of electrical currents if she had lived a century later. The medical armamentarium of the nineteenth century did not have the necessary weaponry, however, and her father knew it: "No doctor will ever do her any good; that is perfectly plain. The best in the world have had charge of her for 3 years and haven't made an inch of progress toward a cure" (*Ltrs-Rogers*, 406). Clemens had two options for dealing with Jean's seizures. He could pursue alternatives that offered little hope, or he could do nothing and remove all hope. He was a parent. He made the obvious, understandable choice. He didn't give up. He provided hope.

Jean's seizures were so incapacitating that Clemens was driven to alternative therapies when traditional medicine failed, but the argument in favor of nontraditional therapy may be even more compelling for medical problems that are less severe (particularly when the patient is disabled from the illness). If the level of illness is high but the amount of disease is minimal, as was the case for neurasthenia, there is a great deal of benefit to be derived from placebo and its variants. And with the neurasthenic it did not seem to matter which remedy was employed. George Beard's electrotherapy program (one hundred to three hundred dollars for a three-to-six-month session), Weir Mitchell's rest cure, Rachel Gleason's hydrotherapy, Newton's "mind-cure" (with a fifteen-thousand-dollar charge to the Langdons), and Pinkham's Vegetable Compound (the bargain in the batch at one to two dollars a bottle) were all successful. The main idea was to do *something*, and then let the patient's faith take over; in 1903, a Brooklyn neurologist observed that neurasthenics "are peculiarly liable to suggestion, and the physician who fails to avail himself of its use drops one of the most important articles out of his list of remedial agents. The history of quackery is full of lessons as to the efficacy of faith as the prime agent in healing."[17]

This is not to downplay the role of alternative medicine in dealing with the maladies of humanity. Dr. Alvan Feinstein has observed that "when an ailment such as hysterical paralysis involves highly complex cultural or psychodynamic sources, the orthodox approaches of authoritative professors of neurology, neurosurgery, or even psychiatry may all be ineffectual. A surprising, dramatic unorthodox cure may then be achieved by a charismatic faith healer or a visit to the Shrine of Lourdes." Spiro reminds us that there is an important distinction in the goals of the two types of therapists: "Doctors sometimes cure disease, whereas healers help illness."[18] Traditional physicians strive to cure diseases, and they sometimes forget that it is possible to relieve a tremendous number of symptoms even when they cannot cure a single disease. On the other hand, nontraditional healers never lose track of how they can best help their patients deal with the symptoms that create their distress.

> Alternative medicine practitioners spend time with patients, talking to them and dealing with their problems in a personal as well as medical way. As psychoanalysts have come to realize, their specific rites may be less important than the time they spend and the connections they establish. Placebic communications should not be taken as sham, for different approaches have different symbolic and unexplained meanings for patients. Someone with muscle aches and pains may benefit from a massage or acupuncture, but so will someone who is lonely, and maybe even the patient with headaches.[19]

The nineteenth-century physician Dr. Worthington Hooker noted that homeopathy and the other nontraditional sects attracted patients with chronic complaints. These patients seemed to be always seeking a panacea. The practices of alternative care practitioners seemed especially suited to such patients, whose defining characteristic is that they are "always getting better, but never get well."[20] Dr. Robert Cabot (1868–1939), a leading physician of his era, had a strong interest in the spiritual aspects of medicine even as a medical student at Harvard Medical School in the 1890s. His senior paper, entitled "The Medical Bearing of Mind-Cure," studied Christian Science healing and the medical effects of faith. He expanded the study in 1908 and examined a group of patients who claimed benefit from Christian Science. Cabot found he could divide the patients into two groups. Some had evidence of physical disease, while others had no apparent physical cause for their complaints; Cabot found that mind cure was particularly beneficial for the latter group.[21]

For people who are intrinsically healthy but in desperate need of assurance, alternative medicine often seems preferable to traditional medicine. A major reason for this stems from the tendency of alternative medical sects to present the most positive interpretation of a patient's clinical status, on the premise that negative news can lead to severe damage of a mental or spiritual (and possibly even physical) nature. The "worried well" want nothing more intensely than they want support and hope and reassurance, and alternative medicine's emphasis on hope may be its greatest tool. No one wants to hear bad news, and bad news is not a component of the vocabulary of nontraditional medicine. No one wants to be told that his symptoms are "in his head" either. Even though alternative medicine has been likened to a form of parapsychiatry, its practitioners are well aware of the pejorative implications of such a viewpoint, and they would never hint at such a possibility, as Dr. Surendra Kelwala noted in a letter to the *Journal of the American Medical Association* in 1998: "Patients would rather seek alternative therapies that purport to cure by physical means—e.g., acupuncture, chiropractic, herbal concoctions—than see a psychiatrist or acknowledge that the benefits of alternative medicine mostly lie in faith and are mediated through the mind."[22]

In Samuel Clemens's lifetime, traditional medicine was no more successful than its competition. Since then, technological advances have made allopathic medicine more effective against many types of disease and have allowed it to separate itself from its many competitors. Yet, in spite of (and to some extent, because of) its advances in diagnostic and therapeutic prowess, orthodox medicine has failed to extinguish its competition—if anything, the advances of allopathy have paradoxically made it the major contributor to the continued success of alternative medicine. The toxicity of old-fashioned allopathic medicine created a role for its competitors; a somewhat different toxicity of modern-day allopathic medicine has sustained the success of the same competitors today, in addition to a host of newer alternative versions.

The greatest sin of science-driven conventional medicine may be in its potential for destroying hope, regardless of whether the patient suffers from "disease" or "illness." Bad news has to be given far too often, and it is never what the patient wants to hear. Conventional medicine not only is disadvantaged in comparison to alternative medicine by its need to report unpleasant information, but it is further disadvantaged by the problems inherent in doing it well. Giving bad news is very difficult even for the most sensitive and empathic communicator, and many times it may not be done at all well (particularly by physicians whose entire training has emphasized the medicine of the soma rather than the medicine of the psyche). Frank Davidoff has given the most important principle in delivering bad news: "Although it is important to give bad news, it is unforgivable to give bad news badly." For the doctor, the fact that the message's content is "bad" is the most important part of the message; for the patient, the fact that the message was delivered "badly" is of overwhelming importance. It is easier on the doctor's emotional state if he can deliver bad news in the same impersonal manner in which the news correspondent reports the day's events, but such a degree of detachment on the part of the physician makes the exchange much harder on the patient. Giving a patient bad news without providing emotional support is an unacceptable practice that has been likened to "dropping truth fragmentation bombs."[23]

The epitome of delivering bad news badly can be observed in doctors whose communication methods include "hanging the crepe," the practice of purposefully exaggerating the seriousness of an illness and routinely prognosticating a dismal outcome. The physician may rationalize that this is an approach of kindness, as it prepares the patient and family for the worst and spares them from painful surprises if the patient's condition deteriorates. On the other hand, if the patient does better than predicted, the doctor will gain personal credit for succeeding against overwhelming odds. In reality, it is an intellectually dishonest approach that causes its own brand of pain. The true purpose of hanging crepe is to benefit the reputation of the physician, who always comes out looking good whether the patient rallies or dies. It has been compared to the proposal of seventeenth-century mathematician and philosopher Blaise Pascal in the utility of believing in God—if God exists, the believer benefits immensely; if God does not exist, nothing has been lost by making the wager.[24] Samuel Clemens accused President McKinley's physicians of hanging the crepe after the president was shot on September 6, 1901: "The news of the President! We never got it until yesterday evening, when a N.Y. paper wandered into the camp. I doubt if it is serious. Otherwise, they would not have moved him. Doctors (and politicians) always get all the advertising they can out of a case; making it desperate, and then fetching it out all right, after they've sucked the profit out of it" (*Ltrs-Rogers*, 470).

In recent years, it has been estimated that 42 percent of Americans use at least one unconventional therapy (relaxation techniques, chiropractic, therapeutic massage, homeopathy, special diets, and so forth).[25] They do so for the same reasons Samuel Clemens did. Much of this is self-administered, as it was during the heyday of patent medicine, but a significant number will also seek therapy from alternative care providers. About one-third of the unconventional practices involve overtly unscientific theories that clash with the tenets of scientific medicine, including "energy healing" with crystals, spiritual healing, herbal medicine, homeopathy, and chiropractic.[26] The majority of those who currently use unconventional therapy do so for treatment of chronic conditions such as back pain and insomnia. Advocates of complementary and alternative therapies consider such treatments to be more helpful than traditional medical therapy for conditions that are chronic and debilitating, such as headaches and back problems.[27] As Spiro notes, "alternative practices and placebos help only certain kinds of diseases—those whose physiologic disturbances dribble out like water from a garden hose rather than those that pour out like the torrent of a fire hose."[28]

Patients do not pursue alternative treatment for self-limited problems only. They also look to nontraditional treatment for serious medical problems ("disease"), but not exclusively—83 percent also consult a medical doctor for the same ailment (although the majority will not tell their medical doctor about the alternative treatment).[29] Jane Clemens was never reluctant to call upon an allopathic physician when her own "experiments" with her family's health seemed unsuccessful, and Samuel Clemens blended traditional medicine with its complementary versions throughout his lifetime. Finley Peter Dunne's character "Mr. Dooley" explains why some patients may feel a need to seek two separate systems to gain relief from their ailments: "If the Christyan Scientists had some science an' th' doctors more Christyanity, it wudden't make anny diff'rence which ye call in."[30]

When he saw the pile of crutches and eyeglasses at the shrine of healing at Lourdes, George Bernard Shaw is said to have asked, "But where are the wooden legs and glass eyes?" The "quack" Dr. J. R. Newton, who cured the paralysis of Livy Langdon and hundreds of others who were similarly afflicted, protested against the suggestion that his accomplishments were miracles: "If a leg were to grow where one had been cut off it would be a miracle," Newton observed, "but we have no record that it was ever done."[31] Clemens similarly recognized that many alternative care providers had success in the treatment of "illness," but he also realized that these approaches could not cure "disease." He had no objection to patients seeking help from nontraditional practitioners (especially if they derived psychological benefit from doing so), but he did express concern about restrictive treatment systems that confined the patient's options by forbidding the concomitant use of traditional medical therapies.

> Within the last quarter of a century, in America, several sects of curers have appeared under various names and have done notable things in the way of healing ailments without the use of medicines. There are the Mind Cure, the Faith Cure, the Prayer Cure, the Mental-Science Cure and the Christian-Science Cure; and apparently they all do their miracles with the same old powerful instrument—*the patient's imagination*. Differing names, but no difference in the process. . . . They all achieve some cures, there is no question about it; and the Faith Cure and the Prayer Cure probably do no harm when they do no good, since they do not forbid the patient to help out the cure with medicines if he wants to; but the others bar medicines, and claim ability to cure every conceivable human ailment through the application of their mental forces alone. They claim ability to cure malignant cancer, and other affections which have never been cured in the history of the race. There would seem to be an element of danger here. It has the look of claiming too much, I think. (*Christian Sci.*, 36–37)

Present-day clinicians share Clemens's concern that nontraditional medical care may rob the patient with "disease" of opportunities to benefit from effective therapy. "Although we can talk ourselves into love or even charity, we cannot slow down a cancer by will or hope alone," notes Spiro. "Placebos may help symptoms, but they do not help diseases."[32]

This distinction is not lost on most advocates of alternative medicine. The truth of the matter is that alternative medicine is not really alternative. Alternative medicine is parallel medicine. It is not used in place of traditional medicine—it is used along with orthodox medicine. It truly is complementary medicine. Patients usually see a medical doctor before consulting with an alternative care practitioner, or they may see both healers simultaneously, but they do not typically desert orthodox medicine in favor of nontraditional medicine.[33] The relationship between alternative medicine and standard medical care is not either/or, but both/ and. The complementary relationship between traditional medicine and its competitors became even more complicated as the improvements in the quality of allopathic medicine provided patients with an even greater freedom to dispassionately assess the alternatives, as Clemens described: "To heal the body of its ills and pains is a mighty benefaction, but in our day our physicians and surgeons work a thousand miracles—prodigies which would have ranked as miracles fifty years ago—and they have so greatly extended their domination over disease that we feel so well protected that we are able to look with a good deal of composure and absence of hysterics upon the claims of new competitors in that field" (*Christian Sci.*, 267–68).

Even though patients may seek either traditional or nontraditional approaches for their chronic symptoms that defy explanation or effective treatment, they always tend to "come home" to standard medical care when significant pathology is evident. In "The Metaphysics of Holism," Neil J. Elgee observed that "even the unsophisticated user of the holistic chiropractor becomes acutely nonalternative when the chest pain starts to squeeze."[34]

Patients who pursue alternative health care approaches are not necessarily rejecting the benefits of standard medicine. Many of them have a broad view of health care, and they envision their physician as a single component of a much larger system. Such patients usually are firm believers in the importance of being personally responsible for their health and of personal autonomy.[35] Sam Clemens was such a person. "Now what I contend is that my body is my own, at least, I have always so regarded it," Clemens argued. "If I do it harm through my experimenting it is I who suffer, not the state. And if I indulge in dangerous experiments the state don't die. I attend to that. . . . So I want liberty to do as I choose with my physical body and experiment as much as possible" (*MT Speaking*, 386–87). To a large extent, patients who pursue complementary and alternative medical practices today share the attitudes of patients in Samuel Clemens's day who sought therapy from water cure and osteopathic treatments. Their philosophies encompassed a holistic approach to health, often tempered by experiences that had altered their perspective on life. They tended to belong to a cultural group interested in environmentalism, committed to feminism, and fascinated by issues of spirituality.[36]

There is yet another force, even more basic than the desire for control and autonomy, that drives the search for newer and better approaches to medical care. That force is the hope that there is some solution out there, somewhere, that is capable of resolving the current predicament. Dr. Michael Sergeant has recently described the motivating factors that lead Americans to pursue alternative medical care, which are no different from the influences that drove Samuel Clemens's quest for better forms of medical treatment a century earlier.

> [T]he reason people seek alternative medicine has nothing to do with how well it works, with the perception that the practitioners spend more time, or with its position as the latest fad . . . people choose alternative medicine for the same reason people turn to religions, cults, psychics, and faith healers.
>
> It harkens back to how fragile life is. Everyone is one heartbeat away from death. In the blink of an eyelash, we will all be sick, alone, dead, and forgotten. These inevitable truths are omnipresent and overbearing. Therefore, we as an inherently fearful and superstitious people clutch at anything that will give us power or the perception of power over these events. We invent spirits, souls, and reincarnations to evade the inevitable. Magical thinking is one way to avoid the "unbearable" sorrow of life. Alternative treatments are popular because the magic of "something out there that we don't understand" beats the system. If there were a scientific basis for them, they would simply melt into standard practice, and they would lose their allure. The higher one's level of education and wealth and the more one has to lose, the more vulnerable one is to being seduced by alternative medicine. Although the poor may give in to witch doctors, incantations, and some magic potion, the educated wait until the deception rises to jargon-laden pseudoscience, until they, too, are deluded by the fantasy.[37]

Clemens's search for medical options led him to a remarkable insight. As much as he came to admire the advances of scientific medicine, he also discovered that traditional physicians were wrong when they asserted that patients could not benefit from "nonscientific" alternative systems.

Even as a young reporter for the *San Francisco Daily Morning Call* in 1864, he posed an essential question to his readers: "Who can decide when Doctors disagree?"[38] He found that the alternative methods of medical care were successful, but only to the extent that the patient had faith in them. He realized that his extensive pursuits of the optimal treatments for his wife and children had largely been acts of foolish despair. As he helplessly watched the death of those closest to him, one by one, Clemens came to understand that death can never be defeated: "Disease! that is the main force, the diligent force, the devastating force! It attacks the infant the moment it is born; it furnishes it one malady after another: croup, measles, mumps, bowel-troubles, teething pains, scarlet fever, and other childhood specialties. It chases the child into youth and furnishes it some specialties for that time of life. It chases the youth into maturity; maturity into age and age into the grave" (*WIM&OPW*, 427).

Clemens not only learned of the futility of fighting death, but in the despondency of his lonely final years he came to see that death may be the greatest boon to humanity. The goal of medicine, then, should not be the defeat of death (which will always have its final say), but instead the enhancement of the quality of life. Medical technology can weaken disease (which is the agent of death), and will continue to get better and better in doing so, but it may not always improve the patient's condition. Clemens understood that the benefit a patient receives from a patent medicine, a sham operation, a prayer, or a chiropractic treatment is related less to the therapy itself than to the patient's belief in it. In a letter to the *New York Sunday Mercury* of 1867, he argued for preservation of diversity in medical choices, noting that "there has always been a variance of choice under which system a citizen preferred to find his way across the Styx, and he enjoyed in this State till now the privilege of choosing the rower who was to aid in ferrying him over in Charon's boat" (*CT-1*, 228).[39]

Samuel Clemens knew that there was much more to healing than could be derived from the specific philosophies and methods of the allopaths, homeopaths, osteopaths, and all of their numerous competitors.

The power which a man's imagination has over his body to heal it or make it sick is a force which none of us is born without. The first man had it, the last one will possess it. If left to himself, a man is most likely to use only the mischievous half of the force—the half which invents imaginary ailments for him and cultivates them; and if he is one of these very wise people, he is quite likely to scoff at the beneficent half of the force and deny its existence. And so, to heal or help that man, *two* imaginations are required: his own and some outsider's. The outsider, B, must imagine that *his* incantations are the healing-power that is curing A, and A must imagine that this is so. I think it is not so, at all; but no matter, the cure is effected, and that is the main thing. The outsider's work is unquestionably valuable; so valuable that it may fairly be likened to the essential work performed by the engineer when he handles the throttle and turns on the steam; the actual power is lodged exclusively in the engine, but if the engine were left alone it would never start of itself. Whether the engineer be named Jim, or Bob, or Tom, it is all one—his services are necessary, and he is entitled to such wage as he can get you to pay. Whether he be named Christian Scientist, or Mental Scientist, or Mind Curist, or King's-Evil Expert, or

Hypnotist, it is all one; he is merely the Engineer; he simply turns on the same old steam and the engine does the whole work. (*Christian Sci.*, 84–85)

Although he never practiced medicine, Samuel Clemens had discovered the mysterious force that underlies every successful interaction between a patient and a healer—the positive and caring interaction of one human being with another.

Appendix 1

A BRIEF FAMILY MEDICAL HISTORY

Mark Twain

Samuel Langhorne Clemens (1935–1910). Clemens was born prematurely and was small and sickly as a child. He was treated with a number of allopathic medicines throughout his youth, and his mother also treated him with popular patent medicines and other home remedies. As an adult, he was known for his heavy smoking habit (cigars) and regular alcohol use. He had recurrent problems with colds, bronchitis, gout, and rheumatism and occasional difficulties with abscesses and boils ("carbuncles"), particularly when traveling. He suffered from incapacitating angina in his later years and died from cardiac causes.

Wife

Olivia ("Livy") Langdon Clemens (1845–1904). A number of controversies surround Livy Clemens's health status, with ongoing debate about the relative contributions of physical illness and psychological factors in her overall condition. She grew up in a well-to-do family. She has been described by some as chronically frail and weak, and in many ways her medical history is consistent with features of the "neurasthenia" that was a popular diagnosis of the era. At age sixteen she fell on the ice and was bedridden for two years in a state of paralysis. She was treated successfully by a faith healer after traditional medical treatments failed. She suffered from serious medical illnesses at times, including infection with typhoid fever. In later years, she had typical manifestations of severe and disabling congestive heart failure, possibly aggravated by hyperthyroidism. Clemens's desire to improve her health led him to seek any promising treatment that might be available and exposed him to many of the competing health care systems of the nineteenth century.

Parents

John Marshall Clemens (1798–1847). Samuel Clemens's father was a lawyer, storekeeper, and judge and has been described as a dour and humorless man. He worried about his health and consumed large quantities of patent medicines, according to his son Orion. He died of pneumonia when Sam was twelve years of age, and young Sam looked through a keyhole to observe his father's autopsy on the family dining room table (an event that, according to the speculation of some, caused severe psychological trauma to the youngster).

Jane Lampton Clemens (1803–1890). Jane married John Clemens after she was spurned by a medical student. She was bright, energetic, and eclectic in her interests and a major influence on Samuel Clemens. She was constantly worried about the health of her children (a not unrealistic concern, considering the child mortality statistics of the times and that three of her six children did not live past the age of ten years). She subscribed to popular health-oriented literature and was eager to try any new preventative on her children, no matter how vile, in the interest of keeping them healthy. Samuel Clemens accompanied her on a trip to a rural faith healer who cured her toothache. Much of Aunt Polly in *The Adventures of Tom Sawyer* is derived from Jane Clemens, including her passion for patent medicines such as Perry Davis's Pain-Killer. She was healthy throughout most of her long life but had features of dementia in her later years.

Siblings

Orion Clemens (1825–1897). Orion was Samuel Clemens's oldest brother. He was an honest and hardworking failure in careers in journalism, politics, storekeeping, law, chicken farming, and inventing. An unsuccessful visionary and a model for fickleness in religion and politics, Orion did not have any major medical problems.

Pamela Clemens Moffett (1827–1904). Eight years the senior of Samuel, Pamela was always close to her famous brother, and they remained confidants throughout their lives. She was intelligent, kind, and sensitive, and she served as the model for Tom Sawyer's fictional cousin Mary. Samuel Clemens characterized her as a lifelong invalid, but she lived well into her seventies.

Pleasant Hannibal Clemens (1828 or 1829?). Virtually nothing is known about the third child of John and Jane Clemens. He lived only about three months.

Margaret L. Clemens (1830–1839). Margaret was the Clemens's fourth child. She died of "bilious fever" before Samuel was four years of age.

Benjamin Clemens (1832–1842). Benjamin was close to his younger brother Samuel and died suddenly after a brief illness when Samuel was six years old.

Henry Clemens (1838–1858). Samuel was probably closer to Henry, his youngest sibling, than to any of the other Clemens children. Henry followed Samuel into the steamboating industry on the Mississippi River and died as a result of a steamboat explosion in which he sustained severe lung damage from inhaling steam. Samuel felt personally responsible for his death and had mixed emotions about the medical care Henry received after the explosion; he suspected that an overdose of morphine by poorly trained medical school graduates may have been the immediate cause of death, but he was also very appreciative of the kindness displayed by Henry's doctors.

Children

Langdon Clemens (1870–1872). Clemens's first child and only son, Langdon was born prematurely and was chronically ill throughout his brief life. Clemens took personal responsibility (probably incorrectly) for the child's death after Langdon's blanket slipped off in cold weather while the child was under Clemens's supervision.

Olivia Susan ("Susy") Clemens (1872–1896). Susy, Clemens's oldest daughter, was intelligent, creative, and precocious. Her father considered her a prodigy, and she began writing his biography when she was thirteen. She had aspirations in music and literature, but she was limited by poorly characterized problems with fragile health throughout her life. She dropped out of Bryn Mawr College for uncertain reasons after the first year. She traveled with her family in Europe in quest of medical treatments for the chronic problems of her mother and youngest sister, Jean. She became bored, moody, and unhappy. She became acutely ill and died of meningitis in Hartford, Connecticut, when her parents were in England. Her tragic death was unavoidable in the pre-antibiotic era, but it caused Samuel Clemens to become further embittered against the mainstream medical profession.

Clara Langdon Clemens (1874–1962). Clara was the second of Samuel Clemens's three daughters and the only child still alive at the time of his death. As a child, she did not have the severe medical problems of her two sisters. She became responsible for much of the care of her mother in the later years of Olivia Langdon Clemens's life. She developed emotional problems after her mother's death and spent the better part of the next year in a sanatorium. She later became an advocate of Christian Science, in spite of her father's earlier vicious attacks on the sect. She died in southern California at the age of eighty-eight.

Jane ("Jean") Lampton Clemens (1880–1909). Jean was Clemens's youngest child. She was infected with scarlet fever at the age of two and was generally in poor health after that. She suffered from spells of unusual behavior that were eventually diagnosed as seizures. Clemens first learned about osteopathy when he took Jean to Sweden to be treated by Jonas Kellgren, and he became a strong advocate of osteopathic care after Jean seemed to improve. Jean had intervals of freedom from the seizures, which worsened after stressful life events such as the death of her mother in 1904. She spent most of the last five years of her life in sanatoriums, with little contact with her father. She died in her morning bath on Christmas Eve 1909, apparently following a seizure.

THE LEGACY OF NEURASTHENIA

Political parties disband and species of animals become extinct, but is it possible for a *disease* to totally disappear? Considering the huge influence of neurasthenia on medicine and society in the Victorian America of Samuel Clemens's lifetime, it may seem odd that the diagnosis is no longer a part of the medical lexicon. This situation creates a number of intriguing questions about diagnoses in general and neurasthenia in particular. First of all, what exactly *is* a "diagnosis"? Is it a social construct, akin to a political organization, that exists at the whim of the people who created it? Or is it a biological process, equivalent to a species of plant or animal, regulated by the rules of nature? And what *was* this thing called "neurasthenia"? Was it a physical disease, a psychiatric disorder, or simply an affectation of the well-to-do and educated? And, whatever it was, if neurasthenia no longer exists, *where* did it go?

The answers to these questions require an understanding of the term *diagnosis* and the process used by doctors to "make a diagnosis." In its simplest form, a diagnosis is an abstract image, an icon that has been created to represent a disease. The brain of every physician contains a picture of every disease that he knows anything about; his mental collection of disease images serves as his private reference library whenever he attempts to define the nature of a patient's sickness. Each template is the "perfect" representation of a disease, the "classic case," an idealized image that never is seen in real life.[1] As the physician accumulates information about a patient's illness, he continually compares his patient's features to his collection of disease templates. He may seek additional information from the physical examination and from laboratory studies to narrow down the number of acceptable matches between his patient's situation and the many pictures of disease he has in his head. When the patient's clinical picture makes an acceptably good fit with one particular disease template, the name associated with that template becomes the patient's "diagnosis."

"Making the diagnosis" is of paramount importance to both the physician and the patient. If a diagnosis cannot be established, the physician has no basis for defining the patient's therapy nor for providing the patient with prognostic information that will help the patient understand what the future may hold. The doctor faces an awkward situation when a diagnosis is elusive. Even so, the difficulties are even greater for the patient; without a diagnosis, the patient has no explanation for (and, perhaps, even no legitimization of) the symptoms.

The process of making a diagnosis is fraught with significant limitations. The physician's mental library of disease models is limited to those diseases that are known to him and that fit within the scope of his medical belief system. Each school of medical care—be it allopathic, homeopathic, chiropractic, or Christian Science—is limited by the constraints of its own templates and its own vocabulary of disease, and each one requires its patients to subscribe to the same unique terminology and philosophy. Allopathic medicine has an extensive (but not unlimited) collection of templates to apply to a patient with headaches—there are headaches that are caused by the stress-induced contraction of neck muscles ("tension headaches"); there are headaches that result from infection of the sinuses; there are headaches that are caused by brain tumors; there are headaches that occur when blood vessels in the brain contract and dilate excessively ("migraine headaches"). Almost all allopathic doctors have mental models for all of these headache types that assist in the process of making a diagnosis, but very few allopathic doctors have a mental model for a headache that begins when his patient's enemy jabs a pin through a voodoo doll.

A patient cannot benefit fully from a course of treatment prescribed by a doctor, and will probably refuse to even consider it, unless both patient and doctor share a common medical belief system. If a patient understands the basis of his allopathic doctor's assessment that his headaches are probably stress-induced, he has a very good chance of benefiting from the recommendations of relaxation techniques and over-the-counter pain medications. On the other hand, if the patient is convinced that his headaches are caused by an enemy's witchcraft, an allopathic doctor's treatments will be useless to him. He cannot be helped by physical therapy or anti-inflammatory medicine if he believes his pain comes from the malevolence of the devil. He needs a doctor who knows how to reverse his enemy's hex; he needs a therapist whose templates for headache include an image of headache by voodoo. It is not even necessary for his doctor to know that *some* headaches can arise from sinus infections or brain tumors or migraines, since those things did not cause *his* headache. Dr. Clifton Meador discusses this phenomenon in a case report of a poorly educated man who was near death after a hex had been pronounced upon him by a voodoo priest. The man recovered after his family doctor was able to convince him that the hex had been reversed. Meador then presents a second case of a patient who died with the mistaken belief that he was suffering from widespread malignancy; at autopsy, only a small nodule of cancer could be identified. Meador suggests that the second man's death may represent a variation of the first man's "hex"; each case can be viewed as an illness caused by the *belief* of the patient that he was ill.[2]

It may be disconcerting for patients to realize that a doctor's library of diagnostic templates is neither constant nor fixed. In medicine, the diagnostic possibilities are not static. As medical knowledge increases, new diagnostic templates can be developed, older templates can undergo modification, and outdated templates can be destroyed. It was impossible to develop an accurate template for AIDS (the acquired immunodeficiency syndrome) until medical scientists discovered the human immunodeficiency virus (HIV) that was the cause of AIDS. This does not negate the experience of the many patients who suffered from AIDS before the virus was found; it simply means that they could not be given an explanation for *why* they were sick. For both patient and physician, there is nothing more frustrating than the presence of symptoms that cannot be explained. It happened in the pre-HIV era of the AIDS epidemic, and it happens at some time in the history of every disease that has ever afflicted a human being.

If a patient has symptoms that do not match any available diagnostic template (that is, the patient has symptoms that defy diagnosis), the patient has no hope for rational treatment nor any reasonable expectation of cure. A doctor's inability to match the patient's symptoms with a disease template eventually creates tension in the doctor-patient relationship. As time goes by, the physician who cannot find a logical template that will fit the symptoms may come to question whether the patient's symptoms are "real," especially if the patient doesn't look sick. At the same time, the patient may begin to doubt the competence of the physician, suspecting that the doctor is poorly educated and does not possess the proper template or lacks the skills necessary to match the symptoms to the correct template.

Symptoms that defy diagnosis create a stalemate between doctor and patient. The patient may decide to resolve the conundrum by seeking another doctor who might be better trained or might even turn to an alternative health care system in the hope that *its* disease templates are a better match for his symptoms. Another option is for medicine to create newer disease templates as an explanation for otherwise unexplained symptom complexes. This was the approach that created "neurasthenia." Neurasthenia became extremely useful for patients and doctors alike; it had a very generous template that included symptoms of virtually every description—almost anyone could fit the neurasthenic model at one time or another, which was useful to doctors who would otherwise be at a loss to explain odd symptoms. Neurasthenia was a useful diagnosis for patients. It had positive connotations for its victims by proclaiming that they were intelligent, they were refined, and they were diligent workers. Neurasthenia gave rise to a variety of therapeutic options. Neurasthenia was a *very* good fit for the Gilded Age in every way.

The invention of a new disease such as neurasthenia is a mechanism for resolving the tension that occurs when doctors and patients disagree on the nature of an illness. Physicians take seriously only the disorders that come from pathological processes, even though many patients suffer most from the malaise of their human existence. Doctors have templates for the diseases that are listed in the medical textbooks, but not for the illnesses that are created from the misery of their patients' lives. As the physician looks harder to find disease, it is easier to overlook the patient's illness. Illness and disease exist on two separate planes, and it is impossible to sharpen the focus on one without blurring the perception of the other.

The need to create a diagnosis such as neurasthenia is driven by the presence of patients who suffer with symptoms that continue unabated for months and years. This is never an issue for self-resolving sicknesses that clear up in a short time. It does not matter whether the disease is a respiratory infection or a sprained ankle—for medical problems that are limited in severity and duration, "disease" and "illness" run on the same track, and they frequently cross the finish line in a dead heat. In such cases, the doctor and the patient share the same vantage point, and the "disease" that the doctor hopes to cure is not readily separable from the "illness" that causes the patient's suffering. The patient's dysfunction comes to an end when the pathological process is eliminated. In the classic model of acute disease, both doctor and patient share the same goal of returning the patient to health as soon as possible; in the meantime, the "sick role" creates a brief and acceptable pardon from the duties and responsibilities of daily life as the patient submits himself to medical care.

The situation becomes more complicated for patients who suffer from chronic symptoms. For some of these patients, the source of the problem may not be a well-defined "disease" process, creating a situation that can generate great tension between doctor and patient. It appears that one person may not be holding up his end of the contract—the patient suspects that the physician is overlooking the diagnosis, and the physician speculates that there may be no diagnosis to be found.

The "rules of sickness" seem to be a major issue only to the traditional physician (alternative medical practitioners do not fret about the meaning of any given diagnosis and are generally more concerned with alleviating symptoms). Tensions arise between a patient and a doctor whose prior training and personal prejudice cause him to view somatization as a type of malingering rather than a medical disease, even though it may be more accurate to view patients with somatization disorders as people who are truly victims of a terribly severe disease process—they are suffering from "existential pain."[3] In order to cope, some patients seem to adopt a sick role that they can never fully relinquish, or even admit to having, and physicians struggle with the challenge of breaking through impenetrable barriers. Mehl-Madrona has described this challenge:

> Looking within a chronically ill person's soul and finding the healing resources hidden there can be a little like stealing fire from the gods. Sometimes the coping mechanisms we have learned to deal with an illness end up keeping us sick. People develop habits that nurture and maintain illness. Since, when we are sick these habits seem helpful, we become extremely reluctant to change them. Often these habits help us manage and contain otherwise unbearable emotion.[4]

Such conflicts can be eliminated if the physician can apply an "official" medical definition (that is, a "diagnosis") to a specific constellation of symptoms that are shared by groups of patients. By creating a diagnosis, the doctor can transform a patient's "illness" into a legitimate "disease." Neurasthenia became a legitimate target for medical therapy when it was defined as a disease process, even though the basis for neurasthenia as a human malady may have been more sociological than physiological. As noted by Robert Martensen in a 1994 discussion, "the disease construct of neurasthenia illustrates the complexity of relationships between diagnostic categories, culture, disease, patients and providers. In particular, neurasthenia helped make sense of symptoms that otherwise would have been found reprehensible, such as an inability to function in the home or office."[5]

Neurasthenia utilized the "vocabulary of nerves" to enhance the status of its sufferers, and in an era when the role of women was quickly changing, neurasthenia could be either a powerful tool for strong women or an indicator of weakness in women of lower status. "First-hand observations of how the nervous sufferer interacts with others show how women can use their self-diagnosed cases of nerves to negotiate their way through a series of complex social networks in high-stress or rapidly changing social settings," Dona Davis notes. "Nerves is best viewed not as the product of status but as a tool for negotiating status."[6] When disorders such as neurasthenia or chronic fatigue syndrome are accepted as "real" diseases by the medical profession, patients are able to avoid the pejorative implications of the "somatization" by which the illness manifests itself; they also gain the advantages associated with having a chronic disease (which include legitimization of their symptoms, increased compassion for their suffering, and more diligent efforts to find a cure).

The invention of a new disease such as neurasthenia can come about only when the social and medical conditions of an era create a niche for a new diagnosis. When neurasthenia was first described in 1869 by Dr. George Beard in *A Practical Treatise on Nervous Exhaustion (Neurasthenia)*, there was a real need for a disease that explained the malaise of the overworked and overstressed brain workers of the Gilded Age. It was an impressive feat for Beard to announce that a new disease had arrived in the land; it was even more remarkable that Beard's invention was so readily able to root and spread itself across the country, a medical kudzu that quickly became recognized as "the American disease." The diffusion of conditions such as neurasthenia throughout a population has been compared to the transmission of viruses; their raison d'être is their primitive need to self-replicate, an activity that requires them to infect one host cell after another in their drive to sustain their own existence. In a sense, though, a malady such as neurasthenia is neither a virus nor a disease; instead, it takes on the most destructive properties of each and becomes "a virulent idea, a maladaptive social construction of disease." Such illnesses can be seen as "infectious agents that, like microbes, have virulence factors, affect hosts with particular vulnerabilities, are disseminated through a variety of vectors, and are promoted or inhibited by various components of the social ecology."[7]

Every human being is susceptible to the development of neurasthenic symptoms. No one can avoid the occasional vague symptoms of uncertain and indefinable unhappiness, often combined with a sense that something is just not right with the world. This sensation of personal malaise and distress is usually fueled by a recent acceleration of the interpersonal or social stresses of daily living. To feel helpless, hopeless, overwhelmed, undervalued, or unloved can create some of the most distressing physical symptoms that a human being can experience. This discomfort of body and spirit creates a misery that often provokes a search for the source of the anguish and ennui that have diminished the joy of existence. Visits to the doctor's office commonly create one more level of frustration; the physician can discover no evidence of a physical disease and is left with advising the sufferer that the symptoms may be coming from depression or anxiety or excessive worry or too much work. The inability to identify the source of the stress creates even more stress and worsening symptoms. Depression and anxiety and excessive worry and too much work all suggest personal failure and a personal responsibility for one's plight. Doctors rarely endear themselves to patients by suggesting such possibilities, which are deemed unacceptable explanations by the majority of patients. This is where the nineteenth century's "neurasthenia" and its descendants of the twentieth and twenty-first centuries have found their niche.

Both physicians and patients need a mutually acceptable template of disease that is sufficient to explain the somatic symptoms of fatigue, malaise, and irritability. "Depression" and "anxiety" are concepts that work well for physicians but are not acceptable to many patients, who would much prefer to have a diagnosis of a physical ailment.[8] "Neurasthenia," the American disease, became the nineteenth-century resolution to the doctor-patient conflict in semantics. If a patient had insufficient "nerve force" to deal with the stresses of modern life, it was hardly his fault. He had every right to feel depressed or anxious *about* his disease, but anxiety and depression were *not* his disease (they were simply the *symptoms* of his neurasthenia). By inventing neurasthenia, physicians of the nineteenth century created an explanation that both they and their patients could accept. If a diagnosis has an image that is acceptable to the victim, the illness itself can take over as the culturally permissible surrogate that gives the sufferer permission to publicly exhibit the full scope of what would otherwise be a personal and private distress. A patient who is depressed or anxious is far better able to cope with distress when the medical profession proclaims that the source of suffering is entirely out of that individual's control. The advantages are immense, as Stephen Ross explained in 1999.

> The symptoms may prompt the sufferer to ascribe the distress to a physical illness... suggesting to the sufferer that she has been hurt, poisoned, or infected. Once integrated, this framework can induce a somatic preoccupation that becomes self-validating and self-reinforcing.... Social, economic, and legal factors may further promote consolidation. Those who suffer... may be relieved of social obligations and may be provided with sympathy and support.[9]

If a scientific basis for a disorder cannot eventually be determined, however, it may lose its status as a disease and revert back to being a collection of ill-defined symptoms. Although patients continue to have the same symptoms as those suffered by neurasthenics, the diagnosis no longer exists, and thus the symptoms no longer represent a disorder to be treated. In the absence of a disease, patients with neurasthenic symptoms are unlikely to receive therapy from physicians trained in allopathic medicine. Patients with poorly defined symptoms that do not match any specific diagnosis constitute an immense population. Although the symptoms may be nonspecific, they are also chronic, unexplainable, severe, and often debilitating. It is this plight that drives patients to explore the options of alternative medicine.

Nontraditional practitioners never fail to give validity to a patient's symptoms. This willingness to accept the patient at face value underlies much of the success of alternative medicine. Traditional physicians have only one way to validate a patient's symptoms, and that is by translating the symptoms into a diagnosis. Without a diagnosis, the patient can have no disease; without a diagnosis, the patient's symptoms cannot be interpreted, and they may not even be real. In the absence of a common language, there is no reason for any further interaction between the patient and the doctor. Nineteenth-century medicine developed the diagnosis of neurasthenia so that it *would* have a mechanism to negotiate with the patients who experienced nonspecific symptoms. Doctors could diagnose neurasthenia, but patients were also allowed to declare themselves neurasthenic if they chose to do so. The disappearance of neurasthenia created another diagnostic void and communication impasse that could only be broken by the invention of new diagnoses. Although neurasthenia no longer exists, at least in official medical jargon, it probably never went away. Instead, it simply changed its name with changing times.

As medical science learned the details of glucose metabolism in fueling the body's energy needs, "hypoglycemia" became one of the twentieth century's substitutes for neurasthenia. The concept of an insufficient supply of glucose was a simple variation of neurasthenia's inadequate nerve force, and hypoglycemia became a popular diagnosis for patients who experienced a spectrum of bodily complaints that included fatigue, pain, numbness, tingling, lethargy, poor stamina, and mental dullness. The diagnosis was often made by the patient but was also found to be acceptable by some physicians. Surprisingly little attention was paid to the fact that the typical patient had perfectly normal blood sugar metabolism, and the continued attribution of symptoms to a presumed abnormality of glucose regulation allowed the nondisease of "hypoglycemia" to become epidemic. The reason for the popularity of the hypoglycemia diagnosis was simple enough—the diagnosis conferred the same benefits that came from having neurasthenia a century earlier:

> Consider the advantages of hypoglycemia: to start, the diagnosis is socially acceptable. Rather than endure a "psychologic" or otherwise stigmatizing condition the patient may suffer from a respectable metabolic illness and enjoy the corresponding status and privileges.
>
> Of course, the very act of attributing discomfort to hypoglycemia may provide some relief from the perplexing and ambiguous symptoms. Moreover, the patient's explanation, although primitive, is compatible with our basic cultural belief that illness is physiologic—not due to demons. Most people today link "energy level" and vitality to blood sugar; they can easily believe and persuade others to believe that abnormal sugar metabolism account for their weird complaints, signs and symptoms.
>
> Too, hypoglycemia promises the patient an opportunity to deal actively and easily with the complaints: by simply following certain dietary prescriptions—or dietary rituals—the patient can hope to cope cheaply and effectively with and master the symptoms, or at least enjoy the comforts of compulsive behavior. Thus, hypoglycemia provides all at once a socially acceptable problem, a quasi-physiologic explanation and the promise of a relatively inexpensive and successful self-help program.[10]

Hypoglycemia was just one of neurasthenia's many replacement diagnoses. The list includes "chronic fatigue syndrome," "irritable bowel syndrome," "fibromyalgia," "noncardiac chest pain," "tension headache," "chronic pelvic pain," "temporomandibular joint dysfunction," and "multiple chemical sensitivity." Despite the many diagnoses that have arisen to replace neurasthenia, they have a substantial overlap in their manifestations, none of which differ substantially from the symptoms George Beard ascribed to neurasthenia. The similarities among neurasthenia's descendants are so much greater than their differences that there is question as to whether they should even be considered distinct syndromes.[11] Collectively, these illnesses with their sometimes intense body-focused symptoms are referred to as somatization disorders. "Somatization" is the modern terminology for what used to be neurasthenia. The revision in nomenclature may not be as important as the realization that "[c]hanging the language we use will not make these illnesses go away."[12]

Chronic fatigue syndrome is one of the latest versions of neurasthenia.[13] The new chronic fatigue parallels the old neurasthenia in many ways. Its sufferers experience incapacitating exhaustion that requires them to severely reduce their level of activity. They commonly have generalized malaise, aching of muscles and joints, weakness of muscles, a subjective feeling of feverishness, dizziness or light-headedness, irritability, depression, anxiety, and problems with concentration and memory. As a result of the marked reduction in their ability to function, many chronic fatigue patients are not able to maintain a full-time job, but instead spend many of their hours seeking restorative treatment in order to maintain a very minimal level of functioning. (The term *nervous breakdown*, with its obvious neurasthenic overtones, continues to be popular with patients to describe their psychiatric problems, and some psychiatrists argue that "neurasthenia" should be restored as a legitimate objective diagnosis.)[14]

There is little doubt that new replacements for neurasthenia will arise in the future. Not every diagnosis is suitable for this purpose. The diagnosis must fit in with the existing disease taxonomy of the era. Suffering from "the vapors" was once a popular disorder but is no longer culturally sanctioned. No contemporary patient or physician could suggest the diagnosis without becoming the target of ridicule. Newer disease models continue to appear. "In a previous era, spirits and demons oppressed us . . . they have been replaced by our contemporary concern about invisible viruses, chemicals, and toxins."[15] Suitable diagnoses depend upon a sufficient polarity in the culture for the positive and negative extremes to be readily distinguished ("the vapors" could be a valid diagnosis when the intrinsic delicacy of women was easily contrasted with the coarser nature and cruder sensitivities of men, but progressive equalization of the genders made the "vapors" a less viable diagnosis). It is also important for the illness to be apparent to others (as with the "swoon" of the vapors sufferer, and the lassitude of the neurasthenia victim). Finally, the illness should allow an otherwise unavailable escape from cultural tensions. This need for escape creates chronic, unrelenting symptomatology that defies medical treatment. Neurasthenia and "the vapors" went away when their sociological niches disappeared, only to be replaced by chronic fatigue syndrome and sick building syndrome. The template for neurasthenia is no longer used or seen as valid. This creates an interesting historical dilemma—if neurasthenia doesn't exist, what did neurasthenics really have? It is reasonable to argue that they really *did* have neurasthenia.

Every generation develops its own explanations for the unanswered mysteries of the universe on the basis of its own scientific discoveries and its own models of scientific "truth." The work products of Edison and Darwin—electricity and evolution—were the hot topics of the late nineteenth century that created a scientific template for "nervous exhaustion" as a depletion of the life-giving electrical force, predominantly afflicting those who have evolved as humanity's most sensitive and fragile life forms. Eventually, though, paradigms are forced to shift as science marches on. The science of the twentieth century became the science of infection, immunology, and penicillin. Neurasthenia stopped making sense. The arrival of immunoglobulins, lymphocytes, and antibiotics forced the departure of "nerve force" from the medical lexicon. But patients with neurasthenic symptoms remained, and medicine readily found other explanations to fill in the gaps left by neurasthenia's departure from the diagnostic scene. The need to stick a name on every assortment of symptoms persisted (as it always will), and the twentieth century's scientific paradigm of immunity quickly created new maladies that could provide viable and fresh explanations for weakness and malaise. Conceptual diseases such as chronic Epstein-Barr virus infection, systemic candidiasis, and environmental hypersensitivity all arose from (and then were blended back into) a fuzzy image of an impaired immune system, in much the same way that neurasthenia grew out of the notion of a weakened nerve force. For the twentieth-century sufferer who had other symptoms that did not quite fit an immunological mechanism, varying amalgams of the physiology-pathology-psychology complex could be used to create fibromyalgia, sick building syndrome, hormone imbalance, irritable bowel syndrome, multiple chemical sensitivities, temporomandibular joint syndrome, and hypoglycemia. When medical science could not pin down a specific pathological process for patients who were forever sickly, always fatigued, and chronically distressed, these modern-day offshoots of neurasthenia were malleable enough to explain anything that was wrong with their body or with their life, without really explaining anything at all.

Appendix 3

ONE OF THE CHOICEST
HUMAN BEINGS IN THE WORLD

Dr. Clarence Charles Rice (1853–1935) had a substantial influence on the way Samuel Clemens viewed medical issues. Rice was Clemens's personal physician for many years, and he also became a close personal friend. Rice was a nose and throat specialist who was house physician for the Metropolitan Opera, and he had appointments to the faculty and administrative staffs of the New York Postgraduate Medical School and Hospital and many other professional organizations. His patients included performers such as Enrico Caruso, Edwin Booth, and Lillian Russell. Clemens had great admiration for Rice, both professionally and personally, and described the doctor as "a physician of great reputation, and one of the choicest human beings in the world. I go bail for him" (*Ltrs-Rogers*, 742).

The medical care that Rice provided for Clemens included surgical procedures. Clemens's notebook records the performance of an operation: "Dr. Rice cut my palate" (*N&J-3*, 332). On October 14, 1887, Clemens was frustrated with the slowness of his recovery from the surgery, reporting that "I had my palate cut out several days ago, and it promises to never get well again."[1] The exact nature of this operation is unclear, but it may have been for an impacted wisdom tooth or dental abscess, as suggested by another notebook entry. "Have Dr. Rice cut my palate, or pull it out by the roots" (*N&J-3*, 335). After the operation, Rice continued to provide medical services for the family; in August 1888, Clemens wrote a check to Rice for $105 for professional services to Clemens, Livy, and Susy (*N&J-3*, 477). Five years later, when he was suffering from a hernia provoked by a chronic cough, Clemens reported that he was "in bed, and waiting for Dr. Rice" (*Ltrs-Rogers*, 29).

Rice was also the man who introduced Clemens to Henry Huttleston Rogers, the millionaire Standard Oil executive and financier who successfully guided Clemens out of bankruptcy. Rice, Rogers, and Clemens developed a close relationship that was based on friendship as well as professional interactions, and Rice became the butt of good-natured jesting by Clemens. Some of the joking was personal in nature, shared with Rogers in written correspondence. Defects in Rice's character were implied by Clemens's lighthearted jesting, but as a whole the commentary speaks of a close and mutual respect.

> If I were lazier—like Rice—nothing could keep me from retiring. (*Ltrs-Rogers*, 378)

> Pretty soon, at this rate, it will become Rice to speak of me as *Mr.* Clemens—yes, and even *Colonel.* I don't like to suggest it to him myself, but you might remind him. He is [a] man who has a passion for titles—when they are conferred upon him. (*Ltrs-Rogers*, 391)

> [A]s for cigars, they are 3 1/2 cent apiece, and there is no way for a really conscientious economist to do but steal them. It shames me to do this, and it makes a good deal of talk; but I feel as Rice does about such matters: that it is better to be economical than honest, as a general thing. I have learned many useful things from Rice. (*Ltrs-Rogers*, 396)

> I do not get entirely over my lameness, and the gout has never kept up its threatenings so long before. Certainly the righteous do have a rough time of it in this world, I wish I was like Rice. (*Ltrs-Rogers*, 597)

Clemens did not overlook Rice's role as a physician while poking fun at the doctor. In what may well have been an "inside joke," Clemens reminded his friend Rogers, tongue in cheek, about how the two of them had observed Rice's shortcomings as a diagnostician and his propensity for charging outrageous fees:

> As to Rice . . . there must be something outstanding between you and me and him on medical consultations there in his office. He has never settled up on those, I think. Then there were those men whom he was treating for something that he called gastritis and charging them burglar rates. I never said a word, though those people were merely drunk, that was all. I could have given that thing away, but I didn't. He must owe us something on that. (*Ltrs-Rogers*, 113)

The involvement of a famous millionaire like Rogers and a world-famous celebrity like Clemens in one of Rice's formal medical consultations seems unlikely. It is possible that the "medical consultations" in question represented some sociable alcohol consumption in Rice's office by the three close friends, with resultant intoxication and abdominal distress.

In a similar lampooning of Rice's practice methods, Clemens even suggested to Rogers that the doctor would create new medical problems for his patients, just so he would have something to treat and charge them for: "Mrs. Crane [Susan Langdon Crane, Olivia Clemens's foster sister] runs down every little while and buys Rice's professional help. . . . She and Rice are great friends. Rice breeds some kind of an animal in her nose—an octopus, I think—and then charges her for letting on to take it out. He *is* the most ingenious cuss!" (*Ltrs-Rogers*, 130). The jesting did not all originate with Clemens. Rogers shared Clemens's pleasure in cheerfully ridiculing Rice's methods of practice. In a letter to Clemens, Rogers portrayed the doctor as an outdated practitioner. "If you do not want to come to Fairhaven, why don't you say so? Why this indefinite talk? Why this feigned sickness? Rice has been to Fairhaven with Calomel and leeches for two weeks, hoping to get relief himself by experimenting with you" (*Ltrs-Rogers*, 593).

Clemens had a very comfortable personal relationship with Rice that is reflected in the personal and professional barbs that were shared with Rogers. He also had great trust in Rice as a physician. However, his faith in Dr. Rice as a medical authority was not absolute, and he did not always seek Rice's opinion when he needed to make critical medical decisions. In 1900, the Clemens family was eager to return to the United States from London, but not at the risk of a setback in the health of Jean (whose epilepsy was being successfully treated—or so it seemed—by the osteopathic methods of Dr. Henrik Kellgren). Clemens decided that he would move the family back only if he could be confident that Jean would receive the same type of treatment she had been getting from Kellgren. Clemens asked his nephew, Samuel Moffett, to question the osteopath Dr. George Helmer in New York to try to determine whether American osteopathic treatment was the equivalent of Kellgren's osteopathic therapy. In spite of the crucial nature of this decision, he purposefully avoided getting any input from Rice: "At last, however, I have gone at the matter in a square way. I have sent a relative to a New York osteopath to ask what he can say, and what he can promise. I am hoping that when I get that report it will determine us to go home a few months hence. Don't tell Rice anything. He does not believe in osteopathy" (*Ltrs-Rogers*, 431).

This statement is critical to an understanding of how Clemens viewed the competing health care systems that surrounded him. There is no doubt that he had great faith and confidence in the clinical abilities and judgment of Dr. Clarence Rice—he allowed the man to cut an incision into his own palate and treat other members of his own family. However, Clemens's opinion was that, as an allopathic physician, Rice could never be entirely objective in his assessment of any competing medical system. Clemens's statement demonstrates his belief that even the most trusted practitioners of allopathic medicine can have their blind side. Only he, Samuel Langhorne Clemens, was capable of making decisions about what was right for his own health and for the well-being of his family.

Notes

Introduction

1. This event was reported in a *New York Times* article of January 21, 1909, entitled "Twain Talks to Doctors" and subtitled "'Dr. Clemens' Describes Imaginary Medical School at His Country Home."

2. Thomas A. Tenney, "Introduction." The conclusion of this famous quote is often mistakenly given as "the report of my death was *greatly exaggerated*."

3. Mark Twain, "Fenimore Cooper's Literary Offenses."

4. Dr. Robert Prichard, who served for many years as the chairman of the department of pathology at Wake Forest University, told each entering class of medical students that the most important thing they would gain from their medical education would be the knowledge that would allow them to protect themselves from other doctors.

5. Mark Twain, "The First Writing-Machines."

6. Clemens wrote this on August 12, 1908 (*Ltrs-Rogers*, 652). Doctors not only "charged so much," but they sometimes charged Clemens more than they charged other patients. In Bombay in 1896, Clemens was treated for a cold by Dr. Sidney Smith, who sent him a bill for 100 rupees (about $27, or $500 in current value) for four visits. After Clemens found out that Dr. Smith charged other wealthy patients 10 rupees per visit, he sent the doctor 40 rupees with a note asking for an explanation of the excessive charge (Robert Cooper, *Around the World with Mark Twain*, 190).

7. Justin Kaplan, *Mr. Clemens and Mark Twain*, 382.

8. See Louis H. Bragman, "The Medical Wisdom of Mark Twain"; Walter J. Friedlander, "Mark Twain, Social Critic, and His Image of the Doctor"; K. Patrick Ober, "The Pre-Flexnerian Reports: Mark Twain's Criticism of Medicine in the United States."

9. John Duffy, *From Humors to Medical Science: A History of American Medicine*, 93–94.

10. Cooper, *Around the World with Mark Twain*, 105, 102–3.

11. Franklin Walker and G. Ezra Dane, eds., *Mark Twain's Travels with Mr. Brown*, 238.

12. Blue mass was a preparation of mercury used as a laxative. It was used to treat patients who suffered from "biliousness" arising from sluggish liver function, a common explanation for many medical symptoms at that time.

13. Alfred Bigelow Paine, ed., *Mark Twain's Notebook*, 218.

14. William Dean Howells, *My Mark Twain*, chap. 21.

15. In his notebooks from 1883 and 1884, inspired by the question of how a physician might embark on the project of writing a drama, Clemens created a list of characters whose first name derived from a medical disorder. The list included "Apoplexy Addison," "Typhoid Billings," "Diphtheria Marsh," "Consumption Babcock," "Paralysis Brown," "Malaria Johnson," "Asphyxia Beedle," "Lockjaw Harris," "Chilblain Batterson," "Dropsy Miller," "Quinsy Warner," "Gangrene Hopkins," "Influenza Smith," "Tuberculosis Butler," and "last of all, the hero—Scrofula St. Augustine." The idea remained a source of amusement for Clemens through the years, and his notes for an unfinished sketch "Indiantown," written around 1899, include an entry about Dr. Bradshaw, who is a character in the story: "Named his children Scarlatina,—named for epidemic outbraks—cholera morbus" (*N&J-3*, 50–53). He used the same idea in the story "Which Was It?" by inventing a character named "Asphyxia Perry." Clemens explained that the girl "owed her singular name to her mother, who was ignorant and romantic, and afflicted her children with any chance name she found in a book, if it had a pretty sound, without stopping to inquire into its pedigree or relationships. She had a son named Solar Plexus" (*WWD&OSW*, 297).

16. Kaplan, *Mr. Clemens and Mark Twain*, 247.

17. Frederick Anderson, ed., *A Pen Warmed Up in Hell: Mark Twain in Protest*, 135–36.

18. On the other hand, Clemens himself in later years developed a despondency about the human condition that caused him to use similar terminology in "Letters from the Earth," in which he defined human life as a mechanical process:

> The human being is a machine. An automatic machine. It is composed of thousands of complex and delicate mechanisms, which perform their functions harmoniously and perfectly, in accordance with laws devised for their governance, and over which the man himself has no authority, no mastership, no control. For each of these thousands of mechanisms the Creator has planned an enemy, whose office is to harass it, pester it, persecute it, damage it, afflict it with pains, and miseries, and ultimate destruction. (*WIM&OPW*, 427)

19. James L. Gibbons and S. L. Miller, "An Image of Contemporary Hospital Chaplaincy."

20. Lewis Mehl-Madrona, *Coyote Medicine: Lessons from Native-American Healing*, 33.

21. Leon Eisenberg, "Why Is There a Conflict between Complementary/Alternative Medicine and the Medical Establishment?"

22. Horacio Fabrega, Jr., "Medical Validity in Eastern and Western Traditions."

23. Michael B. Frank and Harriet Elinor Smith, eds., *Mark Twain's Letters, Volume 6, 1874–1875*, 582.

1. A Sickly, Precarious, Tiresome, and Uncertain Child

1. Dixon Wecter, *Sam Clemens of Hannibal*, 80.

2. R. I. Holcombe, *History of Marion County, Missouri, 1884*, 915.

3. Dahlia Armon and Walter Blair, "Biographical Directory."

4. Wecter, *Sam Clemens of Hannibal*, 55.
5. Ibid., 111.
6. Ibid., 55.
7. Ibid., 43.

2. Allopathic Medicine: Taking Heroic Measures

1. John Harley Warner, *The Therapeutic Perspective: Medical Practice, Knowledge, and Identity in America, 1820–1885*, 63.
2. As traditional medicine became increasingly science-based in the twentieth century, it discarded these concepts, which are compatible with the notion of "holistic medicine." Paradoxically, the attitudes traditional medicine left behind were incorporated into the various brands of "alternative" or "complementary" medicine that came into being. Because the philosophies of alternative medical sects are very similar to the holistic approaches that were shed by the "old" orthodox medicine, it can be argued that it is really traditional medicine that has changed its position from its "holistic" beginnings, and thus the mainstream medicine of today is the true "alternative" medicine. See Don G. Bates, "Why Not Call Modern Medicine 'Alternative'?"
3. Charles E. Rosenberg, "The Therapeutic Revolution: Medicine, Meaning, and Social Change in Nineteenth-Century America."
4. Warner, *Therapeutic Perspective*, 92.
5. This is in direct contrast to contemporary medical practice, where the need to conceptualize microscopic, genetic, and biochemical processes has become an essential skill. In the provocative chapter "Who Has Seen a Blood Sugar?" from his book by the same name, Dr. Frank Davidoff observes that the blood sugars of his patients with diabetes were "very real to me . . . almost tangible," even though he had never *seen* one. "How can something invisible be so real?" he asks. "Perhaps that isn't such a mystery when you consider that the essence of medical education is to create those very intangibles, the mental models of anatomical structure, physiological function, and pathophysiological dislocations . . . woven together into a truly extraordinary conceptual structure, a whole virtual world. Over time, that world becomes so real, so tangible, that once we have entered it, we never quite leave it" (*Who Has Seen a Blood Sugar? Reflections on Medical Education*, 96).
6. Doris Webster and Samuel Webster, "Whitewashing Jane Clemens."
7. Wecter, *Sam Clemens of Hannibal*, 55–56.
8. In 1847, the town of Hannibal had fifteen physicians to care for its population of three thousand (Donald H. Welsh, "Sam Clemens' Hannibal, 1836–1838").

3. Scarlet Fever Will Be True to You

1. Both the yellow fever virus and its *Aedes aegypti* mosquito vector were believed to have been imported from Africa as a side effect of the slave trade.
2. K. David Patterson, "Yellow Fever Epidemics and Mortality in the United States, 1693–1905." Memphis was devastated by yellow fever epidemics in 1873 (when up to four thousand people died) and again in 1878 (when there were more than five thousand deaths, representing about 10 percent of the city's population).
3. Whether the epidemic described by Pamela actually was yellow fever is not certain. It is known that yellow fever traveled as far upriver as Cairo, Illinois (Patter-

son, "Yellow Fever Epidemics"), and it is certainly possible that it could have gone the extra distance to Hannibal. The fact that the outbreak occurred during the winter months, after the typical summertime mosquito season, seems unusual. The taxonomy of infectious illnesses was far from complete, and the outbreak may have represented some other infectious illness associated with jaundice.

4. The measles epidemic was actually in 1844 (R. Kent Rasmussen, *Mark Twain A to Z: The Essential Reference to His Life and Writings*, 41). According to the *History of Marion County*, measles broke out in Hannibal in the spring of 1844 "with uncommon virulence." Nearly forty people died from the outbreak, and there were seven deaths from measles in a single day (Holcombe, *History of Marion County*, 900).

5. Cyril Clemens, *Mark Twain the Letter Writer*, 102.

6. The greatest risk for death from measles occurs when the infected patient is very old or very young. As Tom Sawyer explained to Huck Finn, "Measles never kills anybody except grown people and babies" (*HH&T*, 184).

7. Ronald D. Greenwood, "An Account of a Scarlatina Epidemic, 1839."

8. S. R. Duncan, S. Scott, and C. J. Duncan, "Modelling the Dynamics of Scarlet Fever Epidemics in the Nineteenth Century"; C. J. Duncan, S. R. Duncan, and S. Scott, "The Dynamics of Scarlet Fever Epidemics in England and Wales in the Nineteenth Century."

9. Greenwood, "Account of a Scarlatina Epidemic." The physician, Dr. D. M. Borland, initiated treatment with the application of mustard to the stomach and extremities. Using typical allopathic therapy, he then proceeded to include "small doses of calomel, repeated every two hours until it operated on the bowels," followed by "cold-pressed castor oil, to keep up a regular but moderate evacuation of the bowels throughout the disease." To decrease the swelling and pain of the tonsils, he recommended that a mixture of vinegar and turpentine "be rubbed on until it produced an eruption, which it generally did in the course of a few hours, and with the happiest effect." Next, Borland had the patient sponged every half-hour with a mixture of water and cold vinegar "with the most gratifying results ... Indeed, sponging was the sheet-anchor of my hopes" (ibid.).

10. Barry M. Gray, "Streptococcal Infections."

11. In a dinner speech in 1909, Clemens recalled another example of deafness that came from meningitis, or "brain fever," that had been caused by scarlet fever. "Helen Keller ... that marvelous girl, that wonderful southern girl, that girl who was stone deaf, blind, and dumb from scarlet-fever when she was a baby eighteen months old ... the most marvelous person of her sex that has existed on this earth since Joan of Arc" (*MT Speaking*, 642).

12. As he witnessed Jim's remorse and anguish for unfairly punishing his innocent daughter, Huck began to understand Jim as being something more than the runaway property of another man. By sharing his shame and sadness, Jim allowed Huck to see that they were fellow human beings who shared the same pains and guilts. As Huck saw Jim "setting there with his head down betwixt his knees, moaning and mourning to himself," the boy had an episode of enlightenment that moved him past the restrictions of his upbringing: "I do believe he cared just as much for his people as white folks does for their'n. It don't seem natural, but I reckon it's so" (*Huck Finn*, 201).

13. Clemens thought about writing a story based on this experience, featuring the McWilliams family. He had already written three stories about the fictional family, whose experiences paralleled some of the miscommunications, misunderstandings, and misadventures of his own family—"Experience of the McWilliamses with Membranous Croup," "Mrs. McWilliams and the Lightning," and "The McWilliamses

and the Burglar Alarm." Clemens's idea was to have the McWilliamses fumigate their house with sulfuric acid after encountering what would turn out to be a "false case of Scarlet Fever." The acid would ruin all the metalwork in their house, and later they would discover that the presumed scarlet fever was in truth "nothing but a rash" (*N&J-2*, 508).

14. James Osgood (1836–1892), a publisher and a friend of Clemens's, was a poor businessman. Clemens blamed Osgood for low sales of *Life on the Mississippi*, which had been published in 1883.

4. The Cholera Days of '49

1. Rasmussen, *Mark Twain A to Z*, 67.
2. Wecter, *Sam Clemens of Hannibal*, 214.
3. William M. McPheeters, "Epidemic of Cholera in St. Louis in 1849," 79.
4. Wecter, *Sam Clemens of Hannibal*, 213–14.
5. McPheeters, "Epidemic of Cholera in St. Louis," 83.
6. Ibid., 81–84.
7. Ibid., 88.
8. Stephen E. Ambrose, *Undaunted Courage: Meriwether Lewis, Thomas Jefferson, and the Opening of the American West*, 89. Rush provisioned Lewis with fifty dozen Rush's Pills in addition to other drugs, including 1,300 doses of "physic" for use as purgatives, 1,100 doses of "emetic" to cause vomiting, and 3,500 doses of "diaphoretic" to induce sweating, in addition to drugs for blistering and salivation and supplies such as lancets and syringes.
9. McPheeters, "Epidemic of Cholera in St. Louis," 89–90.
10. The modern-day "gallows humor" of medicine refers to the same principle whenever a cynical physician assures his colleagues that there should be no reason for excessive concern when treating a hemorrhaging patient. No matter how severe the bleeding appears to be, the outcome is predictable for every case—sooner or later, the bleeding will *always* stop!
11. Martin Kaufman, *Homeopathy in America: The Rise and Fall of a Medical Heresy*, 2; Ronald V. Loge, " 'Two Dozes of Barks and Opium': Lewis and Clark as Physicians."
12. John F. Burnum, "Medical Vampires."
13. The text was still used by practitioners well into the nineteenth century, as Clemens noted. "In 1861 this deadly book was still working the cemeteries—down in Virginia. For three generations and a half it had been going quietly along, enriching the earth with its slain. Up to its last free day it was trusted and believed in, and its devastating advice taken, as was shown by notes inserted between its leaves" (*£1m Bank-note*, 244).
14. McPheeters, "Epidemic of Cholera in St. Louis," 89–90.
15. Ibid.
16. Ibid., 91.
17. Holcombe, *History of Marion County*, 297; Wecter, *Sam Clemens of Hannibal*, 213.
18. Clemens managed to avoid cholera during his childhood, but the infection eventually caught up with him in 1856, as he mentioned in a May 1869 letter to Livy Langdon. "If my memory serves me I have been bedridden only twice before in 23 years—cholera in St Louis 16 years ago—& 20 hours in Damascus 2 years ago" (*Ltrs-3*, 246).

In *The Innocents Abroad*, Clemens described the details of his 1867 experience with cholera in Damascus.

The last twenty-four hours we stayed in Damascus I lay prostrate with a violent attack of cholera, or cholera morbus, and therefore had a good chance and a good excuse to lie there on that wide divan and take an honest rest. I had nothing to do but
listen to the pattering of the fountains and take medicine and throw it up again. It
was dangerous recreation, but it was pleasanter than traveling in Syria. I had
plenty of snow from Mount Hermon, and, as it would not stay on my stomach,
there was nothing to interfere with my eating it—there was always room for more.
I enjoyed myself very well. Syrian travel has its interesting features, like travel in
any other part of the world, and yet to break your leg or have the cholera adds a
welcome variety to it. . . .
    . . . The very first thing one feels like doing when he gets into camp, all burning
up and dusty, is to hunt up a bath. We followed the stream up to where it gushes
out of the mountainside, three hundred yards from the tents, and took a bath that
was so icy that if I did not know this was the main source of the sacred river, I
would expect harm to come of it. It was bathing at noonday in the chilly source of
the Abana, "River of Damascus," that gave me the cholera, so Dr. B. said. However,
it generally does give me the cholera to take a bath. (*Inn. Abroad*, 470)

Dr. B. was Dr. George Birch of Hannibal. Clemens's illness was apparently more
than a laughing matter at the time, as he later wrote in 1874 after he learned of
Birch's death: "I have always held Dr. Birch in grateful memory because he stood by
me so stanchly when I was dangerously ill in Damascus" (Frank and Smith, eds.,
Twain's Letters, Volume 6, 25).

5. Fire in a Liquid Form

1. A batch of the Pain-Killer was mixed up by combining 5 gallons of alcohol
with 2 1/4 pounds of gum myrrh, 10 ounces of capsicum (the active ingredient of
cayenne pepper), 8 ounces of gum opium, 6 ounces of gum benzoin, and 3 ounces of
gum fuiaic (Stewart H. Holbrook, *The Golden Age of Quackery*, 152–53).
2. Ibid., 155.
3. Ibid., 15.
4. Holbrook, *Golden Age of Quackery*, 154. In truth, when Dr. William McPheeters
was systematically trying to find an effective cholera antidote, the first treatment he
rejected was one recommended by a Dr. Cartwright of St. Louis that consisted of
calomel, capsicum, and camphor. "This compound, instead of arresting the disease,
was found to be positively prejudicial," McPheeters discovered. He determined that
most of the problems from the Cartwright remedy could be attributed to the capsicum, which in many instances increased the severity of the gastritis. McPheeters
abandoned the use of capsicum as "worse than useless" in the treatment of cholera
("Epidemic of Cholera in St. Louis," 89), even as Perry Davis was actively promoting
his capsicum-laden Pain-Killer as the world's best cholera treatment.
5. Wecter, *Sam Clemens of Hannibal*, 213–14.

6. Patent Medicine: The Great American Fraud

1. James Harvey Young, "From Hooper to Hohensee: Some Highlights of American Patent Medicine Promotion."
2. Edgar Marquess Branch and Robert H. Hirst, eds., *Early Tales and Sketches,
Volume 2, 1864–1865*, 235. Benjamin Brandreth, one of America's most successful

patent medicine magnates, was an Englishman who came to New York and started making and selling Brandreth's Pills in the mid-1830s. He achieved immense success and within a few years needed an entire Broadway block for his factory and offices.

3. R. G. Guest, "The Great Patent Medicine Fraud."

4. Clemens's father was also a regular user of patent medicines, although Clemens himself may have been unaware of it at the time. Clemens's brother Orion wrote in 1880 that "our father doctored himself to death. He doctored himself from my earliest remembrance. During the latter part of his life he bought Cook's pills by the box, and took some daily" (Edgar M. Branch, Michael Frank, and Kenneth M. Sanderson, eds., *Mark Twain's Letters, Volume 1, 1853–1866*, 114–16). "Cook's pills" were the invention of Dr. John E. Cooke, a professor of the theory and practice of medicine at Transylvania University in Lexington, Kentucky. In the late 1820s, Cooke developed a new system of medical practice founded on the concept that "miasmata" was the ultimate cause of fever and almost every disease. Miasmata weakened the heart, and as a result the pulse diminished, the circulation worsened, and blood accumulated in the vena cava. The congestion of the vena cava was the eventual cause of disease as it interfered with numerous bodily functions and was particularly detrimental because of its suppression of bile secretion. Health could be restored by increasing the flow of bile and stimulating the weakened organs. The cure for all of this, Cooke maintained, could be found in Cooke's Pills, cathartic agents consisting of calomel compounded with rhubarb and aloe. Just as Benjamin Rush had found his panacea in Rush's Pills, Cooke similarly found his in Cooke's Pills—calomel and catharsis appear to have been the common denominators for both (Warner, *Therapeutic Perspective*, 47). In the 1840s Cooke's system was attacked vehemently by a medical student who wrote in his thesis, "The Vena-Cavism of Cooke, we thank God, has, like its originator, one foot in the grave," but only after it "set back medicine in the Valley of the Miss[issippi] at least twenty years" (Warner, *Therapeutic Perspective*, 48).

5. Young, "From Hooper to Hohensee."

6. Welsh, "Sam Clemens' Hannibal."

7. When the American Medical Association began its intense attack on the fraudulent patent medicine industry in the early twentieth century, it found Clemens's optimistic entrepreneur to be a useful model for the corruptness of patent medicine practices. "One is carried back to that delightful character of Mark Twain's, 'Colonel Sellers,'" stated the 1912 edition of the AMA's *Nostrums and Quackery* in its report on Murine Eye Remedy. Indeed, the advertising claims of the eye potion were reminiscent of the Colonel's Infallible Imperial Oriental Optic Liniment and Salvation for Sore Eyes: "Murine is Indicated in Cases of Weak Eyes, Inflamed Eyes, Tired Eyes, Strained Eyes, Children's Eyes, Itching Eyes, Blurring Eyes, Red Eyes." Murine's profit margin appears to have been similar to the one aspired to by Colonel Sellers, according to the AMA. "One wonders to what extent the therapeutic action of Murine is due to the price charged for it. If instead of paying $1.00 an ounce—the price charged—the public could buy it for 5 cents a gallon—the estimated cost—would the removal of such a potent psychic influence have any effect on the virtues of the preparation? The question is not one to be lightly disposed of or settled offhand" (*Nostrums and Quackery*, 605).

8. Welsh, "Sam Clemens' Hannibal." In *Tom Sawyer*, "Dr. Robinson" is the name of the character murdered by Injun Joe in the grave-robbing incident. In *Huckleberry Finn*, "Dr. Robinson" is the first person to question the claim of the King and the Duke that they are entitled to the inheritance of Peter Wilks; Robinson recognized that the King's "English accent" was phony.

9. James Harvey Young, "The Paradise of Quacks" and "From Hooper to Hohensee."

10. Clemens's attack on the patent medicine manufacturer was mentioned on a broadcast by radio host Dr. Dean Edell on April 18, 2000 (Cliff Walker, "Mark Twain and the Patent Medicine Ad"). Robert Slotta, a dealer in Mark Twain memorabilia, provided additional information (Slotta, "Mark Twain and the Patent Medicine Ad"). Robert Hirst of the Mark Twain Project confirms that the letter was written to J. H. Todd on November 20, 1905; Clemens dictated the letter to his secretary, Isabel V. Lyon, who wrote it in pencil. Clemens corrected it and signed it but never mailed it. Clemens's biographer Albert Bigelow Paine took it out of the Mark Twain Papers, and his great-grandson, Bigelow Paine Cushman, eventually obtained it and was able to sell it (personal communication, Robert H. Hirst, general editor, Mark Twain Project).

11. Young, "The Paradise of Quacks."

12. Patent medicines lingered on for many years. Perry Davis's Pain-Killer could be purchased in the United States and Canada as late as 1958, and each bottle continued to show the likeness of "Dr." Davis himself on the label—by mid-twentieth century, it was sold as "Liniment," with a parenthetical clarification that it was a liniment of the "Painkiller Brand" (Holbrook, *Golden Age of Quackery*, 155–56).

13. Samuel Hopkins Adams, "The Great American Fraud: The Scavengers." The identity of the servant is uncertain. Clemens identified the man as his butler, English, forty-three years old, "a drinker" for seventeen years, but a "*hard* drinker" in recent times. Clemens described the failure of Oppenheimer's therapy in a letter he wrote in November 1905 to members of Oppenheimer's advisory board: "Two years ago I sent him there on the 16th of February & he began the treatment. A week or two later he brought me the bill for the cure, & he was drunk at the time. I mentioned this to Dr. Oppenheimer, expecting him to smile, for I thought there was a touch of humor in the situation; but he merely said, 'oh, yes, that happens,' which I interpreted to mean that it was a not unusual incident" (*Ltrs-Microfilm-1*, vol. 10, #7191).

14. Clemens probably first contacted Adams about Oppenheimer in late 1905. The Mark Twain Papers contain a December 18, 1905, letter from Adams to Clemens in which Adams apologized for his delay in following up "in the matter of the Oppenheimer treatment" due to personal illness (MTP, #35071). In a letter written on July 28, 1906, Adams told Clemens he was "about ready to take up the Oppenheimer matter" and planned to have an article ready for *Collier's* by September. Adams asked Clemens to send him "any other material on hand which would be of value to me" and offered to visit Clemens if he had any additional information Adams could use in his article (MTP, #35520).

15. Adams, "The Great American Fraud." Adams's gratitude was evident from a letter he wrote to Clemens on August 10, 1906: "Your extremely interesting collection of Oppenheimer letters reached me safely, and I thank you heartily for them. What an extraordinary exhibit it is of mixed vanity and carelessness" (MTP, #35535).

16. Ibid. Although he was very grateful for the information Clemens had obtained, Adams wanted to be certain Clemens had the final word as to how his involvement was going to be portrayed. Prior to the publication of the article, Adams wrote to Clemens on August 10, 1906, in order to clarify the matter: "As there is no definite understanding of how far I could rightly make use of this material, I suggest that I send you that part of my 'copy' which deals with the Advisory Governors, for revision, as a safeguard against my involving you in the matter" (MTP, #35535). Adams

sent Clemens a rough draft of the article on August 29, prior to publication (MTP, #35552). Clemens responded promptly, sending Adams the letter signed as "Mark Twain" that was featured in the article. The letter from "Mark Twain" seems to have been Clemens's own idea, according to Adams's note of gratitude to Clemens on September 7, 1906: "I thank you for returning the manuscript, and particularly for your letter, which I am only too glad to publish. It puts the case so conclusively that I even feel a sort of sneaking sympathy for the eminent name-lenders" (MTP, #35565). Clemens's involvement in Adams's crusade seems to have been initiated by Clemens himself, and as the publication date for "The Scavengers" approached, Adams told Clemens, "I shall be most glad at any time to follow up any similar trails which you may suggest" (MTP, #35565). Adams's entire series was later published as a book, *The Great American Fraud*. The book states that the chapter entitled "The Scavengers" was "reprinted from 'Collier's Weekly,' September, 22, 1906," but all of the references to Clemens and Oppenheimer that appeared in the original article were left out of the book, with no explanation for the deletions. See Samuel Hopkins Adams, *The Great American Fraud*, 112–22.

17. James Harvey Young, *American Self-Dosage Medicines: An Historical Perspective*, 8–9.

18. *Nostrums and Quackery*, 605. The statute was focused on preventing the distribution of adulterated food (as exposed by Upton Sinclair's novel *The Jungle* in 1906); drug regulations to protect the public from misbranded patent medications were of secondary importance. The act made no effort to restrict dangerous drugs or deal with false advertising (Paul M. Wax, "Elixirs, Diluents, and the Passage of the 1938 Federal Food, Drug, and Cosmetic Act").

19. Cramp, *Nostrums and Quackery and Pseudo-Medicine*, 212.

20. Holbrook, *Golden Age of Quackery*, 16; Cramp, *Nostrums and Quackery and Pseudo-Medicine*, 690.

21. *Nostrums and Quackery*, 691.

22. Martin Gardner, *Fads and Fallacies in the Name of Science*, 229.

7. The Autopsy: "Dissection by the Doctors!"

1. Rasmussen, *Mark Twain A to Z*, 248.

2. Armon and Blair, "Biographical Directory," 339, 348.

3. Wecter, *Sam Clemens of Hannibal*, 116.

4. Ibid., 116–17.

5. Ron Powers, *Dangerous Water: A Biography of the Boy Who Became Mark Twain*, 204–6.

6. Ibid., 284.

7. Ibid., 287; Andrew Hoffman, *Inventing Mark Twain: The Lives of Samuel Langhorne Clemens*, 54.

8. The Great Dr. Joseph McDowell

1. E. J. Goodwin, *A History of Medicine in Missouri*, 37–38.

2. James Walter Wilson, "Joseph Nash McDowell, M.D."

3. James Thomas Flexner, *Doctors on Horseback: Pioneers of American Medicine*, 222.

4. Estelle Brodman, "The Great Eccentric."

5. H. Dwight Weaver and Paul A. Johnson, *Adventures at Mark Twain Cave*, 25.

6. Brodman, "The Great Eccentric."

7. Weaver and Johnson, *Adventures at Mark Twain Cave*, 25.

8. Wilson, "Joseph Nash McDowell."

9. Flexner, *Doctors on Horseback*, 221.

10. Sam Clemens was very much aware of the risks associated with suboptimal medical education: "A half-educated physician is not valuable. He thinks he can cure everything" (R. Kent Rasmussen, *The Quotable Mark Twain: His Essential Aphorisms, Witticisms, and Concise Opinions*, 211).

11. Goodwin, *History of Medicine in Missouri*, 129; Lonnie R. Speer, *Portals to Hell: Military Prisons of the Civil War*, 47.

12. Wilson, "Joseph Nash McDowell."

13. Ibid.

14. Bob Smith, Mark Twain Cave, personal communication (reference to Charles Van Ravenswaay, *St. Louis: An Informal History of the City and Its People, 1764–1865*, ed. Candace O'Connor [St. Louis: Missouri Historical Society Press, 1991]).

15. Brodman, "The Great Eccentric."

16. Flexner, *Doctors on Horseback*, 279.

17. Brodman, "The Great Eccentric."

18. Speer, *Portals to Hell*, 50.

19. Wecter, *Sam Clemens of Hannibal*, 301.

20. For the gate of iron, see letter of Eugene Connor to Harold Meloy, November 29, 1966, on file at Mammoth Cave National Park (personal communication, Charles DeCroix, Park Ranger, Mammoth Cave National Park); for the door of thick wood, see Weaver and Johnson, *Adventures at Mark Twain Cave*, 21. In *The Adventures of Tom Sawyer*, Judge Thatcher sealed the door to prevent children from entering and getting lost in the cave, and in so doing he unknowingly blocked Injun Joe's egress.

21. *The Medical Repository* (New York), n.s. 3 (1817): 187–89; Samuel L. Mitchill, letter, *Transactions of the American Antiquarian Society*, 1 (1820): 318–21; Angelo I. George, *Mummies, Catacombs, and Mammoth Cave* (Louisville: George Publishing Company, 1994).

22. Wilson, "Joseph Nash McDowell."

23. Weaver and Johnson, *Adventures at Mark Twain Cave*, 29.

24. Harold Meloy, "Medics at Mammoth Cave."

25. Chuck DeCroix, personal communication.

26. Victor Fischer et al., eds., "Jim's 'Ghost' Story"; Armon and Blair, "Biographical Directory," 330.

27. From the *Hannibal Gazette*, February 25, 1847:

At the distance of two miles south of the City, and near a half mile from the river, is a somewhat celebrated cave, called "Simms Cave" from the name of a gentleman, who exploded [sic] it, and made saltpetre therefrom. This Cave, in later years obtained, an unexampled celebrity and notoriety from the circumstance of its mouth being fortified, by an iron door, the deposite of ordinance, and some 500 stand of small arms therein, and other sepulchural [sic] indications. Without accounting for the objects of this fortification, it need not be stated, that many strange and curious speculations and reports were rife, at the time, through the country. We may only remark that this event was just previous to, and while the premonitory rumors prevailed of the present Mexican war.

From the *Hannibal Gazette*, November 4, 1847:

> In one place we saw the sarcophagus of Dr. McDowell's child, which has been suspended some years, in this quite *[sic]* resting place. The cavern belongs to the Doct. and in it he had once cannon, and 500 stand of arms for the invasion of Mexico; a scene, which excited not little talk at the time; and comment since. He is now erecting a octogonal towers *[sic]* in St. Louis near Cheotcau's pond; a dissecting room: the lower story of which it is said, will be fortified with these same arms. Such are some of Dr McDowell's eccentriaties *[sic]*.

28. The interactions between Jim Lampton and the McDowell family eventually became even more intimate and complex. In the late 1850s, Dr. John J. McDowell, one of McDowell's sons, was taken in as a boarder by Lampton and his wife, Ella (Armon and Blair, "Biographical Directory," 330). Young McDowell claimed he was fleeing from the animosity of Joseph Nash McDowell's second wife, and years later he stated that the Lamptons "were so kind to me that I never left them. I have felt as one of the family ever since that day" (Armon and Blair, "Biographical Directory," 334). Clemens, who had little respect for Ella (he characterized her as a "loud vulgar beauty" [*Inds.*, 98] and "a coarse, vain, rude, exacting idiot" [Armon and Blair, "Biographical Directory," 330]), viewed the social arrangements between McDowell and the Lamptons as far less innocent: "Young Dr. John McDowell boarded with them, followed them from house to house; an arrant scandal to everybody with eyes—but Jim hadn't any, and believed in the loyalty of both of them. God took him at last, the only good luck he ever had after he met Ella. . . . Doctor John and Ella continued together" (*Inds.*, 98).

29. Victor Doyno, "Textual Addendum." The segment remained unknown until the misplaced first half of Clemens's manuscript was discovered in 1990. The episode has subsequently been published as "Jim and the Dead Man" and has also been referred to as "the cadaver episode" (Michael Patrick Hearn, ed., *The Annotated Huckleberry Finn*, 447).

30. *Adventures of Huckleberry Finn*, Comprehensive Edition, 62.

31. Wecter, *Sam Clemens of Hannibal*, 301.

9. Hydropathic Medicine: The Flush Times

1. As a farm boy, Priessnitz observed that injuries and abnormalities of horses' hooves seemed to heal sooner after bathing with cold water, and he learned the art of "water cure" from an old man who used the system to treat diseases of cattle. After being thrown off a horse, Priessnitz was convinced that he hastened the healing of his own serious bruises and fractures by using a wet towel as a bandage and drinking cold water. He determined that induction of profuse sweating made the use of cold water even more effective (Marshall Scott Legan, "Hydropathy in America: A Nineteenth Century Panacea").

2. Ibid.

3. John W. Dodds, *The Age of Paradox: A Biography of England, 1841–1851*, 369.

4. McPheeters, "Epidemic of Cholera in St. Louis," 90.

5. Clemens commented that the springs may not have been as profitable as might have been predicted due to the large number of patients who either "forget to pay for the benefits they have received" or who "confess at once that they are penni-

less" (*ET&S-1*, 273). It is likely that Samuel Clemens fell into at least one of those categories.

6. This attitude spilled over to other aspects of Clemens's life. He was a believer in science and technology. His unyielding belief in the potential of the flawed typesetter invented by James Paige led him to unwisely invest large sums of money in the machine, which eventually led to his bankruptcy (John Lauber, *The Inventions of Mark Twain*, 264–65).

7. Laura E. Skandera-Trombley, *Mark Twain in the Company of Women*, 82.

8. Jervis Langdon, Livy's father, purchased Quarry Farm in 1869. When he died the following year, Langdon left the property to his adopted daughter Susan Langdon Crane and her husband. Clemens spent most of his summers at Quarry Farm between 1871 and 1889 and did much of his most important writing there.

9. Edward Douglas Branch, *The Sentimental Years, 1836–1860*, 264.

10. Legan, "Hydropathy in America."

11. Rasmussen, *Mark Twain A to Z*, 275.

12. Susan E. Cayleff, "Gender, Ideology, and the Water-Cure Movement," 88.

13. John Cooley, ed., *Mark Twain's Aquarium: The Samuel Clemens–Angelfish Correspondence, 1905–1910*, 262.

14. Legan, "Hydropathy in America."

15. *The Water-Cure Journal* reported that more than a thousand water-cure physicians were in practice in March 1851, even though the American Hydropathic Institute—which claimed to be the world's first medical school based on the principals of hydrotherapy—did not actually open in New York City until later in 1851. A medical degree could be earned in as little as three months; the diploma signed by the faculty stated, "We certify that ____ has diligently attended the Lectures and Instructions of this Institute, and has acquired such thorough knowledge of the Principles and Practice of Medicine, Surgery, and Obstetrics, as to merit confidence as a Water-Cure Physician" (Harry B. Weiss and Howard R. Kemble, *The Great American Watercure Craze: A History of Hydropathy in the United States*, 33–34).

The New York Hydropathic School opened in 1853 and after three years of operation changed its name to the New York Hygeio-Therapeutic College. Its proprietor petitioned the New York state legislature for a charter but met opposition from the allopathic physician who was the chairman of the Committee on Medical Schools; however, the legislature eventually granted the charter in 1857. Other hydropathic medical schools that opened between 1853 and 1860 included the New Jersey Hydropathic Collegiate Institute, the Philadelphia Private Hydropathic College, the Hydropathic College and Institute in Loretta, Pennsylvania, and the Franklin Water-Cure and Physiological School near Winchester, Tennessee.

16. Skandera-Trombley, *Mark Twain in the Company of Women*, 83–84.

17. As with most other nineteenth-century "irregular" medical practitioners, the Gleasons eventually became more diverse in their methodology, extending the scope of their practice to include electrical treatment, Swedish movements, Swedish rest cure, and homeopathic treatment. In fact, the hydrotherapy movement in general became more eclectic as it evolved into a system with an increasing focus on issues of hygiene and public health. For example, when Clara Barton (Civil War humanitarian and founder of the American Red Cross) sought out the water cure treatment in 1876 for her problems with "prostration of the nervous system," her therapy included not only internal and external water (cold bathing) but also fresh air, exercise, a simple diet (including fruit and graham crackers and avoidance of stimulants such as tea or coffee), rest, and freedom from tight corsets or other restrictive clothing

(Allen D. Spiegel, "The Role of Gender, Phrenology, Discrimination, and Nervous Prostration in Clara Barton's Career").

18. Rasmussen, *Mark Twain A to Z*, 465.

19. Resa Willis, *Mark and Livy: The Love Story of Mark Twain and the Woman Who Almost Tamed Him*, 75; Skandera-Trombley, *Mark Twain in the Company of Women*, 96.

20. Norman Gevitz, *The D.O.'s: Osteopathic Medicine in America*, 123.

21. Cayleff, "Gender, Ideology, and the Water-Cure Movement," 96–97.

22. Hydrotherapy continues to be an accepted medical treatment in the Czech Republic, where patients go for typical three-week visits to thirty-seven spa centers, located near natural mineral springs. The various spa districts specialize in treatment of specific disorders. The spas visited by Clemens and his family are still actively in use; Marianske Lazne specializes in gynecologic disorders, and Frantiskovy Lazne emphasizes the treatment of children's diseases. Like the American water cures of the nineteenth century, these spas have an eclectic approach that includes clinical medicine, rehabilitation, physical therapy, and lifestyle modifications in diet, exercise, and stress reduction. As with the hydropathic medicine of an earlier age, the water therapy may be administered internally (as with ingestion of local spring water to aid the digestion of ulcer patients) or externally (with effervescent carbon dioxide baths used for hypertension and alternating hot and cold water baths for patients with circulatory problems). As with virtually all nontraditional medical systems, physiological rationalizations for the treatment are readily offered by its advocates; for example, underwater massage with pressurized water is said to mimic the effect of exercise on nerve endings, thereby improving the circulation (Susan Thorne, "Spas Accepted Part of Health Care in Czech Republic").

23. Clemens was intrigued by the "specialization" of the various spas for particular health problems, as he had noted seven years earlier, when he wrote "Aix-les-Bains,"

> But what I came here for, five weeks ago, was the baths. My right arm was disabled with rheumatism. To sit at home in America and guess out the European bath best fitted for a particular ailment or combination of ailments, it is not possible, and it would not be a good idea to experiment in that way, anyhow. There are a great many curative baths on the Continent, and some are good for one disease but bad for another. So it is necessary to let your physician name a bath for you. As a rule, Americans go to Europe to get this advice, and South Americans go to Paris for it. Now and then an economist chooses his bath himself and does a thousand miles of railroading to get to it, and then the local physicians tell him he has come to the wrong place. He sees that he has lost time and money and strength, and almost the minute he realizes this he loses his temper. I had the rheumatism and was advised to go to Aix, not so much because I had that disease as because I had the promise of certain others. What they were was not explained to me. (*CT-2*, 8)

24. Carl Dolmetsch, *"Our Famous Guest": Mark Twain in Vienna*, 222.

25. Hygiene involved much more than personal cleanliness. The scope of poor hygiene included inadequacies in the quality of air, lighting, ventilation, or food and drink; it encompassed either excesses or deficiencies in physical activity, digestion, or "passions." Fortunately, the Langdons had a good income and were not likely to suffer from a state of deprivation; nor were they ostentatious or extravagant people, and so they were not at high risk for suffering from illnesses brought about by gluttony, according to the principles of hydropathic medicine.

10. Neurasthenia: The American Disease

1. Dona L. Davis, "George Beard and Lydia Pinkham: Gender, Class, and Nerves in Late Nineteenth Century America." In the sketch "Marienbad, a Health Factory," Clemens parodied the clients of European spas who continued to have an obsessive focus on their livers as the regulator of their health.

> Go where you will, hide where you may, you cannot escape that word liver; you overhear it constantly—in the street, in the shop, in the theater, in the music grounds. When you see two or a dozen people of ordinary bulk talking together, you know they are talking about their livers.... After a few days you will begin to notice that out of these people's talk a gospel is framing itself and next you will find yourself believing it. It is this—that a man is not what his rearing, his schooling, his beliefs, his principles make him, he is what his liver makes him; that with a healthy liver he will have the clear-seeing eye, the honest heart, the sincere mind, the loving spirit, the loyal soul, the truth and trust and faith that are based as Gibraltar is based, and that with an unhealthy liver he must and will have the opposite of all these, he will see nothing as it really is, he cannot trust anybody, or believe in anything, his moral foundations are gone from under him. (*Complete Essays*, 106)

2. Susan E. Abbey and Paul E. Garfinkel, "Neurasthenia and Chronic Fatigue Syndrome: The Role of Culture in the Making of a Diagnosis."
3. George F. Drinka, *The Birth of Neurosis: Myth, Malady, and the Victorians*, 191.
4. John Stea and William Fried, "Remedies for a Society's Debilities: Medicines for Neurasthenia in Victorian America."
5. Davis, "George Beard and Lydia Pinkham."
6. Stea and Fried, "Remedies for a Society's Debilities"; A. D. Wood, "The Fashionable Diseases: Women's Complaints and Their Treatment in Nineteenth-Century America."
7. Davis, "George Beard and Lydia Pinkham"; Stea and Fried, "Remedies for a Society's Debilities."
8. Stea and Fried, "Remedies for a Society's Debilities." Black cohosh (*Cimicifuga racemosa*) remains a popular "natural remedy," and it is heavily marketed for women's health needs. Mainstream medicine is starting to take a look at herbal products such as black cohosh and is finding that many do indeed possess pharmacological activity; see S. Lieberman, "A Review of the Effectiveness of *Cimicifuga racemosa* (Black Cohosh) for the Symptoms of Menopause." Interestingly, as women's health concerns have shifted from worries about "inadequate nerve force" to issues of estrogen deficiency, black cohosh has stopped being a stimulant and has started functioning as an estrogen (at least for the purposes of its marketing; presumably, what it *really* does or does not do for women has remained constant). In 2000, black cohosh was available in several versions over the Internet. One formulation, sold as "Ex-Stress," in its marketing follows the Lydia Pinkham tradition of treating women for their nerve problems: "Ex-Stress is an herbal formula that synergistically combines valerian, hops and black cohosh to enhance the relaxing effects of these herbs traditionally used for their calming effects." In contrast, the marketers of "Black Cohosh Extract" had caught up with the times, touting the fact that "Black Cohosh contains substances called phytoestrogens that have an effect similar to the female hormone estrogen. These estrogenic compounds are used to help support the female

reproductive system and cycle." Some marketers are willing to have it both ways, and the same company that sells black cohosh as "Ex-Stress" has another black cohosh product named "Change-O-Life" that it bills as "a popular women's formula, with herbs traditionally used for menopausal support." The producer of these products also has a disclaimer that warns the public (and the lawyers) that these compounds are "not intended to diagnose, treat, cure or prevent any disease."

9. Davis, "George Beard and Lydia Pinkham."

10. Willis, *Mark and Livy*, 24–26.

11. Skandera-Trombley, *Mark Twain in the Company of Women*, 82.

12. Susan E. Cayleff, "'Prisoner of Their Own Feebleness': Women, Nerves, and Western Medicine—A Historical Overview."

13. Susan K. Harris, *The Courtship of Olivia Langdon and Mark Twain*, 33.

14. Nancy Roth, "Electrotherapy, Nineteenth-Century Neurasthenia, and the Case of Alice James."

15. Robert L. Martensen, "Was Neurasthenia a 'Legitimate Morbid Entity'?"

16. Willis, *Mark and Livy*, 25.

17. Skandera-Trombley, *Mark Twain in the Company of Women*, 83–84.

18. Ibid., 84–88.

11. Dr. Newton, the Quack

1. Harold Aspiz, "Mark Twain and 'Doctor' Newton."

2. A. E. Newton, *The Modern Bethesda, or The Gift of Healing Restored*, 294.

3. Skandera-Trombley, *Mark Twain in the Company of Women*, 87–88, 92. The term *Pott's disease* as used by Taylor appears to be no more than a general designation for scoliosis (in contrast to its current use as an eponym for tuberculosis of the spine), as indicated by his *The Mechanical Treatment of Angular Curvature, or Pott's Disease of the Spine*. Paralysis related to tuberculous Pott's disease occurs when a vertebral body collapses due to bony destruction by the infection, with resulting impingement on the spinal cord. This is not reversible. The tuberculous infection, which enters through the respiratory tract and is disseminated throughout the body, would persist and lead to a wasting death unless treated with specific antibiotics (which were not to be available for another century). Tuberculosis was the "consumption" of the nineteenth century, an infection with recurring fevers and sweats, a disease of wasting and death, but certainly not the disease of Olivia Langdon Clemens. As noted by Dr. Leon Eisenberg, paralysis can be cured by faith healing when it is the result of a conversion reaction, but the documentation of any cure of a patient with paralysis caused by an inflammatory disease or tumor is "rare or absent" (Eisenberg, "Why Is There a Conflict?").

4. The spelling was changed to "Susy" when she grew older.

5. His letter to Clara also contains a reference to the illness and death of Clemens's first child. Just as "Hosannah Maria's" illness originated from a drive in the rain, Clemens's only son, Langdon, became ill in 1872 following exposure to inclement weather while under Clemens's supervision. The illness ultimately resulted in the death of the child (for which Clemens took personal blame and never forgave himself). In addition, the doll's deafness appears to borrow from the history of boyhood friend Tom Nash, who developed an infection and lost his hearing and speech after falling through the ice of the frozen Mississippi River.

12. Electrotherapy: Taking Charge with the Current Fad

1. Dennis Stillings, "A Survey of the History of Electrical Stimulation for Pain to 1900."

2. Nicholas Anthony Cambridge, "Electrical Apparatus Used in Medicine before 1900."

3. Stillings, "Survey of the History of Electrical Stimulation."

4. In another variation, mouth electrodes and rectal electrodes were used to enhance the absorption of medications believed to enter the body best through its mucous membranes. As was the case with bleeding by leeches, being a true believer in the therapeutic plan would seem to have been a crucial prerequisite for receiving the treatment in this manner.

5. Nancy Roth, "American Electrotherapy."

6. Quacks also recognized a good thing when they saw it, and electricity had many obvious attractions to the charlatan. In 1790 James Graham of Edinburgh decreed himself president of the Council of Health and invented the "celestial bed." Also known as the "medico-magnetico-musico-electrical bed," this device consisted of a group of electrical devices supported by forty glass pillars and was guaranteed to cure infertility. The "electric belt" was introduced in the early nineteenth century; it consisted of small square plates of zinc connected with copper wires and actually did generate an electric current. Later versions such as the Pulvermacher Electric Belt (consisting of a series of wooden cylinders joined by a flexible belt, each cylinder wrapped in zinc and copper wires and soaked in vinegar before wearing) became increasingly popular and were recommended for treatment of "all nervous, chronic and functional diseases" (Nancy Roth, "The Great Patent Medicine Era").

7. John S. Haller Jr., "Medical Cataphoresis: Electrical Experimentation and Nineteenth Century Therapeutics."

8. In this letter to Emilie Rogers, Clemens touted billiards as a cure-all for a multitude of ailments. For a while, he seemed to believe that billiards was the panacea he had been seeking. Clemens told Rogers, "The billiard table is better than the doctors. It is driving out the heartburn in a most promising way." He attributed some of the benefit of billiards to the physical activity involved, as the physical positioning used to play the game "brings into play every muscle in the body and exercises them all." Clemens demonstrated his usual enthusiasm for his newest health-generating discovery: "If Mr. Rogers will take to daily billiard he can do without the doctors" (*Ltrs-Rogers*, 619–20).

9. James derived little benefit from the unpleasant electricity treatments. It was her opinion that electrotherapy had the "starching properties of the longest Puritan dissent" (Roth, "Electrotherapy").

10. Newton, *The Modern Bethesda*, 140, 160.

11. Eugene D. Robin, "The Cult of the Swan-Ganz Catheter: Overuse and Abuse of Pulmonary Flow Catheters," citing W. A. Silverman, *Retrolental Fibroplasia: A Modern Parable* (New York, Grune and Stratton, 1980). Silverman made his comment in a discussion of the earlier treatments of premature infants with high concentrations of oxygen. Although the treatment seemed to be a rational approach at the time it was initiated, it was later discovered to cause blindness.

12. Clemens described Livy's symptoms of orthopnea and paroxysmal nocturnal dyspnea that are typical of patients with severe congestive heart failure: "Livy was sitting up in bed, with her head bent forward—she had not been able to lie down for seven months. . . . Five times in the last four months she spent an hour and more

fighting violently for breath, and she lived in the awful fear of death by strangulation" (*Autob/MTA*, 345). On August 11, 1902, Livy suffered one of her frightening episodes of paroxysmal dyspnea that was accompanied by a terrifying sense of impending doom, as Clemens described in his autobiography. "I was wakened by a cry. I saw Mrs Clemens standing on the opposite side of the room, leaning against the wall for support, and panting. She said, 'I am dying.'" Even then, when Clemens consulted a physician, he was advised that Livy's symptoms were related to nervous problems and required rest therapy. "I helped her back to the bed and sent for Dr. Leonard, a New York physician. He said it was a nervous break-down and that nothing but absolute rest, seclusion and careful nursing could help her" (*Autob/MTA*, 331). Even as Livy approached her death from cardiac disease, Clemens continued to envision his wife's medical problems in terms of the imagery of neurasthenia: "she would not rest. She could not rest. She never was intended to rest. She had the spirit of a steam engine in a frame of flesh. It was always racking that frame with its tireless energy; it was always exiting of it labors that were beyond its strength" (*Autob/MTA*, 327).

13. The Rest Cure

1. Mark Olfson, "The Weir Mitchell Rest Cure."
2. S. Weir Mitchell, *Fat and Blood: An Essay on the Treatment of Certain Forms of Neurasthenia and Hysteria*, 49. Charlotte Perkins Gilman, treated for neurasthenia by Mitchell, disagreed with his prohibitions from writing and his recommendations that she lead a "domestic" lifestyle. This experience prompted her to write the short story "The Yellow Wallpaper," which described the evolution of her illness from nervous exhaustion to psychotic depression as a result of the restrictions of Mitchell's "rest cure" (Anne Hudson Jones, "Literature and Medicine: Narratives of Mental Illness").
3. "The Hospital Hotel."
4. Geoffrey C. Ward and Dayton Duncan, *Mark Twain: An Illustrated Biography*, 182.
5. Years later, Webster's son would come to his father's defense by discussing the neurasthenia that had thwarted the productivity of Clemens's publisher: "Starting a new publishing house on such an enormous scale, with worries and long hours, had broken his health. He spent the summer of 1887 at Far Rockaway, coming to the office when he could. His neuralgia was terrific. His mother and father came down to visit him and were shocked at his condition. He was very irritable, and the slightest thing would bring an outburst. His mother was often hurt by his irascibility, but the rest of the household understood the situation" (*MTBM*, 387).

14. Osteopathy: The Medicine of Manipulation

1. Norman Gevitz, "Osteopathic Medicine: From Deviance to Difference."
2. S. R. Mercer, "The First Century of Osteopathic Medicine in the United States of America."
3. Joel D. Howell, "The Paradox of Osteopathy."
4. Mercer, "First Century of Osteopathic Medicine."
5. Still had at least one more link to Samuel Clemens—an early postcard of

Clemens's boyhood home showed Dr. Still as an incidental passerby (M. M. Brashear, "Dr. Still and Mark Twain").

6. Dolmetsch, *"Our Famous Guest,"* 261.

7. Mark Twain to Henry James, April 17, 1900, in Jason Gary Horn, *Mark Twain and William James: Crafting a Free Self,* 168.

8. Brashear, "Dr. Still and Mark Twain."

9. Due to the perceived superiority of European medicine, American physicians who had a background of wealth and education frequently trained in Paris from the 1820s through the 1860s. Medical care was observational rather than interventional, and large amounts of information on the natural history of specific disease processes were collected. The Paris school initiated the use of simple statistics to assess the outcomes of patient management, and nothing was taken on faith—all therapies were open to doubt until they were proved to be effective by the collection and thoughtful interpretation of numerical data. To many traditionalists, however, the observational and numerical approach of the Paris school seemed cold, sterile, and antisocial as it reduced patients and therapies to statistics. By the 1860s, the prime destination for the European-bound American physician-in-training shifted from France to Germany. Vienna was the center of attention. Opportunities abounded for intensive clinical experience, education in pathological anatomy, and exposure to medical specialties. In contrast to the observational approaches of the French, the German method was strongly based in laboratory science. For the allopathic physicians who believed in the aggressive therapeutic orientation of American medicine, neither the Germans nor the French seemed to have much commitment to actually treating their patients: "Viennese and Parisian clinicians were, in American eyes . . . excellent scientists but poor healers" (Warner, *Therapeutic Perspective,* 199).

10. Through the years that Clemens lived in Hartford, most of his family's medical care was provided by two homeopathic doctors, Dr. Cincinnatus Taft and (after Taft's death) Dr. Edward Kellogg. When Susy developed meningitis, it appears that Kellogg was not consulted. Instead, Clemens's Nook Farm neighbor, Dr. William Porter Jr., attended Susy in her illness and signed her death certificate. Porter attended Rush Medical School in Chicago before graduating in 1882 from what is now Northwestern University. As was common for the better-trained physicians of that era, his education included two years of postgraduate study in Paris and Vienna. Porter was not as close to the Clemens family as Taft or Kellogg had been, but he was a member of the closely bound Nook Farm community of Hartford, and he knew Clemens as a neighbor. (Once, when Clemens could not get a good telephone connection to St. Louis, he called upon Porter so that he could use the doctor's phone; Porter's connection was not any better, and Clemens became enraged and destroyed Porter's telephone by attacking it with the doctor's cane.) See John F. Reed, "Samuel Clemens and Family: The Hartford Connection and Hartford Physicians."

11. "Mark Twain, Osteopath."

12. Ibid. In November 1896, Vermont became the first state to legalize the practice of osteopathy. The final state to do so was Mississippi, in 1973. California had passed a referendum in 1962 that stopped the licensing of osteopathic physicians, but the California Supreme Court voided the referendum, and osteopathy was reestablished in California in 1974 (Mercer, "First Century of Osteopathic Medicine").

13. This is a recurring theme for all groups that oppose "regular medicine." During the influenza epidemic of 1918–1919, osteopaths collected data that were purported to show that their treatments resulted in lower mortality figures than those of the allopathists (Norman Gevitz, "Sectarian Medicine").

14. Rasmussen, *Mark Twain A to Z,* 78.

15. The Plasmon Cure

1. Earlier, Rogers had bailed Clemens out from the bankruptcy that had been brought on by his unwise investments in an unsuccessful typesetter. Clemens saw Plasmon as an opportunity to show Rogers that he was a shrewd businessman, in spite of his prior failure. Rogers was not impressed, believing that Plasmon was an equally unwise investment (*Ltrs-Rogers*, 437).

2. Rudolf Virchow (1821–1902) is considered the "father of pathology." He was a highly respected researcher and political leader, and he led important public health reforms in Berlin.

16. Lies That Help and Lies That Hurt

1. Ami Schattner and Merav Tal, "Truth Telling and Patient Autonomy: The Patient's Point of View."

2. Mehl-Madrona, *Coyote Medicine*, 262.

3. William G. Porter, "Truth-Telling and Hope: The Dilemma of Modern Medicine."

4. K. B. Thomas, "General Practice Consultations: Is There Any Point in Being Positive?"

5. Peter A. Ubel, "Truth in the Most Optimistic Way."

6. John Lantos, *Do We Still Need Doctors?* 84.

7. For more on the cynical and caustic *Letters*, which Clemens wrote in 1909, see Rasmussen, *Mark Twain A to Z*, 280–82.

8. Michael LaCombe, "Letters of Intent."

9. Porter, "Truth-Telling and Hope."

10. Typhoid fever, also referred to as enteric fever, is caused by an infection with salmonella bacteria. The disease is transmitted through direct contact with an infected individual or through ingestion of contaminated food. Person-to-person spread is a particularly important mechanism of dissemination, as demonstrated by the case of "typhoid Mary," a cook in the early twentieth century who spread infection to approximately fifty other people. Typhoid fever is usually associated with high fever, abdominal pain, and enlargement of the liver and spleen. Other features can include diarrhea, a rash that is characterized by "rose spots," and neuropsychiatric features that can include confusion or delirium. Before the era of antibiotics, the death rate was around 15 percent; the survivors were often ill for weeks, with an interval of debilitation that might last for months (R. B. Hornick et al., "Typhoid Fever: Pathogenesis and Immunologic Control").

11. This fictional physician was irascible, opinionated, and stubborn, but also a man of good intentions. In many ways he had the same characteristics as Clemens's real-life physician acquaintances, including the famous Dr. Joseph Nash McDowell of St. Louis and the prominent Dr. Daniel St. John Bennett Roosa of New York.

12. Modern-day medical ethicists support Clemens's position that one of the physician's responsibilities is to help the patient bear the burden of disease. When a physician presents the entire truth to the patient in the name of "informed consent," he may not be acting in his patient's best interest: "If we tell patients about bad outcomes and they consent, then they are responsible, not us. Rather than a way of sharing power, truth telling and the process of seeking consent has become a way of evading accountability" (Lantos, *Do We Still Need Doctors?* 89–90).

13. Willis, *Mark and Livy*, 62–65.

14. Livy's death was attributed to heart failure caused by hyperthyroidism (Reed, "Samuel Clemens and Family"). Twain biographer Dixon Wecter states that "on August 12 [1902] Livy fell gravely ill, her long suffering with goiter and heart disease having an adverse effect, one condition upon the other—'nervous prostration,' the family called it" (Dixon Wecter, ed., *The Love Letters of Mark Twain*, 338–39). In a 1904 letter to Henry Rogers, Clemens described the severity of his wife's symptoms: "The past week has been awful—she has had bad nights, and been obliged to sit up in bed for hours, in order to get her breath—and she is only a shadow. Three nights ago her pulse went up to *192*, and nothing but a subcutaneous injection of brandy brought her back to life. Her pulse usually oscillates between 115 and 140" (*Ltrs-Rogers*, 558). Her symptoms are typical for congestive heart failure, and the rapid heart rate would be compatible with (but not proof of) a hyperthyroid state.

15. In a letter to Rogers written on February 28, 1903, Clemens complained: "Consound it, Clara tells me the Rices are coming here to dinner Tuesday Evening March 3, an engagement 2 weeks old, and swears she told me of it at the time—which is mere sick-room veracity; she never told me till to-day" (*Ltrs-Rogers*, 520).

16. "Autonomy is almost certainly the most important value 'discovered' in medical and research ethics in the last two decades," according to a 1986 book on the subject of informed consent (Ruth Faden and Tom Beauchamp, *A History and Theory of Informed Consent*, 18).

17. William Ruddick, "Hope and Deception."

18. A discussion in the *Lancet* in 1993 took a stance consistent with Clemens's viewpoint: "Let us be honest: hardly anyone—relative, partner, nurse, or doctor—sticks rigidly to total truth-telling. There is often something held back, just as there is in ordinary life. Those who make a point of telling their neighbours everything they 'have a right to know' about what is going on around them will not usually be congratulated on their impeccable ethics" (Thurston Brewin, "How Much Ethics Is Needed to Make a Good Doctor?").

19. Mark Twain, letter to Dr. Wilberforce W. Baldwin, May 15, 1904, in Clemens, *Mark Twain the Letter Writer*, 102.

17. Homeopathic Medicine: Dilutions of Grandeur

1. H. David Crombie, "Our Famous Victorian: A Humorist's Life of Sadness."

2. Reed, "Samuel Clemens and Family."

3. Ibid. Following Taft's death, his widow apparently told Clemens about a newspaper article that may have cast her husband in a less than perfect light. In a letter of July 10, 1884, Clemens asked Ellen Taft to send him the article so that he could respond to the writer's comments:

> Not that I wish to take up the writer and *answer* him, but a passing reference to some of his remarks will furnish me a pretext for coming out and telling the Hartford people traits of Dr. Taft which every person already knows—for the very graces of character and conduct which you mention in your letter were among the prominent and conspicuous features of the Dr Taft which the world had daily before their eyes, and they were the things spoken of in a taken-for-granted way when he was talked of. Do you get my idea? I do not wish to seem to be defending Dr Taft; for to Hartford people that would be like defending light, and warmth, and water. (*Ltrs-Microfilm-2*, vol. 2, #8928)

Clemens proceeded to characterize Taft as one "of the great and good who have finished their work, and passed out from our vision, and become holy to us." In another letter to Taft's widow, Clemens told her that the doctor had "grown sacred to me, and to many beside, who were not of his household and his blood" (*Ltrs-Microfilm-2*, vol. 2, #3000).

4. Reed, "Samuel Clemens and Family."

5. The other greatest institution was the Children's Theatre, of which Clemens was president.

6. In 1877, the *New York Daily Tribune* pointed out the detrimental aspects of medical sectarianism by describing a situation in which an inmate of the Philadelphia Home for Aged and Infirm Colored Persons "became a lunatic." Two homeopaths certified the man's insanity, but the allopath who was required to sign an authorization for transfer hesitated; he was fearful that he would be expelled from the county medical society if it appeared he was acting on the advice of homeopaths. In the meantime, the patient resolved the dilemma by jumping from a fourth-story window. The editor of the *Daily Tribune* suggested that the incident should provide a lesson for the allopaths: homeopaths "at least knew a lunatic when they saw him" (Kaufman, *Homeopathy in America*, 117–18).

7. Ibid., 128–31. Clemens and Roosa interacted not only as patient and doctor but also in a social and business context. Roosa's central role in this debate undoubtedly influenced Clemens's views on the politics of medicine and the validity of allowing competition among medical systems.

8. Hahnemann was also responsible for devising the term *allopathy* to diminish the image of traditional medicine by suggesting that orthodox physicians were nothing more than just another medical sect.

9. Hahnemann used sequential dilutions of 1:10 (one part "medicine" in ten parts water), and it was fairly standard to repeat thirty sequential 1:10 dilutions in order to produce the final homeopathic solution (identified as "30X"). At some point in the dilution process, known as the dilution limit, the solution contains only one molecule of medicine; after that, there is no active substance in any of the subsequent dilutions. It has been calculated that, at a standard 30X dilution, a patient would have to drink 7,874 gallons of a solution in order to ingest one molecule of the "active" substance. For some homeopathic treatments, the standard dilution is 200C (200 sequential one-hundred-fold dilutions); by the time the final dilution is created, the solution will contain one molecule of medicine per 10^{400} molecules of water. To put this in perspective, the entire universe is estimated to contain 10^{80} molecules (Robert Park, *Voodoo Science: The Road from Foolishness to Fraud*, 53).

10. Mark Twain, *Extract from Captain Stormfield's Visit to Heaven*, 103.

11. Franklin R. Rogers, ed., *Mark Twain's Satires and Burlesques*, 43.

12. Ted J. Kaptchuk and David M. Eisenberg, "Varieties of Healing, 1: Medical Pluralism in the United States."

13. The coexistence was not entirely peaceful, as "the Michigan State Legislature had, in effect, put the lion and the lamb in the same cage, the lecture halls and laboratories at Ann Arbor," and faculty interactions included a fistfight between the dean of the homeopathic school and the allopathic professor of surgery (Martin Kaufman, "Homeopathy in America: The Rise and Fall and Persistence of a Medical Heresy").

14. Gevitz, "Sectarian Medicine."

15. Kaufman, *Homeopathy in America*, 30.

16. Robert P. Hudson, "Abraham Flexner in Perspective: American Medical Education, 1865–1910"; Lester S. King, "The Flexner Report of 1910."

17. Kenneth M. Ludmerer, *Learning to Heal: The Development of American Medical Education*, 178–80.

18. Howard S. Berliner, "A Larger Perspective on the Flexner Report."

19. Ober, "Pre-Flexnerian Reports."

20. Since the demise of Hahnemann's homeopathy, there has been a resurgence of interest in "homeopathic medicine" as a component of the "holistic" approach of the alternative health movement. This new homeopathy is not practiced by physicians, however, but is a form of popular healing. Similar to the concepts of Hahnemann, homeopathic remedies are believed to work by creating an artificial illness that resembles the one being treated. This new "vibrational" illness moves a sick person from a state of illness to one of health. Using concepts of quantum physics, the plants from which the medicines are prepared have their own "vibrational signatures" or energetic frequencies that are the active components of the treatment. As was the case with Hahnemann's homeopathy, it is stated that the "memory of water" permits the electromagnetic energy from the medicines to interact with the body, even though none of the original substance remains in the dose administered to the patient (Jason R. Raabe, "Nontraditional Health Care Systems in the Western World"). Controversy has continued to swirl around the homeopathic movement, and there have been ongoing concerns about the safety and efficacy of homeopathic treatments as the alternative medicine industry has grown. According to one critic, homeopathy has been rejuvenated "from a historical curiosity into a $250-million-a-year scam. Its so-called remedies . . . are the equivalent of a car with no engine . . . [and] are marketed for everything from colds to cancer" (Andrew A. Skolnick, "FDA Petitioned to 'Stop Homeopathy Scam'"). Most homeopathic products were on the market before the Food, Drug, and Cosmetic Act of 1938 was passed, and as a result they were exempted from the requirement that they be proved safe. When the law was amended in 1962 to require that drugs also be shown to be effective, homeopathic drugs were again made exempt. Critics of homeopathy suggest that if the FDA applied the same standards to homeopathic remedies that it used for other therapies—including the requirement that treatments must be proved effective if they are to remain on the market—homeopathy would become extinct.

21. Kaufman, *Homeopathy in America*, 110, 122.

18. Placebo Effect: Curing Warts with Spunk-Water

1. Kaufman, *Homeopathy in America*, 40, 45.

2. Herbert Benson and Richard Friedman, "Harnessing the Power of the Placebo Effect and Renaming It 'Remembered Wellness'"; Janet Jackson, *Truth, Trust, and Medicine*, 8; Benson and Friedman, "Harnessing the Power of the Placebo Effect"; Jackson, *Truth, Trust, and Medicine*, 19.

3. Howard Brody, "The Placebo Effect: Implications for the Study and Practice of Complementary and Alternative Medicine"; Arif Kahn, Heather A. Warner, and Walter A. Brown, "Symptom Reduction and Suicide Risk in Patients Treated with Placebo in Antidepressant Clinical Trials: An Analysis of the Food and Drug Administration Database"; Dennis S. Charney et al., "National Depressive and Manic-Depressive Association Consensus Statement on the Use of Placebo in Clinical Trials of Mood Disorders"; Laura Bienenfeld, William Frishman, and Stephen P. Glasser, "The Placebo Effect in Cardiovascular Disease"; Benson and Friedman, "Harnessing the Power of the Placebo Effect"; Andre M. van Rij et al., "Chelation Therapy for Intermittent Claudication: A Double-Blind, Randomized, Controlled Trial."

4. Eisenberg, "Why Is There a Conflict?"

5. Legan, "Hydropathy in America."

6. Şahin Yazar and Erdal Başaran, "Efficacy of Silver Nitrate Pencils in the Treatment of Common Warts"; Peter Stern and Norman Levine, "Controlled Localized Heat Therapy in Cutaneous Warts"; S. Gibbs et al., "Local Treatments for Cutaneous Warts (Cochrane Review)."

7. Michel Labreque et al., "Homeopathic Treatment of Plantar Warts."

8. Peter C. Gotzsche, "Trials of Homoeopathy"; Jan P. Vandenbroucke, "Homoeopathy Trials: Going Nowhere"; Klaus Linde et al., "Are the Clinical Effects of Homoeopathy Placebo Effects? A Meta-Analysis of Placebo-Controlled Trials."

9. Some assessments of placebo therapy have suggested that the response to placebo may not be significantly different from the effect of no therapy at all. (See Asbjørn Hrobjartsson and Peter C. Gøtzsche, "Is the Placebo Powerless? An Analysis of Clinical Trials Comparing Placebo with No Treatment.") However, the patients who are on "no treatment" *do* receive clinical attention as they participate in therapeutic trials, and this clinical attention may well be the equivalent of a placebo effect. (See Ezekiel J. Emanuel and Franklin G. Miller, "The Ethics of Placebo-Controlled Trials—a Middle Ground.") Clinical trials can compare whether the agent under study is better than placebo, or better than clinical attention (which may be therapeutic in its own right), but they cannot test whether the agent is better than "nothing." (See Andrew C. Leon, "Placebo Protects Subjects from Nonresponse: A Paradox of Power.")

10. Howard M. Spiro, *The Power of Hope: A Doctor's Perspective*; Howard M. Spiro, "Fat, Foreboding, and Flatulence."

11. Benson and Friedman, "Harnessing the Power of the Placebo Effect"; Donna Kalauokalani et al., "Lessons from a Trial of Acupuncture and Massage for Low Back Pain: Patient Expectations and Treatment Effects."

12. Mehl-Madrona, *Coyote Medicine*, 193; Newton, *The Modern Bethesda*, 140; Ted J. Kaptchuk, "The Placebo Effect in Alternative Medicine: Can the Performance of a Healing Ritual Have Clinical Significance?"

13. Alvan R. Feinstein, "The Placebo Effect."

14. In a letter to the *Lancet* in 1985, Dr. J. N. Blau suggested that "the doctor who fails to have a placebo effect on his patients should become a pathologist" (Feinstein, "Placebo Effect").

15. "The royal touch for scrofula" represented the belief that the monarchs of England had the power to cure scrofula (tuberculosis of the lymph glands, also known as the "king's evil") by touching the patient and hanging a gold coin around his or her neck. Oliver Wendell Holmes noted that this treatment seems patently illogical, and he suggested that those who claimed to be cured did not truly have scrofula—some of the "cured" had a disease that was psychological in origin. Their belief that their "scrofula" would be cured with the touch of the king allowed their imaginary illness to disappear. Other patients may have feigned illness in order to get the gold coin from the king. Clemens agreed with Holmes's assessment, as reflected in the comments of Hank Morgan in *A Connecticut Yankee in King Arthur's Court*: "in all such crowds there were many people who only imagined something was the matter with them, and many who were consciously sound but wanted the immortal honor of fleshly contact with a king, and yet others who pretended to illness in order to get the piece of coin that went with the touch" (*Conn. Yankee*, 334).

16. Dr. Leon Eisenberg has discussed the reasons patients may benefit from their interactions with any type of therapist. Whether they seek consultation from a traditionally trained physician or an alternative healer, patients will derive relief from the

very idea that they being cared for, from interacting with someone who can help dismiss their worst fears, and from receiving a plan of therapy that indicates there is "something to do to make matters better" (Eisenberg, "Why Is There a Conflict?").

17. Geraldine M. Leydon et al., "Faith, Hope, and Charity: An In-Depth Interview Study of Cancer Patients' Information Needs and Information-Seeking Behavior"; Mehl-Madrona, *Coyote Medicine*, 119.

19. Anything ... Except Christian Science

1. Gardner, *Fads and Fallacies*, 221.

2. Ober, "Pre-Flexnerian Reports."

3. Each of the various spas specialized in specific disorders, and Clemens's family had personal experience with the "Austrian cold water cure" at Kaltenleutgeben. The results there did not match their expectations, and neither Olivia nor Jean derived the hoped-for health benefit. Clemens's disappointment with the experience at Kaltenleutgeben was not the immediate trigger for the story "At the Appetite Cure," however. He expressed reservations about the effectiveness of the cold-water cure in July 1898, as the course was nearing completion, but he had finished writing "At the Appetite Cure" several months earlier.

4. Of course, the rich were the only people who would pay money to starve. A larger part of the world's population would not have been able to afford the luxury of paying for such a privilege (and, in any case, they had already discovered that it was no trouble to starve for free).

5. Edith Colgate Salsbury, ed., *Susy and Mark Twain: Family Dialogues*, 226–27.

6. To improve vision, mind cure would have to alter the ability of the lens to focus an image on the retina. This would require either a change in the physical properties of the lens or a physical alteration of the distance between the lens and the retina. In contrast, pain is subjective in nature, and no physical changes are necessary to improve headaches and abdominal pain—mind cure needs only to influence the sufferer's perceptions or beliefs about the intensity of the symptoms. The alteration of such perceptions is at the root of most alternative care therapies.

7. Jean-Martin Charcot (1825–1893) is considered by some to be the founder of modern neurology. He is known for the "Charcot joint," a condition of joint destruction that results from impaired muscular support caused by underlying nerve dysfunction (usually on the basis of conditions such as syphilis or diabetes). Charcot had an intense interest in "hysteria," which he believed to result from hereditary weakness of the nervous system combined with a traumatic event that triggered the progressive and irreversible problems associated with the disorder. He suspected that hysteria was similar to a state of hypnosis, and he became an expert in the technique of hypnosis so that he might better study his patients with hysteria. He believed that only hysterics were capable of being hypnotized. His students included Alfred Binet, Pierre Janet, and Sigmund Freud, all of whom also used hypnosis (which they believed to be a psychological rather than a neurological process).

8. In 1883, Playfair characterized Weir Mitchell's rest cure as "the greatest advance of which practical medicine can boast in the last quarter of the century" (Olfson, "The Weir Mitchell Rest Cure").

9. Simon Wessely, "Old Wine in New Bottles: Neurasthenia and 'ME.'"

10. Graham (1794–1851) was the son and grandson of minister-physicians. A minister himself with no medical background, he became interested in health and nutrition when he joined the temperance movement. Advocating a lifestyle that included

healthy dietary habits, exercise, and personal hygiene, "Sylvester Graham preached his gospel of whole wheat grain, moderation, exercise, and hygiene with the fervor of an evangelist" (Duffy, *From Humors to Medical Science*, 88).

11. Rennie B. Schoepflin, "Christian Science Healing in America."

12. Ibid.

13. According to Pamela's grandson, Samuel Charles Webster, she "was tolerant toward Christian Science but never completely convinced. I remember that the doctor came to see her at least once a week. But she did have an aversion to medicine. As a child in Tennessee she had been the victim of the current craze for medical experiment" (*MTBM*, 397).

14. Similar cases have resulted in substantial legal problems for Christian Science. A former Christian Scientist filed a lawsuit in 1996 in response to the death of his sixteen-month-old son. The child, who had been treated by prayer only, had died of meningitis in 1977. The suit resulted in a ruling that put an end to Medicare and Medicaid payments to Christian Scientists—the federal judge determined that the payments violated the constitutional separation of church and state ("Judge Rules Against Medicare, Medicaid Payments to Christian Science Caregivers").

15. In 1956, Clara wrote *Awake to a Perfect Day; My Experience with Christian Science*, in which she attempted to explain her father's opinions on Eddy.

16. Schoepflin, "Christian Science Healing in America."

20. Faith: Believing What You Know Ain't So

1. T. McNichol, "The New Faith in Medicine"; C. Wallis, "Faith and Healing: Can Prayer, Faith, and Spirituality Really Improve Your Physical Health? A Growing and Surprising Body of Scientific Evidence Says They Can."

2. R. P. Sloan, E. Bagiella, and T. Powell, "Religion, Spirituality, and Medicine."

3. Dale A. Matthews, *The Faith Factor: Proof of the Healing Power of Prayer*, 51.

4. Robert L. Hatch et al., "The Spiritual Involvement and Beliefs Scale: Development and Testing of a New Instrument."

5. Stephen G. Post, Christina M. Puchalski, and David M. Larson, "Physicians and Patient Spirituality: Professional Boundaries, Competency, and Ethics."

6. Thomas J. Csordas, "Elements of Charismatic Persuasion and Healing."

7. Mehl-Madrona, *Coyote Medicine*, 16–17.

8. Frank Davidoff, "Weighing the Alternatives: Lessons from the Paradoxes of Alternative Medicine."

9. Ibid.

10. Eisenberg, "Why Is There a Conflict?"

11. Sloan, Bagiella, and Powell, "Religion, Spirituality, and Medicine."

12. Mehl-Madrona, *Coyote Medicine*, 287.

13. Clemens continued the passage by describing the similarities of what he had witnessed to the healing methods Jesus had used in the same region, centuries earlier:

> Christ knew how to preach to these simple, superstitious, disease-tortured creatures: He healed the sick. They flocked to our poor human doctor this morning when the fame of what he had done to the sick child went abroad in the land, and they worshiped him with their eyes while they did not know as yet whether there was virtue in his simples or not. The ancestors of these—people precisely like them in color, dress, manners, customs, simplicity—flocked in vast multitudes after Christ, and when they saw Him make the afflicted whole with a word, it is no

wonder they worshiped Him. No wonder His deeds were the talk of the nation. No wonder the multitude that followed Him was so great that at one time—thirty miles from here—they had to let a sick man down through the roof because no approach could be made to the door; no wonder His audiences were so great at Galilee that He had to preach from a ship removed a little distance from the shore; no wonder that even in the desert places about Bethsaida, five thousand invaded His solitude, and He had to feed them by a miracle or else see them suffer for their confiding faith and devotion; no wonder when there was a great commotion in a city in those days, one neighbor explained it to another in words to this effect: "They say that Jesus of Nazareth is come!"

Well, as I was saying, the doctor distributed medicine as long as he had to distribute, and his reputation is mighty in Galilee this day. (*Inn. Abroad*, 474–75)

14. One of his contemporaries described Birch as "rather heavy set a plain, old fashioned Gentleman that cares more for substance than show, and hartily despises meanness, parade and vanity" (*Ltrs-2*, 132). On the excursion, Clemens and Birch made a special trip in order to get a flask of the water from the pool at Bethesda, which, according to the biblical account in John 5:4, has miraculous healing powers. Clemens write his mother: "Dr. Birch, of Hannibal, has got a bottle of water which he & I got out of the Pool of Bethesda, in Jerusalem one Sunday morning when the angel wasn't around" (*Ltrs-2*, 130).

15. Some researchers argue that distant healing and healing by prayer are as amenable to scientific study as any other medical intervention. See John A. Astin, Elaine Harkness, and Edzard Ernst, "The Efficacy of 'Distant Healing': A Systematic Review of Randomized Trials." Others suggest that matters of faith and trust cannot be tested by scientific methods, and they argue that it is not even necessary to do so. Once it is recognized that faith can be helpful for people who are in need of ways to cope with illness, suffering, disability, and death, they argue, it becomes as inappropriate to use science as a means of authenticating spiritual beliefs as it would be to employ faith to corroborate scientific data—"research on the effects of religion and spirituality on health should avoid attempting to validate God through scientific methods" (John T. Chibnall, Joseph M. Jeral, and Michael A. Cerullo, "Experiments on Distant Intercessory Prayer: God, Science, and the Lesson of Massah").

16. E. Targ and K. S. Thomson, "Can Prayer and Intentionality Be Researched? Should They Be?"

21. Any Mummery Will Cure, if the Patient's Faith Is Strong in It

1. It is fair to point out that allopathic physicians were not quacks and charlatans who prescribed therapies they knew to be ineffective and worthless. Instead, they trusted their treatment programs without question or hesitation and were as likely to use bleeding and purgatives for themselves and their families as for their patients. When ten members of Benjamin Rush's family had remitting fevers in 1795, all were cured with a total of twenty-four bleedings in a single month. "I submitted to two of them in one day," Rush reported. "Our infant of 6 weeks old was likewise bled twice, and thereby rescued from the grave" (Rosenberg, "Therapeutic Revolution"). Even as Rush reported that his own bleedings created a "faintness which threatened the extinction of my life," he interpreted his recovery as a testimony to the benefits of bleeding (Eisenberg, "Why Is There a Conflict"?).

2. Kaufman, *Homeopathy in America*, 7.

3. Warner, *Therapeutic Perspective*, 33.

4. This prescription was a caricature of prescriptions that Clemens had discovered in a 1743 medical textbook (James's *A Medicinal Dictionary*), which he lampooned in "A Majestic Literary Fossil." James's book included the prescription for "Alexander's Golden Antidote." As Clemens interpreted the *Dictionary* 's recommendations, it appeared to him that the antidote "is good for—well, pretty much everything. It is probably the old original first patent-medicine." He then wrote the details of the prescription:

Take of Afarabocca, Henbane, Carpobalsamum, each two Drams and a half; of Cloves, Opium, Myrrh, Cyperus, each two Drams; of Opobalsamum, Indian Leaf, Cinnamon, Zedoary, Ginger, Coftus, Coral, Cassia, Euphorbium, Gum Tragacanth, Frankincense, Styrax Calamita, Celtic, Nard, Spignel, Hartwort, Mustard, Saxifrage, Dill, Anise, each one Dram; of Xylaloes, Rheum, Ponticum, Alipta Moschata, Castor, Spikenard, Galangals, Opoponax, Anacardium, Mastich, Brimstone, Peony, Eringo, Pulp of Dates, red and white Hermodactyls, Roses, Thyme, Acorns, Pennyroyal, Gentian, the Bark of the Root of Mandrake, Germander, Valerian, Bishops Weed, Bay-berries, long and white Pepper, Xylobalsamum, Carnabadium, Macodonian, Parsley-seeds, Lovage, the Seeds of Rue, and Sinon, of each a Dram and a half; of pure Gold, pure Silver, Pearls not perforated, the Blatta Byzantina, the Bone of the Stag's Heart, of each the Quantity of fourteen Grains of Wheat; of Sapphire, Emerald, and Jasper Stones, each one Dram; of Haslenut, two Drams; of Pellitory of Spain, Shavings of Ivory, Calamus Odoratus, each the Quantity of twenty-nine Grains of Wheat; of Honey or Sugar a sufficient Quantity. (*£1m Bank-note*, 258)

This prescription is reproduced by Clemens in *Those Extraordinary Twins*, which contains a slapstick version of the same cynical criticisms of allopathic medicine that he made in "A Majestic Literary Fossil." In *Twins*, Dr. Claypool writes a prescription for Alexander's Golden Antidote when one of the Siamese twins is wounded. Clemens was obviously intrigued by the prescriptions in *A Medicinal Dictionary*; in "A Majestic Literary Fossil" he not only lists the ingredients of the "Golden Antidote" but also writes out the contents of "Aqua Limacum," which uses some of the same ingredients—including cloves, herbs, and animal dung—that composed the prescription concocted by Dr. Bradshaw in *"Which Was It?"*

Aqua Limacum. Take a great Peck of Garden-snails, and wash them in a great deal of Beer, and make your Chimney very clean, and set a Bushel of Charcoal on Fire; and when they are thoroughly kindled, make a Hole in the Middle of the Fire, and put the Snails in, and scatter more Fire amongst them, and let them roast till they make a Noise; then take them out, and, with a Knife and coarse Cloth, pick and wipe away all the green froth: Then break them, Shells and all, in a Stone Mortar. Take also a Quart of Earth-worms, and scour them with Salt, divers times over. Then take two Handfuls of Angelica and lay them in the Bottom of the Still; next lay two Handfuls of Celandine; next a Quart of Rosemary-flowers; then two Handfuls of Bearsfoot and Agrimony; then Fenugreek; then Turmerick; of each one Ounce: Red Dock-root, Bark of Barberry-trees, Wood-sorrel, Betony, of each two Handfuls.— Then lay the Snails and Worms on the top of the Herbs; and then two Handfuls of Goose Dung, and two Handfuls of Sheep Dung. Then put in three Gallons of Strong Ale, and place the pot where you mean to set Fire under it: Let it stand all Night, or longer; in the Morning put in three Ounces of Cloves well beaten, and a small Quantity of Saffron, dry'd to Powder; then six Ounces of Shavings of

Hartshorn, which must be uppermost. Fix on the Head and Refrigeratory, and distil according to Art. (*£1m Bank-note*, 259)

5. Kaufman, *Homeopathy in America*, 6–7.

6. Quinine is an effective therapy for malaria. At that time, malaria was not recognized as an infectious disease but instead was considered to be "a noxious miasm or effluvium arising from decaying organic matter that contributed to a variety of pathological conditions" and an entity that "engrafted itself" into all diseases (Warner, *Therapeutic Perspective*, 69–70).

7. Kaufman, *Homeopathy in America*, 13.

8. "Suppressed itch" is a homeopathic term: Hahnemann's third principle of homeopathy was that chronic diseases were caused by a miasm, or evil spirit, that pervaded the body, which he referred to as a "suppressed itch" or "psora." Hahnemann believed that the aggressive therapies of the allopathic physicians kept the "psora" suppressed so that it could not display itself as skin eruptions, and thus tended to prolong the course of chronic diseases. According to Hahnemann, ailments ranging from asthma to insanity were the result of allopathic treatment of the "suppressed itch" (Kaufman, *Homeopathy in America*, 26). Clemens's joke comes from having an allopathic physician not only diagnose "suppressed itch" (which is a purely homeopathic "disease"), but then paradoxically treat "the itch" with the aggressive allopathic methods that (according to homeopathic principles) created the disease in the first place. In reality, "suppressed itch" would not have been part of the vocabulary of any allopathic physician, and any homeopathic physician who would diagnose "suppressed itch" would never have employed the "heroic measures" prescribed by Dr. Bradshaw. When Dug Hapgood later develops severe abdominal pain after ingesting Bradshaw's gut-wrenching allopathic prescription, Bradshaw—unaware that Hapgood took the medicine—speculates that Hapgood also suffers from "suppressed itch." Bradshaw, ignorant of the fact that he himself is responsible for Hapgood's misery, speculates that the "itch" might actually be a contagious disease; he gleefully predicts that his discovery is bound to "make a stir in the medical world" (*WWD&OSW*, 292), overlooking the fact that his fanciful bastardization of allopathic and homeopathic dogma would not be acceptable to either group of practitioners.

9. W. R. Houston, "The Doctor Himself as a Therapeutic Agent."

10. Spiro, *The Power of Hope*, 146.

11. Ruth Macklin, "The Ethical Problems with Sham Surgery in Clinical Research."

12. A. Branthwaite and P. Cooper, "Analgesic Effects of Branding in Treatment of Headaches"; Daniel E. Moerman and Wayne B. Jonas, "Deconstructing the Placebo Effect and Finding the Meaning Response."

13. Mark Twain, letter to Dr. Wilberforce W. Baldwin, May 15, 1904, in Clemens, *Mark Twain the Letter Writer*, 102.

14. This phenomenon is not limited to therapeutic intervention but also applies to diagnostic testing. In the current era of sophisticated medical technology, diagnostic methods are frequently overutilized due to patient expectations and physician insecurities. Excessive and unnecessary laboratory testing commonly leads to the discovery of results that fall outside the "normal range." These results are often clinically irrelevant; by definition, 5 percent of a healthy population will have a result that is outside the "normal range" for any particular test. Even so, the fact that a test falls outside the range of "normal" will usually trigger further testing in order to resolve the matter. Eventually the patient and doctor find themselves in the same predicament as the fictional Brer Rabbit (invented by Clemens's friend Joel Chandler

Harris), whose curiosity led him to initiate his unwise assault on the mysterious Tar-Baby. Once stuck in the tar, Brer Rabbit only made his situation worse by punching and kicking to free himself from his tarry trap. Similarly, unnecessary laboratory testing can create a medical Tar-Baby in which the physician and patient play the role of Brer Rabbit—the initial laboratory test stimulates a clinical cascade of further testing, with each test being more expensive and risky than the previous one. See K. Patrick Ober, "Uncle Remus and the Cascade Effect in Clinical Medicine: Brer Rabbit Kicks the Tar-Baby."

15. Kaufman, *Homeopathy in America*, 11.

16. Rosenberg, "Therapeutic Revolution." Clemens and Sir William Osler (1849–1919) were acquaintances. They met in 1881 in Montreal, where Osler was on the McGill Medical College faculty. Clemens had been visiting in Montreal to satisfy a Canadian publication requirement for protecting the copyright of his works. At the end of his visit, he was honored by a group of about a hundred dignitaries with a farewell dinner; Osler was a member of the group. Osler later served on the faculty at the University of Pennsylvania and then became physician in chief at the Johns Hopkins Medical School before he moved to Oxford University in 1905 to become Regius Professor of Medicine. When Clemens was given an honorary degree at Oxford in 1907, Osler hosted a luncheon to honor him (John C. Carson, "Mark Twain's Georgia Angel-Fish Revisited"). Clemens mentioned Osler at least once in writing, in a tribute to William Dean Howells: "Is it true that the sum of a man's mentality touches noon at forty and then begins to wane toward setting? Dr. Osler is charged with saying so. Maybe he said it, maybe he didn't" (CT-2, 722).

17. William Osler, *The Principles and Practice of Medicine*; Richard L. Golden, "Osler's Legacy: The Centennial of *The Principles and Practice of Medicine*." Clemens knew of one other characteristic separating man from other creatures: "Man is the only animal that blushes—or needs to" (*Foll. Equat.*, 256).

18. Spiro, *The Power of Hope*, 248; Joann Troutmann Banks, "Mrs. Woolf in Harley Street."

19. Paul B. Fontanarosa and George D. Lundberg, "Alternative Medicine Meets Science."

20. Bernard L. Stein, "Explanatory Notes," 471.

22. Old Age and Broken Health

1. Joseph Goodman (1838–1917) was the owner and editor of the Virginia City (Nevada) *Territorial Enterprise* who hired Clemens as a reporter during his stint in Nevada in the early 1860s. Goodman's open-minded approach as editor was important to Clemens's development as a writer, and the two remained lifelong friends.

2. Bragman, "Medical Wisdom of Mark Twain."

3. William R. Phillips, "Patients, Pills, and Professionals: The Ethics of Placebo Therapy."

4. Abraham Verghese, "The Physician as Storyteller."

5. Rosenberg, "Therapeutic Revolution."

6. Spiro, *The Power of Hope*, 189.

7. Salsbury, ed., *Susy and Mark Twain*, 394.

8. Janet Smith, ed., *Mark Twain on the Damned Human Race*, 41–42.

9. "Medical therapeutics changed in some ways remarkably little in the 2 millennia preceding 1800" (Rosenberg, "Therapeutic Revolution"); "Medicine in 1804

had evolved very little in the 2000 years from the time of Galen and Hippocrates" (Loge, "'Two Dozes of Barks and Opium'"); "[M]edical therapeutics in the early and mid-nineteenth century had in some respects changed little from that practiced over two millennia earlier" (Warner, *Therapeutic Perspective*, 163).

10. Ignaz Semmelweis (1818–1865) was a Hungarian physician who demonstrated that there was a 12 percent rate of fatal postpartum sepsis in the patients of his medical colleagues who did not wash their hands between autopsies and deliveries; he contrasted this to the 3 percent death rate when the delivery was performed by midwives, who did not perform autopsies. Through these famous observations, Semmelweis demonstrated the benefit of hand washing in the prevention of the spread of infection. His findings were severely attacked; he was banished from his hospital post, eventually to die in a mental hospital of a self-inflicted wound from a contaminated scalpel. A 1999 editorialist came to the same conclusion reached by Clemens a century earlier: "Although Semmelweis is feted in our era, in his own time he was denounced and driven out of his job, his country, and perhaps, his mind, dying in a mental institution at the age of 47" (Steven N. Goodman, "Probability at the Bedside: The Knowing of Chances or the Chances of Knowing?").

11. Mark Twain, *Tom Sawyer Abroad*, 142.

Afterword: Hell Is of No Consequence to a Person Who Doesn't Live There

1. Eisenberg, "Why Is There a Conflict?"
2. Davidoff, *Who Has Seen a Blood Sugar?* 10. Davidoff's perspective is consistent with the views presented by Susan Sontag in *Illness as a Metaphor*.
3. Allen F. Shaughnessy, "Alternative Views on Alternative Medicine."
4. Alfred Bigelow Paine, *Mark Twain: A Biography*, 1010.
5. Clemens repeats here the criticisms of the outdated medical practices of the American frontier physician that had been his focus in "A Majestic Literary Fossil."
6. Chaichana Nimnuan et al., "How Many Functional Somatic Syndromes?"
7. Chaichana Nimnuan, Matthew Hotopf, and Simon Wessely, "Medically Unexplained Symptoms: An Epidemiological Study in Seven Specialities."
8. Neil Scheurich, "Hysteria and the Medical Narrative."
9. Simon Wessely, "Responding to Mass Psychogenic Illness"; Nortin M. Hadler, "If You Have to Prove You Are Ill, You Can't Get Well: The Object Lesson of Fibromyalgia."
10. Clemens's burlesque is two-tiered here. "Suppressed itch" is a homeopathic diagnosis, and Bradshaw was an allopathic physician who would never have used the term. More important, Bradshaw's treatment was going to be the same regardless of his diagnosis (which is often the case for alternative medical regimens), and there was no reason for him to suggest a diagnosis of "suppressed itch"—he could just as easily have given an allopathic diagnosis such as "neurasthenia."
11. Aspiz, "Mark Twain and 'Doctor' Newton."
12. "Thought for the Day." Shaw (1818–1885), who used the pseudonym "Josh Billings," was a popular American humorist and friend of Samuel Clemens's.
13. Victoria Maizes et al., "Integrative Medical Education: Development and Implementation of a Comprehensive Curriculum at the University of Arizona."
14. This observation, made by character Harry Brierly, is found in chapter 31, which was written by Warner (Rasmussen, *Mark Twain A to Z*, 171). Warner made other observations about medical practice in chapter 21:

Whether medicine is a science, or only an empirical method of getting a living out of the ignorance of the human race, Ruth found before her first term was over at the medical school that there were other things she needed to know quite as much as that which is taught in medical books, and that she could never satisfy her aspirations without more general culture.

"Does your doctor know anything—I don't mean about medicine, but about things in general, is he a man of information and good sense?" once asked an old practitioner. "If he doesn't know anything but medicine the chance is he doesn't know that." (*Gilded Age*, 194)

15. Spiro, *The Power of Hope*, 86.
16. H. Gilbert Welch and Jon D. Lurie, "Teaching Evidence-Based Medicine: Caveats and Challenges."
17. Stea and Fried, "Remedies for a Society's Debilities."
18. Feinstein, "Placebo Effect"; Spiro, *The Power of Hope*, 136.
19. Spiro, *The Power of Hope*, 245.
20. Kaufman, *Homeopathy in America*, 46.
21. T. Andrew Dodds, "Richard Cabot: Medical Reformer during the Progressive Era (1809–1920)."
22. Surendra Kelwala, "Why Patients Use Alternative Medicine."
23. Davidoff, "Weighing the Alternatives."
24. Mark Siegler, "Pascal's Wager and the Hanging of Crepe."
25. David M. Eisenberg et al., "Trends in Alternative Medicine Use in the United States, 1990–1997."
26. Edward W. Campion, "Why Unconventional Medicine?"
27. David M. Eisenberg et al., "Perceptions about Complementary Therapies Relative to Conventional Therapies among Adults Who Use Both: Results from a National Survey."
28. Spiro, "Fat, Foreboding, and Flatulence."
29. David M. Eisenberg et al., "Unconventional Medicine in the United States: Prevalence, Costs, and Patterns of Use."
30. Finley Peter Dunne, *Mr. Dooley's Opinions*, 9. "Mr. Dooley" was a popular newspaper commentator whose observations about American life were similar to those of Sam Clemens. His creator, Finley Peter Dunne, was a billiard-playing crony of Clemens's; Clemens chose Dunne "to be one of the few select members of his Human Race Luncheon Club, organized to damn the species" (Milton Meltzer, *Mark Twain Himself: A Pictorial Biography*, 246).
31. Spiro, *The Power of Hope*, 83; Newton, *The Modern Bethesda*, 115.
32. Robert Kreisberg, "We Blew It"; Spiro, *The Power of Hope*, 76.
33. Eisenberg et al., "Perceptions about Complementary Therapies."
34. Neil J. Elgee, "The Metaphysics of Holism: Laughter in Carnival with Alternative Medicine."
35. Eisenberg et al., "Perceptions about Complementary Therapies."
36. John A. Astin, "Why Patients Use Alternative Medicine: Results of a National Study."
37. Michael J. Sergeant, "More on Alternative Medicine."
38. In a newspaper article with the headline "Row among the Doctors," Clemens described "a nice little breeze between the practitioners." After a man by the name of John Ferguson took strychnine with the intention of ending his life, a Dr. Elliott was called, and he promptly declared the case to be beyond any hope of recovery. A Dr. DeCastro was then called, and as the new physician on the scene DeCastro

"emeticized, purged and pumped him, till the poison had no show." After Ferguson's recovery, the original physician (Dr. Elliott) suggested that the man had not taken any poison at all; instead, Elliott proposed, the druggist had suspected the patient's suicidal intention and substituted a benign chemical for the requested strychnine. A chemist named Dickey supported Dr. Elliott's claim that the patient *did not* receive strychnine, while the druggist Riley backed up Dr. DeCastro's contention that he *did* dispense strychnine. Clemens concluded his article by restating the uncertainty: "Thus the matter stands. Who can decide when Doctors disagree?" (*Cl. of Call*, 151).

39. In Greek mythology, it is Charon's responsibility to ferry the souls of the dead over the River Styx to the home of Hades, the god of death.

Appendix 2. The Legacy of Neurasthenia

1. Davidoff, *Who Has Seen a Blood Sugar?* 3–6.
2. Clifton Meador, "Hex Death: Voodoo Magic or Persuasion?"
3. Spiro, *The Power of Hope*, 3.
4. Mehl-Madrona, *Coyote Medicine*, 213.
5. Martensen, "Neurasthenia."
6. Davis, "George Beard and Lydia Pinkham."
7. Stephen E. Ross, "'Memes' as Infectious Agents in Psychosomatic Illness."
8. The diagnosis of depression is perceived by many as a personal failing, making it an undesirable explanation for lethargy and weakness. It is an entirely different matter to be the victim of a viral infection—the sufferer is an innocent bystander, and there is no disgrace in having a "chronic Epstein-Barr virus infection." In fact, there may even be a component of prestige when the illness is most virulent for those who are poised to accomplish the greatest success. The exhausted twentieth-century American with the "yuppie virus" (attributed to "chronic Epstein-Barr virus infection") was a direct descendant of the nineteenth-century neurasthenia victim.
9. Ross, "'Memes' as Infectious Agents."
10. Joel Yager and Roy T. Young, "Non-Hypoglycemia Is an Epidemic Condition."
11. Nimnuan et al., "How Many Functional Somatic Syndromes?"; S. Wessely, C. Nimnuan, and M. Sharpe, "Functional Somatic Syndromes: One or Many?"
12. Ian R. McWhinney, Ronald M. Epstein, and Tom R. Freeman, "Rethinking Somatization."
13. Donna B. Greenberg, "Neurasthenia in the 1980s: Chronic Mononucleosis, Chronic Fatigue Syndrome, and Anxiety and Depressive Disorders"; Wessely, "Old Wine in New Bottles."
14. I. Hickie, D. Hadzi-Pavlovic, and C. Ricci, "Reviving the Diagnosis of Neurasthenia."
15. Wessely, "Responding to Mass Psychogenic Illness."

Appendix 3. One of the Choicest Human Beings in the World

1. Hamlin Hill, ed., *Mark Twain's Letters to His Publishers, 1867–1910*, 235.

References

Abbey, Susan E., and Paul E. Garfinkel. "Neurasthenia and Chronic Fatigue Syndrome: The Role of Culture in the Making of a Diagnosis." *American Journal of Psychiatry* 148 (1991): 1638–46.

Adams, Samuel Hopkins. *The Great American Fraud.* N.P.: P. F. Collier and Son, 1905, 1906.

———. "The Great American Fraud: The Scavengers." *Collier's* 37 (September 22, 1906): 16–18, 24–25.

Ambrose, Stephen E. *Undaunted Courage: Meriwether Lewis, Thomas Jefferson, and the Opening of the American West.* New York: Simon and Schuster, 1996.

Anderson, Frederick. *A Pen Warmed Up in Hell: Mark Twain in Protest.* New York: Harper Colophon, 1972.

Anderson, Frederick, William M. Gibson, and Henry Nash Smith, eds. *Selected Mark Twain–Howells Letters, 1872–1910.* Cambridge: Belknap Press of Harvard University Press, 1967.

Anderson, Frederick, Michael B. Frank, and Kenneth M. Sanderson, eds. *Mark Twain's Notebooks and Journals, Volume I, 1855–1873.* Berkeley: University of California Press, 1975.

Anderson, Frederick, Lin Salamo, and Bernard L. Stein, eds., *Mark Twain's Notebooks and Journals, Volume II, 1877–1883.* Berkeley: University of California Press, 1975.

Apple, Rimma D. *Women, Health, and Medicine in America.* New York: Garland, 1990.

331

Armon, Dahlia, and Walter Blair. "Biographical Directory." In *Huck Finn and Tom Sawyer among the Indians and Other Unfinished Stories,* 299–351. Berkeley: University of California Press, 1989.

Aspiz, Harold. "Mark Twain and 'Doctor' Newton." *American Literature* 44 (March 1972): 130–36.

Astin, John A. "Why Patients Use Alternative Medicine: Results of a National Study." *Journal of the American Medical Association* 279 (1998): 1548–53.

Astin, John A., Elaine Harkness, and Edzard Ernst. "The Efficacy of 'Distant Healing': A Systematic Review of Randomized Trials." *Annals of Internal Medicine* 132 (2000): 903–10.

Baender, Paul, ed. *What Is Man? and Other Philosophical Writings.* Berkeley: University of California Press, 1973.

Baer, Hans A. "The American Dominative Medical System as a Reflection of Social Relations in the Larger Society." *Social Sciences and Medicine* 28 (1989): 1103–12.

Banks, Joann Troutmann. "Mrs. Woolf in Harley Street." *Lancet* 351 (1998): 1124–26.

Bates, Don G. "Why Not Call Modern Medicine 'Alternative'?" *Perspectives in Biology and Medicine* 43 (2000): 502–18.

Benson, Herbert, and Richard Friedman. "Harnessing the Power of the Placebo Effect and Renaming It 'Remembered Wellness.'" *Annual Review of Medicine* 47 (1996): 193–99.

Berliner, Howard S. "A Larger Perspective on the Flexner Report." *International Journal of Health Services* 5 (1975): 573–92.

Bienenfeld, Laura, William Frishman, and Stephen P. Glasser. "The Placebo Effect in Cardiovascular Disease." *American Heart Journal* 132 (1996): 1207–21.

Blair, Walter, ed. *Mark Twain's Hannibal, Huck, and Tom.* Berkeley: University of California Press, 1969.

Bragman, Louis H. "The Medical Wisdom of Mark Twain." *Annals of Medical History* 7 (1925): 425–39.

Branch, Edgar M., ed. *Clemens of the "Call": Mark Twain in San Francisco.* Berkeley: University of California Press, 1969.

Branch, Edgar M., Michael Frank, and Kenneth M. Sanderson, eds. *Mark Twain's Letters, Volume 1, 1853–1866.* Berkeley: University of California Press, 1988.

Branch, Edgar Marquess, and Robert H. Hirst, eds. *Early Tales and Sketches, Volume 1, 1851–1864.* Berkeley: University of California Press, 1979.

————. *Early Tales and Sketches, Volume 2, 1864–1865.* Berkeley: University of California Press, 1981.

Branch, Edward Douglas. *The Sentimental Years, 1836–1860.* New York: Appleton-Century, 1934.

Branthwaite, A., and P. Cooper. "Analgesic Effects of Branding in Treatment of Headaches." *British Medical Journal* 282 (1981): 1576–78.

Brashear, M. M. "Dr. Still and Mark Twain." *Journal of the American Osteopathic Association* 73 (1973): 67–71.

Brewin, Thurston. "How Much Ethics Is Needed to Make a Good Doctor?" *Lancet* 341 (1993): 161–63.

Brodman, Estelle. "The Great Eccentric." *Washington University Magazine* 50 (December 1980): 5–11.

Brody, Howard. "The Placebo Effect: Implications for the Study and Practice of Complementary and Alternative Medicine." In *The Role of Complementary and Alternative Medicine: Accommodating Pluralism*, ed. Daniel Callahan, 74–83. Washington, D.C.: Georgetown University Press, 2002.

Browning, Robert Pack, Michael B. Frank, and Lin Salamo, eds. *Mark Twain's Notebooks and Journals, Volume III, 1883–1891.* Berkeley: University of California Press, 1979.

Bui, Anh Quynh, et al., eds. *Microfilm Edition of Mark Twain's Manuscript Letters Now in the Mark Twain Papers, The Bancroft Library.* 11 vols. Berkeley: Bancroft Library, 2001.

————. *Microfilm Edition of Mark Twain's Previously Unpublished Letters.* 8 vols. Berkeley: Bancroft Library, 2001.

Burnum, John F. "Medical Vampires." *New England Journal of Medicine* 314 (1986): 1250–51.

Cambridge, Nicholas Anthony. "Electrical Apparatus Used in Medicine before 1900." *Proceedings of the Royal Society of Medicine* 70 (1977): 635–41.

Campion, Edward W. "Why Unconventional Medicine?" *New England Journal of Medicine* 328 (1993): 282–83.

Carson, Gerald. *One For a Man, Two For a Horse: A Pictorial History, Grave and Comic, of Patent Medicines.* New York: Bramhall House, 1961.

Carson, John C. "Mark Twain's Georgia Angel-fish Revisited." *Mark Twain Journal* 36:1 (spring 1998): 16–18.

Cayleff, Susan E. "Gender, Ideology, and the Water-Cure Movement." In *Other Healers: Unorthodox Medicine in America*, ed. Norman Gevitz, 82–98. Baltimore: Johns Hopkins University Press, 1988.

————. "'Prisoner of Their Own Feebleness': Women, Nerves, and Western Medicine—A Historical Overview." *Social Science and Medicine* 26 (1988): 1199–1208.

Charney, Dennis S., et. al. "National Depressive and Manic-Depressive Association Consensus Statement on the Use of Placebo in Clinical Trials of Mood Disorders." *Archives of General Psychiatry* 59 (2002): 262–70.

Chibnall, John T., Joseph M. Jeral, and Michael A. Cerullo. "Experiments on Distant Intercessory Prayer: God, Science, and the Lesson of Massah." *Archives of Internal Medicine* 161 (2001): 2529–36.

Clemens, Clara. *My Father, Mark Twain.* New York: Harper and Brothers, 1931.

Clemens, Cyril. *Mark Twain the Letter Writer.* Boston: Meador Publishing, 1932.

Clemens, Susy. *Papa: An Intimate Biography of Mark Twain.* Garden City, N.Y.: Doubleday, 1985.

Cooley, John, ed. *Mark Twain's Aquarium: The Samuel Clemens–Angelfish Correspondence, 1905–1910.* Athens: University of Georgia Press, 1991.

Cooper, Robert. *Around the World with Mark Twain.* New York: Arcade Publishing, 2000.

Cramp, A. J. *Nostrums and Quackery and Pseudo-Medicine.* Chicago: Press of the American Medical Association, 1936.

Crombie, H. David. "Our Famous Victorian: A Humorist's Life of Sadness." *Connecticut Medicine* 66 (2002): 107–8.

Csordas, Thomas J. "Elements of Charismatic Persuasion and Healing." *Medical Anthropology Quarterly* 2 (1988): 121–42.

Davidoff, Frank. "Weighing the Alternatives: Lessons from the Paradoxes of Alternative Medicine." *Annals of Internal Medicine* 129 (1998): 1068–70.

————. *Who Has Seen a Blood Sugar? Reflections on Medical Education.* Philadelphia: American College of Physicians, 1996.

Davis, Dona L. "George Beard and Lydia Pinkham: Gender, Class, and Nerves in Late Nineteenth Century America." *Health Care for Women International* 10 (1989): 93–114.

DeVoto, Bernard, ed. *Letters from the Earth,* by Mark Twain. New York: Perennial Library, Harper and Row, 1974.

Dodds, John W. *The Age of Paradox: A Biography of England, 1841–1851.* London: Gollancz, 1953.

Dodds, T. Andrew. "Richard Cabot: Medical Reformer during the Progressive Era (1809–1920)." *Annals of Internal Medicine* 119 (1993): 417–22.

Dolmetsch, Carl. "Austria (Austria-Hungary)." In *The Mark Twain Encyclopedia*, ed. J. R. LeMaster and James D. Wilson, 49–53. New York and London: Garland Publishing, 1993.

———. *"Our Famous Guest": Mark Twain in Vienna*. Athens: University of Georgia Press, 1992.

Donegan, Jane B. *"Hydropathic Highway to Health": Women and Water-Cure in Antebellum America*. New York: Greenwood Press, 1986.

Doyle, Arthur Conan. "The Blue Carbuncle." In *The Adventures of Sherlock Holmes*, 149–70. Oxford, Oxford University Press, 1993.

Doyno, Victor. "Textual Addendum." In *Adventures of Huckleberry Finn*, by Mark Twain, 374. New York: Random House, 1996.

Drinka, George F. *The Birth of Neurosis: Myth, Malady, and the Victorians*. New York. Simon and Schuster, 1984.

Duffy, John. *From Humors to Medical Science: A History of American Medicine*. 2d ed. Urbana and Chicago: University of Illinois Press, 1993.

Duncan, C. J., S. R. Duncan, and S. Scott. "The Dynamics of Scarlet Fever Epidemics in England and Wales in the Nineteenth Century." *Epidemiology and Infection* 117 (1996): 493–99.

Duncan, S. R., S. Scott, and C. J. Duncan. "Modelling the Dynamics of Scarlet Fever Epidemics in the Nineteenth Century." *European Journal of Epidemiology* 16 (2000): 619–26.

Dunne, Finley Peter. *Mr. Dooley's Opinions*. New York: R. H. Russell, 1901.

Eisenberg, David M., et al. "Perceptions about Complementary Therapies Relative to Conventional Therapies among Adults Who Use Both: Results from a National Survey." *Annals of Internal Medicine* 135 (2001): 344–51.

———. "Trends in Alternative Medicine Use in the United States, 1990–1997." *Journal of the American Medical Association* 280 (1998): 1569–75.

———. "Unconventional Medicine in the United States: Prevalence, Costs, and Patterns of Use." *New England Journal of Medicine* 328 (1993): 246–52.

Eisenberg, Leon. "Why Is There a Conflict between Complementary/Alternative Medicine and the Medical Establishment?" In *Education of Health Professionals in Complementary/Alternative Medicine*, ed. Mary Hager, 39–73. New York: Josiah Macy Jr. Foundation, 2001.

Elgee, Neil J. "The Metaphysics of Holism: Laughter in Carnival with Alternative Medicine." *Pharos* (fall 1995): 18–20.

Emanuel, Ezekiel J., and Franklin G. Miller. "The Ethics of Placebo-Controlled Trials—a Middle Ground." *New England Journal of Medicine* 345 (2001): 915–19.

Fabrega, Horacio, Jr. "Medical Validity in Eastern and Western Traditions." *Perspectives in Biology and Medicine* 45 (2002): 395–415.

Faden, Ruth, and Tom Beauchamp. *A History and Theory of Informed Consent.* New York: Oxford University Press, 1986.

Fatout, Paul, ed. *Mark Twain Speaking.* Iowa City: University of Iowa Press, 1976.

Feinstein, Alvan R. "The Placebo Effect." In *Education of Health Professionals in Complementary/Alternative Medicine,* ed. Mary Hager, 74–91. New York: Josiah Macy Jr. Foundation, 2001.

Fischer, Victor, et al., eds. "Jim's 'Ghost' Story." In *Adventures of Huckleberry Finn,* by Mark Twain, 463–470. Berkeley: University of California Press, 2001.

Fischer, Victor, Michael B. Frank, and Dahlia Armon, eds. *Mark Twain's Letters, Volume 3, 1869.* Berkeley: University of California Press, 1992.

Fischer, Victor, Michael B. Frank, and Lin Salamo, eds. *Mark Twain's Letters, Volume 4, 1870–1871.* Berkeley: University of California Press, 1995.

Flexner, Abraham. *Medical Education in the United States and Canada.* New York: Carnegie Foundation for the Advancement of Teaching, 1910.

Flexner, James Thomas. *Doctors on Horseback: Pioneers of American Medicine.* New York: Viking Press, 1944.

Fontanarosa, Paul B., and George D. Lundberg. "Alternative Medicine Meets Science." *Journal of the American Medical Association* 280 (1998): 1618–19.

Frank, Michael B., and Harriet Elinor Smith, eds. *Mark Twain's Letters, Volume 6, 1874–1875.* Berkeley: University of California Press, 2002.

Friedlander, Walter J. "Mark Twain, Social Critic, and His Image of the Doctor." *Annals of Internal Medicine* 77 (1972): 1007–10.

Gardner, Martin. *Fads and Fallacies in the Name of Science.* New York: Dover Publications, 1957.

Gerber, John C., Paul Baender, and Terry Firkins, eds. *The Adventures of Tom Sawyer, Tom Sawyer Abroad, Tom Sawyer Detective.* Berkeley: University of California Press, 1980.

Gevitz, Norman. *The D.O.'s: Osteopathic Medicine in America.* Baltimore: Johns Hopkins University Press, 1982.

————. "Osteopathic Medicine: From Deviance to Difference." In *Other Healers: Unorthodox Medicine in America*, ed. Norman Gevitz, 124–57. Baltimore: Johns Hopkins University Press, 1988.

————. "Sectarian Medicine." *Journal of the American Medical Association* 257 (1987): 1636–40.

Gibbons, James L., and S. L. Miller. "An Image of Contemporary Hospital Chaplaincy." *Journal of Pastoral Care* 43 (1989): 355–61.

Gibbs, S., et al. "Local Treatments for Cutaneous Warts (Cochrane Review)." *Cochrane Library*, vol. 4. Oxford: Update Software, 2001.

Gibson, William M., ed. *Mark Twain's Mysterious Stranger Manuscripts*. Berkeley: University of California Press, 1969.

Golden, Richard L. "Osler's Legacy: The Centennial of *The Principles and Practice of Medicine*." *Annals of Internal Medicine* 116 (1992): 255–60.

Goodman, Steven N. "Probability at the Bedside: The Knowing of Chances or the Chances of Knowing?" *Annals of Internal Medicine* 130 (1999): 604–6.

Goodwin, E. J. *A History of Medicine in Missouri*. St. Louis: W. L. Smith, 1905.

Gotzsche, Peter C. "Trials of Homoeopathy." *Lancet* 341 (1993): 1533.

Gray, Barry M. "Streptococcal Infections." In *Bacterial Infections of Humans: Epidemiology and Control*, ed. Alfred S. Evans and Philip S. Brachman, 673–711. 3d ed. New York: Plenum Medical Book Co., 1998.

Greenberg, Donna B. "Neurasthenia in the 1980s: Chronic Mononucleosis, Chronic Fatigue Syndrome, and Anxiety and Depressive Disorders." *Psychosomatics* 31 (1990): 129–37.

Greenwood, Ronald D. "An Account of a Scarlatina Epidemic, 1839." *Illinois Medical Journal* 150 (1976): 147–48.

Grimes, Absalom. *Absalom Grimes: Confederate Mail Runner.* New Haven: Yale University Press, 1926.

Guest, R. G. "The Great Patent Medicine Fraud." *Applied Therapeutics* 8 (1966): 449–61.

Hadler, Nortin M. "If You Have to Prove You Are Ill, You Can't Get Well: The Object Lesson of Fibromyalgia." *Spine* 21 (1996): 2397–2400.

Haller, John S., Jr. *American Medicine in Transition, 1840–1910*. Urbana: University of Illinois Press, 1981.

————. "Medical Cataphoresis: Electrical Experimentation and Nineteenth Century Therapeutics." *New York State Journal of Medicine* 85 (1985): 257–61.

Harris, Susan K. *The Courtship of Olivia Langdon and Mark Twain.* Cambridge: Cambridge University Press, 1996.

Hatch, Robert L., et al. "The Spiritual Involvement and Beliefs Scale: Development and Testing of a New Instrument." *Journal of Family Practice* 46 (1998): 476–86.

Hearn, Michael Patrick, ed. *The Annotated Huckleberry Finn.* New York: W. W. Norton and Co., 2001.

Hechtlinger, Adelaide. *The Great Patent Medicine Era.* New York: Galahad Books, 1970.

Hickie, I., D. Hadzi-Pavlovic, and C. Ricci. "Reviving the Diagnosis of Neurasthenia." *Psychological Medicine* 27 (1997): 989–94.

Hill, Hamlin, ed. *Mark Twain's Letters to His Publishers, 1867–1910.* Berkeley: University of California Press, 1967.

Hirst, Robert H. "'Permission to Drink Anything': Mark Twain's Letters to Eduard Pötzl." *Bancroftiana* 121 (fall 2002): 10

Hoffman, Andrew. *Inventing Mark Twain: The Lives of Samuel Langhorne Clemens.* New York: William Morrow and Co., 1997.

Holbrook, Stewart H. *The Golden Age of Quackery.* New York: Macmillan Co., 1959.

Holcombe, R. I. *History of Marion County, Missouri, 1884.* St. Louis: E. F. Perkins, 1884.

Horn, Jason Gary. *Mark Twain and William James: Crafting a Free Self.* Columbia: University of Missouri Press, 1996.

Hornick, R. B., et al. "Typhoid Fever: Pathogenesis and Immunologic Control." *New England Journal of Medicine* 283 (1970): 686–91.

"The Hospital Hotel." *Journal of the American Medical Association* 26 (1896): 94.

Houston, W. R. "The Doctor Himself as a Therapeutic Agent." *Annals of Internal Medicine* 11 (1938): 1416–25.

Howell, Joel D. "The Paradox of Osteopathy." *New England Journal of Medicine* 341 (1999): 1465–68.

Howells, William D. *My Mark Twain.* New York: Harper and Brothers, 1910.

Hrobjartsson, Asbjørn, and Peter C. Gøtzsche. "Is the Placebo Powerless? An Analysis of Clinical Trials Comparing Placebo with No Treatment." *New England Journal of Medicine* 344 (2001): 1594–1602.

Hudson, Robert P. "Abraham Flexner in Perspective: American Medical Education, 1865–1910." *Bulletin of the History of Medicine* 46 (1972): 545–61.

Jackson, Janet. *Truth, Trust, and Medicine.* London and New York: Routledge, 2001.

Jonas, Wayne B., Ted J. Kaptchuk, and Klaus Linde. "A Critical Overview of Homeopathy." *Annals of Internal Medicine* 138 (2003): 393–99.

Jones, Anne Hudson. "Literature and Medicine: Narratives of Mental Illness." *Lancet* 350 (1977): 359–61.

"Judge Rules against Medicare, Medicaid Payments to Christian Science Caregivers." *Winston-Salem Journal*, August 9, 1996, A9.

Kahn, Arif, Heather A. Warner, and Walter A. Brown. "Symptom Reduction and Suicide Risk in Patients Treated with Placebo in Antidepressant Clinical Trials: An Analysis of the Food and Drug Administration Database." *Archives of General Psychiatry* 57 (2000): 311–17.

Kalauokalani, Donna, et al. "Lessons from a Trial of Acupuncture and Massage for Low Back Pain: Patient Expectations and Treatment Effects." *Spine* 26 (2001): 1418–24.

Kaplan, Justin. *Mr. Clemens and Mark Twain*. New York: Simon and Schuster, 1966.

Kaplan, Marty. "Ambushed by Spirituality." *Time Magazine*, June 24, 1996, p. 62.

Kaptchuk, Ted J. "The Placebo Effect in Alternative Medicine: Can the Performance of a Healing Ritual Have Clinical Significance?" *Annals of Internal Medicine* 136 (2002): 817–25.

Kaptchuk, Ted J., and David M. Eisenberg. "The Persuasive Appeal of Alternative Medicine." *Annals of Internal Medicine* 129 (1998): 1061–65.

———. "Varieties of Healing, 1: Medical Pluralism in the United States." *Annals of Internal Medicine* 135 (2001): 189–95.

Kaufman, Martin. "Homeopathy in America: The Rise and Fall and Persistence of a Medical Heresy." In *Other Healers: Unorthodox Medicine in America*, ed. Norman Gevitz, 99–123. Baltimore: Johns Hopkins University Press, 1988.

———. *Homeopathy in America: The Rise and Fall of a Medical Heresy*. Baltimore: Johns Hopkins University Press, 1971.

Kelwala, Surendra. "Why Patients Use Alternative Medicine" (letter). *Journal of the American Medical Association* 280 (1998): 1660–61.

King, Lester S. "The Flexner Report of 1910." *Journal of the American Medical Association* 251 (1984): 1079–86.

———. "Medical Sects and Their Influence." *Journal of the American Medical Association* 248 (1982): 1221–24.

Kiskis, Michael J., ed. *Mark Twain's Own Autobiography: The Chapters from the "North American Review."* Madison: University of Wisconsin Press, 1990.

Kreisberg, Robert. "We Blew It." *New England Journal of Medicine* 332 (1995): 945–49.

Labreque, Michel, et al. "Homeopathic Treatment of Plantar Warts." *Canadian Medical Association Journal* 146 (1992): 1749–53.

LaCombe, Michael. "Letters of Intent." In Howard Spiro et al., eds., *Empathy and the Practice of Medicine: Beyond Pills and the Scalpel*, 54–66. New Haven: Yale University Press, 1993.

Lantos, John. *Do We Still Need Doctors?* New York: Routledge, 1997.

Lauber, John. *The Inventions of Mark Twain*. New York: Hill and Wang, 1990.

Leary, Lewis, ed. *Mark Twain's Correspondence with Henry Huttleston Rogers, 1893–1909*. Berkeley: University of California Press, 1969.

Legan, Marshall Scott. "Hydropathy in America: A Nineteenth Century Panacea." *Bulletin of the History of Medicine* 45 (1971): 267–80.

Leon, Andrew C. "Placebo Protects Subjects from Nonresponse: A Paradox of Power." *Archives of General Psychiatry* 57 (2000): 329–30.

Leydon, Geraldine M., et al. "Faith, Hope, and Charity: An In-Depth Interview Study of Cancer Patients' Information Needs and Information-Seeking Behavior." *Western Medical Journal* 173 (2000): 26–31.

Lieberman, S. "A Review of the Effectiveness of *Cimifuga racemosa* (Black Cohosh) for the Symptoms of Menopause." *Journal of Women's Health* 7 (1998): 525–29.

Linde, Klaus, et al. "Are the Clinical Effects of Homoeopathy Placebo Effects? A Meta-Analysis of Placebo-Controlled Trials." *Lancet* 350 (1997): 834–43.

Loge, Ronald V. "'Two Dozes of Barks and Opium': Lewis and Clark as Physicians." *Pharos* 59 (summer 1996): 26–31.

Ludmerer, Kenneth M. *Learning to Heal: The Development of American Medical Education*. Baltimore: Johns Hopkins University Press, 1985.

Macklin, Ruth. "The Ethical Problems with Sham Surgery in Clinical Research." *New England Journal of Medicine* 341 (1999): 992–96.

Maizes, Victoria, et al. "Integrative Medical Education: Development and Implementation of a Comprehensive Curriculum at the University of Arizona." *Academic Medicine* 77 (2002): 851–60.

"Mark Twain, Osteopath." *New York Times*, February 28, 1901.

Martensen, Robert L. "Was Neurasthenia a 'Legitimate Morbid Entity'?" *Journal of the American Medical Association* 271 (1994): 1243.

Matthews, Dale A. *The Faith Factor: Proof of the Healing Power of Prayer.* New York: Penguin Books, 1999.

McCullough, Joseph B., and Janice McIntire-Strasburg, eds. *Mark Twain at the "Buffalo Express."* DeKalb: Northern Illinois University Press, 1999.

McNichol, T. "The New Faith in Medicine." *USA Today Weekend,* April 5–7, 1996, p. 4.

McPheeters, William M. "Epidemic of Cholera in St. Louis in 1849." In *A History of Medicine in Missouri,* by E. J. Goodwin, 71–92. St. Louis: W. L. Smith, 1905.

McWhinney, Ian R., Ronald M. Epstein, and Tom R. Freeman. "Rethinking Somatization." *Annals of Internal Medicine* 126 (1997): 747–50.

Meador, Clifton. "Hex Death: Voodoo Magic or Persuasion?" *Southern Medical Journal* 85 (1992): 244–47.

Mehl-Madrona, Lewis. *Coyote Medicine: Lessons from Native American Healing.* New York: Simon and Schuster, 1997.

Meloy, Harold. "Medics at Mammoth Cave." Typescript. Mammoth Cave National Park Library, 1972.

Meltzer, Milton. *Mark Twain Himself: A Pictorial Biography.* Columbia: University of Missouri Press, 2002.

Mercer, S. R. "The First Century of Osteopathic Medicine in the United States of America." *Transactions and Studies of the College of Physicians of Philadelphia* 45 (1978): 127–36.

Mitchell, S. Weir. *Fat and Blood: An Essay on the Treatment of Certain Forms of Neurasthenia and Hysteria.* 3d ed. Philadelphia: J. B. Lippincott and Co., 1884.

Moerman, Daniel E., and Wayne B. Jonas. "Deconstructing the Placebo Effect and Finding the Meaning Response." *Annals of Internal Medicine* 136 (2002): 471–76.

Newton, A. E. *The Modern Bethesda, or The Gift of Healing Restored.* New York: Newton Publishing Co., 1879.

Nimnuan, Chaichana, et al. "How Many Functional Somatic Syndromes?" *Journal of Psychosomatic Research* 51 (2001): 549–57.

Nimnuan, Chaichana, Matthew Hotopf, and Simon Wessely. "Medically Unexplained Symptoms: An Epidemiological Study in Seven Specialities." *Journal of Psychosomatic Research* 51 (2001): 361–67.

Nostrums and Quackery. Chicago: American Medical Association Press, 1912.

Ober, K. Patrick "The Pre-Flexnerian Reports: Mark Twain's Criticism of Medicine in the United States." *Annals of Internal Medicine* 126 (1997): 157–63.

———. "Uncle Remus and the Cascade Effect in Clinical Medicine: Brer Rabbit Kicks the Tar-Baby." *American Journal of Medicine* 82 (1987): 1009–13.

Olfson, Mark. "The Weir Mitchell Rest Cure." *Pharos* 51 (summer 1988): 30–32.

Osler, William. *The Principles and Practice of Medicine.* 1st ed. New York: Appleton, 1892.

Paine, Alfred Bigelow. *Mark Twain: A Biography.* New York: Harper and Brothers, 1912.

Paine, Alfred Bigelow, ed. *Mark Twain's Letters.* 2 vols. New York: Harper and Brothers, 1917.

———. *Mark Twain's Notebook.* New York: Harper and Brothers, 1935.

Park, Robert. *Voodoo Science: The Road from Foolishness to Fraud.* New York: Oxford University Press, 2000.

Patterson, K. David. "Yellow Fever Epidemics and Mortality in the United States, 1693–1905." *Social Science and Medicine* 34 (1992): 855–65.

Peabody, Francis W. "The Care of the Patient." *Journal of the American Medical Association* 88 (1927): 877–82.

Phillips, William R. "Patients, Pills, and Professionals: The Ethics of Placebo Therapy." *Pharos* 44 (1981): 21–25.

Porter, William G. "Truth-Telling and Hope: The Dilemma of Modern Medicine." *North Carolina Medical Journal* 60 (1999): 142–48.

Post, Stephen G., Christina M. Puchalski, and David M. Larson. "Physicians and Patient Spirituality: Professional Boundaries, Competency, and Ethics." *Annals of Internal Medicine* 132 (2000): 578–83.

Powers, Ron. *Dangerous Water: A Biography of the Boy Who Became Mark Twain.* New York: Basic Books, 1999.

Raabe, Jason R. "Nontraditional Health Care Systems in the Western World." *MD News Piedmont Triad,* June 2000, 15–18.

Rasmussen, R. Kent. *Mark Twain A to Z: The Essential Reference to His Life and Writings.* New York: Facts on File, 1995.

———. *The Quotable Mark Twain: His Essential Aphorisms, Witticisms, and Concise Opinions.* Lincolnton, Ill.: Contemporary Books, 1997.

Ravin, James G. "Mark Twain in Ohio: The Novelist's Visits with Some of His Medical Opinions." *Ohio Medicine* 85 (1989): 858–63.

Reed, John F. "Samuel Clemens and Family: The Hartford Connection and Hartford Physicians." *American Journal of Surgery* 141 (1981): 401–10.

Robin, Eugene D. "The Cult of the Swan-Ganz Catheter: Overuse and Abuse of Pulmonary Flow Catheters." *Annals of Internal Medicine* 103 (1985): 445–49.

Rogers, Franklin R., ed. *Mark Twain's Satires and Burlesques*. Berkeley: University of California Press, 1967.

Rosenberg, Charles E. "The Therapeutic Revolution: Medicine, Meaning, and Social Change in Nineteenth-Century America." *Perspectives in Biology and Medicine* 20 (1977): 485–506.

Rosner, Fred. "Religion and Medicine." *Archives of Internal Medicine* 161 (2001): 1811–12.

Ross, Stephen E. "'Memes' as Infectious Agents in Psychosomatic Illness." *Annals of Internal Medicine* 131 (1999): 867–71.

Roth, Nancy. "American Electrotherapy." *Medical Instrumentation* 10 (1976): 302–3.

———. "Electrotherapy, Nineteenth-Century Neurasthenia, and the Case of Alice James." *Medical Instrumentation* 15 (1981): 116.

———. "The Great Patent Medicine Era." *Medical Instrumentation* 11 (1977): 302–3.

———. "The Nineteenth-Century Revival of Electrotherapy." *Medical Instrumentation* 11 (1977): 236–37.

Ruddick, William. "Hope and Deception." *Bioethics* 13 (1999): 343–57.

Salsbury, Edith Colgate, ed. *Susy and Mark Twain: Family Dialogues*. New York: Harper and Row, 1965.

Schattner, Ami, and Merav Tal. "Truth Telling and Patient Autonomy: The Patient's Point of View." *American Journal of Medicine* 113 (2002): 66–69.

Scheurich, Neil. "Hysteria and the Medical Narrative." *Perspectives in Biology and Medicine* 43 (2000): 461–76.

Schoepflin, Rennie B. "Christian Science Healing in America." In *Other Healers: Unorthodox Medicine in America*, ed. Norman Gevitz, 192–214. Baltimore: Johns Hopkins University Press, 1988.

Scott, George Ryley. *The Story of Baths and Bathing*. London, T. Werner Laurie, 1939.

Sergeant, Michael J. "More on Alternative Medicine" (letter). *Annals of Internal Medicine* 132 (2000): 675.

Shaughnessy, Allen F. "Alternative Views on Alternative Medicine (letter)." *Annals of Internal Medicine* 131 (1999): 229.

Siegler, Mark. "Pascal's Wager and the Hanging of Crepe." *New England Journal of Medicine* 293 (1975): 853–57.

Skandera-Trombley, Laura E. *Mark Twain in the Company of Women.* Philadelphia: University of Pennsylvania Press, 1994.

Sklar, Kathryn Kish. "All Hail to Pure Cold Water." In *Women and Health in America,* ed. Judith W. Leavitt, 239–46. Madison: University of Wisconsin Press, 1984.

Skolnick, Andrew A. "FDA Petitioned to 'Stop Homeopathy Scam.'" *Journal of the American Medical Association* 272 (1994): 1154–56.

Sloan, R. P., E. Bagiella, and T. Powell. "Religion, Spirituality, and Medicine." *Lancet* 353 (1999): 664–67.

Sloan, Richard P., et al. "Should Physicians Prescribe Religious Activities?" *New England Journal of Medicine* 342 (2000): 1913–16.

Slotta, Robert. "Mark Twain and the Patent Medicine Ad." Letter to Internet. Mark Twain Forum, July 20, 2000.

Smith, Harriet Elinor, Richard Bucci, and Lin Salamo, eds. *Mark Twain's Letters, Volume 2, 1867–1868.* Berkeley: University of California Press, 1990.

Smith, Janet, ed. *Mark Twain on the Damned Human Race.* New York: Hill and Wang, 1962.

Sontag, Susan. *Illness as a Metaphor.* New York: Farrar, Straus, and Giroux, 1978.

Speer, Lonnie R. *Portals to Hell: Military Prisons of the Civil War.* Mechanicsville, Pa.: Stackpole Books, 1997.

Spiegel, Allen D. "The Role of Gender, Phrenology, Discrimination, and Nervous Prostration in Clara Barton's Career." *Journal of Community Health* 20 (1995): 501–26.

Spiro, Howard M. "Fat, Foreboding, and Flatulence." *Annals of Internal Medicine* 130 (1999): 320–22.

———. *The Power of Hope: A Doctor's Perspective.* New Haven: Yale University Press, 1998.

Stea, John, and William Fried. "Remedies for a Society's Debilities: Medicines for Neurasthenia in Victorian America." *New York State Journal of Medicine* 93 (1993): 120–27.

Stein, Bernard L. "Explanatory Notes." In *A Connecticut Yankee in King Arthur's Court,* by Mark Twain, 455–75. Berkeley: University of California Press, 1984.

Stern, Peter, and Norman Levine. "Controlled Localized Heat Therapy in Cutaneous Warts." *Archives of Dermatology* 128 (1992): 945–48.

Stillings, Dennis. "A Survey of the History of Electrical Stimulation for Pain to 1900." *Medical Instrumentation* 9 (1975): 255–59.

Straus, Joshua L., and Stephanie von Ammon Cavanaugh. "Placebo Effects: Issues for Clinical Practice in Psychiatry and Medicine." *Psychosomatics* 37 (1996): 315–26.

Targ, E., and K. S. Thomson. "Can Prayer and Intentionality Be Researched? Should They Be?" *Alternative Therapies in Health and Medicine* 3 (1997): 92–96.

Tenney, Thomas A. "Introduction." *Mark Twain Journal* 37 (1999): 3–5.

Thomas, K. B. "General Practice Consultations: Is There Any Point in Being Positive?" *British Medical Journal* 294 (1987): 1200–1202.

Thorne, Susan. "Spas Accepted Part of Health Care in Czech Republic." *Canadian Medical Association Journal* 153 (1995): 94–95.

"Thought for the Day." *Winston-Salem Journal,* July 8, 2000, p. E6.

Tuckey, John S., ed. *Mark Twain's Which Was the Dream? and Other Symbolic Writings of the Later Years.* Berkeley: University of California Press, 1968.

Twain, Mark. *Adventures of Huckleberry Finn.* New York: Charles L. Webster and Co., 1885.

———. *Adventures of Huckleberry Finn.* Comprehensive Edition. New York: Random House, 1996.

———. *The Adventures of Tom Sawyer.* Hartford: American Publishing Co., 1876.

———. "Aix-les-Bains." In *Mark Twain: Collected Tales, Sketches, Speeches, and Essays, 1891–1910,* ed. Louis J. Budd, 1–14. New York: Library of America, 1992.

———. *The American Claimant.* New York: Charles L. Webster and Co., 1892.

———. "At the Appetite Cure." In *The Man That Corrupted Hadleyburg and Other Stories and Essays,* 147–66. New York: Harper and Brothers, 1900.

———. *The Autobiography of Mark Twain.* Ed. Charles Neider. New York: Harper and Row, 1959.

———. "Bible Teaching and Religious Practice." In *Mark Twain on the Damned Human Race,* ed. Janet Smith, 40–45. New York: Hill and Wang, 1962.

———. "Boy's Manuscript." In *The Adventures of Tom Sawyer, Tom Sawyer Abroad, Tom Sawyer Detective,* ed. John C. Gerber, Paul Baender, and Terry Firkins, 419–51. Berkeley: University of California Press, 1980.

———. *Christian Science*. New York and London: Harper and Brothers, 1907.

———. "Christian Science and the Book of Mrs. Eddy." In *Mark Twain: Collected Tales, Sketches, Speeches, and Essays, 1891–1910,* ed. Louis J. Budd, 371–89. New York: Library of America, 1992.

———. "The Chronicle of Young Satan." In *Mark Twain's Mysterious Stranger Manuscripts,* ed. William M. Gibson, 35–174. Berkeley: University of California Press, 1969.

———. "Concerning the Answer to That Conundrum." *Twain's World.* CD-ROM. Parsippani, N.J.: Bureau Development, 1993.

———. *A Connecticut Yankee in King Arthur's Court.* New York: Charles L. Webster and Co., 1889.

———. "Corn-Pone Opinions." In *Mark Twain: Collected Tales, Sketches, Speeches, and Essays, 1891–1910,* ed. Louis J. Budd, 507–11. New York: Library of America, 1992.

———. "Curing a Cold." In *The Celebrated Jumping Frog of Calaveras County and Other Sketches,* 67–75. New York: C. H. Webb, 1867.

———. "The Danger of Lying in Bed." In *Mark Twain: Collected Tales, Sketches, Speeches, and Essays, 1852–1890,* ed. Louis J. Budd, 510–13. New York: Library of America, 1992.

———. "Dinner Speech" [Businessman's Dinner for Henry H. Rogers, April 3, 1909]. In *Mark Twain Speaking,* ed. Paul Fatout, 640–43. Iowa City: University of Iowa Press, 1976.

———. "Dinner Speech" [New York Postgraduate Medical School and Hospital Dinner]. In *Mark Twain Speaking,* ed. Paul Fatout, 631–36. Iowa City: University of Iowa Press, 1976.

———. "Dinner Speech" [Society on Medical Jurisprudence]. In *Mark Twain Speaking,* ed. Paul Fatout, 429–31. Iowa City: University of Iowa Press, 1976.

———. "Dr. Loeb's Incredible Discovery." In *Mark Twain: Collected Tales, Sketches, Speeches, and Essays, 1891–1910,* ed. Louis J. Budd, 648–51. New York: Library of America, 1992.

———. "Enthusiastic Eloquence." In *Early Tales and Sketches, Volume 2, 1864–1865,* ed. Edgar Marquess Branch and Robert H. Hirst, 235. Berkeley: University of California Press, 1981.

———. "Extract from an Article in 'The Radical,' January 916." In *Letters from the Earth,* ed. Bernard DeVoto, 81–83. New York: Perennial Library, Harper and Row, 1974.

———. *Extract from Captain Stormfield's Visit to Heaven.* New York: Harper and Brothers, 1909.

————. "The Facts Concerning the Recent Carnival of Crime in Connecticut." In *The Stolen White Elephant, Etc.,* 106–30. Boston: James R. Osgood and Co., 1882.

————. "Fenimore Cooper's Literary Offenses." In *How to Tell a Story and Other Essays,* 93–116. New York: Harper and Brothers, 1897.

————. "The First Writing-Machines." In *The Complete Essays of Mark Twain,* ed. Charles Neider, 324–26. Garden City, N.Y.: Doubleday and Co., 1963.

————. *Following the Equator.* Hartford: American Publishing Co., 1897.

————. "Goldsmith's Friend Abroad Again." In *A Pen Warmed Up in Hell: Mark Twain in Protest,* ed. Frederick Anderson, 131–52. New York: Harper Colophon, 1972.

————. "Indiantown." In *Mark Twain's Which Was the Dream? and Other Symbolic Writings of the Later Years,* ed. John S. Tuckey, 153–78. Berkeley: University of California Press, 1968.

————. *The Innocents Abroad.* Hartford: American Publishing Co., 1869.

————. "Letters from the Earth." In *What Is Man and Other Philosophical Writings,* ed. Paul Baender, 401–54. Berkeley: University of California Press, 1973.

————. "L'Homme Qui Rit." In *Mark Twain's Satires and Burlesques,* ed. Franklin R. Rogers, 42–48. Berkeley: University of California Press, 1967.

————. *Life on the Mississippi.* Boston: James R. Osgood and Co., 1883.

————. "A Majestic Literary Fossil." In *The Million Pound Bank Note and Other New Stories,* 241–60. New York: Charles L. Webster and Co., 1893.

————. "Man's Place in the Animal World." In *Mark Twain: Collected Tales, Sketches, Speeches, and Essays, 1891–1910,* ed. Louis J. Budd, 213–15. New York: Library of America, 1992.

————. "The Man That Corrupted Hadleyburg." In *The Man That Corrupted Hadleyburg and Other Stories and Essays,* 1–83. New York: Harper and Brothers, 1900.

————. "Marienbad, a Health Factory." In *The Complete Essays of Mark Twain,* ed. Charles Neider, 99–109. Garden City, N.Y.: Doubleday and Co., 1963.

————. "My Debut as a Literary Person." In *The Man That Corrupted Hadleyburg and Other Stories and Essays,* 84–127. New York: Harper and Brothers, 1900.

————. *No. 44, The Mysterious Stranger.* In *Mark Twain's Mysterious Stranger*

Manuscripts, ed. William M. Gibson, 221–405. Berkeley: University of California Press, 1969.

———. "Official Physic." In *Mark Twain: Collected Tales, Sketches, Speeches, and Essays, 1852–1890,* ed. Louis J. Budd, 228–230. New York: Library of America, 1992.

———. "On the Decay of the Art of Lying." In *The Stolen White Elephant, Etc.,* 217–25. Boston: James R. Osgood and Co., 1882.

———. "Personal Habits of the Siamese Twins." In *Sketches New and Old,* 208–12. Hartford: American Publishing Co., 1875.

———. *The Prince and the Pauper.* Boston: James R. Osgood and Co., 1882.

———. *Pudd'nhead Wilson and Those Extraordinary Twins.* Hartford: American Publishing Co., 1894.

———. "Remarks on Osteopathy." In *Mark Twain Speaking,* ed. Paul Fatout, 384–88. Iowa City: University of Iowa Press, 1976.

———. *Roughing It.* Hartford: American Publishing Co., 1872.

———. "Row among the Doctors." In *Clemens of the "Call": Mark Twain in San Francisco,* ed. Edgar M. Branch, 151. Berkeley: University of California Press, 1969.

———. "Seventieth Birthday Dinner Speech." In *Mark Twain: Collected Tales, Sketches, Speeches, and Essays, 1891–1910,* ed. Louis J. Budd, 713–18. New York: Library of America, 1992.

———. "Three Thousand Years among the Microbes." In *Mark Twain's Which Was the Dream? and Other Symbolic Writings of the Later Years,* ed. John S. Tuckey, 433–553. Berkeley: University of California Press, 1968.

———. *Tom Sawyer Abroad.* New York: Charles Webster and Co., 1894.

———. "Tom Sawyer's Conspiracy." In *Mark Twain's Hannibal, Huck, and Tom,* ed. Walter Blair, 163–242. Berkeley: University of California Press, 1969.

———. *A Tramp Abroad.* Hartford: American Publishing Co., 1880.

———. "The Turning Point in my Life." In *What Is Man? and Other Philosophical Writings,* ed. Paul Baender, 455–64. Berkeley: University of California Press, 1973.

———. "Two Little Tales." In *Mark Twain: Collected Tales, Sketches, Speeches, and Essays, 1891–1910,* ed. Louis J. Budd, 496–506. New York: Library of America, 1992.

———. "Villagers of 1840–3." In *Huck Finn and Tom Sawyer among the Indians and Other Unfinished Stories,* 93–108. Berkeley: University of California Press, 1989.

————. "Was It Heaven? or Hell?" In *The $30,000 Bequest and Other Stories*, 68–102. New York: Harper and Brothers, 1906.

————. *Which Was It?* In *Mark Twain's Which Was the Dream? and Other Symbolic Writings of the Later Years*, ed. John S. Tuckey, 179–432. Berkeley: University of California Press, 1968.

————. "William Dean Howells." In *Mark Twain: Collected Tales, Sketches, Speeches, and Essays 1891–1919*, ed. Louis J. Budd, 723–30. New York: Library of America, 1992.

Twain, Mark, and Charles Dudley Warner. *The Gilded Age*. Hartford: American Publishing Co., 1873.

"Twain Talks to Doctors: 'Dr. Clemens' Describes Imaginary Medical School at His Country Home." *New York Times*, January 21, 1909.

Twain's World. CD-ROM. Parsippany, N.J.: Bureau Development, 1993.

Tyler, Alice F. *Freedom's Ferment: Phases of American Social History to 1860*. Minneapolis: University of Minnesota Press, 1944.

Ubel, Peter A. "Truth in the Most Optimistic Way." *Annals of Internal Medicine* 134 (2001): 1142–43.

Vandenbroucke, Jan P. "Homoeopathy Trials: Going Nowhere." *Lancet* 350 (1997): 824.

Van Rij, Andre M., et al. "Chelation Therapy for Intermittent Claudication: A Double-Blind, Randomized, Controlled Trial." *Circulation* 90 (1994): 1194–99.

Verghese, Abraham. "The Physician as Storyteller." *Annals of Internal Medicine* 135 (2001): 1012–17.

Walker, Cliff. "Mark Twain and the Patent Medicine Ad." Letter to Internet. Mark Twain Forum, July 14, 2000.

Walker, Franklin, and G. Ezra Dane, eds., *Mark Twain's Travels with Mr. Brown*. New York: Alfred A. Knopf, 1940.

Wallis, C. "Faith and Healing: Can Prayer, Faith, and Spirituality Really Improve Your Physical Health? A Growing and Surprising Body of Scientific Evidence Says They Can." *Time* 147 (1996): 58.

Ward, Geoffrey C., and Dayton Duncan. *Mark Twain: An Illustrated Biography*. New York: Alfred A. Knopf, 2001.

Warner, John Harley. *The Therapeutic Perspective: Medical Practice, Knowledge, and Identity in America, 1820–1885*. Princeton: Princeton University Press, 1997.

Wax, Paul M. "Elixirs, Diluents, and the Passage of the 1938 Federal Food, Drug, and Cosmetic Act." *Annals of Internal Medicine* 122 (1995): 456–61.

Weaver, H. Dwight, and Paul A. Johnson. *Adventures at Mark Twain Cave.* Jefferson City, Mo.: Discovery Enterprises, 1972.

Webster, Doris, and Samuel Webster. "Whitewashing Jane Clemens." *Bookman* 51 (1925): 531–35.

Webster, Samuel Charles, ed. *Mark Twain, Business Man.* Boston: Little, Brown and Co., 1946.

Wecter, Dixon. *Sam Clemens of Hannibal.* Boston: Houghton Mifflin Co., 1952.

Wecter, Dixon, ed. *The Love Letters of Mark Twain.* New York: Harper and Brothers, 1949.

Weiss, Harry B., and Howard R. Kemble. *The Great American Water-cure Craze: A History of Hydropathy in the United States.* Trenton, N.J.: The Past Times Press, 1967.

Welch, H. Gilbert, and Jon D. Lurie. "Teaching Evidence-Based Medicine: Caveats and Challenges." *Academic Medicine* 75 (2000): 235–40.

Welsh, Donald H. "Sam Clemens' Hannibal, 1836–1838." *Midcontinent American Studies Journal* 3 (spring 1962): 28–43.

Wessely, Simon. "Old Wine in New Bottles: Neurasthenia and 'ME.'" *Psychological Medicine* 20 (1990): 35–53.

———. "Responding to Mass Psychogenic Illness." *New England Journal of Medicine* 342 (2000): 129–30.

Wessely, S., C. Nimnuan, and M. Sharpe. "Functional Somatic Syndromes: One or Many?" *Lancet* 354 (1999): 936–39.

Willis, Resa. *Mark and Livy: The Love Story of Mark Twain and the Woman Who Almost Tamed Him.* New York: Atheneum Publishers, 1992.

Wills, Garry. "Introduction." In *Christian Science,* by Mark Twain, xxxi–xxxvii. New York: Oxford University Press, 1996.

Wilson, James Walter. "Joseph Nash McDowell, M.D." *Register of the Kentucky Historical Society* 65 (1967): 324–40; 68 (1970): 341–69.

Wood, A. D. "The Fashionable Diseases: Women's Complaints and Their Treatment in Nineteenth-Century America." *Journal of Interdisciplinary History* 4 (1973): 25–52.

Yager, Joel, and Roy T. Young. "Non-Hypoglycemia Is an Epidemic Condition." *New England Journal of Medicine* 291 (1974): 907–8.

Yazar, Şahin, and Erdal Başaran. "Efficacy of Silver Nitrate Pencils in the Treatment of Common Warts." *Journal of Dermatology* 21 (1994): 329–33.

Young, James Harvey. *American Self-Dosage Medicines: An Historical Perspective.* Lawrence: Coronado Press, 1974.

―――. "From Hooper to Hohensee: Some Highlights of American Patent Medicine Promotion." *Journal of the American Medical Association* 204 (1968): 100–104.

―――. "The Paradise of Quacks." *New York State Journal of Medicine* 93 (1993): 127–33.

Index